*Oracle Press*™

Oracle PL/SQL Programming

Scott Urman

Osborne **McGraw-Hill**

Berkeley New York St. Louis San Francisco
Auckland Bogotá Hamburg London Madrid
Mexico City Milan Montreal New Delhi Panama City
Paris São Paulo Singapore Sydney
Tokyo Toronto

Osborne **McGraw-Hill**
2600 Tenth Street
Berkeley, California 94710
U.S.A.

For information on translations or book distributors outside the U.S.A., or to arrange bulk purchase discounts for sales promotions, premiums, or fund-raisers, please contact Osborne **McGraw-Hill** at the above address.

Oracle PL/SQL Programming

67890 DOC 9987

ISBN 0-07-882176-2

Acquisitions Editor
Wendy Rinaldi

Project Editor
Nancy McLaughlin

Technical Editor
Tim Smith

Copy Editor
Judith Brown

Proofreader
Patricia Mannion

Indexer
David Heiret

Computer Designer
Jani Beckwith

Illustrators
Loretta Au
Leslee Bassin

Quality Control Specialist
Joe Scuderi

Series Design
Jani Beckwith

Cover Design
Ted Mader Associates

Oracle Press™

Oracle PL/SQL Programming

About the Author

Scott Urman is a Senior Technical Analyst in the
Language Group of Oracle Worldwide Technical
Support, where he aids users of Oracle's various
language products (PL/SQL, OCI, and the Oracle
Precompilers). In addition, he reviews Oracle
technical documentation, writes white papers
on Oracle languages, and makes technical
presentations both inside Oracle and at meetings
of Oracle user's groups.

This book is dedicated to the technical analysts and management
team at Oracle Worldwide Technical Support.
Never have I worked with people as dedicated,
technically proficient, supportive, and fun-loving.
No matter what people may say,
this is a great organization that is truly world-class.

Contents at a Glance

Contents

Acknowledgments

When I was first offered the opportunity to work on this book, I was told that five months to write a 500 page book about PL/SQL was an impossibility. I scoffed at my detractors, threw caution to the winds, and dove in. Now, five months of caffeine later, I'm tempted to agree. Sunrises are very beautiful, but I think I've seen too many of them recently. However, I've put my heart, soul, and most of my sleep into this project, and I'm very pleased with the result. I hope that you agree with me, and find this volume useful.

There were a number of people who should be acknowledged for their invaluable help with this project. Thanks to Tim Smith at Oracle for your insightful and detailed review—it was interesting switching roles with you. I look forward to reviewing *your* material again so I don't have to include your suggestions, and you can put mine in. Thanks also to Wendy Rinaldi and Nancy McLaughlin at Osborne for cajoling me into finishing on time. Also thanks to the management team at Oracle Technical Support for their assistance, support, and suggestions, and most importantly for the time to finish this properly. And of course, thanks to my family and friends (you know who you are) for their comments and advice.

I used a number of resources during the development of this book, including several Oracle manuals. These include the *PL/SQL User's Guide and Reference*, *Oracle7 Server Application Developer's Guide, Oracle7 Server Administrator's*

Guide, Oracle7 Server SQL Reference, Oracle7 Server Concepts Manual, and *Programmer's Guide to the Pro*C Precompiler.*

If you have any comments about this book, I can be reached via e-mail at **surman@us.oracle.com**. I apologize for any errors (I think we got them all) and welcome any thoughts for the sequel (or should that be SQL?).

Introduction

O racle is an extremely powerful and flexible relational database system. Along with this power and flexibility comes complexity, however. In order to design useful applications based on Oracle, it is necessary to understand how Oracle manipulates the data stored within the system. PL/SQL is an important tool that is designed for data manipulation, both internally (within Oracle) and externally (in your own applications). PL/SQL is available in a variety of environments, each of which has different advantages.

After reading this book, you should be able to use PL/SQL easily and effectively in your own applications. It's designed to help you understand PL/SQL and appreciate the power of this unique language. Once you are familiar with the basics of PL/SQL, the book can also serve as a reference manual for day-to-day programming questions.

Intended Audience

This book is meant to be both a user's guide and a reference to PL/SQL. It is appropriate both for the experienced programmer who just needs to know the syntax for PL/SQL and its advanced features, and for the novice programmer who is not familiar with other third-generation languages. A general familiarity with

Oracle (connecting to and using the database, basic SQL, etc.) will be helpful, but is not required before reading.

How to Use This Book

This book is divided into 12 chapters and 4 appendices. Chapter 1 is an introduction, Chapters 2-6 describe the syntax and semantics of PL/SQL, and Chapters 7-11 describe the advanced features of the language, including the built-in packages. Chapter 12 covers performance and tuning, and the 4 appendices offer a valuable medley of reference information.

Chapter 1: Introduction to PL/SQL

This chapter introduces PL/SQL and describes some of the major features of the language. It also discusses the different versions of PL/SQL and which database versions they correspond to. The chapter concludes with a description of the database schema used as an example throughout the book.

Chapter 2: PL/SQL Syntax and Constructs

This chapter describes the syntax of PL/SQL. Topics included are the structure of a PL/SQL program, variables and types, expressions and operators, and control structures (loops and conditional statements). The chapter concludes with advice on PL/SQL style and how to write code that is readable and easily maintained.

Chapter 3: SQL Within PL/SQL

This chapter covers the SQL statements available within PL/SQL—the data manipulation commands that run the database. It also describes the built-in SQL functions and the details of transaction control.

Chapter 4: Cursors

This chapter contains a detailed discussion of cursors and how they are used to manipulate large quantities of data. It includes the syntax for declaring and using cursors, as well as a description of cursor attributes and examples that demonstrate how to use cursor variables.

Chapter 5: Procedures, Functions, Packages, and Triggers

This chapter describes the different types of program units available in PL/SQL: procedures, functions, packages, and triggers. The syntax and meaning of each type is discussed, as are the differences between them. The chapter explains how to use functions in SQL statements, how roles and procedures interact, and the relationship between stored subprograms and the data dictionary.

Chapter 6: Error Handling

Error handing is crucial to any well-designed application. This chapter describes how to use PL/SQL exceptions to ensure that your program is robust and able to handle run-time exception conditions. It also includes guidelines for the effective use of exceptions.

Chapter 7: PL/SQL Execution Environments

PL/SQL can be run from a variety of environments. This chapter compares the merits of client-side vs. server-side PL/SQL, and details the use of PL/SQL in SQL*Plus, the Oracle precompilers, OCI, and the Developer 2000 suite of tools.

Chapter 8: Testing and Debugging

This chapter describes several different methods of debugging your PL/SQL applications. You'll get to practice these techniques by solving three common PL/SQL problems. The chapter concludes with a discussion of the software development process and how to carry it out effectively in PL/SQL.

Chapter 9: Intersession Communication

This chapter describes the two built-in packages available for communicating directly between database sessions: database pipes (DBMS_PIPE) and database alerts (DBMS_ALERT). Specific examples are included, along with a comparison between the two packages.

Chapter 10: Dynamic PL/SQL

Dynamic PL/SQL is a powerful programming technique that allows you to write extremely flexible programs. This chapter discusses the DBMS_SQL package, which implements dynamic PL/SQL; it also explains how the package can be used to overcome the PL/SQL restriction whereby only DML statements are allowed.

Chapter 11: Database Jobs and File I/O

The UTL_FILE package allows PL/SQL to read from and write to operating system files. The DBMS_JOB package allows you to schedule PL/SQL jobs (in the form of stored procedures) so that they run automatically at specified times. Both packages are discussed in detail here, with examples.

Chapter 12: Performance and Tuning

A properly written PL/SQL program should not only produce the correct result, but should also determine this result as efficiently as possible. Several performance and tuning techniques are discussed in this chapter, including the use of the shared pool, how to tune SQL statements, and how to use the Oracle array interface.

Appendix A: Reserved Words in PL/SQL

This appendix lists the keywords reserved by PL/SQL and by the database itself.

Appendix B: Guide to Supplied Packages

This appendix describes all of the built-in packages available in PL/SQL. These packages implement such things as file I/O, job scheduling, intersession communication, dynamic programming, and management of the shared pool.

Appendix C: Glossary of PL/SQL Features

This appendix contains an alphabetical list of the various features available in PL/SQL. A brief description of each is included, along with a reference to the chapter that describes the topic in detail.

Appendix D: The Data Dictionary

This appendix describes the data dictionary views that are relevant to the PL/SQL programmer.

An Added Bonus...

All of the sample code that you'll see in this book is available in electronic form on the World Wide Web! Check out Osborne's Oracle Press Web page at **http://www.osborne.com/oracle**.

CHAPTER 1

Introduction to PL/SQL

PL/SQL is a sophisticated programming language used to access an Oracle database from various environments. PL/SQL is integrated with the database server, so that the PL/SQL code can be processed quickly and efficiently. In this chapter we will discuss the reasons for PL/SQL and its development, the major features of the language, and the importance of knowing the PL/SQL and database versions. The chapter concludes with a description of the database tables used as examples throughout the book.

What Is PL/SQL?

Oracle is a relational database. The language used to access a relational database is *Structured Query Language* (*SQL*—often pronounced *sequel*). SQL is a flexible, efficient language, with features designed to manipulate and examine relational data. For example, the following SQL statement will delete all students who are majoring in Nutrition from the database:

```
DELETE FROM students
  WHERE major = 'Nutrition';
```

(The database tables used in this book, including **students**, are described at the end of this chapter.)

SQL is a *fourth-generation language*. This means that the language describes what should be done, but not how to do it. In the DELETE statement just shown, for example, we don't know how the database will actually determine which students are majoring in Nutrition. Presumably, the server will have to loop through all the students in some order, to determine the proper entries to delete. But the details of this are hidden from us.

Third-generation languages, such as C or COBOL, are more procedural in nature. A program in a third-generation language (3GL) implements a step-by-step algorithm to solve the problem. For example, we could accomplish the DELETE operation with something like this:

```
LOOP over each student record
  IF this record has major = 'Nutrition' THEN
    DELETE this record;
  END IF;
END LOOP;
```

Each language has advantages and disadvantages. Fourth-generation languages such as SQL are generally fairly simple (compared to third-generation languages) and have fewer commands. 4GLs also insulate the user from the underlying data structures and algorithms. In some cases, however, the procedural constructs available in 3GLs are useful to express a desired program. This is where PL/SQL comes in—it combines the power and flexiblity of SQL (a 4GL) with the procedural constructs of a 3GL.

PL/SQL stands for Procedural Language/SQL. As its name implies, PL/SQL extends SQL by adding constructs found in other procedural languages, such as:

- Variables and types
- Control structures such as IF-THEN-ELSE statements and loops
- Procedures and functions

Procedural constructs are integrated seamlessly with Oracle SQL, resulting in a structured, powerful language. For example, suppose we want to change the major for a student. If the student doesn't exist, then we want to create a new record. We could do this with the following PL/SQL code:

```
DECLARE
    /* Declare variables which will be used in SQL statements */
    v_NewMajor VARCHAR2(10) := 'History';
    v_FirstName VARCHAR2(10) := 'Scott';
    v_LastName VARCHAR2(10) := 'Urman';
BEGIN
    /* Update the students table. */
    UPDATE students
      SET major = v_NewMajor
      WHERE first_name = v_FirstName
      AND last_name = v_LastName;
    /* Check to see if the record was found. If not, then we need
       to insert this record. */
    IF SQL%NOTFOUND THEN
      INSERT INTO students (ID, first_name, last_name, major)
        VALUES (10020, v_FirstName, v_LastName, v_NewMajor);
    END IF;
END;
```

This example contains two different SQL statements (UPDATE and INSERT) as well as several variable declarations, and the conditional IF statement.

PL/SQL is unique in that it combines the flexibility of SQL with the power and configurability of a 3GL. All of the necessary procedural constructs are there, together with the database access. The result is a robust, powerful language, well-suited for designing complex applications.

Client-Server Model

Many database applications are built using the client-server model. The program itself resides on a client machine and sends requests to a database server for information. The requests are done with SQL. Typically, this results in many network trips, one for each SQL statement. This is illustrated by the diagram on the left-hand side of Figure 1-1. Compare this with the situation on the right, however. Several SQL statements can be bundled together into one PL/SQL block and sent to the server as a single unit. This results in less network traffic and a faster application.

Even when the client and the server are both running on the same machine, performance is increased. In this case, there isn't any network, but packaging SQL statements still results in a simpler program that makes fewer calls to the database.

Standards

Oracle7 supports the ANSI (American National Standards Institute) standard for the SQL language, as defined in ANSI document X3.135-1992, "Database Language SQL." This standard, commonly known as SQL92 (or SQL2), defines the SQL language only. It does not define the 3GL extensions to the language that PL/SQL provides. SQL92 has three compliance levels: Entry, Intermediate, and Full. Oracle7 Release 7.2 complies with the Entry SQL92 standards, as certified by the National Institute for Standards and Technology (NIST). Oracle is working with ANSI to ensure that future versions of Oracle and PL/SQL comply with the full standard.

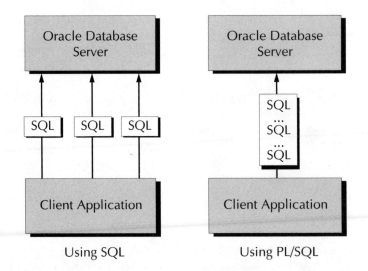

FIGURE 1-1. *PL/SQL in a client-server environment*

Features of PL/SQL

PL/SQL has a number of different features and capabilities, which are best illustrated by example. This section describes some of the main features of the language. We will be examining these features in detail throughout this book.

Block Structure

The basic unit in PL/SQL is a *block*. All PL/SQL programs are made up of blocks, which can be nested within each other. Typically, each block performs a logical unit of work in the program; thus different tasks are separated from each other. A block has the following structure:

DECLARE
> *Declarative section—PL/SQL variables, types, cursors,
> and local subprograms go here.*

BEGIN
> *Executable section—procedural and SQL statements go here.
> This is the main section of the block, and the only one
> that is required.*

EXCEPTION
> *Exception handling section—error handling statements go
> here.*

END;

Only the executable section is required; the declarative and exception handling sections are optional. The different sections of the block separate different functions of a PL/SQL program.

PL/SQL is based on the Ada third-generation language. Many of the constructs available in Ada can also be found in PL/SQL. These include the block structure. Other Ada features which are found in PL/SQL include exception handling the syntax for declaring procedures and functions, and packages. Throughout this book, we will see examples of the similarities between Ada and PL/SQL.

Error Handling

The exception handling section of the block is used for responding to run-time errors encountered by your program. By separating the error handling code from the main body of the program, the structure of the program itself is clear. For example, the following PL/SQL block demonstrates an exception handling section which logs the error received, along with the current time and the user who encountered the error:

```
DECLARE
  v_ErrorCode NUMBER;              -- Code for the error
  v_ErrorMsg  VARCHAR2(200);       -- Message text for the error
  v_CurrentUser VARCHAR2(8);       -- Current database user
  v_Information VARCHAR2(100);     -- Information about the error
BEGIN
  ...
EXCEPTION
  WHEN OTHERS THEN
    -- Assign values to the log variables, using built-in
    -- functions.
    v_ErrorCode := SQLCODE;
    v_ErrorMsg := SQLERRM;
    v_CurrentUser := USER;
    v_Information := 'Error encountered on ' ||
      TO_CHAR(SYSDATE) || ' by database user ' || v_CurrentUser;
    -- Insert the log message into log_table.
    INSERT INTO log_table (code, message, info)
      VALUES (v_ErrorCode, v_ErrorMsg, v_Information);
END;
```

Variables and Types

Information is transmitted between PL/SQL and the database with *variables*. A variable is a storage location which can be read from or assigned to by the program. In the above example, **v_CurrentUser**, **v_ErrorCode**, and **v_Information** are all variables. Variables are declared in the declarative section of the block.

Every variable has a specific *type* associated with it. The type defines what kind of information the variable can hold. PL/SQL variables can be of the same type as database columns:

```
DECLARE
  v_StudentName   VARCHAR2(20);
  v_CurrentDate   DATE;
  v_NumberCredits NUMBER(3);
```

or they can be of additional types:

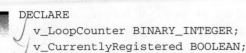

```
DECLARE
  v_LoopCounter BINARY_INTEGER;
  v_CurrentlyRegistered BOOLEAN;
```

PL/SQL also supports user-defined types—tables and records. User-defined types allow you to customize the structure of the data your program manipulates:

```
DECLARE
  TYPE t_StudentRecord IS RECORD (
    FirstName   VARCHAR2(10),
    LastName    VARCHAR2(10),
    CurrentCredits NUMBER(3)
  );
  v_Student t_StudentRecord;
```

Looping Constructs

PL/SQL supports different kinds of loops. A *loop* allows you to execute the same sequence of statements repeatedly. For example, the following block uses a *simple loop* to insert the numbers 1 through 50 into **temp_table**:

```
DECLARE
  v_LoopCounter BINARY_INTEGER := 1;
BEGIN
  LOOP
    INSERT INTO temp_table (num_col)
      VALUES (v_LoopCounter);
    v_LoopCounter := v_LoopCounter + 1;
    EXIT WHEN v_LoopCounter > 50;
  END LOOP;
END;
```

Another type of loop, a *numeric FOR loop*, can be used as well. This looping construct provides a simpler syntax. We can accomplish the same thing as the above example with

```
BEGIN
  FOR v_LoopCounter IN 1..50 LOOP
    INSERT INTO temp_table (num_col)
      VALUES (v_LoopCounter);
  END LOOP;
END;
```

Cursors

A *cursor* is used to process multiple rows retrieved from the database. Using a cursor, your program can step through the set of returned rows one at a time, processing each one in its turn. For example, the following block will retrieve the first and last names of all students in the database:

```
DECLARE
  v_FirstName VARCHAR2(20);
  v_LastName  VARCHAR2(20);
  -- Cursor declaration. This defines the SQL statement to
  -- return the rows.
  CURSOR c_Students IS
    SELECT first_name, last_name
      FROM students;
BEGIN
  -- Begin cursor processing.
  OPEN c_Students;
  LOOP
    -- Retrieve one row.
    FETCH c_Students INTO v_FirstName, v_LastName;
    -- Exit the loop after all rows have been retrieved.
    EXIT WHEN c_Students%NOTFOUND;
    /* Process data here */
  END LOOP;
  -- End processing.
  CLOSE c_Students;
END;
```

PL/SQL and the Different Versions of Oracle

PL/SQL is contained within the Oracle server. The first version of PL/SQL, 1.0, was released with Oracle version 6. Oracle7 contains PL/SQL 2.0. Each subsequent release of the database contains an associated version of PL/SQL. This is outlined in Table 1-1, which also lists the major new features incorporated in each release.

This book discusses PL/SQL versions 2.0 through 2.3. Features that are available only in specific releases are highlighted by icons, as shown here:

 This paragraph discusses a feature available with PL/SQL 2.1 and higher, such as the DBMS_SQL package.

 This paragraph discusses a feature available with PL/SQL 2.2 and higher, such as cursor variables.

 This paragraph discusses a feature available with PL/SQL 2.3 and higher, such as the UTL_FILE package.

Oracle Release	PL/SQL Release	Features Added or Changed
6	1.0	(Initial version)
7.0	2.0	• CHAR datatype changed to fixed-length • Subprograms (procedures, functions, packages, and triggers) • User-defined composite types (tables and records) • Intersession communication with the DBMS_PIPE and DBMS_ALERT packages • Output in SQL*Plus or SQL*DBA with the DBMS_OUTPUT package
7.1	2.1	• User-defined subtypes • Ability to use user-defined functions in SQL statements • Dynamic PL/SQL with the DBMS_SQL package
7.2	2.2	• Cursor variables • User-defined constrained subtypes • Ability to schedule PL/SQL batch processing with the DBMS_JOB package
7.3	2.3	• Enhancements to cursor variables (ability to fetch on the server) • File I/O with the UTL_FILE package PL/SQL table attributes and tables of records • Triggers stored in compiled form

TABLE 1-1.   *Corresponding Versions of Oracle and PL/SQL*

It is important to be aware of the PL/SQL release you are using so you can take advantage of the appropriate features. When you connect to the database, the initial string will contain the database version. For example,

```
Connected to:
Personal ORACLE7 Release 7.1.4.1.0 - Production Release
PL/SQL Release 2.1.4.0.0 - Production
```

and

```
Connected to:
Oracle7 Server Release 7.2.2.3.0 - Production Release
With the distributed, replication and parallel query options
PL/SQL Release 2.2.2.3.0 - Production
```

are both valid initial strings. Note that the PL/SQL release corresponds to the database release.

The majority of the examples in this book were created with Personal Oracle 7.1.4.1.0, running under Microsoft Windows 3.1. The examples for PL/SQL 2.2 and 2.3 were done against Oracle databases running on a Unix system. All of the screen shots were taken under Windows, with Personal Oracle running as the database server.

Example Tables

The examples used in this book operate on a common set of database tables that implement a registration system for a college. There are three main tables: **students**, **classes**, and **rooms**. These contain the main entities necessary for the system. In addition to these main tables, the **registered_students** table contains information about students who have signed up for classes. The following sections detail the structure of these tables, with the SQL necessary to create them.

REMEMBER
The online versions of all the scripts in this book can be found on the World Wide Web at http://www.osborne.com/oracle.

student_sequence
The **student_sequence** sequence is used to generate unique values for the primary key of **students**.

```
CREATE SEQUENCE student_sequence
  START WITH 10000
  INCREMENT BY 1;
```

students
The **students** table contains information about students attending the school.

```
CREATE TABLE students (
  id                NUMBER(5) PRIMARY KEY,
```

```
   first_name       VARCHAR2(20),
   last_name        VARCHAR2(20),
   major            VARCHAR2(30),
   current_credits  NUMBER(3)
   );

INSERT INTO students
   (id, first_name, last_name, major, current_credits)
   VALUES (10000, 'Scott', 'Smith', 'Computer Science', 0);

INSERT INTO students
   (id, first_name, last_name, major, current_credits)
   VALUES (10001, 'Margaret', 'Mason', 'History', 0);

INSERT INTO students
   (id, first_name, last_name, major, current_credits)
   VALUES (10002, 'Joanne', 'Junebug', 'Computer Science', 0);

INSERT INTO students
   (id, first_name, last_name, major, current_credits)
   VALUES (10003, 'Manish', 'Murgratroid', 'Economics', 0);

INSERT INTO students
   (id, first_name, last_name, major, current_credits)
   VALUES(10004, 'Patrick', 'Poll', 'History', 0);

INSERT INTO students
   (id, first_name, last_name, major, current_credits)
   VALUES (10005, 'Timothy', 'Taller', 'History', 0);

INSERT INTO students
   (id, first_name, last_name, major, current_credits)
   VALUES (10006, 'Barbara', 'Blues', 'Economics', 0);

INSERT INTO students
   (id, first_name, last_name, major, current_credits)
   VALUES (10007, 'David', 'Dinsmore', 'Music', 0);

INSERT INTO students
   (id, first_name, last_name, major, current_credits)
   VALUES (10008, 'Ester', 'Elegant', 'Nutrition', 0);

INSERT INTO students
   (id, first_name, last_name, major, current_credits)
```

```
    VALUES (10009, 'Rose', 'Riznit', 'Music', 0);

INSERT INTO students
    (id, first_name, last_name, major, current_credits)
    VALUES (10010, 'Rita', 'Razmataz', 'Nutrition', 0);
```

major_stats

The **major_stats** table holds statistics generated about different majors.

```
CREATE TABLE major_stats (
   major          VARCHAR2(30),
   total_credits  NUMBER,
   total_students NUMBER);
```

rooms

The **rooms** table holds information about the classrooms available.

```
CREATE TABLE rooms (
   room_id          NUMBER(5) PRIMARY KEY,
   building         VARCHAR2(15),
   room_number      NUMBER(4),
   number_seats     NUMBER(4),
   description      VARCHAR2(50)
   );

INSERT INTO rooms
   (room_id, building, room_number, number_seats, description)
   VALUES (99999, 'Building 7', 310, 1000, 'Large Lecture Hall');

INSERT INTO rooms
   (room_id, building, room_number, number_seats, description)
   VALUES (99998, 'Building 6', 101, 500, 'Small Lecture Hall');

INSERT INTO rooms
   (room_id, building, room_number, number_seats, description)
   VALUES (99997, 'Building 6', 150, 50, 'Discussion Room A');

INSERT INTO rooms
   (room_id, building, room_number, number_seats, description)
   VALUES (99996, 'Building 6', 160, 50, 'Discussion Room B');

INSERT INTO rooms
```

```
    (room_id, building, room_number, number_seats, description)
    VALUES (99995, 'Building 6', 170, 50, 'Discussion Room C');

INSERT INTO rooms
    (room_id, building, room_number, number_seats, description)
    VALUES (99994, 'Music Building', 100, 10, 'Music Practice Room');

INSERT INTO rooms
    (room_id, building, room_number, number_seats, description)
    VALUES (99993, 'Music Building', 200, 1000, 'Concert Room');

INSERT INTO rooms
    (room_id, building, room_number, number_seats, description)
    VALUES (99992, 'Building 7', 300, 75, 'Discussion Room D');

INSERT INTO rooms
    (room_id, building, room_number, number_seats, description)
    VALUES (99991, 'Building 7', 310, 50, 'Discussion Room E');
```

classes

The **classes** table describes the classes available for students to take.

```
CREATE TABLE classes (
    department       CHAR(3),
    course           NUMBER(3),
    description      VARCHAR2(2000),
    max_students     NUMBER(3),
    current_students NUMBER(3),
    num_credits      NUMBER(1),
    room_id          NUMBER(5),
    CONSTRAINT classes_department_course
        PRIMARY KEY (department, course),
    CONSTRAINT classes_room_id
        FOREIGN KEY (room_id) REFERENCES rooms (room_id)
    );

INSERT INTO classes
    (department, course, description, max_students,
     current_students, num_credits, room_id)
    VALUES ('HIS', 101, 'History 101', 30, 0, 4, 99999);

INSERT INTO classes
```

```
   (department, course, description, max_students,
    current_students, num_credits, room_id)
   VALUES ('HIS', 301, 'History 301', 30, 0, 4, 99995);

INSERT INTO classes
   (department, course, description, max_students,
    current_students, num_credits, room_id)
   VALUES ('CS', 101, 'Computer Science 101', 50, 0, 4, 99998);

INSERT INTO classes
   (department, course, description, max_students,
    current_students, num_credits, room_id)
   VALUES ('ECN', 203, 'Economics 203', 15, 0, 3, 99997);

INSERT INTO classes
   (department, course, description, max_students,
    current_students, num_credits, room_id)
   VALUES ('CS', 102, 'Computer Science 102', 35, 0, 4, 99996);

INSERT INTO classes
   (department, course, description, max_students,
    current_students, num_credits, room_id)
   VALUES ('MUS', 410, 'Music 410', 5, 0, 3, 99994);

INSERT INTO classes
   (department, course, description, max_students,
    current_students, num_credits, room_id)
   VALUES ('ECN', 101, 'Economics 101', 50, 0, 4, 99992);

INSERT INTO classes
   (department, course, description, max_students,
    current_students, num_credits, room_id)
   VALUES ('NUT', 307, 'Nutrition 307', 20, 0, 4, 99991);
```

registered_students

The **registered_students** table contains information about the classes that students are currently taking.

```
CREATE TABLE registered_students (
   student_id NUMBER(5) NOT NULL,
   department CHAR(3)    NOT NULL,
   course     NUMBER(3) NOT NULL,
```

```
   grade       CHAR(1),
   CONSTRAINT rs_grade
     CHECK (grade IN ('A', 'B', 'C', 'D', 'E')),
   CONSTRAINT rs_student_id
     FOREIGN KEY (student_id) REFERENCES students (id),
   CONSTRAINT rs_department_course
     FOREIGN KEY (department, course)
     REFERENCES classes (department, course)
   );

INSERT INTO registered_students
   (student_id, department, course, grade)
   VALUES (10000, 'CS', 102, 'A');

INSERT INTO registered_students
   (student_id, department, course, grade)
   VALUES (10002, 'CS', 102, 'B');

INSERT INTO registered_students
   (student_id, department, course, grade)
   VALUES (10003, 'CS', 102, 'C');

INSERT INTO registered_students
   (student_id, department, course, grade)
   VALUES (10000, 'HIS', 101, 'A');

INSERT INTO registered_students
   (student_id, department, course, grade)
   VALUES (10001, 'HIS', 101, 'B');

INSERT INTO registered_students
   (student_id, department, course, grade)
   VALUES (10002, 'HIS', 101, 'B');

INSERT INTO registered_students
   (student_id, department, course, grade)
   VALUES (10003, 'HIS', 101, 'A');

INSERT INTO registered_students
   (student_id, department, course, grade)
   VALUES (10004, 'HIS', 101, 'C');

INSERT INTO registered_students
   (student_id, department, course, grade)
```

```
       VALUES (10005, 'HIS', 101, 'C');

INSERT INTO registered_students
   (student_id, department, course, grade)
   VALUES (10006, 'HIS', 101, 'E');

INSERT INTO registered_students
   (student_id, department, course, grade)
   VALUES (10007, 'HIS', 101, 'B');

INSERT INTO registered_students
   (student_id, department, course, grade)
   VALUES (10008, 'HIS', 101, 'A');

INSERT INTO registered_students
   (student_id, department, course, grade)
   VALUES (10009, 'HIS', 101, 'D');

INSERT INTO registered_students
   (student_id, department, course, grade)
   VALUES (10010, 'HIS', 101, 'A');

INSERT INTO registered_students
   (student_id, department, course, grade)
   VALUES (10008, 'NUT', 307, 'A');

INSERT INTO registered_students
   (student_id, department, course, grade)
   VALUES (10010, 'NUT', 307, 'A');

INSERT INTO registered_students
   (student_id, department, course, grade)
   VALUES (10009, 'MUS', 410, 'B');

INSERT INTO registered_students
   (student_id, department, course, grade)
   VALUES (10006, 'MUS', 410, 'E');
```

RS_audit

The **RS_audit** table is used to record changes made to **registered_students**.

```
CREATE TABLE RS_audit (
  change_type    CHAR(1)      NOT NULL,
  changed_by     VARCHAR2(8)  NOT NULL,
  timestamp      DATE         NOT NULL,
  old_student_id NUMBER(5),
  old_department CHAR(3),
  old_course     NUMBER(3),
  old_grade      CHAR(1),
  new_student_id NUMBER(5),
  new_department CHAR(3),
  new_course     NUMBER(3),
  new_grade      CHAR(1)
  );
```

log_table

The **log_table** table is used to record Oracle errors.

```
CREATE TABLE log_table (
  code              NUMBER,
  message           VARCHAR2(200),
  info              VARCHAR2(100)
  );
```

temp_table

The **temp_table** table is used to store temporary data that is not necessarily relevant to the other information.

```
CREATE TABLE temp_table (
  num_col    NUMBER,
  char_col   VARCHAR2(60)
  );
```

debug_table

The **debug_table** table is used by the Debug package to hold PL/SQL debugging information. (We'll develop the Debug package in Chapter 8.)

```
CREATE TABLE debug_table (
  linecount   NUMBER,
  debug_str   VARCHAR2(100)
  );
```

Summary

This chapter has presented a broad overview of PL/SQL, including the purpose of the language and the major features. We've discussed the importance of PL/SQL and database versions, and how they correspond. The chapter concluded with a description of the example tables used in this book. In the next chapter we will begin our detailed exploration of the language, starting with the syntax and constructs of PL/SQL.

CHAPTER 2

PL/SQL Syntax and Constructs

Before talking about the advanced features of PL/SQL, we must cover its basic syntax. Syntax rules form the building blocks of any programming language, PL/SQL included. This chapter discusses the components of a PL/SQL block, variable declarations and data types—the basic procedural constructs—and gives a brief introduction to cursors and subprograms. It also covers PL/SQL style, presenting techniques that can help you write easily understood code.

All PL/SQL statements are either procedural or SQL statements. *Procedural statements* include variable declarations, procedure calls, and looping constructs. *SQL statements* are used to access the database. This chapter focuses on the procedural statements of PL/SQL, and Chapters 3 and 4 cover SQL statements.

The PL/SQL Block

The basic unit in any PL/SQL program is a block. All PL/SQL programs are composed of blocks, which can occur sequentially (one after the other) or nested (one inside the other). There are several different kinds of blocks:

- ■ *Anonymous blocks* are generally constructed dynamically and executed only once.

- ■ *Named blocks* are anonymous blocks with a label that gives the block a name. These are also generally constructed dynamically and executed only once.

- ■ *Subprograms* are procedures, packages, and functions that are stored in the database. These blocks generally don't change once they are constructed, and they are executed many times. Subprograms are executed explicitly via a call to the procedure, package, or function.

- ■ *Triggers* are named blocks that are also stored in the database. They also generally don't change once they are constructed and are executed many times. Triggers are executed implicitly whenever the triggering event occurs. The triggering event is a data manipulation language (DML) statement executed against a table in the database. DML statements include INSERT, UPDATE, and DELETE.

For example, the following is an anonymous PL/SQL block that inserts a single row into the classes table:

```
DECLARE
   /* Declare variables to be used in the block. */
   v_Department        CHAR(3)     := 'ECN';
   v_Course            NUMBER(3)   := 203;
   v_Description       VARCHAR2(20) := 'Economics 203';
   v_MaxStudents       NUMBER := 15;
   v_CurrentStudents   NUMBER := 0;
   v_NumCredits        NUMBER := 3;
   v_RoomID            NUMBER := 99997;
BEGIN
   /* Add a row to the classes table, using the values of the
      variables. */
   INSERT INTO classes (department, course, description, max_students,
                   current_students, num_credits, room_id)
      VALUES (v_Department, v_Course, v_Description, v_MaxStudents,
```

```
                   v_CurrentStudents, v_NumCredits, v_RoomID);
END;
```

In order to name this block, we put a label before the DECLARE keyword, as in the next example. The label can optionally appear after the END keyword as well. Labels will be discussed in more detail later in this chapter.

```
<<l_AddNewRow>>
DECLARE
  /* Declare variables to be used in the block. */
  v_Department       CHAR(3)   := 'ECN';
  v_Course           NUMBER(3) := 203;
  v_Description      VARCHAR2(20) := 'Economics 203';
  v_MaxStudents      NUMBER := 15;
  v_CurrentStudents  NUMBER := 0;
  v_NumCredits       NUMBER := 3;
  v_RoomID           NUMBER := 99997;
BEGIN
  /* Add a row to the classes table, using the values of the
     variables. */
  INSERT INTO classes (department, course, description, max_students,
                       current_students, num_credits, room_id)
    VALUES (v_Department, v_Course, v_Description, v_MaxStudents,
            v_CurrentStudents, v_NumCredits, v_RoomID);
END l_AddNewRow;
```

We can make this block into a stored procedure by replacing the **DECLARE** keyword with the **CREATE PROCEDURE** keywords. Procedures are discussed in more detail in Chapter 5. Again, notice that the procedure name is used after the **END** keyword:

```
CREATE PROCEDURE AddNewRow AS
  /* Declare variables to be used in the block. */
  v_Department       CHAR(3)   := 'ECN';
  v_Course           NUMBER(3) := 203;
  v_Description      VARCHAR2(20) := 'Economics 203';
  v_MaxStudents      NUMBER := 15;
  v_CurrentStudents  NUMBER := 0;
  v_NumCredits       NUMBER := 3;
  v_RoomID           NUMBER := 99997;
BEGIN
  /* Add a row to the classes table, using the values of the
     variables. */
```

```
    INSERT INTO classes (department, course, description, max_students,
                    current_students, num_credits, room_id)
      VALUES (v_Department, v_Course, v_Description, v_MaxStudents,
             v_CurrentStudents, v_NumCredits, v_RoomID);
END AddNewRow;
```

Finally, we can construct a trigger on the classes table to verify that the room ID specified actually exists, and signal an error if it doesn't. Triggers are discussed in more detail in Chapter 5 as well. This trigger will be called whenever a new row is inserted into the classes table or an existing row is updated.

```
CREATE OR REPLACE TRIGGER CheckRoomID
  BEFORE INSERT OR UPDATE OF room_id
  ON classes
  FOR EACH ROW
DECLARE
  /* Temporary variable to hold the room ID */
  v_RoomID   NUMBER(5);
BEGIN
  /* Check to see if the room ID is valid by querying the
     rooms table. */
  SELECT room_id
    into v_RoomID
    FROM rooms
    where room_id = :new.room_id;
EXCEPTION
  WHEN NO_DATA_FOUND THEN
    /* We will get here when the room ID is not found. In this case
       raise an error indicating that the room ID is not valid. This
       will also cause the INSERT statement to fail. */
    RAISE_APPLICATION_ERROR(-20000, :new.room_id || ' is not a ' ||
       ' valid room');
END CheckRoomID;
```

The above functionality can also be accomplished through a declarative integrity constraint, but the trigger allows us to raise a more meaningful error message.

Basic Block Structure

All blocks have three distinct sections—the declarative section, executable section, and exception section. Only the executable section is required; the other two are optional. For example, here is an anonymous block with all three sections:

```
DECLARE
  /* Start of declarative section */
  v_StudentID NUMBER(5) := 10000;  -- Numeric variable initialized
                                   -- to 10,000
  v_FirstName VARCHAR2(20);        -- Variable-length character string
                                   -- with maximum length of 20
BEGIN
  /* Start of executable section */
  -- Retrieve first name of student with ID 10,000
  SELECT first_name
    INTO v_FirstName
    FROM students
    WHERE id = v_StudentID;
EXCEPTION
  /* Start of exception section */
  WHEN NO_DATA_FOUND THEN
    -- Handle the error condition
    INSERT INTO log_table (info)
      VALUES ('Student 10,000 does not exist!');
END;
```

The *declarative section* is where all variables, cursors, and types used by this block are located. Local procedures and functions can also be declared in this section. These subprograms will be available for this block only. The remainder of this chapter explains the declarative section in more detail.

The *executable section* is where the work of the block is done. Both SQL statements and procedural statements can appear in this section. Chapters 3 and 4 cover the contents of the executable section.

Errors are handled in the *exception section*. Code in this section is not executed unless an error occurs. Chapter 6 deals with the exception section and how it is used to detect and handle errors.

The keywords DECLARE, BEGIN, EXCEPTION, and END delimit each section. The final semicolon is also required—this is a syntactic part of the block. Based on this, the skeleton of an anonymous block looks like this:

```
DECLARE
  /* Declarative section is here */
BEGIN
  /* Executable section is here */
EXCEPTION
  /* Exception section is here */
END;
```

NOTE
The DECLARE keyword is not necessary when creating a subprogram. In fact, it is an error to use it. However, DECLARE is required when creating a trigger. See Chapter 5 for more information.

If the declarative section is absent, the block starts with the BEGIN keyword. If the exception section is absent, the EXCEPTION keyword is omitted and the END keyword followed by a semicolon finishes the block. So a block with just the executable section would be structured like this:

```
BEGIN
  /* Executable section is here */
END;
```

while a block with declarative and executable sections, but no exception section, would look like this:

```
DECLARE
  /* Declarative section is here */
BEGIN
  /* Executable section is here */
END;
```

Lexical Units

Any PL/SQL program is made up of lexical units—the building blocks of a language. Essentially, a *lexical unit* is a sequence of characters, in the character set allowed for the PL/SQL language. This character set includes

■ Upper- and lowercase letters A-Z and a-z

■ Digits 0-9

- White space: tabs, spaces, and carriage returns
- Mathematical symbols: + – * / < > =
- Punctuation symbols: ( ) { } [ ] ? ! ~ ; : . ' " @ # % $ ^ & _ ¦

Any symbol in the character set, and only the symbols in the character set, can be used as part of a PL/SQL program. Like SQL, PL/SQL is not case-sensitive. Thus, upper- and lowercase letters are equivalent, except inside quoted strings.

The standard PL/SQL character set is part of the ASCII character set. ASCII is a single-byte character set, which means that every character can be represented as one byte of data. This limits the total number of characters to 256. Oracle does have support for other multibyte character sets, which have more than 256 characters. These are necessary to represent languages that do not use the English alphabet. A full discussion of multibyte characters is beyond the scope of this book—consult the Oracle documentation for more information.

Lexical units can be classified as identifiers, delimiters, literals, and comments.

Identifiers

Identifiers are used to name PL/SQL objects, such as variables, cursors, and subprograms. Identifiers consist of a letter optionally followed by any sequence of characters including letters, numbers, dollar signs, underscores, and pound signs. Other characters are illegal. The maximum length for an identifier is 30 characters, and all characters are significant. For example, here are some legal identifiers:

```
x
v_StudentID
TempVar
v1
v2_
social_security_#
```

Here are some illegal identifiers:

```
x+y                              -- Illegal character +
_temp_                           -- Must start with a letter,
                                    not an underscore
First Name                       -- Illegal space
This_is_a_really_long_identifier -- More than 30 characters
1_variable                       -- Can't start with a digit
```

Since PL/SQL is not case-sensitive, the following identifiers all mean the same thing to PL/SQL:

```
Room_Description
room_description
ROOM_DESCRIPTION
rOOm_DEscriPTIOn
```

It is good programming practice to have a consistent naming scheme for identifiers and to make them descriptive. See the section "PL/SQL Style Guide" at the end of this chapter for more information.

Reserved Words

Many identifiers, known as *reserved words* (or keywords), have special meaning to PL/SQL. It is illegal to use these words to name your own identifiers. For example, BEGIN and END are used to delimit PL/SQL blocks. Thus you cannot use them as variable names. For example, the following declarative section is illegal and will generate a compile error:

```
DECLARE
  begin number;
```

These words are only reserved when used as identifiers by themselves. They can appear within other identifiers. The following declarative section is legal:

```
DECLARE
  v_BeginDate  DATE;
```

In this book, reserved words are written in uppercase to improve readability. See the section "PL/SQL Style Guide" at the end of this chapter for more information. Appendix A contains a complete list of reserved words.

Quoted Identifiers

If you want to make an identifier case-sensitive, include characters such as spaces, or use a reserved word, you can enclose the identifier in double quotation marks. For example, all of the following are legal and distinct identifiers:

```
"A number"
"Linda's variable"
"x/y"
"X/Y"
```

Like nonquoted identifiers, the maximum length of a quoted identifier is 30 characters (not including the double quotes). Any printable character is legal as part of a quoted identifier except a double quote.

Quoted identifiers can be useful when you want to use a PL/SQL reserved word in an SQL statement. PL/SQL reserves more words than SQL (this is also indicated by the chart in Appendix A). For example, if you wanted to query a table with a column called "exception" (a reserved word) you could access it with

```
DECLARE
  v_Exception    VARCHAR2(10);
BEGIN
  SELECT "EXCEPTION"
    INTO v_Exception
    FROM exception_table;
END;
```

Note that **"EXCEPTION"** is in uppercase. All identifiers are stored in uppercase in the data dictionary, unless explicitly created as a quoted identifier and lowercase in the table CREATE statement.

I don't recommend using reserved words for identifiers, even though it is legal. It is poor programming style and can make the program more difficult to understand. The only case where this may become necessary is when a database table uses a PL/SQL reserved word for a column name. Because PL/SQL has more reserved words than SQL, a table may have a column that is a PL/SQL reserved word, but not an SQL reserved word. The **exception_table** table in the previous example illustrates this case.

TIP
Although **exception_table** can still be used in PL/SQL, it is better to rename the offending column. If the table definition cannot be changed, a view can be created with an alternate name for the column. This view can then be used in PL/SQL. For example, suppose we created **exception_table** with

```
CREATE TABLE exception_table (
  exception       VARCHAR2(20),
  date_occurred   DATE);
```

Given this definition, we can create a view with

```
CREATE VIEW exception_view (
  exception_description    VARCHAR2(20),
  date_occurred            DATE);
```

The column can now be referred to as **exception_description**, which is not reserved.

Delimiters

Delimiters are symbols (either a single character or a sequence of characters) that have special meaning to PL/SQL. They are used to separate identifiers from each other. Table 2-1 includes the delimiters available to PL/SQL.

Symbol	Description
+	Addition operator
–	Subtraction operator
*	Multiplication operator
/	Division operator
=	Equality operator
<	Less-than operator
>	Greater-than operator
(	Initial expression delimiter
)	Final expression delimiter
;	Statement terminator
%	Attribute indicator
,	Item separator
.	Component selector
@	Database link indicator
'	Character string delimiter
"	Quoted string delimiter
:	Bind variable indicator
**	Exponentiation operator
<>	Not-equal-to operator
!=	Not-equal-to operator (equivalent to <>)
~=	Not-equal-to operator (equivalent to !=)
^=	Not-equal-to operator (equivalent to ~=)
<=	Less-than-or-equal-to operator
>=	Greater-than-or-equal-to operator
:=	Assignment operator

TABLE 2-1. *PL/SQL Delimiters*

Symbol	Description
=>	Association operator
..	Range operator
¦¦	String concatenation operator
<<	Begin label delimiter
>>	End label delimiter
--	Single line comment indicator
/*	Initial multiline comment indicator
*/	Final multiline comment indicator
<space>	Space
<tab>	Tab character
<cr>	Carriage return

TABLE 2-1.   *PL/SQL Delimiters* (continued)

Literals

A *literal* is a character, numeric, or boolean value that is not an identifier.
As an example, −23.456 and NULL are both literals. The boolean, character, and
numeric types are discussed in the section "PL/SQL Types" later in this chapter.

Character Literals

Character literals, also known as *string literals,* consist of one or more characters
delimited by single quotes. Character literals can be assigned to variables of type
CHAR or VARCHAR2 without conversion. For example, all of the following are
legal string literals:

```
'12345'
'Four score and seven years ago...'
'100%'
' " '
```

All string literals are considered to have the datatype CHAR. Any printable
character in the PL/SQL character set can be part of a literal, including another
single quote. Since a single quote is also used to delimit the literal, to include a
single quote as part of the string, place two single quotes next to each other. For
example, to put the string "Mike's string" into a literal, we would use

```
'Mike''s string'
```

Thus, in PL/SQL, the string that consists of just a single quote would be identified by

```
''''
```

The first single quote delimits the start of the string, the next two identify the only character in the string (which happens to be a single quote), and the fourth quote delimits the end of the string. Note that this is different from the literal

```
''
```

which denotes a zero-length string. In PL/SQL, the zero-length string literal is considered identical to NULL.

Numeric Literals

A numeric literal represents either an integer or real value. Numeric literals can be assigned to variables of type NUMBER without conversion. These are the only literals that are valid as part of arithmetic expressions. Integer literals consist of an optional sign (+ or –) followed by digits. No decimal point is allowed for an integer literal. The following are legal integer literals:

```
123
-7
+12
0
```

A real literal consists of an optional sign followed by digits containing one decimal point. The following are all legal real literals:

```
-17.1
23.0
3.
```

Even though **23.0** and **3.** actually contain numbers with no fractional part, they are still considered real literals by PL/SQL. Real literals can also be written using scientific notation if desired. The following are also legal real literals:

```
1.345E7
9.87E-3
-7.12e+12
```

After the **E** or **e**, there can be only an integer literal. The **E** stands for "exponent" and can be interpreted as "times 10 to the power of." So the preceding three values can also be read as

```
1.345E7 = 1.345 times 10 to the power of 7
        = 1.345 x 10,000,000
        = 13,450,000
9.87E-3 = 9.87 times 10 to the power of -3
        = 9.87 x .001
        = 0.00987
-7.12e+12 = -7.12 times 10 to the power of 12
          = -7.12 x 1,000,000,000,000
          = -7,120,000,000,000
```

(The commas are included for readability—commas are not allowed in numeric literals.)

Boolean Literals
There are only three possible boolean literals: TRUE, FALSE, and NULL. These values can only be assigned to a boolean variable. Boolean literals represent the truth or falsity of conditions and are used in IF and LOOP statements.

Comments

Comments improve readability and make your programs more understandable. They are ignored by the PL/SQL engine. There are two kinds of comments: single-line comments and multiline or C-style comments.

Single-line Comments
A single-line comment starts with two dashes and continues until the end of the line (delimited by a carriage return). Given this PL/SQL block,

```
DECLARE
  v_Department  CHAR(3);
  v_Course      NUMBER;
BEGIN
  INSERT INTO classes (department, course)
    VALUES (v_Department, v_Course);
END;
```

we can add single-line comments to make this block more understandable. For example:

```
DECLARE
  v_Department  CHAR(3);   -- Variable to hold the 3 character
```

```
                                -- department code
  v_Course        NUMBER;    -- Variable to hold the course number
BEGIN
  -- Insert the course identified by v_Department and v_Course
  -- into the classes table in the database.
  INSERT INTO classes (department, course)
    VALUES (v_Department, v_Course);
END;
```

NOTE
If the comment extends over more than one line, the double dash (--)
is necessary at the start of each line.

Multiline Comments

Multiline comments start with the **/*** delimiter and end with the ***/** delimiter. This is
the same style of comments as used in the C language. For example:

```
DECLARE
  v_Department  CHAR(3);    /* Variable to hold the 3 character
                               department name */
  v_Course      NUMBER;    /* Variable to hold the course number */
BEGIN
  /* Insert the course identified by v_Department and v_Course
     into the classes table in the database. */
  INSERT INTO classes (department, course)
    VALUES (v_Department, v_Course);
END;
```

Multiline comments can extend over as many lines as desired. However, they
cannot be nested. One comment has to end before another can begin. The
following block is illegal because it contains nested comments.

```
BEGIN
  /* We are now inside a comment. If we were to begin another
     comment such as /* this */ it would be illegal. */
  NULL;
END;
```

Variable Declarations

Communication with the database takes place via variables in the PL/SQL block.
Variables are memory locations, which can store data values. As the program runs,

the contents of variables can and do change. Information from the database can be assigned to a variable, or the contents of a variable can be inserted into the database. These variables are declared in the declarative section of the block. Every variable has a specific type as well, which describes what kind of information can be stored in it. Types are discussed shortly.

Declaration Syntax

Variables are declared in the declarative section of the block. The general syntax for declaring a variable is

>   *variable_name type* [CONSTANT] [NOT NULL] [:= *value*];

where *variable_name* is the name of the variable, *type* is the type, and *value* is the initial value of the variable. For example, the following are all legal variable declarations:

```
DECLARE
    v_Description      VARCHAR2(50);
    v_NumberSeats      NUMBER := 45;
    v_Counter          BINARY_INTEGER := 0;
```

Any legal PL/SQL identifier can be used as a variable name. PL/SQL identifiers are defined in the earlier section "Lexical Units." VARCHAR2, NUMBER and BINARY_INTEGER are valid PL/SQL types. In this example, **v_NumberSeats** and **v_Counter** are both initialized, to 45 and 0 respectively. If a variable is not initialized, such as **v_Description**, it is assigned the nonvalue NULL by default. If NOT NULL is present in the declaration, then the variable must be initialized. Furthermore, it is illegal to assign NULL to a variable constrained to be NOT NULL in the executable or exception section of the block. The following declaration is illegal because **v_TempVar** is constrained to be NOT NULL, but is not initialized:

```
DECLARE
    v_TempVar   NUMBER NOT NULL;
```

We can correct this by assigning a default value to **v_TempVar**, for example:

```
DECLARE
    v_TempVar   NUMBER NOT NULL := 0;
```

If CONSTANT is present in the variable declaration, the variable must be initialized, and its value cannot be changed from this initial value. A constant variable is treated as read-only for the remainder of the block. Constants are often used for values that are known when the block is written. For example:

```
DECLARE
   c_MinimumStudentID  CONSTANT NUMBER(5) := 10000;
```

If desired, the keyword DEFAULT can be used instead of := as well

```
DECLARE
   v_NumberSeats   NUMBER DEFAULT 45;
   v_Counter       BINARY_INTEGER DEFAULT 0;
   v_FirstName     VARCHAR2(20) DEFAULT 'Scott';
```

There can be only one variable declaration per line in the declarative section. The following section is illegal, since two variables are declared on the same line:

```
DECLARE
   v_FirstName, v_LastName  VARCHAR2(20);
```

The correct version of this block would be

```
DECLARE
   v_FirstName VARCHAR2(20);
   v_LastName  VARCHAR2(20);
```

Variable Initialization

Many languages do not define what uninitialized variables contain. As a result, uninitialized variables can contain random or unknown values at run time. This is not good programming style. In general, it is best to initialize a variable if its value can be determined.

PL/SQL, however, does define what an uninitialized variable contains—it is assigned the nonvalue NULL. NULL simply means "missing or unknown value." As a result, it is logical that NULL be assigned by default to any uninitialized variable. This is a unique feature of PL/SQL. Many other programming languages (C and Ada included) do not define the behavior for uninitialized variables.

PL/SQL Types

All PL/SQL types are either scalar, composite, or reference. Scalar datatypes do not have any components within the type, while composite types do. A reference type

```
        SCALAR TYPES                          COMPOSITE TYPES
Numeric Family:      Character Family:    TABLE
  NUMBER               VARCHAR2           RECORD
  DEC                  VARCHAR
  DECIMAL              CHAR
  DOUBLE PRECISION     CHARACTER
  INTEGER              LONG                    REFERENCE TYPES
  INT                                      REF CURSOR
  NUMERIC            Raw Family:
  REAL                 RAW
  SMALLINT             LONG RAW
  BINARY_INTEGER
  NATURAL            Date Family:
  POSITIVE             DATE

Boolean Family:      Rowid Family:
  BOOLEAN              ROWID

Trusted Family:
  MLSLABEL
```

FIGURE 2-1.   *PL/SQL types*

is a pointer to another type. Figure 2-1 lists all of the PL/SQL types, and they are described in the following sections.

PL/SQL types are defined in a package called STANDARD. The contents of this package are available to any PL/SQL block. Besides types, package STANDARD defines the built-in SQL and conversion functions available in PL/SQL.

Scalar Types

The legal scalar types consist of the same types valid for a database column, with a number of additions. Scalar types can be divided into seven families—numeric, character, raw, date, rowid, boolean, and trusted—each of which is described in the following sections.

Numeric Family
Types in the numeric family store integer or real values. There are two basic types—NUMBER and BINARY_INTEGER. Variables of type NUMBER can hold either an integer or real quantity, and variables of type BINARY_INTEGER can hold only integers.

Declaration	Assigned Value	Stored Value
NUMBER;	1234.5678	1234.5678
NUMBER(3);	123	123
NUMBER(3);	1234	Error—exceeds precision
NUMBER(3,4);	123.4567	123.4567
NUMBER(3,4);	123.45678	123.4568[1]
NUMBER(3, –3)	1234	1000[2]
NUMBER(3, –1)	1234	1230[2]

TABLE 2-2. *Precision and Scale Values*

[1] If the assigned value exceeds the scale, the stored value is rounded to the number of digits specified by the scale.
[2] If the scale is negative, the stored value is rounded to the number of digits specified by the scale, to the left of the decimal point.

NUMBER   This type can hold a numeric value, either integer or floating point. It is the same as the number database type. The syntax for declaring a number is

    NUMBER (*P,S*);

where *P* is the precision and *S* is the scale. The precision is the number of digits in the value, and the scale is the number of digits to the right of the decimal point. Both precision and scale are optional, but if scale is present, precision must be present as well. Table 2-2 shows different combinations of precision and scale and their meanings.

The maximum precision is 38 and the scale ranges from –84 to 127.

A *subtype* is an alternate name for a type, which can optionally constrain the legal values for a variable of the subtype. Subtypes are explained in detail in the "User-Defined Subtypes" section later in this chapter. There are a number of subtypes that are equivalent to NUMBER, which essentially rename the NUMBER datatype, since none of them are constrained. You may want to use an alternate name for readability, or for compatibility with datatypes from other databases. These are the equivalent types:

- DEC
- DECIMAL

- DOUBLE PRECISION
- INTEGER
- INT
- NUMERIC
- REAL
- SMALLINT

BINARY_INTEGER   The NUMBER type is stored in a decimal format, which is optimized for accuracy and storage efficiency. Because of this, arithmetic operations can't be performed directly on NUMBERs. In order to compute using numeric quantities, NUMBERs must be converted into a binary type. The PL/SQL engine will do this automatically before computations are done and convert the results back to NUMBER afterwards.

However, if you have a value that won't be stored in the database, but will only be used for computations, the BINARY_INTEGER datatype is available. This datatype is used to store signed integer values, which range from –2147483647 to +2147483647. It is stored in a 2's complement binary format, which means that it is available for computations without conversion. Loop counters are often of type BINARY_INTEGER.

Like NUMBER, there are subtypes defined for BINARY_INTEGER. Unlike the NUMBER subtypes, however, the BINARY_INTEGER subtypes are *constrained*, which means that they can only hold restricted values. Variables of subtype NATURAL can have values from 0 to 2147483647, and variables of subtype POSITIVE can have values from 1 to 2147483647.

Character Family
Variables in the character family are used to hold strings, or character data. The types in the character family are VARCHAR2, CHAR, and LONG.

VARCHAR2   This type behaves similarly to the VARCHAR2 database type. Variables of type VARCHAR2 can hold variable-length character strings, with a maximum length. The syntax for declaring a VARCHAR2 variable is

    VARCHAR2(*L*);

where *L* is the maximum length of the variable. The length is required—there is no default. The maximum length for a VARCHAR2 variable is 32,767 bytes. Note that a VARCHAR2 database column can only hold 2000 bytes. If a VARCHAR2 PL/SQL variable is more than 2000 bytes, it can only be inserted into a database column of type LONG, which has a maximum length of 2 gigabytes. Likewise, LONG data cannot be selected into a VARCHAR2 variable unless it is 2,000 bytes or less in length.

The length of a VARCHAR2 is specified in bytes, not in characters. The actual data is stored in the character set for your database, which could be ASCII or EBCDIC Code Page 500, for example. If the database character contains multibyte characters, the maximum number of characters that a VARCHAR2 variable can hold may be less than the length specified. This is because a single character may take more than one byte to represent.

The subtype VARCHAR is equivalent to VARCHAR2.

CHAR   Variables of this type are fixed-length character strings. The syntax for declaring a CHAR variable is

    CHAR(L);

where L is the maximum length, in bytes. Unlike VARCHAR2, however, specifying the length is optional. If it is not specified, it defaults to 1. Since CHAR variables are fixed-length, they are blank-padded if necessary to fill out the maximum length. Because they are blank-padded, CHAR variables won't necessarily match in a character comparison. See the section "Boolean Expressions" later in this chapter for more information on character comparisons.

The maximum length of a CHAR variable is 32,767 bytes. The maximum length of a CHAR database column is 255 bytes. Therefore, if a CHAR variable contains more than 255 bytes, it can only be inserted into a VARCHAR2 or LONG database column. Similarly, LONG data can only be selected into a CHAR variable if it is less than 32,767 bytes.

Like VARCHAR2, the length of a CHAR variable is specified in bytes, not characters. If the database character set contains multibyte characters, then the maximum number of characters a CHAR variable can hold may be less than the length specified.

CHARACTER is a subtype for CHAR, with the same restrictions. VARCHAR2 and CHAR variables have significantly different comparison semantics (see the section "Boolean Expressions" later in this chapter for more information).

LONG   Unlike the database LONG type, which can hold up to 2 gigabytes of data, the PL/SQL LONG type is a variable-length string with a maximum length of 32,760 bytes. LONG variables are very similar to VARCHAR2 variables. Similar to the behavior for VARCHAR2 variables, if a LONG database column contains more than 32,760 bytes of data, it cannot be selected into a PL/SQL LONG variable. However, since the maximum length of a PL/SQL LONG is less than a database

LONG, a PL/SQL LONG can be inserted into a database column of type LONG with no restrictions.

Raw Family

The types in the raw family are used to store binary data. Character variables are automatically converted between character sets by Oracle if necessary. This can happen if the data is being passed via a database link between two databases, each using different character sets. This will not happen for raw variables.

RAW   RAW variables are similar to CHAR variables, except that they are not converted between character sets. The syntax for specifying a RAW variable is

  RAW(*L*);

where *L* is the length in bytes of the variable. RAW is used to store fixed-length binary data. Unlike character data, RAW data is not converted between character sets when transmitted between two different databases. The maximum length of a RAW variable is 32,767 bytes. The maximum length of a RAW database column is 255 bytes. So if the data is more than 255 bytes in length, it cannot be inserted into a RAW database column. It can be inserted, however, into a LONG RAW database column, which has a maximum length of 2 gigabytes. Similarly, if the data in a LONG RAW database column is more than 32,767 bytes in length, it cannot be selected into a PL/SQL RAW variable.

LONG RAW   LONG RAW data is similar to LONG data, except that PL/SQL will not convert between character sets. The maximum length of a LONG RAW variable is 32,760 bytes. Again, since the maximum length of a database LONG RAW column is 2 gigabytes, if the actual length of the data is more than 32,760 bytes in length, it cannot be selected into a PL/SQL LONG RAW variable. But since the maximum length of a PL/SQL LONG RAW will fit into a database LONG RAW, there are no restrictions on insertion of PL/SQL LONG RAWs into a database LONG RAW.

Date Family

There is only one type in the date family—DATE. The DATE PL/SQL type behaves the same way as the DATE database type. The DATE type is used to store both date and time information, including the century, year, month, day, hour, minute, and second. A DATE variable is 7 bytes, with one byte for each component (century through second).

   Values are usually assigned to DATE variables via the TO_DATE built-in function. This allows character variables to be converted to DATE variables with ease. Likewise, the TO_CHAR function can convert from DATE to character. The built-in conversion functions are described in the "Converting Between Datatypes" section later in this chapter, and also in Chapter 3.

Rowid Family

The only type in the rowid family is ROWID. The ROWID PL/SQL type is the same as the database ROWID pseudocolumn type. It can hold a *rowid*, which can be thought of as a unique key for every row in the database. Rowids are stored internally as a fixed-length binary quantity, whose length varies between operating systems. In order to manipulate rowids, they can be converted to character strings via the built-in function ROWIDTOCHAR. The output of this function is an 18-character string with this format:

```
BBBBBBBB.RRRR.FFFF
```

where BBBBBBBB identifies the block within a database file, RRRR the row within the block, and FFFF the file number. Each component of a rowid is represented as a hexadecimal number. For example, the rowid

```
0000001E.00FF.0001
```

identifies the 30th block, the 255th row within this block, in file 1. Rowids are not generally constructed by a PL/SQL program; they are selected from the ROWID pseudocolumn of a table. This value can then be used in the where clause of a subsequent UPDATE or DELETE statement.

Boolean Family

The only datatype in the Boolean family is BOOLEAN. Booleans are used in PL/SQL control structures, such as IF-THEN-ELSE and LOOP statements. A BOOLEAN value can hold TRUE, FALSE, or NULL only. Thus, the following PL/SQL is illegal since 0 is not a valid BOOLEAN value:

```
DECLARE
  v_ContinueFlag  BOOLEAN := 0;
```

Trusted Family

The only datatype in the trusted family is MLSLABEL. This datatype is used in Trusted Oracle to store variable-length binary labels. With standard Oracle, variables and table columns of type MLSLABEL can only hold the value NULL. Internally, MLSLABEL variables are between 2 and 5 bytes in length. However, they can be converted to and from a character variable automatically. The maximum length of a character representation of an MLSLABEL is 255 bytes.

Composite Types

The two composite types available in PL/SQL are records and tables. A *composite type* is one that has components within it. A variable of a composite type contains one or more scalar variables. The composite types are discussed in the "PL/SQL Records and Tables" section later in this chapter.

Reference Types

 PL/SQL 2.2 ...and HIGHER Once a variable is declared of a scalar or composite type in PL/SQL, the memory storage for this variable is allocated. The variable names this storage and is used to refer to it later in the program. However, there is no way to deallocate the storage and still have the variable remain available—the memory is not freed until the variable is no longer in scope. (See the section "Variable Scope and Visibility" later in this chapter for information on scope.) A reference type does not have this restriction. A *reference type* in PL/SQL is the same as a pointer in C. A variable that is declared of a reference type can point to different storage locations over the life of the program.

The only reference type available with PL/SQL 2.2 is REF CURSOR. This type, also known as a cursor variable, will be discussed in detail in Chapter 4. Future versions of PL/SQL will likely have additional reference types.

Using %TYPE

In many cases, a PL/SQL variable will be used to manipulate data stored in a database table. In this case, the variable should have the same type as the table column. For example, the **first_name** column of the **students** table has type VARCHAR2(20). Based on this, we can declare a variable as follows:

```
DECLARE
  v_FirstName    VARCHAR2(20);
```

This is fine, but what happens if the definition of **first_name** is changed? Say the table is altered and **first_name** now has type VARCHAR2(25). Any PL/SQL code that uses this column would have to be changed, as shown here:

```
DECLARE
  v_FirstName   VARCHAR2(25);
```

If you have a large amount of PL/SQL code, this can be a time-consuming and error-prone process. Rather than hardcode the type of a variable in this way, you can use the %TYPE attribute. This attribute is appended to a table column reference, or another variable, and returns its type. For example:

```
DECLARE
  v_FirstName  students.first_name%TYPE;
```

By using %TYPE, **v_FirstName** will have whatever type the **first_name** column of the **students** table has. The type is determined each time the block is run for anonymous and named blocks, and whenever stored objects (procedures, functions, and so on) are compiled. %TYPE can also be applied to an earlier PL/SQL variable declaration. The following example shows various applications of the %TYPE attribute:

```
DECLARE
  v_RoomID      classes.room_id%TYPE;     -- Returns NUMBER(5)
  v_RoomID2     v_RoomID%TYPE;            -- Returns NUMBER(5)
  v_TempVar     NUMBER(7,3) NOT NULL := 12.3;
  v_AnotherVar  v_TempVar%TYPE;           -- Returns NUMBER(7,3)
```

If %TYPE is applied to a variable or column that is constrained to be NOT NULL (such as **classes.room_id** or **v_TempVar**), the type it returns does not have this restriction. The preceding block is still legal, since even though **v_RoomID**, **v_RoomID2**, and **v_AnotherVar** are not initialized, they can hold NULL values.

It is good programming style to use %TYPE, since it makes a PL/SQL program more flexible and able to adapt to changing database definitions.

User-Defined Subtypes

PL/SQL 2.1 ...and HIGHER A subtype is a PL/SQL type that is based on an existing type. A subtype can be used to give an alternate name for a type, which describes its intended use. PL/SQL defines several subtypes (for example DECIMAL and INTEGER are subtypes of NUMBER) in package STANDARD. With PL/SQL 2.1 and higher, you can define subtypes as well, in addition to the predefined subtypes. The syntax is

SUBTYPE *new_type* IS *original_type*;

where *new_type* is the name of the new subtype, and *original type* refers to the base type. The base type can be a predefined type or subtype, or a %TYPE reference. For example:

```
DECLARE
  SUBTYPE T_LoopCounter IS NUMBER;  -- Define the new subtype
```

```
v_LoopCounter    T_LoopCounter;    -- Declare a variable of
                                   -- the subtype
SUBTYPE T_NameType IS students.first_name%TYPE;
```

The SUBTYPE definition cannot be constrained directly in the definition. The following block is illegal:

```
DECLARE
  SUBTYPE T_LoopCounter IS NUMBER(4);  -- Illegal constraint
```

There is a workaround for this, however. You can declare a dummy variable of the desired type (with the constraint) and use %TYPE in the SUBTYPE definition:

```
DECLARE
  v_DummyVar   NUMBER(4);  -- Dummy variable, won't be used
  SUBTYPE T_LoopCounter is v_DummyVar%TYPE;   -- Returns NUMBER(4)
  v_Counter  T_LoopCounter;
```

Variable declarations using an unconstrained subtype can also constrain the type:

```
DECLARE
  SUBTYPE   T_Numeric IS NUMBER; -- Define unconstrained subtype,
  v_Counter is T_Numeric(5);    -- but a constrained variable
```

A subtype is considered to be in the same family as its base type.

Converting Between Datatypes

PL/SQL can handle conversions between different families among the scalar datatypes. Within a family, you can convert datatypes with no restrictions, except for constraints imposed on the variables. For example, a CHAR(10) variable cannot be converted into a VARCHAR2(1) variable, since there is not enough room. Likewise, precision and scale constraints may prohibit conversion between NUMBER(3,2) and NUMBER(3). In cases of constraint violations, the PL/SQL compiler will not issue an error, but you may get a run-time error, depending on the values in the variables to be converted.

In general, the composite datatypes cannot be converted between each other, since they are too dissimilar. You can write a function to perform this conversion if necessary, however, based on the meaning of the datatypes in your program.

There are two types of conversions, regardless of the type: implicit and explicit.

Function	Description	Available Families for Conversion
TO_CHAR	Converts its argument to a VARCHAR2 type, depending on the optional format specifier.	Numeric, date
TO_DATE	Converts its argument to a DATE type, depending on the optional format specifier.	Character
TO_NUMBER	Converts its argument to a NUMBER type, depending on the optional format specifier.	Character
RAWTOHEX	Converts a RAW value to a hexadecimal representation of the binary quantity.	Raw
HEXTORAW	Converts a hexadecimal representation into the equivalent binary quantity.	Character (must be in a hexadecimal representation)
CHARTOROWID	Converts a character representation of a ROWID into the internal binary format.	Character (must be in the 18-character rowid format)
ROWIDTOCHAR	Converts an internal binary ROWID variable into the 18-character external format.	Rowid

TABLE 2-3. *PL/SQL and SQL Datatype Conversion Functions*

Explicit Datatype Conversion

The built-in conversion functions available in SQL are also available in PL/SQL. Table 2-3 gives brief descriptions of these functions. When desired, you can use these functions to convert explicitly between variables in different datatype families. For more information and examples on using these conversion functions, see Chapter 3.

Implicit Datatype Conversion

PL/SQL will automatically convert between datatype families when possible. For example, the following block retrieves the current number of credits for student 10002:

```
DECLARE
  v_CurrentCredits  VARCHAR2(5);
BEGIN
  SELECT current_credits
    INTO v_CurrentCredits
    FROM students
    WHERE id = 10002;
END;
```

In the database, **current_credits** is a NUMBER(3) field. But **v_CurrentCredits** is a VARCHAR2(5) variable. PL/SQL will automatically convert the numeric data into a character string and then assign it to the character variable. PL/SQL can convert between

- Characters and numbers

- Characters and dates

Even though PL/SQL will implicitly convert between datatypes, it is good programming practice to use an explicit conversion function. In the next example, this is done with the TO_CHAR function:

```
DECLARE
  v_CurrentCredits  VARCHAR2(5);
BEGIN
  SELECT TO_CHAR(current_credits)
    INTO v_CurrentCredits
    FROM students
    WHERE id = 10002;
END;
```

The advantage of this is that an explicit format string can also be used in the TO_CHAR function, if desired. It also makes the intent of the program clearer and emphasizes the type conversion.

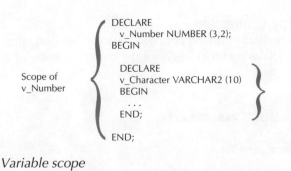

FIGURE 2-2. *Variable scope*

Automatic datatype conversion can also take place when PL/SQL is evaluating expressions, which are described fully in the section "Expressions and Operators" later in this chapter. The same guidelines apply there as well; however, use of an explicit conversion function is recommended.

Variable Scope and Visibility

The *scope* of a variable is the portion of the program in which the variable can be accessed. For a PL/SQL variable, this is from the variable declaration until the end of the block. When a variable goes out of scope, the PL/SQL engine will free the memory used to store the variable, since it can no longer be referenced. Figure 2-2 illustrates this. **v_Character** is in scope only in the inner block; after the END of the inner block, it is out of scope. The scope of **v_Number** ranges until the END of the outer block. Both variables are in scope in the inner block.

The *visibility* of a variable is the portion of the program where the variable can be accessed without having to qualify the reference. The visibility is always within the scope; if a variable is out of scope, it is not visible. Consider Figure 2-3. At location 1, both **v_AvailableFlag** and **v_SSN** are in scope and are visible. At location 2, the same two variables are in scope, but only **v_AvailableFlag** is still visible. The redeclaration of **v_SSN** as a CHAR(11) variable has hidden the NUMBER(9) declaration. All four variables are in scope at location 2, but only three are visible—**v_AvailableFlag**, **v_StartDate**, and the CHAR(11) **v_SSN**. By location 3, **v_StartDate** and the CHAR(11) **v_SSN** are no longer in scope and hence are no longer visible. The same two variables are in scope and visibility as in location 1—**v_AvailableFlag** and the NUMBER(9) **v_SSN**.

If a variable is in scope but is not visible, how does the program reference it? Consider Figure 2-4. This is the same block as Figure 2-3, but a label **<<l_Outer>>**

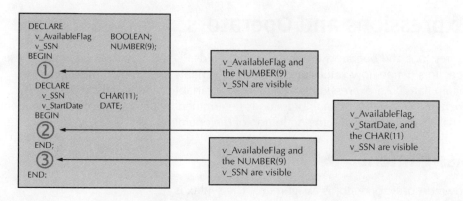

FIGURE 2-3.   *Scope and visibility*

has been added to the outer block. (Labels are discussed in more detail in the "PL/SQL Control Structures" section later in this chapter.) At location 2, the NUMBER(9) **v_SSN** is not visible. However, we can refer to it using the label, as

```
l_Outer.v_SSN
```

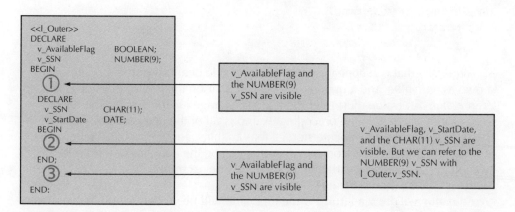

FIGURE 2-4.   *Using a label to reference a variable*

Expressions and Operators

Expressions and operators are the glue that holds PL/SQL variables together. These operators define how values are assigned to variables and how these values are manipulated. An *expression* is a sequence of variables and literals, separated by *operators*. The value of an expression is determined by the values of its component variables and literals and the definition of the operators.

Assignment

The most basic operator is assignment. The syntax is

> *variable* := *expression*;

where *variable* is a PL/SQL variable and *expression* is a PL/SQL expression. Assignments are legal in the executable and exception handling sections of a block. The following example illustrates some assignments:

```
DECLARE
  v_String1   VARCHAR2(10);
  v_String2   VARCHAR2(15);
  v_Numeric   NUMBER;
BEGIN
  v_String1 := 'Hello';
  v_String2 := v_String1;
  v_Numeric := -12.4;
END;
```

A quantity that can appear on the left-hand side of an assignment operator is known as an *lvalue*, and a quantity that can appear on the right-hand side is known as an *rvalue*. An lvalue must refer to an actual storage location, since the rvalue will be written into it. In the preceding example, all of the lvalues are variables. The PL/SQL engine will allocate storage for variables, and the values **'Hello'** and **–12.4** can be put into this storage. An rvalue can be the contents of a storage location (referenced by a variable), or a literal. The example illustrates both cases: **'Hello'** is a literal, and **v_String1** is a variable.

An rvalue will be read from, while an lvalue will be written to. All lvalues are also rvalues.

Expressions

PL/SQL expressions are rvalues. As such, an expression is not valid as a statement by itself—it must be part of another statement. For example, an expression can appear on the right-hand side of an assignment operator, or as part of an SQL statement. The operators that make up an expression, together with the type of their operands, determine the type of the expression.

An *operand* is the argument to an operator. PL/SQL operators take either one argument (unary) or two arguments (binary). For example, the negation operator (–) is a unary operand, while the multiplication operator (*) is a binary operand. Table 2-4 classifies the PL/SQL operators according to their precedence, or priority. Operators with the highest precedence are listed first.

The *precedence* of the operators in an expression determines the order of evaluation. Consider the following numeric expression:

```
3 + 5 * 7
```

Since multiplication has a higher precedence than addition, this expression evaluates to 38 (3 + 35) rather than 56 (8 * 7). You use parentheses in the expression to override the default order of precedence. For example, in the following form, the expression evaluates to 56:

```
(3 + 5) * 7
```

Character Expressions

The only character operator is concatenation (||). This operator attaches two or more strings together. For example, this expression

```
'Hello ' || 'World' || '!'
```

Operator	Type	Description
**, NOT	Binary	Exponentiation, logical negation
+, –	Unary	Identity, negation
*, /	Binary	Multiplication, division
+, –, ||	Binary	Addition, subtraction, string concatenation
=, !=, <, >, <=, >=, IS NULL, LIKE, BETWEEN, IN	Binary (except for IS NULL, which is unary)	Logical comparison
AND	Binary	Logical conjunction
OR	Binary	Logical inclusion

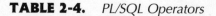

TABLE 2-4.   *PL/SQL Operators*

evaluates to

```
'Hello World!'
```

If all of the operands in a concatenation expression are of type CHAR, then the expression is of type CHAR. If any operand is of type VARCHAR2, then the expression is of type VARCHAR2. String literals are considered to be of type CHAR, so the preceding example evaluates to a CHAR value. The expression assigned to **v_Result** in the following block, however, evaluates to a VARCHAR2 value:

```
DECLARE
  v_TempVar  VARCHAR2(10) := 'PL';
  v_Result   VARCHAR2(20);
BEGIN
  v_Result := v_TempVar || '/SQL';
END;
```

Boolean Expressions

All of the PL/SQL control structures (except GOTO) involve boolean expressions, also known as *conditions*. A *boolean expression* is any expression that evaluates to a boolean value (TRUE, FALSE, or NULL). For example, all of the following are boolean expressions:

```
X > Y
NULL
(4 > 5) OR (-1 != Z)
```

There are three operators that take boolean arguments, and return boolean values—AND, OR, and NOT. Their behavior is described by the truth tables in Figure 2-5. These operators implement standard three-valued logic.

NOT	TRUE	FALSE	NULL
	FALSE	TRUE	NULL

AND	TRUE	FALSE	NULL
TRUE	TRUE	FALSE	NULL
FALSE	FALSE	FALSE	FALSE
NULL	NULL	FALSE	NULL

OR	TRUE	FALSE	NULL
TRUE	TRUE	TRUE	TRUE
FALSE	TRUE	FALSE	NULL
NULL	TRUE	NULL	NULL

FIGURE 2-5. *Truth tables*

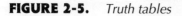

Essentially, AND returns TRUE only if both of its operands are TRUE, and OR returns FALSE only if both of its operands are FALSE.

NULLs add complexity to boolean expressions. NULL means "missing or unknown value." The expression

```
TRUE AND NULL
```

evaluates to NULL because we don't know if the second operand is TRUE or not. For more information, see the section "Null Conditions" later in this chapter.

Comparison, or *relational,* operators take numeric, character, or data operands and return a boolean value. These operators are defined according to the following table:

Operator	Definition
=	Is equal to (equality)
!=	Is not equal to (inequality)
<	Is less than
>	Is greater than
<=	Is less than or equal to
>=	Is greater than or equal to

The IS NULL operator returns TRUE only if its operand is NULL. NULLs cannot be tested using the relational operators because any relational expression with a NULL operand returns NULL.

The LIKE operator is used for pattern matching in character strings, similar to regular expressions in Unix. The underscore character (_) matches exactly one character, and the percent character (%) matches zero or more characters. The following expressions all return TRUE:

```
'Scott' LIKE 'Sc%t'
```

```
'Scott' LIKE 'Sc_tt'
```

```
'Scott' LIKE '%'
```

The BETWEEN operator combines <= and >= in one expression. For example, the following expression returns FALSE,

```
100 BETWEEN 110 AND 120
```

while this expression returns TRUE:

```
100 BETWEEN 90 and 110
```

The IN operator returns TRUE if its first operand is contained in the set identified by the second operand. For example, the following expression returns FALSE:

```
'Scott' IN ('Mike', 'Pamela', 'Fred')
```

If the set contains NULLs, they are ignored, since a comparison with NULL will always return NULL.

PL/SQL Control Structures

PL/SQL, like other third generation languages, has a variety of control structures that allow you to control the behavior of the block as it runs. These structures include conditional statements and loops. It is these structures, combined with variables, that give PL/SQL its power and flexibility.

IF-THEN-ELSE

The syntax for an IF-THEN-ELSE statement is

> **IF** *boolean_expression1* **THEN**
>   *sequence_of_statements1;*
> [**ELSIF** *boolean_expression2* **THEN**
>   *sequence_of_statements2;*]
> ...
> [**ELSE**
>   *sequence_of_statements3;*]
> **END IF**;

where *boolean_expression* is any expression that evaluates to a boolean value, defined in the previous section, "Boolean Expressions." The ELSIF and ELSE clauses are optional, and there can be as many ELSIF clauses as desired. For example, the following block shows an IF-THEN-ELSE statement with one ELSIF clause and one ELSE clause:

```
DECLARE
  v_NumberSeats rooms.number_seats%TYPE;
```

```
   v_Comment VARCHAR2(35);
BEGIN
   /* Retrieve the number of seats in the room identified by ID 99999.
      Store the result in v_NumberSeats. */
   SELECT number_seats
     INTO v_NumberSeats
     FROM rooms
     WHERE room_id = 99999;
   IF v_NumberSeats < 50 THEN
     v_Comment := 'Fairly small';
   ELSIF v_NumberSeats < 100 THEN
     v_Comment := 'A little bigger';
   ELSE
     v_Comment := 'Lots of room';
   END IF;
END;
```

The behavior of the preceding block is the same as the keywords imply. If the first condition evaluates to TRUE, then the first sequence of statements is executed. In this case, the first condition is

```
v_NumberSeats < 50
```

and the first sequence of statements is

```
v_Comment := 'Fairly small';
```

If the number of seats is not less than 50, then the second condition is evaluated:

```
v_NumberSeats < 100
```

If this evaluates to TRUE, then the second sequence of statements is executed:

```
v_Comment := 'A little bigger';
```

Finally, if the number of seats is not less than 100, the final sequence of statements is executed:

```
v_Comment := 'Lots of room';
```

Each sequence of statements is executed only if its associated boolean condition evaluates to TRUE.

In the example, each sequence of statements has only one procedural statement. However, in general, you can have as many statements (procedural or SQL) as desired. The following block illustrates this:

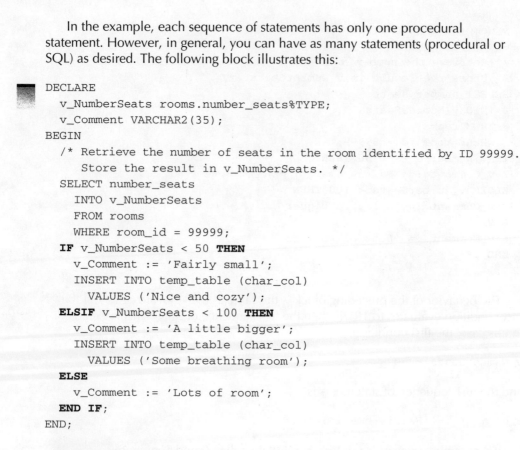

```
DECLARE
  v_NumberSeats rooms.number_seats%TYPE;
  v_Comment VARCHAR2(35);
BEGIN
  /* Retrieve the number of seats in the room identified by ID 99999.
     Store the result in v_NumberSeats. */
  SELECT number_seats
    INTO v_NumberSeats
    FROM rooms
    WHERE room_id = 99999;
  IF v_NumberSeats < 50 THEN
    v_Comment := 'Fairly small';
    INSERT INTO temp_table (char_col)
      VALUES ('Nice and cozy');
  ELSIF v_NumberSeats < 100 THEN
    v_Comment := 'A little bigger';
    INSERT INTO temp_table (char_col)
      VALUES ('Some breathing room');
  ELSE
    v_Comment := 'Lots of room';
  END IF;
END;
```

NOTE
You may have noticed the spelling of ELSIF—there is no E and no space. This syntax comes from the Ada language.

Null Conditions

A sequence of statements in an IF-THEN-ELSE statement is executed only if its associated condition evaluates to TRUE. If the condition evaluates to FALSE or NULL, then the sequence of statements is not executed. Consider the following two blocks as an example:

```
/* Block 1 */
DECLARE
  v_Number1 NUMBER;
```

```
    v_Number2 NUMBER;
    v_Result  VARCHAR2(5);
BEGIN
   ...
   IF v_Number1 < v_Number2 THEN
     v_Result := 'Yes';
   ELSE
     v_Result := 'No';
   END IF;
END;


/* Block 2 */
 DECLARE
v_Number1 NUMBER;
v_Number2 NUMBER;
v_Result VARCHAR2(5);
BEGIN
   ...
   IF v_Number1 >= v_Number2 THEN
     v_Result := 'No';
   ELSE
     v_Result := 'Yes';
   END IF;
END;
```

Do these blocks behave the same? Suppose that **v_Number1** = 3 and
v_Number2 = 7. The condition in block 1 (3 < 7) will thus evaluate to TRUE and
v_Result will be set to 'Yes'. Similarly, the condition in block 2 (3 >= 7) will
evaluate to FALSE, and **v_Result** will also be set to 'Yes'. For any non-NULL values
of **v_Number1** and **v_Number2**, the blocks have the same behavior.

Now suppose that **v_Number1** = 3 but **v_Number2** is NULL. What happens
now? The condition in block 1 (3 < NULL) will evaluate to NULL, so the ELSE
clause will be executed, assigning 'No' to **v_Result**. The condition in block 2 (3 >=
NULL) will also evaluate to NULL, so the ELSE clause will be executed, assigning
'Yes' to **v_Result**. If either **v_Number1** or **v_Number2** is NULL, the blocks behave
differently.

If we add a check for NULL to the preceding blocks, we can make them
behave the same:

```
/* Block 1 */
DECLARE
  v_Number1 NUMBER;
```

```
  v_Number2 NUMBER;
  v_Result  VARCHAR2(5);
BEGIN
  ...
  IF v_Number1 IS NULL OR
        v_Number2 IS NULL THEN
    v_Result := 'Unknown';
  ELSIF v_Number1 < v_Number2 THEN
    v_Result := 'Yes';
  ELSE
    v_Result := 'No';
  END IF;
END;


/* Block 2 */
DECLARE
  v_Number1 NUMBER;
  v_Number2 NUMBER;
  v_Result VARCHAR2(5);
BEGIN
  ...
  IF v_Number1 IS NULL OR
        v_Number2 IS NULL THEN
    v_Result := 'Unknown';
  ELSIF v_Number1 >= v_Number2 THEN
    v_Result := 'No';
  ELSE
    v_Result := 'Yes';
  END IF;
END;
```

The **IS NULL** condition will evaluate to TRUE only if the variable it is checking is NULL. If the variable is not NULL, the condition will evaluate to FALSE. By adding this check to the preceding blocks, we assign 'Unknown' to **v_Result** if either variable is NULL. The block will only check whether **v_Number1** is greater than **v_Number2** if it is assured that both are non-NULL, in which case the remainder of the blocks behave the same.

Loops

PL/SQL provides a facility for executing statements repeatedly, via *loops*. Loops are divided into four categories. Simple loops, WHILE loops, and numeric FOR loops are discussed in the following sections. Cursor FOR loops are discussed in Chapter 4.

Simple Loops

The most basic kind of loops, simple loops, have this syntax:

```
LOOP
  sequence_of_statements;
END LOOP;
```

Sequence_of_statements will be executed infinitely, since this loop has no stopping condition. We can add one via the EXIT statement, which has this syntax:

```
EXIT [WHEN condition];
```

For example, the following block inserts 50 rows into the **temp_table** table.

```
DECLARE
  v_Counter BINARY_INTEGER := 1;
BEGIN
  LOOP
    -- Insert a row into temp_table with the current value of the
    -- loop counter.
    INSERT INTO temp_table
      VALUES (v_Counter, 'Loop index');
    v_Counter := v_Counter + 1;
    -- Exit condition - when the loop counter > 50 we will
    -- break out of the loop.
    IF v_Counter > 50 THEN
      EXIT;
    END IF;
  END LOOP;
END;
```

The statement

EXIT WHEN *condition*;

is equivalent to

```
IF condition THEN
    EXIT;
END IF;
```

so we can rewrite the example with the following block, which behaves exactly the same way:

```
DECLARE
  v_Counter BINARY_INTEGER := 1;
BEGIN
  LOOP
    -- Insert a row into temp_table with the current value of the
    -- loop counter.
    INSERT INTO temp_table
      VALUES (v_Counter, 'Loop index');
    v_Counter := v_Counter + 1;
    -- Exit condition - when the loop counter > 50 we will
    -- break out of the loop.
    EXIT WHEN v_Counter > 50;
  END LOOP;
END;
```

WHILE Loops

The syntax for a WHILE loop is

```
WHILE condition LOOP
    sequence_of_statements;
END LOOP;
```

The *condition* is evaluated before each iteration of the loop. If it evaluates to TRUE, *sequence_of_statements* is executed. If *condition* evaluates to FALSE or NULL, the loop is finished and control resumes after the END LOOP statement. Now we can rewrite the example using a WHILE loop, as follows:

```
DECLARE
  v_Counter BINARY_INTEGER := 1;
BEGIN
```

```
  -- Test the loop counter before each loop iteration to
  -- insure that it is still less than 50.
  WHILE v_Counter <= 50 LOOP
    INSERT INTO temp_table
      VALUES (v_Counter, 'Loop index');
    v_Counter := v_Counter + 1;
  END LOOP;
END;
```

The EXIT or EXIT WHEN statement can still be used inside a WHILE loop to exit the loop prematurely, if desired.

Note that if the loop condition does not evaluate to TRUE the first time it is checked, the loop is not executed at all. If we remove the initialization of **v_Counter** in our example, the condition **v_Counter < 50** will evaluate to NULL, and no rows will be inserted into temp_table:

```
DECLARE
  v_Counter BINARY_INTEGER;
BEGIN
  -- This condition will evaluate to NULL, since v_Counter
  -- is initialized to NULL by default.
  WHILE v_Counter <= 50 LOOP
    INSERT INTO temp_table
      VALUES (v_Counter, 'Loop index');
    v_Counter := v_Counter + 1;
  END LOOP;
END;
```

Numeric FOR Loops

The number of iterations for simple loops and WHILE loops is not known in advance—it depends on the loop condition. Numeric FOR loops, on the other hand, have a defined number of iterations. The syntax is

FOR *loop_counter* IN [REVERSE] *low_bound* .. *high_bound* LOOP
    sequence_of_statements;
END LOOP;

where *loop_counter* is the implicitly declared index variable, *low_bound* and *high_bound* specify the number of iterations, and *sequence_of_statements* is the contents of the loop.

The bounds of the loop are evaluated once. This determines the total number of iterations. *loop_counter* will take on the values ranging from *low_bound* to *high_bound,* incrementing by 1 each time, until the loop is complete. We can rewrite our looping example using a FOR loop as follows:

```
BEGIN
  FOR v_Counter IN 1..50 LOOP
    INSERT INTO temp_table
      VALUES (v_Counter, 'Loop Index');
  END LOOP;
END;
```

Scoping Rules   The loop index for a FOR loop is implicitly declared as a BINARY_INTEGER. It is not necessary to declare it prior to the loop. If it is declared, the loop index will hide the outer declaration in the same way that a variable declaration in an inner block can hide a declaration in an outer block. For example:

```
DECLARE
  v_Counter  NUMBER := 7;
BEGIN
  -- Inserts the value 7 into temp_table.
  INSERT INTO temp_table (num_col)
    VALUES (v_Counter);
  -- This loop redeclares v_Counter as a BINARY_INTEGER, which hides
  -- the NUMBER declaration of v_Counter.
  FOR v_Counter IN 20..30 LOOP
    -- Inside the loop, v_Counter ranges from 20 to 30.
    INSERT INTO temp_table (num_col)
      VALUES (v_Counter);
  END LOOP;
  -- Inserts another 7 into temp_table.
  INSERT INTO temp_table (num_col)
    VALUES (v_Counter);
END;
```

Using REVERSE   If the REVERSE keyword is present in the FOR loop, then the loop index will iterate from the high value to the low value. Notice that the syntax is the same—the low value is still referenced first. For example:

```
BEGIN
  FOR v_Counter in REVERSE 10..50 LOOP
    -- v_Counter will start with 50, and will be decremented by
```

```
       -- 1 each time through the loop.
     NULL;
   END LOOP;
END;
```

Loop Ranges   The high and low values don't have to be numeric literals. They can be any expression that can be converted to a numeric value. For example:

```
DECLARE
  v_LowValue   NUMBER := 10;
  v_HighValue NUMBER := 40;
BEGIN
  FOR v_Counter IN REVERSE v_LowValue .. v_HighValue LOOP
    INSERT INTO temp_table
      VALUES (v_Counter, 'Dynamically specified loop ranges');
  END LOOP;
END;
```

GOTOs and Labels

PL/SQL also includes a GOTO statement. The syntax is

  GOTO *label*;

where *label* is a label defined in the PL/SQL block. Labels are delimited by in double angle brackets. When a GOTO statement is evaluated, control immediately passes to the statement identified by the label. For example, we can implement our looping example with:

```
DECLARE
  v_Counter   BINARY_INTEGER := 1;
BEGIN
  LOOP
    INSERT INTO temp_table
      VALUES (v_Counter, 'Loop count');
    v_Counter := v_Counter + 1;
    IF v_Counter > 50 THEN
      GOTO l_EndOfLoop;
    END IF;
  END LOOP;
```

```
<<l_EndOfLoop>>
  INSERT INTO temp_table (char_col)
    VALUES ('Done!');
END;
```

Restrictions on GOTO

PL/SQL enforces restrictions on the use of GOTO. It is illegal to branch into an inner block, loop, or IF statement. The following illegal example illustrates this.

```
BEGIN
  GOTO L_InnerBlock;   -- Illegal, cannot branch to an inner block.
  BEGIN
    ...
    <<L_InnerBlock>>
    ...
  END;

  GOTO L_InsideIf;   -- Illegal, cannot branch into an IF statement.
  IF x > 3 THEN
    ...
    <<L_InsideIf>>
    INSERT INTO ...
  END IF;
END;
```

If these were legal, then statements inside the IF statement could be executed even if the IF condition did not evaluate to TRUE. In the preceding example, the INSERT statement could be executed if x = 2.

It is also illegal for a GOTO to branch from one IF clause to another:

```
BEGIN
  IF x > 3 THEN
    ...
    GOTO L_NextCondition;
  ELSE
    <<L_NextCondition>>
    ...
  END IF;
END;
```

Finally, it is illegal to branch from an exception handler back into the current block. Exceptions are discussed in Chapter 6.

```
DECLARE
  v_Room  rooms%ROWTYPE;
BEGIN
  -- Retrieve a single row from the rooms table.
  SELECT *
    INTO v_Room
    FROM rooms
    WHERE rowid = 1;
  <<L_Insert>>
  INSERT INTO temp_table (char_col)
    VALUES ('Found a row!');
EXCEPTION
  WHEN NO_DATA_FOUND THEN
    GOTO L_Insert;  -- Illegal, cannot branch into current block
END;
```

Labeling Loops

Loops themselves can be labeled. If so, the label can be used on the EXIT statement to indicate which loop is to be exited. For example:

```
BEGIN
  <<L_Outer>>
  FOR v_OuterIndex IN 1..50 LOOP
    ...
    <<L_Inner>>
    FOR v_InnerIndex IN 2..10 LOOP
      ...
      IF v_OuterIndex > 40 THEN
        EXIT L_Outer;  -- Exits both loops
      END IF;
    END LOOP L_Inner;
END LOOP L_Outer;
```

If a loop is labeled, the label name can optionally be included after the END LOOP statement, as the preceding example indicates.

GOTO Guidelines

Be careful when using GOTO. Unnecessary GOTO statements can create *spaghetti code*—code that jumps around from place to place with no apparent reason and is very difficult to understand and maintain.

Just about all cases where a GOTO could be used can be rewritten using other PL/SQL control structures, such as loops or conditionals. Exceptions can also be used to exit out of a deeply nested loop, rather than branching to the end.

NULL as a Statement

In some cases, you may want to explicitly indicate that no action is to take place. This can be done via the NULL statement. The NULL statement does not do anything; it just serves as a placeholder. For example:

```
DECLARE
  v_TempVar  NUMBER := 7;
BEGIN
  IF v_TempVar < 5 THEN
    INSERT INTO temp_table (char_col)
      VALUES ('Too small');
  ELSIF v_TempVar < 10 THEN
    INSERT INTO temp_table (char_col)
      VALUES ('Just right');
  ELSE
    NULL;  -- Do nothing
  END IF;
END;
```

Pragmas

Pragmas are compiler directives, similar to **#pragma** or **#define** directives in C. They serve as instructions to the PL/SQL compiler. The compiler will act on the pragma during the compilation of the block. For example, the RESTRICT_REFERENCES pragma places restrictions on what kinds of SQL statements can be in a function. In addition to compiling the function as normal, the compiler needs to verify that the restrictions are met. The RESTRICT_REFERENCES pragma is described in Chapter 5. PL/SQL has a number of pragmas, which we will see throughout this book.

Pragmas are another concept that PL/SQL and Ada have in common.

PL/SQL Records and Tables

Both composite types (RECORD and TABLE) are user-defined types. In order to use them, first you define the type and then you declare a variable of that type. The scalar types that we have seen so far are all predefined in package STANDARD. The composite types are defined in your program.

Records

PL/SQL records are similar to C structures. A record provides a way to deal with separate but related variables as a unit. Consider the following declarative section:

```
DECLARE
  v_StudentID   NUMBER(5);
  v_FirstName   VARCHAR2(20);
  v_LastName    VARCHAR2(20);
```

All three of these variables are logically related, since they refer to common fields in the students table. By declaring a record type for these variables, the relationship between them is apparent, and they can be manipulated as a unit. For example:

```
DECLARE
  /* Define a record type to hold common student information */
  TYPE t_StudentRecord IS RECORD (
    StudentID  NUMBER(5),
    FirstName  VARCHAR2(20),
    LastName   VARCHAR2(20));

  /* Declare a variable of this type. */
  v_StudentInfo   t_StudentRecord;
```

The general syntax for defining a record type is

TYPE *record_type* IS RECORD (
  field1 type1 [NOT NULL] [:= *expr1*],
  field2 type2 [NOT NULL] [:= *expr2*],
  ...
  fieldn typen [NOT NULL] [:= *exprn*]);

where *record_type* is the name of the new type, *field* is the name of a field within the record, and *type* is the type of the associated field. A record can have as many fields as desired. Each field declaration looks essentially the same as a variable declaration outside a record, including NOT NULL constraints and initial values. *expr* represents an initial value. Based on this definition, the following is a legal record type:

```
DECLARE
  TYPE t_SampleRecord IS RECORD (
    Count         NUMBER(4),
    Name          VARCHAR2(10)  := 'Scott',
```

```
     EffectiveDate   DATE,
     Description      VARCHAR2(45) NOT NULL := 'Unknown');
  v_Sample1  t_SampleRecord;
  v_Sample2  t_SampleRecord;
```

Similar to declarations not inside record definitions, if a field is constrained to be NOT NULL, then it must have an initial value. Any field without an initial value is initialized to NULL. The DEFAULT keyword can be used instead of := as well.

In order to refer to a field within a record, dot notation is used. The syntax is

record name.field name

The following example shows how fields in **v_Sample1** and **v_Sample2** are referenced:

```
BEGIN
  /* SYSDATE is a built-in function which returns the current
     date and time. */
  v_Sample1.EffectiveDate := SYSDATE;
  v_Sample2.Description := 'Pesto Pizza';
END;
```

A reference like this is an rvalue, so it can be used on either side of an assignment operator.

Record Assignment

In order for one record to be assigned to another, both records must be of the same type. For example, given the previous declarations of **v_Sample1** and **v_Sample2**, the following assignment is legal:

```
v_Sample1 := v_Sample2;
```

Even if you have two different types that happen to have the same field definitions, the records cannot be assigned to each other. The following example is illegal:

```
DECLARE
  TYPE t_Rec1Type IS RECORD (
    Field1 NUMBER,
    Field2 VARCHAR2(5));
  TYPE t_Rec2Type IS RECORD (
    Field1 NUMBER,
    Field2 VARCHAR2(5));
```

```
   v_Rec1 t_Rec1Type;
   v_Rec2 t_Rec2Type;
BEGIN
   /* Even though v_Rec1 and v_Rec2 have the same field names
      and field types, the record types themselves are different.
      This is an illegal assignment. */
   v_Rec1 := v_Rec2;

   /* However, the fields are the same type, so the following
      are legal assignments. */
   v_Rec1.Field1 := v_Rec2.Field1;
   v_Rec2.Field2 := v_Rec2.Field2;
END;
```

A record can also be assigned with a SELECT statement. This will retrieve data from the database and store it into the record. The fields in the record should match the fields in the select list of the query. Chapter 3 describes the SELECT statement in more detail. This is illustrated in the following example:

```
DECLARE
   -- Define a record to match some fields in the students table.
   -- Note the use of %TYPE for the fields.
   TYPE t_StudentRecord IS RECORD (
     FirstName   students.first_name%TYPE,
     LastName    students.last_name%TYPE,
     Major       students.major%TYPE);

   -- Declare a variable to receive the data.
   v_Student   t_StudentRecord;
BEGIN
   -- Retrieve information about student with ID 10,000.
   -- Note how the query is returning columns which match the
   -- fields in v_Student.
   SELECT first_name, last_name, major
     INTO v_Student
     FROM students
     WHERE ID = 10000;
END;
```

Using %ROWTYPE

It is common in PL/SQL to declare a record with the same types as a database row. PL/SQL provides the %ROWTYPE operator to facilitate this. Similar to %TYPE,

%ROWTYPE will return a type based on the table definition. For example, a declaration such as

```
DECLARE
  v_RoomRecord  rooms%ROWTYPE;
```

will define a record whose fields correspond to the columns in the **rooms** table. Specifically, **v_RoomRecord** will look like this:

```
(room_id       NUMBER(5),
 building      VARCHAR2(15),
 room_number   NUMBER(4),
 number_seats  NUMBER(4),
 description   VARCHAR2(50))
```

As with %TYPE, any NOT NULL constraint defined on the column is not included. The length of VARCHAR2 and CHAR columns and the precision and scale for NUMBER columns are included, however.

If the table definition changes, then %ROWTYPE changes along with it. Like %TYPE, %ROWTYPE is evaluated each time an anonymous block is submitted to the PL/SQL engine, and each time a stored object is compiled.

Tables

PL/SQL tables are similar to arrays in C. Syntactically, they are treated like arrays. However, they are implemented differently. In order to declare a PL/SQL table, you first need to define the table type, and then you declare a variable of this type, as the following declarative section illustrates:

```
DECLARE
  /* Define the table type. Variables of this type can hold
     character strings with a max of 10 characters each. */
  TYPE t_CharacterTable IS TABLE OF VARCHAR2(10)
    INDEX BY BINARY_INTEGER;

  /* Declare a variable of this type. This is what actually
     allocates the storage. */
  v_Characters t_CharacterTable;
```

The general syntax for defining a table type is

```
TYPE tabletype IS TABLE OF type INDEX BY BINARY_INTEGER;
```

where *tabletype* is the name of the new type being defined, and *type* is a predefined scalar type, or a reference to a scalar type via %TYPE. In the previous example, *tabletype* is **t_CharacterTable**, and *type* is **VARCHAR2(10)**. The following declarative section illustrates several different PL/SQL table types and variable declarations:

```
DECLARE
  TYPE t_NameTable IS TABLE OF students.first_name%TYPE
    INDEX BY BINARY_INTEGER;
  TYPE t_DateTable IS TABLE OF DATE
    INDEX BY BINARY_INTEGER;
  v_Names t_NameTable;
  v_Dates t_DateTable;
```

The **INDEX BY BINARY_INTEGER** syntax is always required as part of the table definition. This syntax is part of PL/SQL to allow flexibility; but in the future, PL/SQL tables may be able to be indexed by types other than BINARY_INTEGER. For now, up to version 2.3, BINARY_INTEGER is the only type available.

Once the type and the variable are declared, we can refer to an individual element in the PL/SQL table by using the syntax

tablename(*index*)

where *tablename* is the name of a table and *index* is either a variable of type BINARY_INTEGER or a variable or expression that can be converted to a BINARY_INTEGER. Given the declarations for the different table types, we could continue the PL/SQL block with

```
v_Names(1) := 'Scott';
v_Dates(-4) := SYSDATE - 1;  /* SYSDATE -1 evaluates to the time
                                24 hours ago */
```

NOTE
A table reference, like a record or variable reference, is an lvalue since it points to storage that has been allocated by the PL/SQL engine.

Tables vs. Arrays

Syntactically, PL/SQL tables are treated like arrays. However, the actual implementation of a table differs from an array. A PL/SQL table is similar to a database table, with two columns—KEY and VALUE. The type of KEY is BINARY_INTEGER, and the type of VALUE is whatever type is specified in the definition (*type* in the syntax shown earlier).

Given the definition of **t_NameTable** and **v_Names** in the declaration statement shown in the previous section, suppose the following sequence of statements is executed:

```
v_Names(0) := 'Harold';
v_Names(-7) := 'Susan';
v_Names(3) := 'Steve';
```

The data structure will then look like this:

Key	Value
0	Harold
–7	Susan
3	Steve

There are several things to note about PL/SQL tables that are illustrated by this example:

- Tables are unconstrained. The only limit on the number of rows is the values that can be represented by the BINARY_INTEGER type.

- The elements in a PL/SQL table are not necessarily in any particular order. Since they are not stored contiguously in memory like an array, elements can be inserted with arbitrary key values.

- The key values used for a PL/SQL table don't have to be sequential. Any BINARY_INTEGER value or expression can be used for a table index.

An assignment to element *i* in a PL/SQL table actually creates this element. It is very similar to an INSERT operation on a database table. If element *i* is referenced before it has been created, the PL/SQL engine will return this error:

```
ORA-1403: no data found
```

 Prior to version 2.3 of PL/SQL, tables can only hold scalar types. However, version 2.3 lifts this restriction and allows tables of records. The following block is legal only in PL/SQL 2.3 and higher.

```
DECLARE
  TYPE t_StudentTable IS TABLE OF students%ROWTYPE
    INDEX BY BINARY_INTEGER;
  /* Each element of v_Students is a record */
  v_Students t_StudentTable;
```

```
BEGIN
  /* Retrieve the record with id = 10,001 and store it into
     v_Students(10001) */
  SELECT *
    INTO v_Students(10001)
    FROM students
    WHERE id = 10001;
END;
```

Since each element of this table is a record, we can refer to fields within this record via the syntax

table(*index*).*field*

For example, we can continue the previous block with

```
v_Students(10001).first_name := 'Larry';
```

v_Students(10001) refers to a record of type students%ROWTYPE, and a field within this record is **first_name**. A period separates the record and field reference.

Tables of records significantly enhance the functionality of PL/SQL tables, since only one table definition is required to hold information about all the fields of a database table. Prior to version 2.3, a separate table definition is required for each database field.

Table Attributes

PL/SQL **2.3** ...and HIGHER Besides allowing tables of records, PL/SQL 2.3 extends the functionality of PL/SQL tables through table attributes. The syntax for using an attribute is

table.attribute

where *table* is a PL/SQL table reference, and *attribute* is the attribute desired. PL/SQL table attributes are described in Table 2-5 and in the following sections.

Attribute	Type Returned	Description
COUNT	NUMBER	Returns the number of rows in the table
DELETE	N/A	Deletes rows in a table
EXISTS	BOOLEAN	Returns true if the specified entry exists in the table

TABLE 2-5. *PL/SQL 2.3 Table Attributes*

Attribute	Type Returned	Description
FIRST	BINARY_INTEGER	Returns the index of the first row in the table
LAST	BINARY_INTEGER	Returns the index of the last row in the table
NEXT	BINARY_INTEGER	Returns the index of the next row in the table after the specified row
PRIOR	BINARY_INTEGER	Returns the index of the previous row in the table before the specified row

TABLE 2-5. *PL/SQL 2.3 Table Attributes* (continued)

COUNT   This attribute returns the current number of rows in a PL/SQL table. Consider the following block:

```
DECLARE
  TYPE t_NumberTable IS TABLE OF NUMBER
    INDEX BY BINARY_INTEGER;
  v_Numbers t_NumberTable;
  v_Total NUMBER;
BEGIN
  -- Insert 50 rows into the table.
  FOR v_Counter IN 1..50 LOOP
    v_Numbers(v_Counter) := v_Counter;
  END LOOP;

  v_Total := v_Numbers.COUNT;
END;
```

Here, **v_Numbers.COUNT** returns 50, and this value is assigned to **v_Total**.

DELETE   The DELETE attribute removes rows from a PL/SQL table. It is used as follows:

table.DELETE removes all rows in the table,
table.DELETE(*i*) removes the row with index *i* from the table, and
table.DELETE(*i,j*) removes all rows with indices between *i* and *j* from the table.

These are illustrated in the following example:

```
DECLARE
  TYPE t_ValueTable IS TABLE OF VARCHAR2(10)
    INDEX BY BINARY_INTEGER;
  v_Values t_ValueTable;
BEGIN
  -- Insert rows into the table.
  v_Values(1) := 'One';
  v_Values(3) := 'Three';
  v_Values(-2) := 'Minus Two';
  v_Values(0) := 'Zero';
  v_Values(100) := 'Hundred';

  v_Values.DELETE(100);   -- Removes 'Hundred'
  v_Values.DELETE(1,3);   -- Removes 'One' and 'Three'
  v_Values.DELETE;        -- Removes all remaining values
END;
```

NOTE
The DELETE attribute is an entire statement by itself—unlike the other attributes, it is not called as part of an expression.

EXISTS   The statement *table*.EXISTS(*i*) returns TRUE if a row with index *i* is in the table, and FALSE otherwise. This attribute is useful for avoiding the ORA-1403 error, which is raised in reference to a non-existing table element. For example:

```
DECLARE
  t_FirstNameTable IS TABLE OF students.first_name%TYPE
    INDEX BY BINARY_INTEGER;
  FirstNames  t_FirstNameTable;
BEGIN
  -- Insert rows into the table.
  FirstNames(1) := 'Scott';
  FirstNames(3) := 'Joanne';

  -- Check to see if rows exist.
  IF FirstNames.EXISTS(1) THEN
    INSERT INTO temp_table (char_col) VALUES
```

```
          ('Row 1 exists!');
    ELSE
      INSERT INTO temp_table (char_col) VALUES
        ('Row 1 doesn't exist!');
    END IF;
    IF FirstNames.EXISTS(2) THEN
      INSERT INTO temp_table (char_col) VALUES
        ('Row 2 exists!');
    ELSE
      INSERT INTO temp_table (char_col) VALUES
        ('Row 2 doesn''t exist!');
    END IF;
END;
```

After execution of this block, "Row 1 exists!" and "Row 2 doesn't exist!" would be inserted into **temp_table**.

FIRST and LAST   FIRST and LAST return the index of the first and last rows in the PL/SQL table, respectively. Keep in mind that they don't return the key value contained for these rows, just the index. The first row is defined as the row with the lowest index, and the last row is the row with the highest index. For example:

```
DECLARE
  t_LastNameTable IS TABLE OF students.last_name%TYPE
    INDEX BY BINARY_INTEGER;
  v_LastNames  t_LastNameTable;
  v_Index  BINARY_INTEGER;
BEGIN
  -- Insert rows in the table.
  v_LastNames(43) := 'Mason';
  v_LastNames(50) := 'Junebug';
  v_LastNames(47) := 'Taller';

  -- Assigns 43 to v_Index.
  v_Index := v_LastNames.FIRST;

  -- Assigns 50 to v_Index.
  v_Index := v_LastNames.LAST;
END;
```

NEXT and PRIOR   NEXT and PRIOR each take a single argument, similar to DELETE. They return the index of the next element in the table, or the previous

element, respectively. They can be used in a loop which iterates over the entire
table, regardless of the values used the indices. For example:

```
DECLARE
  TYPE t_MajorTable IS TABLE OF students.major
    INDEX BY BINARY_INTEGER;
  v_Majors t_MajorTable;
  v_Index  BINARY_INTEGER;
BEGIN
  -- Insert values into the table.
  v_Majors(-7) := 'Computer Science';
  v_Majors(4) := 'History';
  v_Majors(5) := 'Economics';

  -- Loop over all the rows in the table, and insert them into
  -- temp_table.
  v_Index := v_Majors.FIRST;
  LOOP
    INSERT INTO temp_table (num_col, char_col)
      VALUES (v_Index, v_Majors(v_Index));
    EXIT WHEN v_Index := v_Majors.LAST;
    v_Index := v_Majors.NEXT(v_Index);
  END LOOP;
END;
```

Guidelines for Using PL/SQL Tables

The following list of guidelines should make dealing with PL/SQL tables a little
more straightforward.

1. Keep a separate variable as a row count. This is not quite as necessary in
   PL/SQL 2.3 since the COUNT table attribute is available, but it is still a
   good idea. Since the size of a table is unconstrained, your program should
   keep track of how many rows have been added to the table.

2. Start with index value 1, and increment by 1 for each new element. The
   next element would have index 2, the following 3, and so on. This way, it
   is easy to loop through the elements in the table in a controlled manner.
   Indexing a table this way also makes it possible for the table to be bound
   to a C array, when the PL/SQL block is called from, or embedded in, a
   Pro*C or OCI program. (See Chapter 7 for more information on using
   PL/SQL in Pro*C or OCI.)

3. Remember that an element in a table is not defined until it is explicitly assigned. If you refer to a table element before it has been assigned to, then ORA-1403 (the "no data found" error) will be raised.

4. If you need to delete an entire PL/SQL table, you can assign NULL to it:

```
DECLARE
  TYPE t_NameTable IS TABLE OF students.first_name%TYPE
    INDEX BY BINARY_INTEGER;
  v_Names t_NameTable;
BEGIN
  /* Delete everything in v_Names */
  v_Names := NULL;
END;
```

PL/SQL Style Guide

There are no absolute rules for the style of a program. Program style includes things such as variable names, use of capitalization and white space, and the use of comments. These are not things that will necessarily affect how a program runs—two different styles for the same program will still do the same thing. However, a program that is written with good style will be much easier to understand and maintain than a poorly written program.

Good style means that it will take less time to understand what the program is doing when seeing it for the first time. It will also help you understand what the program is doing, both as you write it and when you see it a month later.

As an example, consider the following two blocks. Which one is easier to understand?

```
declare
x number;
y number;
begin if x < 10 then y := 7; else y := 3; end if; end;
```

```
DECLARE
  v_Test   NUMBER;  -- Variable which will be examined
  v_Result NUMBER;  -- Variable to store the result
BEGIN
  -- Examine v_Test, and assign 7 to v_Result if v_Test < 10.
  IF v_Test < 10 THEN
    v_Result := 7;
```

```
   ELSE
      v_Result := 3;
   END IF;
END;
```

Both blocks accomplish the same thing. However, the program flow in the second one is significantly easier to understand.

   This section covers several points of style. I feel that if you follow these recommendations, you will produce better code. All of the examples in this book follow these guidelines and serve as illustrations of this style of PL/SQL programming.

Style of Comments

Comments are the main mechanism for informing the reader what the purpose of a program is and how it works. I recommend putting comments:

- At the start of each block and/or procedure. These comments should explain what the block or procedure is supposed to do. Especially for procedures, it is important to list which variables or parameters will be read by the procedure (input) and which variables or parameters will be written to by the procedure (output). Also, it is a good idea to list the database tables accessed.

- By each variable declaration. Describe what the variable will be used for. Often, these can simply be one-line comments such as

```
v_SSN CHAR(11);    -- Social Security Number
```

- Before each major section of the block. You don't necessarily need comments around every statement, but a comment explaining the purpose of the next group of statements is useful. The algorithm used may be apparent from the code itself, so it is better to describe the purpose of the algorithm and what the results will be used for, rather than the details of the method.

   It's possible to have too many comments, which just get in the way of the code. When deciding on whether or not a comment is appropriate, ask yourself, "What would a programmer seeing this for the first time want to know?" Remember that the programmer may be yourself a month or two after you write the code!

   Comments should be meaningful and not restate what the PL/SQL code itself says. For example, the following comment doesn't tell us anything more than the PL/SQL does and thus isn't really useful:

```
DECLARE
  v_Temp NUMBER := 0;  -- Assign 0 to v_Temp
```

Style of Variable Names

The key to variable names is to make them descriptive. The declaration

```
x number;
```

doesn't tell us anything about what x will be used for. However,

```
v_StudentID  NUMBER(5);
```

tells us that this variable will probably be used for a student ID number, even without an explanatory comment by the declaration. Keep in mind that the maximum length of a PL/SQL identifier is 30 characters, and all of them are significant. Thirty characters are generally enough for a descriptive name.

The variable name can also tell us the use of the variable. I use a one-letter code separated by an underscore from the rest of the variable to indicate this. For example:

```
v_VariableName     Program variable
e_ExceptionName    User defined exception
t_TypeName         User defined type
p_ParameterName    Parameter to a procedure or function
```

Style of Capitalization

PL/SQL is not case-sensitive. However, I feel that proper use of upper- and lowercase significantly increases program readability. I generally follow these rules:

- Reserved words are in uppercase (BEGIN, DECLARE, ELSIF).
- Built-in functions are in uppercase (SUBSTR, COUNT, TO_CHAR).
- Predefined types are in uppercase (NUMBER(7,2), BOOLEAN, DATE).
- SQL keywords are in uppercase (SELECT, INTO, UPDATE, WHERE).
- Database objects are in lowercase (log_table, classes, students).
- Variable names are in mixed case, with a capital letter for each word in the name (v_HireDate, e_TooManyStudents, t_StudentRecordType).

Style of Indentation

Using *white space* (carriage returns, spaces, and tabs) is one of the simplest things you can do, and it can have the largest effect on program readability. Compare the two identical nested IF-THEN-ELSE constructs shown here:

```
IF x < y THEN IF z IS NULL THEN x := 3; ELSE x := 2; END IF; ELSE
x := 4; END IF;
```

```
IF x < y THEN
  IF z IS NULL THEN
    x := 3;
  ELSE
    x := 2;
  END IF;
ELSE
  x := 4;
END IF;
```

I generally indent each line within a block by two spaces. I indent the contents of a block from the DECLARE..END keywords, and I indent loops and IF-THEN-ELSE statements. SQL statements that are continued over multiple lines are also indented, as in

```
SELECT id, first_name, last_name
  INTO v_StudentID, v_FirstName, v_LastName
  FROM STUDENTS
  WHERE id = 10002;
```

Style in General

As you write more PL/SQL code, you will probably develop your own programming style. These guidelines are by no means required, but I have found them useful in my own PL/SQL development, and I use them in the examples in this book. It is a good idea to show your code to another programmer and ask him or her what it does. If another programmer can describe what the program does and the outline of how it works, then you have documented it well and written in a good style.

In addition, many development organizations have guidelines for good code documentation and style, which can apply to other languages besides PL/SQL as well. The converse is also true: if you have an established C coding style, you can probably adapt it for use in PL/SQL.

Summary

In this chapter, we've covered the basic building blocks of PL/SQL: the structure of a PL/SQL block, variables and datatypes (scalar, composite, and reference), expressions and operators, datatype conversion rules, and the basic control structures. Our discussion of PL/SQL style should help you write more understandable and manageable code. We can now continue in Chapter 3 by adding SQL to the procedural constructs we've already explored.

CHAPTER 3

SQL Within PL/SQL

Structured Query Language (SQL) defines how data in Oracle is manipulated. This is true in PL/SQL as well. The procedural constructs in Chapter 2 become more useful when combined with the processing power of SQL. This chapter discusses the SQL operations that are permitted in PL/SQL and the transaction control statements that guarantee consistency of the data.

SQL Statements

SQL statements can be divided into six categories, as described here. Table 3-1 gives some example statements. The *Oracle7 Server SQL Reference* describes all of the SQL statements in detail.

- **Data manipulation language (DML) statements** change the data in tables, or query data in a database table, but do not change the structure of a table or other object.

■ *Data definition language (DDL) statements* create, drop, or alter the structure of a database object. Commands that change permissions on database objects are also DDL.

■ *Transaction control statements* guarantee the consistency of the data by organizing SQL statements into logical transactions, which either succeed or fail as a unit.

■ *Session control statements* change the settings for a single database connection, for example, to enable SQL tracing.

■ *System control statements* change the settings for the entire database, for example, to enable or disable archiving.

■ *Embedded SQL commands* are used in Oracle precompiler and OCI (Oracle Call Interface) programs.

Using SQL in PL/SQL

The only SQL statements allowed in a PL/SQL program are DML and transaction control statements. Specifically, DDL statements are illegal. EXPLAIN PLAN, although classified as DML, is also illegal. In order to explain why this is the case, we need to look at the way PL/SQL is designed.

In general, a programming language can bind variables in two ways—early or late. *Binding* a variable is the process of identifying the storage location associated

Category	Sample SQL Statements
Data manipulation language (DML)	SELECT, INSERT, UPDATE, DELETE, SET TRANSACTION, EXPLAIN PLAN
Data definition language (DDL)	DROP, CREATE, ALTER, GRANT, REVOKE
Transaction control	COMMIT, ROLLBACK, SAVEPOINT
Session control	ALTER SESSION, SET ROLE
System control	ALTER SYSTEM
Embedded SQL	CONNECT, DECLARE CURSOR, ALLOCATE[1]

TABLE 3-1. *Categories of SQL Statements*

[1] The ALLOCATE embedded SQL command is available with Oracle 7.2 and higher.

with an identifier in the program. In PL/SQL, binding also involves checking the database for permission to access the object referenced. A language that uses *early binding* performs the bind during the compile phase, whereas a language that uses *late binding* postpones the bind until run time. Early binding means that the compile phase will take longer (since the work of binding has to be done), but execution will be faster, since the bind has already been completed. Late binding shortens the compile time but lengthens the execution time.

PL/SQL was intentionally designed to use early binding. This decision was made so that execution of a block would be as fast as possible, with all the database objects having been pre-verified by the compiler. Early binding makes sense in PL/SQL, since blocks can be stored in the database via procedures, functions, packages, and triggers. These objects are stored in compiled form so that when they are needed, they can be loaded from the database into memory and run. (For more information on stored objects, see Chapter 5.) As a result of this design decision, DDL statements are prohibited. Since a DDL statement will modify a database object, the permissions must be validated again. Validating the permissions requires that the identifiers be bound, and in PL/SQL, binding has already been done during the compile phase.

To further illustrate this, consider the following illegal PL/SQL block:

```
BEGIN
  CREATE TABLE temp_table (
    num_value    NUMBER,
    char_value   CHAR(10));
END;
```

In order to compile this, the **temp_table** identifier needs to be bound. This process will check to see whether this table exists. However, the table won't exist until the block is run. But since the block can't even compile, there is no way that it can run.

DML and transaction control statements are the only SQL statements that don't have the potential to modify permissions on database objects, thus they are the only legal statements in PL/SQL.

Using DDL

PL/SQL **2.1** ...and HIGHER There is, however, an alternative. PL/SQL versions 2.1 and higher provide a built-in package, DBMS_SQL. This package allows you to create an SQL statement dynamically at run time, and then execute it. Before executing, this dynamic statement will be parsed by the database. Since the statement doesn't actually get created until run time, the PL/SQL compiler doesn't have to bind it. This allows the block to compile. Chapter 10 describes the DBMS_SQL package in detail.

DML in PL/SQL

DML statements include SELECT, INSERT, UPDATE, and DELETE. Each of these commands operates as its name implies: SELECT returns rows from a database table that match the criteria given by its WHERE clause, INSERT adds rows to a database table, UPDATE modifies the rows in a database table that match the WHERE clause, and DELETE removes rows identified by the WHERE clause. Besides the WHERE clause, these statements can have other clauses, which are described later in this section.

When SQL statements are executed from SQL*Plus, the results are returned to the screen, as shown in Figure 3-1. For an UPDATE, INSERT, or DELETE statement, SQL*Plus returns the number of rows processed. For a SELECT statement, the rows that match the query are echoed to the screen.

Notice the INSERT statement in Figure 3-1:

```
INSERT INTO classes (department, course, description, max_students,
                     current_students, num_credits, room_id)
   VALUES ('CS', 101, 'Computer Science 101', 50, 50, 4, 99998);
```

All of the values that are inserted into the classes table are hardcoded—they are known at the time the statement is written. PL/SQL removes this restriction with

```
                               Oracle SQL*Plus
 File  Edit  Search  Options  Help

SQL> SELECT first_name, last_name, major
  2   FROM students
  3   ORDER BY major;

FIRST_NAME           LAST_NAME            MAJOR
-------------------- -------------------- --------------------------------
Scott                Smith                Computer Science
Joanne               Junebug              Computer Science
Manish               Murgratroid          Economics
Margaret             Mason                History
Patrick              Poll                 History
Timothy              Taller               History

6 rows selected.

SQL> INSERT INTO classes (department, course, description, max_students,
  2                       current_students, num_credits, room_id)
  3      VALUES ('CS', 101, 'Computer Science 101', 50, 50, 4, 99998);

1 row created.

SQL> commit;

Commit complete.

SQL>
```

FIGURE 3-1.   *Results of executing SQL statements in SQL*Plus*

variables. Variables are allowed wherever an expression is allowed in the SQL statement. When used in this manner, they are known as *bind variables*. For example, in the preceding INSERT statement, we could replace the hardcoded description 'Computer Science 101' with a bind variable:

```
DECLARE
  v_CourseDescription  classes.description%TYPE;
BEGIN
  /* Assign to v_CourseDescription */
  v_CourseDescription := 'Computer Science 101';
  INSERT INTO classes (department, course, description, max_students,
                       current_students, num_credits, room_id)
    VALUES ('CS', 101, v_CourseDescription, 50, 50, 4, 99998);
END;
```

Not everything in an SQL statement can be replaced by a variable—only expressions. Notably, the table and column names have to be known. This is required because of early binding—names of Oracle objects have to be known at compile time. By definition, the value of a variable is not known until run time. The DBMS_SQL package can be used to overcome this restriction as well. For more information on DBMS_SQL, see Chapter 10.

SELECT

A SELECT statement retrieves data from the database into PL/SQL variables. The general form of a SELECT statement is shown here:

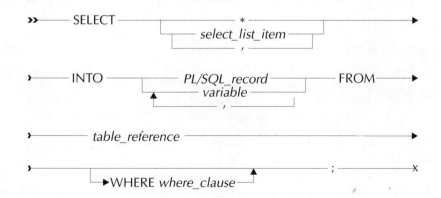

Each component is described in the following table.

SELECT Clause	Description
select_list_item	Column (or expression) to be selected. Each *select list item* is separated by a comma and can optionally be identified by an alias. The complete set of select list items is known as the *select list*. The * syntax is shorthand for the entire row. This will bring back every field in the table, in the order in which the fields were defined.
variable	PL/SQL variable into which a select list item will go. Each variable should be compatible with its associated select list item, and there should be the same number of select list items and output variables.
PL/SQL_record	Can be used instead of a list of variables. The record should contain fields that correspond to the select list, but it allows easier manipulation of the returned data. Records combine related fields together in one syntactic unit, so they can be manipulated as a group as well as individually. Records are described more fully in Chapter 2. If the select list is just *, then this record could be defined as table_reference%ROWTYPE.
table_reference	Identifies the table from which to get the data. Can be a synonym, or a table at a remote database specified with a database link. See the section on table references later in this chapter for more information.
where_clause	Criteria for the query. This clause identifies the row that will be returned by the query. It is made up of boolean conditions joined by the boolean operators, and is also described in more detail later in this chapter.

NOTE
In general, more clauses are available for a SELECT statement than for other statements. These include the ORDER BY and GROUP BY clauses, for example. Clauses will be discussed in more detail in Chapter 4.

The form of the SELECT statement described here should return no more than one row. The WHERE clause will be compared against each row in the table. If it matches more than one row, PL/SQL will return this error message:

```
ORA-1427: Single-row query returns more than one row
```

In this case, you should use a cursor to retrieve each row individually. See Chapter 4 for information about cursors.

The following example illustrates two different SELECT statements:

```
DECLARE
  v_StudentRecord    students%ROWTYPE;
  v_Department       classes.department%TYPE;
  v_Course           classes.course%TYPE;
BEGIN
  -- Retrieve one record from the students table, and store it
  -- in v_StudentRecord. Note that the WHERE clause will only
  -- match one row in the table.
  -- Note also that the query is returning all of the fields in
  -- the students table (since we are selecting *). Thus the
  -- record into which we fetch is defined as students%ROWTYPE.
  SELECT *
    INTO v_StudentRecord
    FROM students
    WHERE id = 10000;

  -- Retrieve two fields from the classes table, and store them
  -- in v_Department and v_Course. Again, the WHERE clause will
  -- only match one row in the table.
  SELECT department, course
    INTO v_Department, v_Course
    FROM classes
    WHERE room_id = 99997;
END;
```

INSERT

The syntax for the INSERT statement is shown here. Notice that there is no WHERE clause directly in the statement (although there could be one in the subquery).

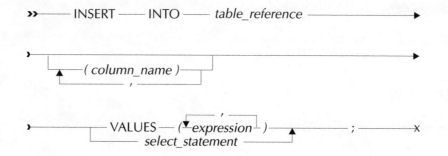

The *table_reference* clause refers to an Oracle table, *column_name* refers to a column in this table, and *expression* is an SQL or PL/SQL expression, as defined in the previous chapter. Table references are discussed in more detail later in this chapter. If the INSERT statement contains a *select_statement*, the select list should match the columns to be inserted.

The following example includes several valid INSERT statements:

```
DECLARE
  v_StudentID  students.id%TYPE;
BEGIN
  -- Retrieve a new student ID number
  SELECT student_sequence.NEXTVAL
    INTO v_StudentID
    FROM dual;

  -- Add a row to the students table
  INSERT INTO students (id, first_name, last_name)
    VALUES (v_StudentID, 'Timothy', 'Taller');

  -- Add a second row, but use the sequence number directly
  -- in the INSERT statement.
  INSERT INTO students (id, first_name, last_name)
    VALUES (student_sequence.NEXTVAL, 'Patrick', 'Poll');
END;
```

The following example is invalid, since the select list of the subquery does not match the columns to be inserted. This statement returns the Oracle "too many values" error ORA-913.

```
INSERT INTO rooms
  SELECT * FROM classes;
```

This next example, however, is legal. It doubles the size of the classes table by inserting a second copy of each row.

```
INSERT INTO classes
  SELECT * FROM classes;
```

UPDATE

The syntax for the UPDATE statement is shown here:

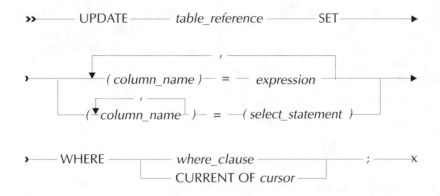

The *table_reference* clause refers to the table being updated, *column* is a column whose value will be changed, and *expression* is an SQL expression as defined in Chapter 2. If the statement contains a *select_statement*, the select list should match the columns in the SET clause.

The following block shows an example of an UPDATE statement.

```
DECLARE
  v_Major            students.major%TYPE;
  v_CreditIncrease   NUMBER := 3;
BEGIN
  -- This UPDATE statement will add 3 to the current_credits
  -- field of all students who are majoring in History.
  v_Major := 'History';
  UPDATE students
    SET current_credits = current_credits + v_CreditIncrease
    WHERE major = V_Major;
END;
```

DELETE

The DELETE statement removes rows from a database table. The WHERE clause of the statement indicates which rows are to be removed. Here is the syntax for the DELETE statement:

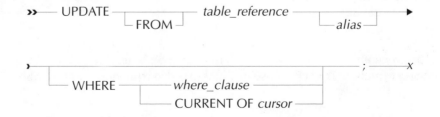

The *table_reference* clause refers to an Oracle table, and the *where_clause* defines the set of rows to be deleted. The special syntax CURRENT OF *cursor* is used with a cursor definition, and will be discussed in Chapter 4. Table references and the WHERE clause are discussed in detail in the sections that follow.

The following block illustrates some different DELETE statements:

```
DECLARE
  v_StudentCutoff  NUMBER;
BEGIN
  v_StudentCutoff := 10;
  -- Delete any classes which don't have enough students registered.
  DELETE FROM classes
    WHERE current_students < v_StudentCutoff;

  -- Delete any Economics students who don't have any credits yet.
  DELETE FROM students
    WHERE current_credits = 0
    AND   major = 'Economics';
END;
```

The WHERE Clause

The SELECT, UPDATE, and DELETE statements all include the WHERE clause as an integral part of their operations. This clause defines which statements make up the *active set*—the set of rows returned by a query (SELECT) or acted upon by an UPDATE or DELETE statement.

A WHERE clause consists of conditions, joined together by the boolean operators AND, OR, and NOT. Conditions usually take the form of comparisons, for example, in the following DELETE statement:

```
DECLARE
  v_Department  CHAR(3);
BEGIN
  v_Department := 'CS';
  -- Remove all Computer Science classes
  DELETE FROM classes
    WHERE department = v_Department;
END;
```

The preceding block will remove all rows in the **classes** table for which the condition evaluates to TRUE (those in which the **department** column = 'CS'). There are several things to note about comparisons such as these, including the importance of variable names and how characters are compared.

Variable Names

Suppose we change the name of the variable in the preceding block from **v_Department** to **department**:

```
DECLARE
 Department  CHAR(3);
BEGIN
  Department := 'CS';
  -- Remove all Computer Science classes
  DELETE FROM classes
    WHERE department = Department;
END;
```

This simple change has a dramatic effect on the results of the statement—the modified block will remove *all* rows in the classes table, not just the ones in which **department** = 'CS'! This happens because of the way the identifiers in an SQL statement are parsed. When the PL/SQL engine sees a condition such as this one,

$$expr1 = expr2$$

expr1 and *expr2* are first checked to see if they match columns in the table being operated upon, then checked to see if they are variables in the PL/SQL block. PL/SQL is not case-sensitive, so in the preceding block both **department** and **Department** are associated with the column in the **classes** table, rather than the variable. This condition will evaluate to TRUE for every row in the table; thus all rows will be deleted.

If the block has a label, we can still use the same name for a variable as a table column by prepending the label to the variable reference. This block has the desired effect, namely, to delete only those rows where **department** = 'CS':

```
<<l_DeleteBlock>>
DECLARE
  Department  CHAR(3);
BEGIN
  Department := 'CS';
  -- Remove all Computer Science classes
  DELETE FROM classes
    WHERE department = l_DeleteBlock.Department;
END;
```

Although this method can be used to get the desired behavior, it is still not good programming style to use the same name for a PL/SQL variable as for a table column. This and other PL/SQL style guidelines are discussed at the end of Chapter 2.

Character Comparisons

When two character values are being compared, as in the previous example, Oracle can use two different kinds of comparison semantics: blank-padded or non-blank-padded. These comparison semantics differ in how character strings of different lengths are compared. Suppose we are comparing two character strings, *string1* and *string2*. For *blank-padded* semantics, the following algorithm is used:

1. If *string1* and *string2* are of different lengths, pad the shorter value with blanks first so that they are both the same length.

2. Compare each string, character by character, starting from the left. Suppose the character in *string1* is *char1,* and the character in *string2* is *char2.*

3. If ASCII(*char1*) < ASCII(*char2*), *string1* < *string2*. If ASCII(*char1*) > ASCII(*char2*), *string1* > *string2*. If ASCII(*char1*) = ASCII(*char2*), continue to the next character in *string1* and *string2*.

4. If the ends of *string1* and *string2* are reached, then the strings are equal.

Using blank-padded semantics, the following conditions will all return TRUE:

```
'abc' = 'abc'
'abc   ' = 'abc'   -- Note the trailing blanks in the first string
'ab' < 'abc'
'abcd' > 'abcc'
```

The *non-blank-padded* comparison algorithm is a little different:

1. Compare each string, character by character, starting from the left. Suppose the character in *string1* is *char1,* and the character in *string2* is *char2.*

2. If ASCII(*char1*) < ASCII(*char2*), *string1* < *string2*. If ASCII(*char1*) > ASCII(*char2*), *string1* > *string2*. If ASCII(*char1*) = ASCII(*char2*), continue to the next character in *string1* and *string2*.

3. If *string1* ends before *string2,* then *string1* < *string2*. If *string2* ends before *string1,* then *string1* > *string2*.

Using non-blank-padded character comparison semantics, the following comparisons will return TRUE:

```
'abc' = 'abc'
'ab' < 'abc'
'abcd' > 'abcc'
```

However, the following comparison will return FALSE since the strings are of different lengths. This is the basic difference between the two comparison methods.

```
'abc   ' = 'abc'  -- Note the trailing blanks in the first string
```

Having defined these two different methods, when is each one used? PL/SQL will use blank-padded semantics only when both values being compared are *fixed-length* values. If either value is variable-length, non-blank-padded semantics are used. The CHAR datatype is fixed-length, and the VARCHAR2 datatype is variable-length. Character literals (enclosed in single quotes) are always considered to be fixed-length.

If a statement isn't acting upon the correct rows, check the datatypes used in the WHERE clause. The following block will *not* delete any rows, since the **v_Department** variable is VARCHAR2 rather than CHAR:

```
DECLARE
 v_Department  VARCHAR2(3);
BEGIN
  v_Department := 'CS';
  -- Remove all Computer Science classes
  DELETE FROM classes
    WHERE department = v_Department;
END;
```

The **department** column of the **classes** table is CHAR. Any computer science classes will thus have a value of 'CS ' for **department** (notice the trailing blank). Since **v_Department** = 'CS' (no trailing blank) and is of a variable-length datatype, the DELETE statement does not affect any rows.

To ensure that your WHERE clauses have the desired effect, make sure that the variables in the PL/SQL block have the same datatype as the database columns to which they are compared. Using %TYPE can guarantee this.

Table References

All of the DML operations reference a table. This reference can in general look like

> *[schema.]table[@dblink]*

where *schema* identifies the owner of the table, and *dblink* identifies a table at a remote database.

In order to establish a database connection, the user's name and password for a particular schema must be provided. Subsequent SQL statements issued during the session will reference this schema by default. If a table reference is unqualified, as in

```
UPDATE students
  SET major = 'Music'
  WHERE id = 10005;
```

then the table name (**students** in this example) must name a table in the default schema. If it does not, then an error such as

```
ORA-942: table or view does not exist
```

or

```
PLS-201: identifier must be declared
```

will be reported. The default schema is the one to which you connect before executing any SQL or PL/SQL commands. If the table is in another schema, then it can be qualified by the schema name, as in

```
UPDATE example.students
  SET major = 'Music'
  WHERE id = 10005;
```

This UPDATE will work if the connection is made to the **example** schema, or to another schema that has been granted the UPDATE privilege on the **students** table.

Database Links

If you have SQL*Net installed on your system, you can take advantage of database links. A *database link* is a reference to a remote database, which can be located on a completely different system from the local database. Here is the form of a DDL statement that creates a database link:

```
CREATE DATABASE LINK link_name
    CONNECT TO username IDENTIFIED BY password
    USING sqlnet_string;
```

The name of the database link, *link_name*, follows the usual rules for a database identifier. *username* and *password* identify a schema on the remote database, and *sqlnet_string* is a valid connect string for the remote database. Assuming that the appropriate schemas have been created and SQL*Net version 2 is installed, the following is an example of a database link creation:

```
CREATE DATABASE LINK example_backup
    CONNECT TO example IDENTIFIED BY example
    USING 'backup_database';
```

For more information on how to install and configure SQL*Net, consult the *SQL*Net User's Guide and Reference*. Given the preceding link, we can now update the students table remotely with

```
UPDATE students@example_backup
    SET major = 'Music'
    WHERE id = 10005;
```

When a database link is used as part of a transaction, the transaction is said to be a *distributed transaction*, since it modifies more than one database. For more information on distributed transactions and their administration and implications, consult the *Oracle7 Server SQL Reference*.

Synonyms

Table references can be complicated, especially if a schema and/or database link is included. In order to make maintenance easier, Oracle allows you to create a synonym for a complicated reference. The *synonym* essentially renames the table reference, similar to an alias for a select list item. However, a synonym is a data dictionary object and is created by the CREATE SYNONYM DDL statement:

CREATE SYNONYM *synonym_name* FOR *reference*;

Replace *synonym_name* with the name of your synonym and *reference* with the object that is referenced. This object can be a table, as in the following example, or it could be a procedure, sequence, or other database object.

```
CREATE SYNONYM backup_students
  FOR students@example_backup;
```

Given this synonym, we can rewrite our distributed UPDATE statement with

```
UPDATE backup_students
  SET major = 'Music'
  WHERE id = 10005;
```

NOTE
Creating a synonym does not grant any privileges on the referenced object—it just provides an alternate name for the object. If the object needs to be referenced from another schema, access to the object should be granted either explicitly or via a role (using the GRANT statement).

Built-in SQL Functions

SQL provides a number of predefined functions that can be called from within an SQL statement. For example, the following SELECT statement uses the UPPER function to return the first names of students, in all uppercase:

```
SELECT UPPER(first_name)
  FROM students;
```

Many SQL functions can be called from PL/SQL procedural statements as well. For example, the following block also uses the UPPER function, but in an assignment statement:

```
DECLARE
  v_FirstName  students.first_name%TYPE;
BEGIN
  v_FirstName := UPPER('Charlie');
END;
```

SQL functions can be divided into categories based on the type of arguments each function expects. The UPPER function, for example, expects a character argument. If you supply an argument that is not in the correct family, it is converted automatically by PL/SQL before the function is called. SQL functions can also be classified as group or single-row functions. A *group function* operates on many rows of data and returns a single result. Group functions are valid only in the select list or HAVING clause of a query. They are not allowed in PL/SQL procedural statements.

COUNT is an example of a group function. *Single-row functions* such as UPPER operate on one value and return another value. They are allowed anywhere an expression is allowed in SQL statements, and also in PL/SQL procedural statements.

The following sections describe built-in functions in detail. Each section lists the syntax, purpose, and where a function is allowed. Examples are also provided. The functions are listed in alphabetical order within each section. Some of the functions take optional arguments. These are indicated by square brackets ([]) in the function syntax.

Character Functions Returning Character Values

These functions all take arguments in the character family (except for CHR) and return character values. The majority of the functions return a VARCHAR2 value, except where noted. The return type of character functions is subject to the same restrictions as the base database type, namely that VARCHAR2 values are limited to 2000 characters and CHAR values are limited to 255 characters. When used in procedural statements, they can be assigned to either VARCHAR2 or CHAR PL/SQL variables.

CHR

Syntax

CHR(*x*)

Purpose   Returns the character that has the value equivalent to *x* in the database character set. CHR and ASCII are opposite functions. CHR returns the character given the character number, and ASCII returns the character number given the character.

Where Allowed   Procedural and SQL statements.

Example

```
SELECT CHR(37) a, CHR(100) b, CHR(101) c
  FROM dual;
A B C
- - -
% d e
```

CONCAT

Syntax

CONCAT(*string1, string2*)

Purpose
Returns *string1* concatenated with *string2*. This function is identical to the || operator.

Where Allowed
Procedural and SQL statements.

Example

```
SELECT CONCAT('Alphabet ', 'Soup') "Dinner"
  FROM dual;
Dinner
-------------
Alphabet Soup
```

INITCAP

Syntax

INITCAP(*string*)

Purpose
Returns *string* with the first character of each word capitalized and the remaining characters of each word in lowercase. Words are separated by spaces or nonalphanumeric characters. Characters that are not letters are unaffected.

Where Allowed
Procedural and SQL statements.

Example

```
SELECT INITCAP('4 scoRE and 7 YEARS ago...') "Speech"
  FROM dual;

Speech
-------------------------
4 Score And 7 Years Ago...
```

LOWER

Syntax

    LOWER(*string*)

Purpose   Returns *string* with all characters in lowercase. Any characters that are not letters are left intact. If *string* has the CHAR datatype, the result is also CHAR. If *string* is VARCHAR2, the result is VARCHAR2.

Where Allowed   Procedural and SQL statements.

Example

```
SELECT LOWER('4 scoRE and 7 YEARS ago...') "Speech"
  FROM dual;
Speech
------------------------
4 score and 7 years ago...
```

LPAD

Syntax

    LPAD(*string1*, *x* [,*string2*])

Purpose   Returns *string1* padded on the left to length *x* with the characters in *string2*. If *string2* is less than *x* characters, it is duplicated as necessary. If *string2* is more than *x* characters, only the first *x* are used. If *string2* is not specified, it defaults to a single blank. Keep in mind that *x* are specified in terms of display length, rather than actual length. If the database character set is multibyte, the display length can be longer than the actual length of the string in bytes. LPAD behaves similarly to RPAD, except that it pads on the left rather than the right.

Where Allowed   Procedural and SQL statements.

Example

```
SELECT LPAD('Short String', 15) "First"
  FROM dual;
```

```
First
---------------
   Short String

SELECT LPAD('Short String', 20, 'XY') "Second"
  FROM dual;
Second
--------------------
XYXYXYXYShort String

SELECT LPAD('Short String', 13, 'XY') "Third"
  FROM dual;
Third
--------------
XShort String
```

LTRIM

Syntax

LTRIM(*string1*, *string2*)

Purpose   Returns *string1* with the leftmost characters appearing in *string2* removed. *string2* defaults to a single blank. The database will scan *string1*, starting from the leftmost position. When the first character not in *string2* is encountered, the result is returned. LTRIM behaves similarly to RTRIM.

Where Allowed   Procedural and SQL statements.

Example

```
SELECT LTRIM('   End of the string') "First"
  FROM dual;
First
-----------------
End of the string

SELECT LTRIM('xxxEnd of the string', 'x') "Second"
  FROM dual;
Second
-----------------
```

```
End of the string

SELECT LTRIM('xyxyxyEnd of the string', 'xy') "Third"
  FROM dual;
Third
----------------
End of the string

SELECT LTRIM('xyxyxxxyEnd of the string', 'xy') "Fourth"
  FROM dual;
Fourth
----------------
End of the string
```

NLS_INITCAP

Syntax

NLS_INITCAP(*string* [,*nlsparams*])

Purpose

Returns *string* with the first character of each word capitalized and the remaining characters of each word in lowercase. *nlsparams* specifies a different sorting sequence than the default for the session. If it is not specified, NLS_INITCAP behaves the same as INITCAP. *nlsparams* can have the form

'NLS_SORT = *sort*'

where *sort* specifies a linguistic sort sequence. For more information on NLS parameters and how they are used, see the *Oracle7 Server SQL Reference*.

Where Allowed   Procedural and SQL statements.

Example

```
SELECT NLS_INITCAP('ijgloo', 'NLS_SORT = Xdutch') "Result"
  FROM dual;
Result
------
IJgloo
```

NLS_LOWER

Syntax

NLS_LOWER(*string* [,*nlsparams*])

Purpose   Returns *string* with all letters in lowercase. Characters that are not letters are left intact. *nlsparams* has the same form and serves the same purpose as in NLS_INITCAP. If *nlsparams* is not included, NLS_LOWER behaves the same as LOWER.

Where Allowed   Procedural and SQL statements.

Example

```
SELECT NLS_LOWER('CITA''DEL', 'NLS_SORT = Xgerman') "Result"
  FROM dual;
Result
---------
citàdel
```

NLS_UPPER

Syntax

NLS_UPPER(*string*, [,*nlsparams*])

Purpose   Returns *string* with all letters in uppercase. Characters that are not letters are left intact. *nlsparams* has the same form and behaves the same as in NLS_INITCAP. If *nlsparams* isn't specified, NLS_UPPER behaves the same as UPPER.

Where Allowed   Procedural and SQL statements.

Example

```
SELECT NLS_UPPER('große', 'NLS_SORT = Xgerman') "Result"
  FROM dual;
Result
------
GROSS
```

REPLACE

Syntax

REPLACE (*string, search_str* [*,replace_str*])

Purpose   Returns *string* with every occurrence of *search_str* replaced with *replace_str*. If *replace_str* is not specified, all occurrences of *search_str* are removed. REPLACE is a superset of the functionality provided by TRANSLATE.

Where Allowed   Procedural and SQL statements.

Example

```
SELECT REPLACE ('This and That', 'Th', 'B') "First"
  FROM dual;
First
-----------
Bis and Bat

SELECT REPLACE ('This and That', 'Th') "Second"
  FROM dual;
Second
---------
is and at

SELECT REPLACE ('This and That', NULL) "Third"
  FROM dual;
Third
-------------
This and That
```

RPAD

Syntax

RPAD(*string1, x* [*,string2*])

Purpose   Returns *string1* padded on the right to length *x* with the characters in *string2*. If *string2* is less than *x* characters, it is duplicated as necessary. If *string2* is more than *x* characters, only the first *x* are used. If *string2* is not specified, it defaults to a single blank. Keep in mind that *x* is specified in terms of display length rather than actual length. If the database character set is multibyte, the display length can be longer than the actual length of the string in bytes. RPAD behaves similarly to LPAD, except that it pads on the right rather than the left.

Where Allowed   Procedural and SQL statements.

Example

```
SELECT RPAD('Nifty', 10, '!') "First"
  FROM dual;
First
----------
Nifty!!!!!

SELECT RPAD('Nifty', 10, 'AB') "Second"
  FROM dual;
Second
----------
NiftyABABA
```

RTRIM

Syntax

> RTRIM(*string1* [,*string2*])

Purpose   Returns *string1* with the rightmost characters appearing in *string2* removed. *string2* defaults to a single blank. The database will scan *string1*, starting from the rightmost position. When the first character not in *string2* is encountered, the result is returned. RTRIM behaves similarly to LTRIM.

Where Allowed   Procedural and SQL statements.

Example

```
SELECT RTRIM('This is a stringxxxxx', 'x') "First"
  FROM dual;
First
----------------
```

```
This is a string

SELECT RTRIM('This is also a stringxxXXxx', 'x') "Second"
  FROM dual;
Second
------------------------
This is also a stringxxXX

SELECT RTRIM('This is a string as well', 'well') "Third"
  FROM dual;
Third
-------------------
This is a string as
```

SOUNDEX

Syntax

SOUNDEX(*string*)

Purpose   Returns the phonetic representation of *string*. This is useful for comparing words that are spelled differently but sound alike. The phonetic representation is defined in *The Art of Computer Programming, Volume 3: Sorting and Searching*, by Donald E. Knuth (Addison-Wesley, 1996). The algorithm for developing the phonetic spelling is as follows:

- Keep the first letter of the string and remove occurrences of a, e, h, i, o, w, and y.

- Assign numbers to the remaining letters as follows:

   1. a, e, h, i, o, w, y

   2. b, f, p, v

   3. c, e, g, j, k, q, s, x, z

   4. d, t

   5. l

   6. m, n

   7. r

■ If two or more numbers are in sequence, remove all but the first.

■ Return the first 4 bytes padded with 0.

Where Allowed   Procedural and SQL statements.

Example

```
SELECT first_name, SOUNDEX(first_name)
  FROM students;
FIRST_NAME           SOUN
-------------------- ----
Scott                S300
Margaret             M626
Joanne               J500
Manish               M520
Patrick              P362
Timothy              T530

SELECT first_name
  FROM students
  WHERE SOUNDEX(first_name) = SOUNDEX('skit');
FIRST_NAME
--------------------
Scott
```

SUBSTR

Syntax

SUBSTR(*string, a* [,*b*])

Purpose   Returns a portion of *string* starting at character *a, b* characters long. If *a* is 0, it is treated as 1 (the beginning of the string). If *b* is positive, characters are returned counting from the left. If *b* is negative, characters are returning starting from the end of *string,* and counting from the right. If *b* is not present, it defaults to the entire string. If *b* is less than 1, NULL is returned. If a floating point value is passed for either *a* or *b,* the value is truncated to an integer first.

Where Allowed   Procedural and SQL statements.

Example

```
SELECT SUBSTR('abc123def', 4, 4) "First"
  FROM dual;
First
----
123d

SELECT SUBSTR('abc123def', -4, 4) "Second"
  FROM dual;
Second
----
3def
```

SUBSTRB

Syntax

SUBSTRB(*string, a* [,*b*])

Purpose   Behaves the same as SUBSTR, except that *a* and *b* are expressed in bytes rather than characters. For a single-byte character string, such as ASCII, SUBSTRB behaves the same as SUBSTR.

Where Allowed   Procedural and SQL statements.

Example (Assuming a Double-Byte Character Set)

```
SELECT SUBSTR("abc123def", 2, 6) "Example"
  FROM DUAL;
Example
-------
bc1
```

TRANSLATE

Syntax

TRANSLATE(*string, from_str, to_str*)

Purpose   Returns *string* with all occurrences of each character in *from_str* replaced by the corresponding character in *to_str*. TRANSLATE is a superset of the functionality provided by REPLACE. If *from_str* is longer than *to_str,* any extra characters in *from_str* not in *to_str* are removed from *string,* since they have no corresponding characters. *to_str* cannot be empty. Oracle interprets the empty string to be the same as NULL, and if any argument to TRANSLATE is NULL, the result is NULL as well.

Where Allowed   Procedural and SQL statements.

Example

```
SELECT TRANSLATE('abcdefghij', 'abcdef', '123456')
  FROM dual;
TRANSLATE(
----------
123456ghij

SELECT TRANSLATE('abcdefghij', 'abcdefghij', '123456')
  FROM dual;
TRANSL
------
123456
```

UPPER

Syntax

UPPER(*string*)

Purpose   Returns *string* with all letters in uppercase. If *string* has datatype CHAR, the return value is also CHAR. If *string* has datatype VARCHAR2, then the return value is VARCHAR2. Any characters that are not letters are left intact in the returned value.

Where Allowed   Procedural and SQL statements.

Example

```
SELECT UPPER('THE quick bROwn Fox jumped over THE LAZY
             dOg...') "Result"
  FROM dual;
```

```
Result
--------------------------------------------------
THE QUICK BROWN FOX JUMPED OVER THE LAZY DOG...
```

Character Functions Returning Numeric Values

These functions take character arguments and return numeric results. The arguments can be either CHAR or VARCHAR2. Although many results are in fact integer values, the return value is simply NUMBER, with no precision or scale defined.

ASCII

Syntax

ASCII(*string*)

Purpose   Returns the decimal representation of the first byte of *string* in the database character set. Notice that this function is still called ASCII even if the character set is not 7-bit ASCII. CHR and ASCII are opposite functions. CHR returns the character given the character number, and ASCII returns the character number given the character.

Where Allowed   Procedural and SQL statements.

Example

```
SELECT ASCII(' ')
  FROM dual;
ASCII('')
---------
       32

SELECT ASCII('a')
  FROM dual;
ASCII('A')
----------
       97
```

INSTR

[handwritten annotations: returns position no. / start search position / no. occurrence]

Syntax

INSTR(*string1*, *string2* [,*a*] [,*b*])

Purpose   Returns the position within *string1* where *string2* is contained. *string1* is scanned from the left, starting at position *a*. If *a* is negative, then *string1* is scanned from the right. The position of the *b*th occurrence is returned. Both *a* and *b* default to 1, which would return the first occurrence of *string2* within *string1*. If *string2* isn't found subject to *a* and *b*, 0 is returned. Positions are relative to the beginning of *string1* regardless of the values of *a* and *b*.

Where Allowed   Procedural and SQL statements.

Example

```
SELECT INSTR('Scott''s spot', 'ot', 1, 2) "First"
  FROM dual;
    First
---------
      11


SELECT INSTR('Scott''s spot', 'ot', -1, 2) "Second"
  FROM dual;
   Second
---------
        3


SELECT INSTR('Scott''s spot', 'ot', 5) "Third"
  FROM dual;
    Third
---------
       11


SELECT INSTR('Scott''s spot', 'ot', 12) "Fourth"
  FROM dual;
   Fourth
---------
        0
```

INSTRB

Syntax

INSTRB(*string1*, *string2* [,*a*] [,*b*])

Purpose   Behaves the same as INSTR, except that *a* and the return value are expressed as bytes. Similar to SUBSTRB, INSTRB behaves the same as INSTR for single-byte character sets.

Where Allowed   Procedural and SQL statements.

Example (Assuming a Double-Byte Character Set)

```
SELECT INSTRB('Scott''s spot', 'ot', 1, 2) "INSTRB"
  FROM dual;
   INSTRB
---------
      21
```

LENGTH

Syntax

LENGTH(*string*)

Purpose   Returns the length of *string* in characters. Since CHAR values are blank-padded, if *string* has datatype CHAR, the trailing blanks are included in the length. If *string* is NULL, the function returns NULL.

Where Allowed   Procedural and SQL statements.

Example

```
SELECT LENGTH('Mary had a little lamb') "Length"
  FROM dual;
   Length
---------
      22
```

LENGTHB

Syntax

LENGTHB(*string*)

Purpose   Behaves the same as LENGTH, except that the return value is expressed in bytes rather than characters. Similar to INSTRB, LENGTHB behaves the same as LENGTH for single-byte character sets.

Where Allowed   Procedural and SQL statements.

Example

```
SELECT LENGTHB('Mary had a little lamb') "Length"
  FROM dual;
  Length
---------
      44
```

NLSSORT

Syntax

NLSSORT(*string* [,*nlsparams*])

Purpose   Returns the string of bytes used to sort *string*. All character values are converted into byte strings such as this for consistency among different database character sets. *nlsparams* behaves the same as it does for NLS_INITCAP. If *nlsparams* is omitted, the default sort sequence for your session is used. For more information on sort sequences, see the "National Language Support" section of the *Oracle7 Server SQL Reference*.

Where Allowed   Procedural and SQL statements.

Example

```
SELECT NLSSORT('Scott') "NLS"
  FROM dual;
NLS
```

```
------------------------------------------------
53636F747400
```

Numeric Functions

These functions take NUMBER arguments and return NUMBER values. The return values of the transcendental and trigonometric functions are accurate to 36 decimal digits.

ABS

Syntax

ABS(*x*)

Purpose   Returns the absolute value of *x*.

Where Allowed   Procedural and SQL statements.

Example

```
SELECT ABS(-7), ABS(7)
  FROM dual;
  ABS(-7)    ABS(7)
--------- ---------
        7         7
```

CEIL

Syntax

CEIL(*x*)

Purpose   Returns the smallest integer greater than or equal to *x*.

Where Allowed   Procedural and SQL statements.

Example

```
SELECT CEIL(18.1), CEIL(-18.1)
  FROM dual;
CEIL(18.1) CEIL(-18.1)
---------- -----------
        19         -18
```

COS

Syntax

COS(*x*)

Purpose   Returns the cosine of *x*. *x* is an angle expressed in radians.

Where Allowed   Procedural and SQL statements.

Example

```
SELECT COS(0), COS(90 * 3.14159265359/180)
  FROM dual;
   COS(0) COS(90*3.14159265359/180)
--------- -------------------------
        1                        -1
```

COSH

Syntax

COSH(*x*)

Purpose   Returns the hyperbolic cosine of *x*.

Where Allowed   Procedural and SQL statements.

Example

```
SELECT COSH(0), COSH(90 * 3.14159265359/180)
  FROM dual;
```

```
COSH(0) COSH(90*3.14159265359/180)
--------- --------------------------
        1                   2.5091785
```

EXP

Syntax

EXP(*x*)

Purpose   Returns *e* raised to the *x*th power. *e* = 2.71828183...

Where Allowed   Procedural and SQL statements.

Example

```
SELECT EXP(1), EXP(2.7)
  FROM dual;
   EXP(1)   EXP(2.7)
--------- ---------
2.7182818 14.879732
```

FLOOR

Syntax

FLOOR(*x*)

Purpose   Returns the largest integer equal to or less than *x*.

Where Allowed   Procedural and SQL statements.

Example

```
SELECT FLOOR(-23.5), FLOOR(23.5)
  FROM dual;
FLOOR(-23.5) FLOOR(23.5)
------------ -----------
        -24          23
```

LN

Syntax

LN(*x*)

Purpose   Returns the natural logarithm of *x*. *x* must be greater than 0.

Where Allowed   Procedural and SQL statements.

Example

```
SELECT LN(100)
  FROM dual;
  LN(100)
---------
4.6051702
```

LOG

Syntax

LOG(*x, y*)

Purpose   Returns the logarithm base *x*, of *y*. The base must be a positive number other than 0 or 1, and *y* can be any positive number.

Where Allowed   Procedural and SQL statements.

Example

```
SELECT LOG(2, 32), LOG(5, 25)
  FROM dual;
LOG(2,32) LOG(5,25)
--------- ---------
        5         2
```

MOD

Syntax

MOD(*x*, *y*)

Purpose   Returns the remainder of *x* divided by *y*. If *y* is 0, *x* is returned.

Where Allowed   Procedural and SQL statements.

Example

```
SELECT MOD(23, 5), MOD(4, 1.3)
  FROM dual;
MOD(23,5) MOD(4,1.3)
--------- ----------
        3         .1
```

NOTE
The MOD function behaves differently from the classical modulus
function when *x* is negative. The classical modulus can be defined as

$$x - y * FLOOR(x/y)$$

POWER

Syntax

POWER(*x*, *y*)

Purpose   Returns *x* raised to the *y*th power. The base *x* and the exponent *y* need not be positive integers, but if *x* is negative, then *y* must be an integer.

Where Allowed   Procedural and SQL statements.

Example

```
SELECT POWER(4, 3), POWER(1.1, 2.6), POWER(25, -2), POWER
   FROM dual;
POWER(4,3)  POWER(1.1,2.6)  POWER(25,-2)  POWER(-2,3)
----------  --------------  ------------  -----------
        64        1.281212         .0016           -8
```

ROUND

Syntax

ROUND(x [,y])

Purpose   Returns x rounded to y places to the right of the decimal point. y defaults to 0, which rounds x to the nearest integer. If y is negative, digits left of the decimal point are rounded. y must be an integer.

Where Allowed   Procedural and SQL statements.

Example

```
SELECT ROUND(1.56), ROUND(1.56, 1), ROUND(12.34, -2)
   FROM dual;
ROUND(1.56)  ROUND(1.56,1)  ROUND(12.34,-2)
-----------  -------------  ---------------
          2            1.6                0
```

SIGN

Syntax

SIGN(x)

Purpose   If x < 0, returns −1. If x = 0, returns 0. If x > 0, returns 1.

Where Allowed   Procedural and SQL statements.

Example

```
SELECT SIGN(-47.3), SIGN(0), SIGN(47.3)
  FROM dual;
SIGN(-47.3)    SIGN(0) SIGN(47.3)
----------- --------- ----------
         -1         0          1
```

SIN

Syntax

SIN(*x*)

Purpose   Returns the sine of *x*, which is an angle expressed in radians.

Where Allowed   Procedural and SQL statements.

Example

```
SELECT SIN(0), SIN(60 * 3.14159265359/180)
  FROM dual;
    SIN(0) SIN(60*3.14159265359/180)
--------- -------------------------
         0                 .8660254
```

SINH

Syntax

SINH(*x*)

Purpose   Returns the hyperbolic sine of *x*.

Where Allowed   Procedural and SQL statements.

Example

```
SELECT SINH(0), SINH(60 * 3.14159265359/180)
  FROM dual;
   SINH(0) SINH(60*3.14159265359/180)
--------- -------------------------
         0                 1.2493671
```

SQRT

Syntax

SQRT(*x*)

Purpose Returns the square root of *x*. *x* cannot be negative.

Where Allowed Procedural and SQL statements.

Example

```
SELECT SQRT(64), SQRT(97.654)
  FROM dual;
 SQRT(64) SQRT(97.654)
--------- ------------
        8    9.8820038
```

TAN

Syntax

TAN(*x*)

Purpose Returns the tangent of *x*, which is an angle expressed in radians.

Where Allowed Procedural and SQL statements.

Example

```
SELECT TAN(0), TAN(-60 * 3.14159265359/180)
  FROM dual;
   TAN(0) TAN(-60*3.14159265359/180)
--------- --------------------------
        0                  -1.732051
```

TANH

Syntax

TANH(*x*)

Purpose

Returns the hyperbolic tangent of *x*.

Where Allowed

Procedural and SQL statements.

Example

```
SELECT TANH(0), TANH(-60 * 3.14159265359/180)
  FROM dual;
  TANH(0) TANH(-60*3.14159265359/180)
--------- ----------------------------
        0                    -.7807144
```

TRUNC

Syntax

TRUNC(*x* [,*y*])

Purpose

Returns *x* truncated (as opposed to rounded) to *y* decimal places. *y* defaults to 0, which truncates *x* to an integer value. If *y* is negative, digits left of the decimal point are truncated.

Where Allowed

Procedural and SQL statements.

Example

```
SELECT TRUNC(-123.456), TRUNC(-123.456, 1), TRUNC(-123.456, -1)
  FROM dual;
TRUNC(-123.456) TRUNC(-123.456,1) TRUNC(-123.456,-1)
--------------- ----------------- ------------------
           -123            -123.4               -120
```

Date Functions

The date functions take arguments of type DATE. Except for the MONTHS_BETWEEN function, which returns a NUMBER, all of the functions return DATE values. Date arithmetic is also discussed in this section.

ADD_MONTHS

Syntax

ADD_MONTHS(*d*, *x*)

Purpose   Returns the date *d* plus *x* months. *x* can be any integer. If the resultant month has fewer days than the month of *d,* the last day of the resultant month is returned. If not, the result has the same day component as *d.* The time component of *d* and the result are the same.

Where Allowed   Procedural and SQL statements.

Example

```
SELECT ADD_MONTHS('02-FEB-91', 1), ADD_MONTHS('19-JAN-87', 1),
       ADD_MONTHS('30-JAN-87', 13)
  FROM dual;
ADD_MONTH ADD_MONTH ADD_MONTH
--------- --------- ---------
02-MAR-91 19-FEB-87 29-FEB-88
```

LAST_DAY

Syntax

LAST_DAY(*d*)

Purpose   Returns the date of the last day of the month that contains *d.* This function can be used to determine how many days are left in the current month.

Where Allowed   Procedural and SQL statements.

Example

```
SELECT LAST_DAY('12-APR-71') "Current",
       LAST_DAY('12-APR-71') - TO_DATE('12-APR-71') "Days Left"
  FROM dual;
Current   Days Left
--------- ---------
30-APR-71        18
```

MONTHS_BETWEEN

Syntax

MONTHS_BETWEEN(*date1*, *date2*)

Purpose   Returns the number of months between *date1* and *date2*. If both *date1* and *date2* have the same day component, or if both are the last days of their respective months, then the result is an integer. Otherwise, the result will contain the fractional portion of a 31-day month.

Where Allowed   Procedural and SQL statements.

Example

```
SELECT MONTHS_BETWEEN('12-APR-71', '12-MAR-97') "First",
       MONTHS_BETWEEN('12-APR-71', '22-MAR-60') "Second"
  FROM dual;
First     Second
--------- ---------
     -311 132.67742
```

NEW_TIME

Syntax

NEW_TIME(*d t, zone1, zone2*)

Purpose   Returns the date and time in time zone *zone2* when the date and time in time zone *zone1* are *d* and *t*. *zone1* and *zone2* are expressed according to the following table:

String	Time Zone
AST	Atlantic Standard Time
ADT	Atlantic Daylight Time
BST	Bering Standard Time
BDT	Bering Daylight Time
CST	Central Standard Time
CDT	Central Daylight Time
EST	Eastern Standard Time
EDT	Eastern Daylight Time
GMT	Greenwich Mean Time
HST	Alaska-Hawaii Standard Time
HDT	Alaska-Hawaii Daylight Time
MST	Mountain Standard Time
MDT	Mountain Daylight Time
NST	Newfoundland Standard Time
PST	Pacific Standard Time
PDT	Pacific Daylight Time
YST	Yukon Standard Time
YDT	Yukon Daylight Time

Where Allowed   Procedural and SQL statements.

Example

```
SELECT TO_CHAR(NEW_TIME(TO_DATE('12-APR-71 12:00:00',
                          'DD-MON-YY HH24:MI:SS'),
                   'PST', 'EST'),
          'DD-MON-YY HH24:MI:SS') "Pacific -> Eastern"
  FROM dual;
Pacific -> Eastern
-----------------
12-APR-71 15:00:00
```

NEXT_DAY

Syntax

NEXT_DAY(*d, string*)

Purpose   Returns the date of the first day named by *string* that is later than the date *d. string* specifies a day of the week in the language of the current session. The time component of the returned value is the same as the time component of *d*. The case of *string* is not significant.

Where Allowed   Procedural and SQL statements.

Example
This example returns the next Thursday after April 12, 1971.

```
SELECT NEXT_DAY('12-APR-71', 'thursday') "Result"
   FROM dual;
Result
--------
15-APR-71
```

ROUND

Syntax

ROUND(*d* [,*format*])

Purpose   Rounds the date *d* to the unit specified by *format*. The available formats (as specified in Table 3-11 of the *SQL Language Reference*) for ROUND and TRUNC are described in Table 3-2. If *format* is not specified, it defaults to 'DD', which rounds *d* to the nearest day.

Where Allowed   Procedural and SQL statements.

Example

```
SELECT ROUND(TO_DATE('12-APR-71'), 'MM') "Nearest Month"
   FROM dual;
Nearest Month
-------------
01-APR-71
```

Format Model	Rounding or Truncating Unit
CC, SCC	Century
SYYYY, YYYY, YEAR, SYEAR, YYY, YY, Y	Year (rounds up on July 1)
IYYY, IY, IY, I	ISO year
Q	Quarter (rounds up on the sixteenth day of the second month of the quarter)
MONTH, MON, MM, RM	Month (rounds up on the sixteenth day)
WW	Same day of the week as the first day of the year
IW	Same day of the week as the first day of the ISO year
W	Same day of the week as the first day of the month
DDD, DD, J	Day
Day, DY, D	Starting day of the week
HH, HH12, HH24	Hour
MI	Minute

TABLE 3-2. *ROUND and TRUNC Date Formats*

SYSDATE

Syntax

```
SYSDATE
```

Purpose   Returns the current date and time, of type DATE. Takes no arguments. When used in distributed SQL statements, SYSDATE returns the date and time of the local database.

Where Allowed   Procedural and SQL statements.

Example

```
SELECT TO_CHAR(SYSDATE, 'Month DD, YYYY HH24:MI:SS') "Now"
  FROM dual;
Now
----------------------------------------------------------------
April  16, 1996 00:14:18
```

TRUNC

Syntax

TRUNC(*d* [,*format*])

Purpose   Returns the date *d* truncated to the unit specified by *format*. The available format models and their effects are the same as ROUND, described in Table 3-2. If *format* is omitted, it defaults to 'DD', which truncates *d* to the nearest day.

Where Allowed   Procedural and SQL statements.

Example

```
SELECT TRUNC(TO_DATE('12-APR-71 13:21:00', 'DD-MON-YY HH24'),
             'Year') "First Day"
  FROM dual;
First Day
---------
01-JAN-71
```

Date Arithmetic

Applying the arithmetic operators to dates and numbers is described according to Table 3-3. Notice that when one date value is subtracted from another, the result is a number.

Examples of valid date arithmetic expressions follow:

```
SELECT SYSDATE, SYSDATE + 1 "Tomorrow"
  FROM dual;
SYSDATE    Tomorrow
---------  ---------
13-NOV-95  14-NOV-95
```

```
SELECT TO_DATE('12-APR-71 12:00:00', 'DD-MON-YY HH24:MI:SS') -
       TO_DATE('15-MAR-71 15:00 -MON-YY
               HH24:MI:SS') "Difference"
  FROM dual
Difference
----------
    27.875
```

Operation	Type of Value Returned	Result
$d1 - d2$	NUMBER	Returns the difference in days between $d1$ and $d2$.[1] This value is expressed as a number, with the real part representing a fraction of a day.
$d1 + d2$	N/A	Illegal—can only subtract two dates.
$d1 + n$	DATE	Adds n days to $d1$ and returns the result.[2] n can be a real number, including a fraction of a day.
$d1 - n$	DATE	Subtracts n days from $d1$ and returns the result. n can be a real number, including a fraction of a day.

TABLE 3-3. *Semantics of Date Arithmetic*

[1] $d1$ and $d2$ represent date values.
[2] n represents a number value.

Conversion Functions

The conversion functions are used to convert between PL/SQL datatypes. PL/SQL will do many of these conversions automatically, via implicit calls to conversion functions. However, you have no control over the format specifiers used in implicit calls made by PL/SQL, and they can make your code more difficult to understand. Consequently, it is good programming style to use explicit conversion functions, explained in this section, rather than relying on PL/SQL's implicit conversions.

CHARTOROWID

Syntax

CHARTOROWID(*string*)

Purpose   Converts a CHAR or VARCHAR2 value containing the external format of a ROWID into the internal binary format. The argument *string* must be an 18-character string containing the external format of a ROWID, as described in Chapter 2. CHARTOROWID is the inverse of ROWIDTOCHAR.

Where Allowed   Procedural and SQL statements.

Example

```
SELECT description
  FROM classes
  WHERE rowid = CHARTOROWID('0000002D.0002.0002');
DESCRIPTION
-------------
Economics 203
```

CONVERT

Syntax

CONVERT(*string, dest_set* [,*source_set*])

Purpose   Converts the character string *string* from the character set identified by *source_set* to the character set identified by *dest_set*. If *source_set* is not specified, it defaults to the character set of the database. Common character sets include those listed here:

Character Set Identifier	Description
US7ASCII	U.S. 7-bit ASCII. This is the character set used by most Unix operating systems and Oracle databases on Unix.
WE8DEC	DEC West European 8-bit.
WE8HP	HP West European LaserJet 8-bit.

F7DEC	DEC French 7-bit.
WE8EBCDIC500	IBM West European EBCDIC Code Page 500.
WE8PC850	IBM PC Code Page 500. This is the character set used by most PC systems and by Oracle running on PCs.
WE8ISO8859P1	ISO-8859-1 West European 8-bit.

For complete conversion, the destination character set should contain a representation of all the characters in the source character set. If not, then a replacement character set is used in the destination. This replacement character is part of the character set definition itself.

Where Allowed   Procedural and SQL statements.

Example (from the *Oracle7 Server SQL Reference*)

```
SELECT CONVERT('Groß', 'WE8HP', 'WE8DEC') "Conversion"
  FROM dual;
Conversion
----------
Groß
```

HEXTORAW

Syntax

HEXTORAW(*string*)

Purpose   Converts the binary value represented by *string* to a RAW value. *string* should contain hexadecimal values. Every two characters in *string* represent one byte of the resultant RAW. HEXTORAW and RAWTOHEX are inverse functions.

Where Allowed   Procedural and SQL statements.

Example

```
INSERT INTO raw_table (raw_column)
  VALUES (HEXTORAW('017D3F'));
```

RAWTOHEX

Syntax

    RAWTOHEX(*rawvalue*)

Purpose   Converts the RAW *rawvalue* to a character string containing the hexadecimal representation. Each byte of *rawvalue* is converted into a two-character string. RAWTOHEX and HEXTORAW are inverse functions.

Where Allowed   Procedural and SQL statements.

Example

```
SELECT raw_column
  FROM raw_table;
RAW_COLUMN
----------
017D3F
```

ROWIDTOCHAR

Syntax

    ROWIDTOCHAR(*rowid*)

Purpose   Converts the ROWID value *rowid* to its external 18-character string representation. ROWIDTOCHAR and CHARTOROWID are inverse functions.

Where Allowed   Procedural and SQL statements.

Example

```
SELECT ROWIDTOCHAR(rowid)
  FROM classes;

ROWIDTOCHAR(ROWID)
------------------
0000002D.0000.0002
0000002D.0002.0002
0000002D.0003.0002
```

TO_CHAR (dates)

Syntax

TO_CHAR(*d* [,*format* [,*nlsparams*]])

Purpose   Converts the date *d* to a VARCHAR2 character string. If *format* is specified, it is used to control how the result is structured. A format string is made up of *format elements*. Each element returns a portion of the date value, such as the month. The date format elements are described in Table 3-4. If *format* is not specified, the default date format for your session is used. If *nlsparams* is specified, it controls the language for the month and day components of the returned string. The format of *nlsparams* is

'NLS_DATE_LANGUAGE = *language*'

where *language* represents the desired language. For more information on TO_CHAR and date format elements, see the *Oracle7 Server SQL Reference*.

Where Allowed   Procedural and SQL statements.

Example

```
SELECT TO_CHAR(SYSDATE, 'DD-MON-YY HH24:MI:SS') "Right Now"
  FROM dual;
Right Now
-----------------
15-NOV-95 01:17:14
```

TO_CHAR (labels)

Syntax

TO_CHAR(*label* [,*format*])

Purpose   Converts the MLSLABEL *label* to a VARCHAR2 type. If specified, the label format *format* is used for the conversion. If not specified, the default label *format* is used. This function is only relevant when using Trusted Oracle. This version of TO_CHAR and TO_LABEL are inverse functions.

Where Allowed   Procedural and SQL statements in a trusted database.

Date Format Element	Description
punctuation	All punctuation symbols are reproduced in the result string.
"*text*"	Text contained in double quotes is likewise reproduced.
AD, A.D.	AD indicator, with or without periods.
AM, A.M.	Ante meridiem indicator, with or without periods.
BC, B.C.	BC indicator, with or without periods.
CC, SCC	Century. SCC returns BC dates as negative values.
D	Day of week (1-7).
DAY[1]	Name of day, padded with blanks to length of nine characters.
DD	Day of month (1-31).
DDD	Day of year (1-366).
DY[1]	Abbreviated name of day.
IW	Week of year (1-52, 1-53) based on the ISO standard.
IYY, IY, I	Last three, two, or one digit(s) of the ISO year.
IYYY	Four-digit year based on the ISO standard.
HH, HH12	Hour of day (1-12).
HH24	Hour of day (0-23).
J	Julian day. The number of days since January 1, 4712 BC. The corresponding output will be an integer value.
MI	Minute (0-59).
MM	Month (1-12). JAN=1, DEC=12.
MONTH[1]	Name of month, padded with blanks to nine characters.
MON[1]	Abbreviated name of month.
PM, P.M.	Post meridiem indicator, with and without periods.
Q	Quarter of year (1-4). JAN-MAR = 1.
RM	Roman numeral month (I-XII). JAN=I, DEC=XII.
RR	Last two digits of year for years in other centuries.
SS	Second (0-59).
SSSSS	Seconds past midnight (0-86399). The format model 'J.SSSSS' will always yield a numeric value.

TABLE 3-4.   *Valid Date Format Elements*

Date Format Element	Description
WW	Week of year (1-53). Week 1 starts on the first day of the year and continues to the seventh day. Thus, the weeks do not necessarily start on Sunday.
W	Week of month (1-5). Weeks are defined as they are for the WW element.
Y, YYY	Year with comma in this position.
YEAR, SYEAR[1]	Year spelled out. SYEAR returns BC dates as negative.
YYYY, SYYYY	Four-digit year. SYYYY returns BC dates as negative.
YYY, YY, Y	Last three, two, or one digit(s) of year.

TABLE 3-4. *Valid Date Format Elements* (continued)

[1]These elements are case-sensitive. For example, 'MON' will return 'JAN' , and 'Mon' will return 'Jan'.

Example
See the *Trusted Oracle7 Server Administrator's Guide*.

TO_CHAR (numbers)

Syntax

    TO_CHAR(*num* [,*format* [,*nlsparams*]])

Purpose   Converts the NUMBER argument *num* to a VARCHAR2. If specified, *format* governs the conversion. Available number formats are described in Table 3-5. If *format* is not specified, the resultant string will have exactly as many characters as necessary to hold the significant digits of *num*. *nlsparams* is used to specify the decimal and group separator, along with the currency symbol. It can have the format

    'NLS_NUMERIC_CHARS = "*dg*" NLS_CURRENCY = "*string*"

where *d* and *g* represent the decimal and group separators, respectively. *string* represents the currency symbol. For example, in the United States the decimal separator is typically a period (.), the group separator is a comma (,), and the currency symbol is $. See the *Oracle7 Server SQL Reference* for complete details on National Language Support.

Where Allowed   Procedural and SQL statements.

Example

```
SELECT TO_CHAR(123456, '99G99G99') "Result"
  FROM dual;
Result
---------
 12,34,56

SELECT TO_CHAR(123456, 'L99G99D99',
              'NLS_NUMERIC_CHARACTERS = '',.''
              NLS_CURRENCY = ''Money'' ') "Result 2"
  FROM dual;
Result 2
-------------
Money12,34.56
```

Format Element	Sample Format String	Description
9	99	Each 9 represents a significant digit in the result. The return value has the number of significant digits equal to the number of 9s, with a leading minus if negative. Any leading zeros are left blank.
0	0999	Returns leading zeros rather than blanks.
0	9990	Returns trailing zeros rather than blanks.
$	$999	Returns value with a leading dollar sign, regardless of the currency symbol. This can be used in addition to leading or trailing zeros.
B	B999	Returns blanks for the integer part of a decimal number when the integer part is zero.
MI	999MI	Returns a negative value with a trailing minus sign rather than a leading minus. A positive value will have a trailing blank.
S	S9999	Returns a leading sign: + for positive numbers, – for negative numbers.
S	9999S	Returns a trailing sign: + for positive numbers, – for negative numbers.

TABLE 3-5.   *Number Format Elements*

Format Element	Sample Format String	Description
PR	99PR	Returns a negative value in *angle_brackets.* A positive value will have a leading and trailing blank.
D	99D9	Returns a decimal point in the specified position. The number of 9s on either side specifies the maximum number of digits.
G	9G999	Returns a group separator in the position specified. G can appear more than once in the format string.
C	C99	Returns the ISO currency symbol in the specified position. C can also appear more than once in the format string.
L	L999	Returns the local currency symbol in the specified position.
,	999,999	Returns a comma in the specified position, regardless of the group separator.
.	99.99	Returns a decimal point in the specified position, regardless of the decimal separator.
V	99V999	Returns a value multiplied by 10^n, where n is the number of 9s after the V. The value is rounded if necessary.
EEEE	9.99EEEE	Returns the value using scientific notation.
RM	RN	Returns the value using uppercase Roman numerals.
rm	rm	Returns the value using lowercase Roman numerals.
FM	FM90.99	Returns a value with no leading or trailing blanks.

TABLE 3-5. *Number Format Elements (continued)*

TO_DATE

Syntax

TO_DATE(*string* [,*format* [,*nlsparams*]])

Purpose   Converts the CHAR or VARCHAR2 *string* into a DATE. *format* is a date format string, as described in Table 3-4. If *format* is not specified, the default date format for the session is used. *nlsparams* is used the same way for TO_DATE as it is for TO_CHAR. TO_DATE and TO_CHAR are inverse functions.

Where Allowed   Procedural and SQL statements.

Example

```
DECLARE
  v_CurrentDate   DATE;
BEGIN
  v_CurrentDate := TO_DATE('January 7, 1973', 'Month DD, YYYY');
END;
```

TO_LABEL

Syntax

TO_LABEL(*string* [,*format*])

Purpose   Converts *string* to a MLSLABEL. *string* can be either VARCHAR2 or CHAR. If specified, *format* is used for the conversion. If *format* is not specified, the default conversion format is used. This function is only relevant in Trusted Oracle. TO_LABEL and TO_CHAR are inverse functions.

Where Allowed   Procedural and SQL statements in a trusted database.

Example
See the *Trusted Oracle7 Server Administrator's Guide.*

TO_MULTI_BYTE

Syntax

TO_MULTI_BYTE(*string*)

Purpose   Returns *string* with all single-byte characters replaced by their equivalent multibyte characters. This function is only relevant if the database character set contains both single-byte and multibyte characters. If not, *string* is returned without change. TO_MULTI_BYTE and TO_SINGLE_BYTE are inverse functions.

Where Allowed   Procedural and SQL statements.

Example

```
SELECT TO_MULTI_BYTE('Hello') "Multi"
  FROM dual;
Multi
----------
Hello
```

TO_NUMBER

Syntax

TO_NUMBER(*string* [,*format* [,*nlsparams*]])

Purpose   Converts the CHAR or VARCHAR2 *string* to a NUMBER value. If *format* is specified, *string* should correspond to the number format (see Table 3-5). *nlsparams* behaves the same as it does for TO_CHAR. TO_NUMBER and TO_CHAR are inverse functions.

Where Allowed   Procedural and SQL statements.

Example

```
DECLARE
  v_Num   NUMBER;
BEGIN
  v_Num := TO_NUMBER('$12345.67', '$99999.99');
END;
```

TO_SINGLE_BYTE

Syntax

TO_SINGLE_BYTE(*string*)

Purpose   Converts all multibyte characters found in *string* to their equivalent single-byte characters. This function is only relevant if the database character set contains both single-byte and multibyte characters. If not, *string* is returned unchanged. TO_SINGLE_BYTE and TO_MULTI_BYTE are inverse functions.

Where Allowed   Procedural and SQL statements.

Example

```
SELECT TO_SINGLE_BYTE('Greetings') "Single"
  FROM dual;
Single
----------
Greetings
```

Group Functions

Group functions return a single result based on many rows, as opposed to single-row functions, which return one result for each row. For example, the COUNT group function returns the number of rows returned. These functions are valid in the select list of a query and the GROUP BY clause only.

Most of these functions can accept qualifiers on their arguments. These qualifiers are DISTINCT and ALL. If the DISTINCT qualifier is passed, then only distinct values returned by the query are considered. The ALL qualifier causes the function to consider all of the values returned by the query. If none is specified, ALL is the default.

AVG

Syntax

AVG([DISTINCT | ALL] *col*)

Purpose   Returns the average of the column values.

Where Allowed   Query select lists and GROUP BY clauses only.

Example

```
SELECT AVG(number_seats)
  FROM rooms;
  AVG(NUMBER_SEATS)
--------------------
        330
```

COUNT

Syntax

```
COUNT(* | [DISTINCT | ALL] col)
```

Purpose   Returns the number of rows in the query. If * is passed, then the total number of rows is returned. If a select list item is passed instead, the non-null values are counted.

Where Allowed   Query select lists and GROUP BY clauses only.

Example

```
SELECT COUNT(*)
  FROM students;
  COUNT(*)
----------
       6

SELECT COUNT(DISTINCT major) "Majors"
  FROM students;
    Majors
----------
         3
```

GLB

Syntax

```
GLB([DISTINCT | ALL] label)
```

Purpose   Returns the greatest lower bound of *label*. This function is meaningful in Trusted Oracle only.

Where Allowed   Query select lists and GROUP BY clauses only, in a trusted database.

Example

See the *Trusted Oracle7 Server Administrator's Guide* for examples and the definition of greatest lower bound.

LUB

Syntax

LUB([DISTINCT | ALL] *label*)

Purpose   Returns the least upper bound of *label*. This function is meaningful in Trusted Oracle only.

Where Allowed   Query select lists and GROUP BY clauses only.

Example

See the trusted *Oracle7 Server Administrator's Guide* for examples and the definition of least upper bound.

MAX

Syntax

MAX([DISTINCT | ALL] *col*)

Purpose   Returns the maximum value of the select list item. DISTINCT and ALL have no effect, since the maximum value would be the same in either case.

Where Allowed   Query select lists and GROUP BY clauses only.

Example

This example returns the length of the longest name in the students table:

```
SELECT MAX(LENGTH(first_name))
  FROM students;
MAX(LENGTH(FIRST_NAME))
----------------------
```

8

MIN

Syntax

MIN([DISTINCT | ALL] *col*)

Purpose   Returns the minimum value of the select list item. DISTINCT and ALL have no effect, since the minimum value would be the same in either case.

Where Allowed   Query select lists and GROUP BY clauses only.

Example

```
SELECT MIN(id)
  FROM students;
  MIN(ID)
---------
   10000
```

STDDEV

Syntax

STDDEV([DISTINCT | ALL] *col*)

Purpose   Returns the standard deviation of the select list item. This is defined as the square root of the variance.

Where Allowed   Query select lists and GROUP BY clauses only.

Example

```
SELECT STDDEV(number_seats)
  FROM rooms;
STDDEV(NUMBER_SEATS)
--------------------
          422.19664
```

SUM

Syntax

SUM([DISTINCT | ALL] *col*)

Purpose   Returns the sum of the values for the select list item.

Where Allowed   Query select lists and GROUP BY clauses only.

Example

```
SELECT department dept, SUM(num_credits)
  FROM classes
  GROUP by department;
DEPT SUM(NUM_CREDITS)
---- ----------------
CS                  4
ECN                 3
HIS                 4
```

VARIANCE

Syntax

VARIANCE([DISTINCT | ALL] *col*)

Purpose   Returns the statistical variance of the select list item. Oracle7 calculates the variance using the formula shown here:

$$\frac{\displaystyle\sum_{i=1}^{n} x_i^{\,2} - \frac{1}{n}\left[\sum_{i=1}^{n} x_i\right]^2}{n-1}$$

In the formula, x_i is a single row value, and n is the total number of elements in the set. If $n = 1$, the variance is defined to be 0.

Where Allowed   Query select lists and GROUP BY clauses only.

Example

```
SELECT VARIANCE(number_seats)
  FROM rooms;
VARIANCE(NUMBER_SEATS)
----------------------
              178250
```

Other Functions

This section lists the remaining functions that do not fit in the previous categories.

DECODE

Syntax

```
DECODE(base_expr, compare1, value1,
                  compare2, value2,
                  ...
                  default)
```

Purpose   The DECODE statement is similar to a series of nested IF-THEN-ELSE statements. The *base_expr* is compared to each of *compare1, compare2,* etc., in sequence. If *base_expr* matches the *i*th *compare* item, the *i*th *value* is returned. If *base_expr* doesn't match any of the *compare* values, *default* is returned.

Each *compare* value is evaluated in turn. If a match is found, the remaining *compare* values, if any, are not evaluated. A NULL *base_expr* is considered equivalent to a NULL *compare* value.

Where Allowed   SQL statements only.

Example

```
SELECT DECODE('abc', 'a', 1,
                     'b', 2,
                     'abc', 3,
                     'd', 4,
                     -1) "Decode 1"
  FROM dual;
Decode 1
```

```
---------
        3

SELECT DECODE(NULL, 'a', 1,
                    NULL, 2) "Decode 2"
  FROM dual;
Decode 2
---------
        2
```

DUMP

Syntax

DUMP(*expr* [,*number_format* [,*start_position*] [,*length*]]])

Purpose   Returns a VARCHAR2 value that contains information about the
internal representation of *expr*. *number_format* specifies the base of the values
returned according to the following table:

number_format	Form of Result
8	Octal notation
10	Decimal notation
16	Hexadecimal notation
17	Single characters

If *number_format* is not specified, the result is returned in decimal notation.
    If *start_position* and *length* are specified, *length* bytes starting at *start_position*
are returned. The default is to return the entire representation. The datatype is
returned as a number corresponding to internal datatypes according to the
following table:

Code	Datatype
1	VARCHAR2
2	NUMBER
8	LONG
12	DATE
23	RAW

24	LONG RAW
69	ROWID
96	CHAR
106	MLSLABEL

Where Allowed   SQL statements only.

Example

```
SELECT first_name, DUMP(first_name) "Dump"
   FROM students
FIRST_NAME          Dump
------------------- ---------------------------------------------
Scott               Typ=1 Len=5: 83,99,111,116,116
Margaret            Typ=1 Len=8: 77,97,114,103,97,114,101,116
Joanne              Typ=1 Len=6: 74,111,97,110,110,101
Manish              Typ=1 Len=6: 77,97,110,105,115,104
Patrick             Typ=1 Len=7: 80,97,116,114,105,99,107
Timothy             Typ=1 Len=7: 84,105,109,111,116,104,121

SELECT first_name, DUMP(first_name, 17) "Dump"
   FROM students
FIRST_NAME          Dump
------------------- ------------------------------------
Scott               Typ=1 Len=5: S,c,o,t,t
Margaret            Typ=1 Len=8: M,a,r,g,a,r,e,t
Joanne              Typ=1 Len=6: J,o,a,n,n,e
Manish              Typ=1 Len=6: M,a,n,i,s,h
Patrick             Typ=1 Len=7: P,a,t,r,i,c,k
Timothy             Typ=1 Len=7: T,i,m,o,t,h,y

SELECT first_name, DUMP(first_name, 17, 2, 4) "Dump"
  FROM students;
FIRST_NAME          Dump
------------------- ------------------------------------
Scott               Typ=1 Len=5: c,o,t,t
Margaret            Typ=1 Len=8: a,r,g,a
Joanne              Typ=1 Len=6: o,a,n,n
Manish              Typ=1 Len=6: a,n,i,s
Patrick             Typ=1 Len=7: a,t,r,i
```

GREATEST

Syntax

> GREATEST(*expr1* [,*expr2*] ...)

Purpose   Returns the greatest expression of its arguments. Each expression is implicitly converted to the type of *expr1* before the comparisons are made. If *expr1* is a character type, non-blank-padded character comparisons are used, and the result has datatype VARCHAR2.

Where Allowed   Procedural and SQL statements.

Example

```
SELECT GREATEST(10, '7', -1)
  FROM dual;
GREATEST(10,'7',-1)
-------------------
                 10
```

GREATEST_LB

Syntax

> GREATEST_LB(*label1* [,*label2*] ...)

Purpose   Returns the greatest lower bound of the list of labels. Each label must have datatype MLSLABEL, RAW MLSLABEL, or be a quoted string literal. This function is valid in Trusted Oracle only.
  For more information, including examples and the definition of the greatest lower bound, see the *Trusted Oracle7 Server Administrator's Guide*.

LEAST

Syntax

> LEAST(*expr1* [,*expr2*] ...)

Purpose   Returns the least value in the list of expressions. LEAST behaves similarly to GREATEST, in that all expressions are implicitly converted to the datatype of the first. All character comparisons are done with non-blank-padded character comparison semantics.

Where Allowed   Procedural and SQL statements.

Example

```
SELECT LEAST('abcd', 'ABCD', 'a', 'xyz') "Least"
  FROM dual;
Least
-----
ABCD
```

LEAST_UB

Syntax

> LEAST_UB(*label1* [,*label2*] ...)

Purpose   Similar to GREATEST_LB, LEAST_UB returns the least upper bound of the list of labels. The labels must have datatype MLSLABEL or be quoted literals. The return value is RAW MLSLABEL. For more information, including examples and the definition of the least upper bound, see the *Trusted Oracle7 Server Administrator's Guide*.

NVL

Syntax

> NVL(*expr1, expr2*)

Purpose   If *expr1* is NULL, returns *expr2*; otherwise, returns *expr1*. The return value has the same datatype as *expr1* unless *expr1* is a character string, in which case the return value has datatype VARCHAR2. This function is useful to ensure that the active set of a query contains no NULL values.

Where Allowed   Procedural and SQL statements.

Example

```
SELECT NVL('non null value', 7) "First",
       NVL(NULL, 'null value') "Second"
  FROM dual;
First          Second
-------------- ----------
non null value null value
```

UID

Syntax

    UID

Purpose   Returns an integer that uniquely identifies the current database user. UID takes no arguments.

Where Allowed   Procedural and SQL statements.

Example
This example shows a sample SQL*Plus session.

```
SQL> connect scott/tiger
Connected.
SQL> SELECT UID
  2    FROM dual;
      UID
---------
        8

SQL> connect system/manager
Connected.
SQL> SELECT UID
  2    FROM dual;
      UID
---------
        5
```

USER

Syntax

USER

Purpose   Returns a VARCHAR2 value containing the name of the current Oracle user. USER takes no arguments.

Where Allowed   Procedural and SQL statements.

Example
This example shows a sample SQL*Plus session.

```
SQL> connect scott/tiger
Connected.
SQL> SELECT USER
  2    FROM dual;
USER
------------------------------
SCOTT

SQL> connect sys/change_on_install
Connected.
SQL> SELECT USER
  2    FROM dual;
USER
------------------------------
SYS
```

USERENV

Syntax

USERENV(*option*)

Purpose   Returns a VARCHAR2 value containing information about the current session, based on *option*. The behavior is described according to the following table:

Value of *option*	Behavior of USERENV(*option*)
'OSDBA'[1]	If the current session has the OSDBA role enabled, returns 'TRUE'; otherwise, returns 'FALSE'. Note that the return value is VARCHAR2, not BOOLEAN.
'LABEL'	Valid in Trusted Oracle only. Returns the current session label. For more information, see the *Trusted Oracle7 Server Administrator's Guide*.
'LANGUAGE'	Returns the language and territory currently used by your session, along with the database character set. These are NLS parameters. The returned value has the form **language_territory.characterset**.
'TERMINAL'	Returns an operating system-dependent identifier for the current session's terminal. For distributed SQL statements, the identifier for the local session is returned.
'SESSIONID'	Returns the auditing session identifier, if the initialization parameter AUDIT_TRAIL is set to TRUE. USERENV('SESSIONID') is not valid in distributed SQL statements.
'ENTRYID'	Returns the available auditing entry identifier, if the initialization parameter AUDIT_TRAIL is set to TRUE. USERENV('ENTRYID') is not valid in distributed SQL statements.

[1] USERENV('OSDBA') is valid in PL/SQL 2.2 (Oracle 7.2) and higher.

Where Allowed   Procedural and SQL statements.

Example

```
SELECT USERENV('TERMINAL'), USERENV('LANGUAGE')
  FROM dual;
USERENV( USERENV('LANGUAGE')
-------- ------------------------------------------
Windows  AMERICAN_AMERICA.WE8ISO8859P1
```

VSIZE

Syntax

VSIZE(*value*)

Purpose Returns the number of bytes in the internal representation of *value*. This information is also returned by the DUMP function. If *value* is NULL, the return value is also NULL.

Where Allowed Procedural and SQL statements.

Example

```
SELECT last_name, VSIZE(last_name) "Size"
  FROM students;
LAST_NAME                Size
-------------------- ---------
Smith                       5
Mason                       5
Junebug                     7
Murgratroid                11
Poll                        4
Taller                      6
```

Pseudocolumns

Pseudocolumns are additional functions that can be called only from SQL statements. Syntactically, they are treated like columns in a table. However, they don't actually exist in the same way that table columns do. Rather, they are evaluated as part of the SQL statement execution.

CURRVAL and NEXTVAL

These two pseudocolumns, CURRVAL and NEXTVAL, are used with sequences. A *sequence* is an Oracle object that is used to generate unique numbers. A sequence is created with the CREATE SEQUENCE DDL command. Once a sequence is created, you can access it with

sequence.CURRVAL

and

    *sequence.*NEXTVAL

where *sequence* is the name of the sequence. CURRVAL returns the current value of the sequence, and NEXTVAL increments the sequence and returns the new value. Both CURRVAL and NEXTVAL return NUMBER values.

    Sequence values can be used in the select list of a query, in the VALUES clause of an INSERT statement, and in the SET clause of an UPDATE statement. They cannot be used in the WHERE clause or in a PL/SQL procedural statement, however. The following are legal examples of using CURRVAL and NEXTVAL:

```
CREATE SEQUENCE student_sequence
  START WITH 10000;

-- This statement will use 10,000 as the id value
INSERT INTO students (id, first_name, last_name)
  VALUES (student_sequence.NEXTVAL, 'Scott', 'Smith');
-- This statement will use 10,001 as the id value
INSERT INTO students (id, first_name, last_name)
  VALUES (student_sequence.NEXTVAL, 'Margaret', 'Mason');

SELECT student_sequence.NEXTVAL "Value"
  FROM dual;  -- Increments the sequence number first
Value
----------
10002

SELECT student_sequence.CURRVAL "Value"
  FROM dual;  -- Returns the current value
Value
----------
10002
```

LEVEL

LEVEL is used only inside a SELECT statement that implements a hierarchical tree walk over a table, via the START WITH and CONNECT BY clauses. The LEVEL pseudocolumn will return the current level of the tree as a NUMBER value. For more information, see the *Oracle7 Server SQL Reference.*

ROWID

The ROWID pseudocolumn is used in the select list of a query. It returns the rowid of that particular row. The external format of a ROWID is an 18-character string, as described in Chapter 2. The ROWID pseudocolumn returns a value of type ROWID. For example, the following query returns all of the rowids in the rooms table:

```
SELECT ROWID
  FROM rooms;

ROWID
------------------
00000045.0000.0002
00000045.0001.0002
00000045.0002.0002
00000045.0003.0002
00000045.0004.0002
```

ROWNUM

ROWNUM will return the current row number in a query. It is useful for limiting the total number of rows, and it is used primarily in the WHERE clause of queries and the SET clause of UPDATE statements. ROWNUM returns a NUMBER value. For example, the following query returns only the first two rows from the students table:

```
SELECT *
  FROM students
  WHERE ROWNUM < 3;
```

The first row has ROWNUM 1, the second has ROWNUM 2, and so on.

NOTE
The ROWNUM value is assigned to a row before a sort is done (via the ORDER BY clause). As a result, you cannot use ROWNUM to retrieve the *n* highest rows in the search order. Consider this statement:

```
SELECT first_name, last_name
  FROM students
```

```
WHERE ROWNUM < 3
ORDER BY first_name;
```

While this statement will return two rows from the students table, sorted by first_name, they won't necessarily be the first two rows in the entire sort order. To guarantee this, it is best to declare a cursor for this query and only fetch the first two rows. Chapter 4 discusses cursors and how to use them.

GRANT, REVOKE, and Privileges

While DDL statements such as GRANT and REVOKE can't be used directly in PL/SQL, they do have an effect on which SQL statements are legal. In order to perform an operation such as INSERT or DELETE on an Oracle table, you need permission to perform the operation. These permissions are manipulated via the GRANT and REVOKE SQL commands.

Object vs. System Privileges

There are two different kinds of privileges—object and system. An *object privilege* allows an operation on a particular object (such as a table). A *system privilege* allows operations on an entire class of objects.

Table 3-6 describes the available object privileges. The DDL object privileges (ALTER, INDEX, REFERENCES) can't be utilized directly in PL/SQL (except for the DBMS_SQL package), since they allow DDL operations on the object in question.

There are many system privileges, for just about any DDL operation possible. For example, the CREATE TABLE system privilege allows the grantee to create tables. The CREATE ANY TABLE system privilege allows the grantee to create tables in other schemas. The *Oracle7 Server SQL Reference* documents all of the available system privileges.

GRANT and REVOKE

The GRANT statement is used to allow another schema access to a privilege, and the REVOKE statement is used to remove the access allowed by GRANT. Both statements can be used for object and system privileges.

GRANT
The basic syntax of GRANT for object privileges is

GRANT *privilege* ON *object* TO *grantee* [WITH GRANT OPTION];

where *privilege* is the desired privilege, *object* is the object to which access is granted, and *grantee* is the user who will receive the privilege. For example, assuming that **userA** is a valid database schema, the following GRANT statement is legal:

```
GRANT SELECT ON classes TO userA;
```

If the WITH GRANT OPTION is specified, then **userA** can in turn grant the privilege to another user. More than one privilege can be specified in one GRANT statement, as in this example:

```
GRANT UPDATE, DELETE ON students TO userA;
```

Object Privilege	Kinds of Objects	Description
ALTER	Tables, sequences	Allows grantee to issue an ALTER statement (such as ALTER TABLE) on the object.
DELETE	Tables, views	Allows grantee to issue a DELETE statement against the object.
EXECUTE	Procedures, functions, packages	Allows grantee to execute the stored PL/SQL object. (Stored objects are discussed in Chapter 5.)
INDEX	Tables	Allows grantee to create an index on the table via the CREATE INDEX command.
INSERT	Tables, views	Allows grantee to issue an INSERT statement against the object.
REFERENCES	Tables	Allows grantee to create a constraint that refers to the table.
SELECT	Tables, views, sequences, snapshots	Allows grantee to issue a SELECT statement against the object.
UPDATE	Tables, views	Allows grantee to issue an UPDATE statement against the object.

TABLE 3-6. *SQL Object Privileges*

For system privileges, the syntax is

> GRANT *privilege* TO *grantee* [WITH ADMIN OPTION];

where *privilege* is the system privilege to be granted, and *grantee* is the user receiving the privilege. If WITH ADMIN OPTION is included, then *grantee* can grant the privilege to other users as well. For example:

```
GRANT CREATE TABLE, ALTER ANY PROCEDURE to userA;
```

Similar to the GRANT statement for object privileges, more than one system privilege can be specified in the same statement.

Since GRANT is a DDL statement, it takes effect immediately and issues an implicit COMMIT after execution.

REVOKE

The syntax for REVOKE for object privileges is

> REVOKE *privilege* ON *object* FROM *grantee* [CASCADE CONSTRAINTS];

where *privilege* is the privilege to be revoked, *object* is the object on which the privilege is granted, and *grantee* is the recipient of the privilege. For example, the following is a legal REVOKE command:

```
REVOKE SELECT ON classes FROM userA;
```

If the CASCADE CONSTRAINTS clause is included and the REFERENCES privilege is being revoked, all referential integrity constraints created by *grantee* with this privilege are dropped as well. Multiple privileges can also be revoked with one statement, as in

```
REVOKE UPDATE, DELETE, INSERT ON students FROM userA;
```

To REVOKE a system privilege, the syntax is

> REVOKE *privilege* FROM *grantee*;

where *privilege* is the system privilege to be revoked, and *grantee* is the user who will no longer have this privilege. For example:

```
REVOKE ALTER TABLE, EXECUTE ANY PROCEDURE FROM userA;
```

Roles

In a large Oracle system, with many different user accounts, administrating privileges can be a challenge. To ease this, Oracle7 provides a facility known as roles. A *role* is essentially a collection of privileges, both object and system. Consider the following series of statements:

```
CREATE ROLE table_query;
GRANT SELECT ON students TO table_query;
GRANT SELECT ON classes TO table_query;
GRANT SELECT ON rooms TO table_query;
```

The **table_query** role has SELECT privileges on three different tables. We can now grant this role to additional users, with

```
GRANT table_query TO userA;
GRANT table_query TO userB;
```

Now, **userA** and **userB** each have SELECT privileges on the three tables. This is easier to administer than the six separate grants that would otherwise have been required.

The role PUBLIC is predefined by Oracle. Every user has been automatically granted this role. Thus, you can issue a statement with this format,

GRANT *privilege* TO PUBLIC;

which grants the privilege to every Oracle user at once.

Oracle7 predefines several other roles, which include common system privileges. These are listed in Table 3-7. The predefined Oracle user SYSTEM is automatically granted all of these roles.

Typically, the CONNECT and RESOURCE roles are granted to the database users who will be creating objects, and just the CONNECT role is granted to users who query objects. Users with just CONNECT would need additional object privileges on the objects that they will need to access.

Transaction Control

A *transaction* is a series of SQL statements that either succeed or fail as a unit. Transactions are a standard part of relational databases and prevent inconsistent data. The canonical example of this is a bank transaction. Consider the following two SQL statements, which implement a transfer of **transaction_amount** dollars between two bank accounts identified as **from_acct** and **to_acct**:

```
UPDATE accounts
  SET balance = balance - transaction_amount
  WHERE account_no = from_acct;
UPDATE accounts
  SET balance = balance + transaction_amount
  WHERE account_no = to_acct;
```

Suppose the first UPDATE statement succeeds, but the second statement fails due to an error (perhaps the database or network went down). The data is now inconsistent—**from_acct** has been debited, but **to_acct** has not been credited. Needless to say, this is not a good situation, especially if you are the owner of **from_acct**. We prevent this by combining the two statements into a transaction, whereby either both statements will succeed, or both statements will fail. This prevents inconsistent data.

A transaction begins with the first SQL statement issued after the previous transaction, or the first SQL statement after connecting to the database. The transaction ends with the COMMIT or ROLLBACK statement.

Role Name	Privileges Granted
CONNECT	ALTER SESSION, CREATE CLUSTER, CREATE DATABASE LINK, CREATE SEQUENCE, CREATE SESSION, CREATE SYNONYM, CREATE TABLE, CREATE VIEW
RESOURCE	CREATE CLUSTER, CREATE PROCEDURE, CREATE SEQUENCE, CREATE TABLE, CREATE PROCEDURE
DBA	All system privileges (with the ADMIN OPTION, so they can be granted again), plus EXP_FULL_DATABASE and IMP_FULL_DATABASE
EXP_FULL_DATABASE	SELECT ANY TABLE, BACKUP ANY TABLE, plus INSERT, UPDATE, DELETE on the system tables **sys.incexp**, **sys.incvid**, and **sys.incfil**
IMP_FULL_DATABASE	BECOME USER

TABLE 3-7. *Predefined System Roles*

COMMIT vs. ROLLBACK

When a COMMIT statement is issued to the database, the transaction is ended, and:

- All work done by the transaction is made permanent.
- Other sessions can see the changes made by this transaction.
- Any locks acquired by the transaction are released.

The syntax for the COMMIT statement is

COMMIT [WORK];

The optional **WORK** keyword is available for increased readability. Until a transaction is committed, only the session executing that transaction can see the changes made by that session. This is illustrated in Figure 3-2. Session A issues the INSERT statement first. Session B issues a query against the **rooms** table, but does not see the INSERT done by session A, since it hasn't been committed. Session A then commits, and the second SELECT by session B will see the new inserted row.

When a ROLLBACK statement is issued to the database, the transaction is ended, and:

- All work done by the transaction is undone, as if it hadn't been issued.
- Any locks acquired by the transaction are released.

The syntax for the ROLLBACK statement is

ROLLBACK [WORK];

Just like COMMIT, the **WORK** keyword is optional and is available for increased readability. An explicit ROLLBACK statement is often used when an error is detected by the program that prevents further work. If a session disconnects from the database without ending the current transaction via COMMIT or ROLLBACK, the transaction is automatically rolled back by the database.

NOTE
SQL*Plus will automatically issue a COMMIT when you exit. The **autocommit** option will issue a COMMIT after every SQL statement, as well. This does not affect the SQL statements inside a PL/SQL block, since SQL*Plus doesn't have control until the block finishes.

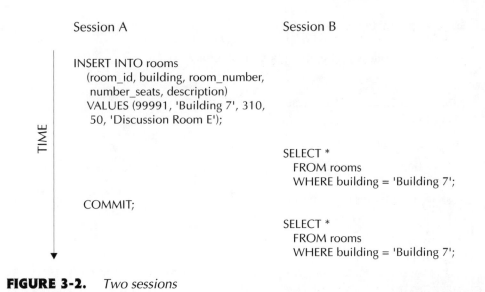

Session A	Session B

INSERT INTO rooms
   (room_id, building, room_number,
   number_seats, description)
   VALUES (99991, 'Building 7', 310,
   50, 'Discussion Room E');	

	SELECT *
	   FROM rooms
	   WHERE building = 'Building 7';

COMMIT;	

	SELECT *
	   FROM rooms
	   WHERE building = 'Building 7';

FIGURE 3-2. *Two sessions*

Savepoints

The ROLLBACK statement undoes the entire transaction, as we have seen. Via the SAVEPOINT command, however, only part of the transaction need be undone. The syntax for SAVEPOINT is

SAVEPOINT *name*;

where *name* is the savepoint's name. Savepoint names follow the usual rules for SQL identifiers (see Chapter 2). Notice that savepoints are not declared in the declarative section, since they are global to a transaction, and the transaction can continue past the end of the block. Once a savepoint is defined, the program can roll back to the savepoint via the following syntax:

ROLLBACK [WORK] TO SAVEPOINT *name*;

When a ROLLBACK TO SAVEPOINT is issued, the following things occur:

- Any work done since the savepoint is undone. The savepoint remains active, however, so it can be rolled back to again if desired.
- Any locks and resources acquired by the SQL statements since the savepoint are released.

■ The transaction is *not* finished, since there are still SQL statements pending.

Consider the following fragment of a PL/SQL block:

```
BEGIN
    INSERT INTO temp_table (char_col) VALUES ('Insert One');
    SAVEPOINT A;
    INSERT INTO temp_table (char_col) VALUES ('Insert Two');
    SAVEPOINT B;
    INSERT INTO temp_table (char_col) VALUES ('Insert Three');
    SAVEPOINT C;
    /* Missing statements here */
    COMMIT;
END;
```

If we put

```
ROLLBACK TO B;
```

in for the missing statements, the third INSERT and SAVEPOINT C will be undone. But the first two INSERTs will be processed. If, on the other hand, we put

```
ROLLBACK TO A;
```

in for the missing statements, the second and third INSERTs will be undone, leaving only the first INSERT.

ROLLBACK TO SAVEPOINT is often used before a complicated section of a transaction. If this part of the transaction fails, it can be rolled back, allowing the earlier part to continue.

Transactions vs. Blocks

It is important to understand the distinction between transactions and PL/SQL blocks. When a block starts, it does not mean that a transaction starts. Likewise, the start of a transaction need not coincide with the start of a block. For example, suppose we issue the following statements from the SQL*Plus prompt.

```
INSERT INTO classes
    (department, course, description, max_students,
     current_students, num_credits, room_id)
  VALUES ('CS', 101, 'Computer Science 101', 50, 10, 4, 99998);
BEGIN
    UPDATE rooms
```

```
      SET room_id = room_id + 1;
  ROLLBACK WORK;
END;
```

Notice that we have issued an INSERT statement and then an anonymous PL/SQL block. The block issues an UPDATE and then a ROLLBACK. This ROLLBACK undoes not only the UPDATE statement, but the prior INSERT as well. Both the INSERT statement and the block are part of the same database session, thus the same transaction.

Similarly, a single PL/SQL block can contain multiple transactions. Consider the following:

```
DECLARE
  v_NumIterations    NUMBER;
BEGIN
  -- Loop from 1 to 500, inserting these values into temp_table.
  -- Commit every 50 rows.
  FOR v_LoopCounter IN 1..500 LOOP
    INSERT INTO temp_table (num_col) VALUES (v_LoopCounter);
    v_NumIterations := v_NumIterations + 1;
    IF v_NumIterations = 50 THEN
      COMMIT;
      v_NumIterations := 0;
    END IF;
  END LOOP;
END;
```

This block will insert the numbers 1 through 500 into **temp_table** and will commit after every 50 rows. So there will be a total of ten transactions during the execution of one block.

Summary

In this chapter, we have discussed the SQL language in general, with particular focus on the DML and transaction control statements allowed in PL/SQL. We've also explored privileges and roles, the built-in SQL functions, and how transactions prevent inconsistent data. In the next chapter, we will discuss cursors, which are used for multirow queries. Cursors will build on the concepts that we looked at in Chapter 2 and have continued in this chapter.

CHAPTER 4

Cursors

In Chapter 3, we discussed how SQL statements can be used in PL/SQL. This functionality is enhanced through the use of cursors, which allow a program to take explicit control of SQL statement processing. In this chapter, we will see how cursors are used for multirow queries and other SQL statements. We will also discuss cursor variables, one of the main new features of PL/SQL 2.2, enhanced in version 2.3.

What Is a Cursor?

In order for the database to process an SQL statement, it needs to allocate memory. This memory is known as the *context area*. The context area is part of the PGA (process global area) and is allocated on the server, as opposed to the client. The PGA and SGA (shared global area) are discussed in more detail in Chapter 12. Information stored in the context area includes the number of rows processed by the statement, a pointer to the parsed representation of the statement, and in the case of a query, the set of rows returned by the query.

A *cursor* is a handle, or pointer, to the context area. Through the cursor, a PL/SQL program can control the context area and what happens to it as the statement is processed. The following PL/SQL block illustrates a cursor fetch loop, in which multiple rows of data are returned using a query.

```
DECLARE
  /* Output variables to hold the results of the query */
  v_StudentID    students.id%TYPE;
  v_FirstName    students.first_name%TYPE;
  v_LastName     students.last_name%TYPE;

  /* Bind variable used in the query */
  v_Major        students.major%TYPE := 'Computer Science';

  /* Cursor declaration */
  CURSOR c_Students IS
    SELECT id, first_name, last_name
      FROM students
      WHERE major = v_Major;
BEGIN
  /* Identify the rows in the active set, and prepare for further
     processing of the data */
  OPEN c_Students;
  LOOP
    /* Retrieve each row of the active set into PL/SQL variables */
    FETCH c_Students INTO v_StudentID, v_FirstName, v_LastName;

    /* If there are no more rows to fetch, exit the loop */
    EXIT WHEN c_Students%NOTFOUND;
  END LOOP;

  /* Free resources used by the query */
  CLOSE c_Students;
END;
```

This example illustrates an *explicit* cursor, in which the cursor name is explicitly assigned to a SELECT statement via the CURSOR..IS statement. An *implicit* cursor is used for all other SQL statements. Processing an explicit cursor involves four steps. For implicit cursors, the PL/SQL engine takes care of these four steps automatically.

Processing Explicit Cursors

The four PL/SQL steps necessary for explicit cursor processing are as follows:

1. Declare the cursor.
2. Open the cursor for a query.
3. Fetch the results into PL/SQL variables.
4. Close the cursor.

The cursor declaration is the only step that goes in the declarative section of a block—the other three steps are found in the executable or exception sections.

Declaring a Cursor

Declaring a cursor defines the name of the cursor and associates it with a SELECT statement. The syntax is

CURSOR *cursor name* IS *select_statement*;

where *cursor name* is the name of the cursor, and *select_statement* is the query to be processed by this cursor. Cursor names follow the usual declaration and scoping rules for PL/SQL identifiers, as described in Chapter 2. Since a cursor name is a PL/SQL identifier, it must be declared before it is referenced. Any SELECT statements are legal, including joins and UNION or MINUS clauses.

NOTE
Select_statement contains no INTO clause. The INTO clause is part of the FETCH statement.

A cursor declaration can reference PL/SQL variables in the WHERE clause. These variables are considered bind variables, as discussed in Chapter 3. Since the usual scoping rules apply, these variables must be visible at the point of the cursor declaration. For example, the following declarative section is legal:

```
DECLARE
  v_Department    classes.department%TYPE;
  v_Course        classes.course%TYPE;
  CURSOR c_Classes IS
    SELECT * from classes
```

```
      WHERE department = v_Department
      AND course = v_Course;
```

The next declarative section is illegal, because **v_Department** and **v_Course** are not declared before they are referenced:

```
DECLARE
  CURSOR c_Classes IS
    SELECT * from classes
      WHERE department = v_Department
      AND course = v_Course;
  v_Department    classes.department%TYPE;
  v_Course        classes.course%TYPE;
```

To ensure that all variables referenced in a cursor declaration are declared before the reference, you can declare all cursors at the end of a declarative section. This is the convention used in this book. The only exception to this is when the cursor name itself is used in a reference, such as the %ROWTYPE attribute. In this case, the cursor must be declared before a reference to it.

Opening a Cursor
The syntax for opening a cursor is

   OPEN *cursor_name*;

where *cursor_name* identifies a cursor that has previously been declared. When a cursor is opened, the following things happen:

- The values of the bind variables are examined.

- Based on the values of the bind variables, the active set is determined.

- The active set pointer is set to the first row.

Bind variables are examined at cursor open time, and only at cursor open time. For example, consider the following PL/SQL block:

```
DECLARE
  v_RoomID        classes.room_id%TYPE;
  v_Building      rooms.building%TYPE;
  v_Department    classes.department%TYPE;
  v_Course        classes.course%TYPE;
  CURSOR c_Buildings IS
```

```
    SELECT building
      from rooms, classes
      where rooms.room_id = classes.room_id
      and department = v_Department
      and course = v_Course;
BEGIN
  -- Assign to bind variables before the cursor OPEN.
  v_Department := 'HIS';
  v_Course := 101;

  -- Open the cursor.
  OPEN c_Buildings;

  -- Reassign the bind variables - this has no effect,
  -- since the cursor is already open.
  v_Department := 'XXX';
  v_Course := -1;
END;
```

When **c_Buildings** is opened, **v_Department** and **v_Course** contain 'HIS' and 101, respectively. These are the values used in the query. Even though **v_Department** and **v_Course** are changed after the OPEN, the active set of the query does not change. This fact is known as *read-consistency* and is designed to ensure the integrity of the data. Read consistency is discussed in more detail in the section "SELECT FOR UPDATE Cursors" later in this chapter. In order for the new values to be examined, the cursor would have to be closed and reopened. The query will see changes made to the database that have been committed prior to the OPEN statement. If another session has made data changes, but has not yet committed them, those changes will not be visible.

The active set (the set of rows that match the query) is determined at cursor open time. The previous query, for example, returns one row ('Building Seven'). The WHERE clause is evaluated against the table or tables referenced in the FROM clause of the query, and any rows for which the condition evaluates to TRUE are added to the active set. A pointer into the set is also established at cursor open time. This pointer indicates which row is to be fetched next by the cursor.

It is legal to open a cursor that is already open. Before the second OPEN, PL/SQL will implicitly issue a CLOSE statement before reopening the cursor. More than one cursor can be open at a time, as well.

Fetching from a Cursor
The INTO clause for the query is part of the FETCH statement. The FETCH statement has two forms,

FETCH *cursor_name* INTO *list_of_variables*;

and

FETCH *cursor_name* INTO *PL/SQL_record*;

where *cursor_name* identifies a previously declared and opened cursor, *list_of_variables* is a comma-separated list of previously declared PL/SQL variables, and *PL/SQL_record* is a previously declared PL/SQL record. In either case, the variable or variables in the INTO clause must be type compatible with the select list of the query. Given the preceding **c_Buildings** cursor declaration, the following FETCH statement is legal:

```
FETCH c_Buildings INTO v_Building;
```

The following example illustrates legal and illegal FETCH statements:

```
DECLARE
  v_Department  classes.department%TYPE;
  v_Course      classes.course%TYPE;
  CURSOR c_AllClasses IS
    SELECT *
      FROM classes;
  v_ClassesRecord  c_AllClasses%ROWTYPE;
BEGIN
  OPEN c_AllClasses;

  -- This is a legal FETCH statement, returning the first
  -- row into a PL/SQL record which matches the select list
  -- of the query.
  FETCH c_AllClasses INTO v_ClassesRecord;

  -- This FETCH statement is illegal, since the select list
  -- of the query returns all 7 columns in the classes table
  -- but we are only fetching into 2 variables.
  FETCH c_AllClasses INTO v_Department, v_Course;
END;
```

After each FETCH, the active set pointer is increased to the next row. Thus, each FETCH will return successive rows in the active set, until the entire set is returned.

The %NOTFOUND attribute, described in the "Cursor Attributes" section, is used to determine when the entire active set has been retrieved. The last fetch will assign NULL to the output variables.

Closing a Cursor

When all of the active set has been retrieved, the cursor should be closed. This tells the PL/SQL engine that the program is finished with the cursor, and the resources associated with it can be freed. These resources include the storage used to hold the active set, as well as any temporary space used for determining the active set. The syntax for closing a cursor is

CLOSE *cursor_name*;

where *cursor_name* identifies a previously opened cursor. Once a cursor is closed, it is illegal to fetch from it. Doing so will yield the Oracle error

```
ORA-1001: Invalid Cursor
```

or

```
ORA-1002: Fetch out of Sequence
```

Similarly, it is illegal to close an already closed cursor.

Cursor Attributes

There are four attributes available in PL/SQL that can be applied to cursors. Cursor attributes are appended to a cursor name in a PL/SQL block and then used in expressions. The attributes are %FOUND, %NOTFOUND, %ISOPEN, and %ROWCOUNT. Each of the following sections refers to the listing in Figure 4-1. For this example, assume that **temp_table** has two rows. The data for these rows is listed here:

num_col	char_col
10	'Hello'
20	'There'

%FOUND   %FOUND is a BOOLEAN attribute. It returns TRUE if the previous FETCH returns a row and FALSE if it doesn't. If %FOUND is checked while the cursor isn't open, ORA-1001 (invalid cursor) is returned. The following table uses the numbered locations in Figure 4-1 to illustrate the behavior of %FOUND.

Location	Value of c_Temp Data%FOUND	Explanation
1	Error: ORA-1001	**c_TempData** hasn't been opened yet. There is no active set associated with it.
2	NULL	Although **c_TempData** has been opened, no fetch has been done. The value of the attribute can't be determined.
3	TRUE	The prior fetch returned the first row in **temp_table**.
4	TRUE	The prior fetch returned the second row in **temp_table**.
5	FALSE	The prior fetch didn't return any data, since all rows in the active set have been retrieved.
6	Error: ORA-1001	**c_TempData** has been closed, clearing all stored information about the active set.

%NOTFOUND   %NOTFOUND behaves opposite to %FOUND—if the prior fetch returns a row, then %NOTFOUND is FALSE. %NOTFOUND returns TRUE only if the prior fetch does not return a row. It is often used as the exit condition for a fetch loop. The following table describes the behavior of %NOTFOUND for the example in Figure 4-1.

Location	Value of c_TempData %NOTFOUND	Explanation
1	Error: ORA-1001	**c_TempData** hasn't been opened yet. There is no active set associated with it.
2	NULL	Although **c_TempData** has been opened, no fetch has been done. The value of the attribute can't be determined.
3	FALSE	The prior fetch returned the first row in **temp_table**.
4	FALSE	The prior fetch returned the second row in **temp_table**.
5	TRUE	The prior fetch didn't return any data, since all rows in the active set have been retrieved.
6	Error: ORA-1001	**c_TempData** has been closed, clearing all stored information about the active set.

```
DECLARE
    -- Cursor declaration
        CURSOR c_TempData IS
        SELECT * from temp_table;
    -- Record to store the fetched data
    v_TempRecord c_TempData%ROWTYPE;
BEGIN
    -- location ①
    OPEN c_Tempdata;                            -- Open cursor
    -- location ②
    FETCH c_TempData INTO v_TempRecord;    -- Fetch first row
    -- location ③
    FETCH c_TempData INTO v_TempRecord;    -- Fetch second row
    -- location ④
    FETCH c_TempData INTO v_TempRecord;    -- Third fetch
    -- location ⑤
    CLOSE c_TempData;
    -- location ⑥
END;
```

FIGURE 4-1.   *A cursor example*

%ISOPEN   This attribute is used to determine whether or not the associated cursor is open. If so, %ISOPEN returns TRUE; otherwise, it returns FALSE. This is illustrated in the next table.

Location	Value of c_Temp Data%ISOPEN	Explanation
1	FALSE	**c_TempData** hasn't been opened yet.
2	TRUE	**c_TempData** has been opened.
3	TRUE	**c_TempData** is still open.
4	TRUE	**c_TempData** is still open.
5	TRUE	**c_TempData** is still open.
6	FALSE	**c_TempData** has been closed.

%ROWCOUNT This numeric attribute returns the number of rows fetched by the cursor so far. If referenced when its associated cursor is not open, ORA-1001 is returned. The behavior of %ROWCOUNT is described in the following table.

Location	Value of c_TempData %ROWCOUNT	Explanation
1	Error: ORA-1001	**c_TempData** hasn't been opened yet. There is no active set associated with it.
2	0	**c_TempData** has been opened, but no fetch has been done.
3	1	The first row from **temp_table** has been fetched.
4	2	The second row from **temp_table** has been fetched.
5	2	Two rows have been fetched from **temp_table** so far.
6	Error: ORA-1001	**c_TempData** has been closed, removing all information about the active set.

Cursor Attribute Comparison Table 4-1 shows the value of all four cursor attributes as the block progresses, for comparison.

Location	c_TempData %FOUND	c_TempData %NOTFOUND	c_TempData %ISOPEN	c_TempData %ROWCOUNT
1	ORA-1001	ORA-1001	FALSE	ORA-1001
2	NULL	NULL	TRUE	0
3	TRUE	FALSE	TRUE	1
4	TRUE	FALSE	TRUE	2
5	FALSE	TRUE	TRUE	2
6	ORA-1001	ORA-1001	FALSE	ORA-1001

TABLE 4-1. *Behavior of All Cursor Attributes*

Processing Implicit Cursors

Explicit cursors are used to process multirow SELECT statements, as we have seen in the previous sections. However, all SQL statements are executed inside a context area and thus have a cursor that points to this context area. This cursor is known as the *SQL cursor*. Unlike explicit cursors, the SQL cursor is not opened or closed by the program. PL/SQL implicitly opens the SQL cursor, processes the SQL statement in it, and closes the cursor afterwards.

The implicit cursor is used to process INSERT, UPDATE, DELETE, and single-row SELECT..INTO statements. The cursor attributes can be applied to the SQL cursor as well. For example, the following block will perform an INSERT statement if the UPDATE statement does not match any rows:

```
BEGIN
  UPDATE rooms
    SET number_seats = 100
    WHERE room_id = 99980;
  -- If the previous UPDATE statement didn't match any rows,
  -- insert a new row into the rooms table.
  IF SQL%NOTFOUND THEN
    INSERT INTO rooms (room_id, number_seats)
      VALUES (99980, 100);
  END IF;
END;
```

We can also accomplish the same thing by using SQL%ROWCOUNT:

```
BEGIN
  UPDATE rooms
    SET number_seats = 100
    WHERE room_id = 99980;
  -- If the previous UPDATE statement didn't match any rows,
  -- insert a new row into the rooms table.
  IF SQL%ROWCOUNT = 0 THEN
    INSERT INTO rooms (room_id, number_seats)
      VALUES (99980, 100);
  END IF;
END;
```

Although SQL%NOTFOUND can be used with SELECT..INTO statements, it is not normally useful to do so. This is because a SELECT..INTO statement will raise the Oracle error

```
ORA-1403: no data found
```

when it does not match any rows. This error causes control to pass immediately to the exception handling section of the block, preventing the check for SQL%NOTFOUND. This is illustrated by the following example:

```
DECLARE
  -- Record to hold room information.
  v_RoomData    rooms%ROWTYPE;
BEGIN
  -- Retrieve information about room ID -1.
  SELECT *
    INTO v_RoomData
    FROM rooms
    WHERE room_id = -1;

  -- The following statement will never be executed, since
  -- control passes immediately to the exception handler.
  IF SQL%NOTFOUND THEN
    INSERT INTO temp_table (char_col)
      VALUES ('Not found!');
  END IF;
EXCEPTION
  WHEN NO_DATA_FOUND THEN
    INSERT INTO temp_table (char_col)
      VALUES ('Not found, exception handler');
END;
```

Exception handling is discussed in detail in Chapter 6. Note that SQL%NOTFOUND can be checked inside a NO_DATA_FOUND exception handler, but it will always evaluate to TRUE at this point.

Cursor Fetch Loops

The most common operation with cursors is to fetch all of the rows in the active set. This is done via a *fetch loop*, which is simply a loop that processes each of the rows in the active set, one by one. The following sections examine several different kinds of cursor fetch loops and their uses.

LOOP..END LOOP

In this first style of fetch loop, the LOOP..END LOOP syntax is used for the cursor processing. Explicit cursor attributes are used to control how many times the loop executes. An example of this type of fetch loop is given here:

```
DECLARE
  -- Declare variables to hold information about the students
  -- majoring in History.
  v_StudentID    students.id%TYPE;
  v_FirstName    students.first_name%TYPE;
  v_LastName     students.last_name%TYPE;

  -- Cursor to retrieve the information about History students
  CURSOR c_HistoryStudents IS
    SELECT id, first_name, last_name
      FROM students
      WHERE major = 'History';
BEGIN
  -- Open the cursor and initialize the active set
  OPEN c_HistoryStudents;
  LOOP
    -- Retrieve information for the next student
    FETCH c_HistoryStudents INTO v_StudentID, v_FirstName, v_LastName;

    -- Exit loop when there are no more rows to fetch
    EXIT WHEN c_HistoryStudents%NOTFOUND;

    -- Process the fetched rows, in this case sign up each
    -- student for History 301 by inserting them into the
    -- registered_students table. Record the first and last
    -- names in temp_table as well.
    INSERT INTO registered_students (student_id, department, course)
      VALUES (v_StudentID, 'HIS', 301);

    INSERT INTO temp_table (num_col, char_col)
      VALUES (v_StudentID, v_FirstName || ' ' || v_LastName);
```

```
  END LOOP;

  -- Free resources used by the cursor
  CLOSE c_HistoryStudents;

  -- Commit our work
  COMMIT;
END;
```

Notice the placement of the EXIT WHEN statement immediately after the FETCH statement. After the last row has been retrieved, **c_HistoryStudents%NOTFOUND** becomes TRUE, and the loop is exited. The EXIT WHEN statement is also before the processing of the data. This is done to ensure that the processing will not handle any NULL rows.

Consider the following loop, which is very similar to the previous one, except that the EXIT WHEN statement has been moved to the end of the loop:

```
DECLARE
  -- Declare variables to hold information about the students
  -- majoring in History.
  v_StudentID    students.id%TYPE;
  v_FirstName    students.first_name%TYPE;
  v_LastName     students.last_name%TYPE;

  -- Cursor to retrieve the information about History students
  CURSOR c_HistoryStudents IS
    SELECT id, first_name, last_name
      FROM students
      WHERE major = 'History';
BEGIN
  -- Open the cursor and initialize the active set
  OPEN c_HistoryStudents;
  LOOP
    -- Retrieve information for the next student
    FETCH c_HistoryStudents INTO v_StudentID, v_FirstName, v_LastName;

    -- Process the fetched rows, in this case sign up each
    -- student for History 101 by inserting them into the
    -- registered_students table. Record the first and last
    -- names in temp_table as well.
    INSERT INTO registered_students (student_id, department, course)
      VALUES (v_StudentID, 'HIS', 101);
```

```
    INSERT INTO temp_table (num_col, char_col)
      VALUES (v_StudentID, v_FirstName || ' ' || v_LastName);


    -- Exit loop when there are no more rows to fetch
    EXIT WHEN c_HistoryStudents%NOTFOUND;

  END LOOP;

  -- Free resources used by the cursor
  CLOSE c_HistoryStudents;

  -- Commit our work
  COMMIT;
END;
```

The last FETCH will return NULL values into **v_StudentID**, **v_FirstName**, and
v_LastName, since there are no more rows in the active set. Since the check is after
the processing, however, these NULL values are inserted into the
registered_students and **temp_table** tables, which is not the desired effect.

WHILE Loops

A cursor fetch loop can also be constructed using the WHILE..LOOP syntax, as
illustrated by the following example:

```
DECLARE
  -- Cursor to retrieve the information about History students
  CURSOR c_HistoryStudents IS
    SELECT id, first_name, last_name
      FROM students
      WHERE major = 'History';

  -- Declare a record to hold the fetched information.
  v_StudentData  c_HistoryStudents%ROWTYPE;
BEGIN
  -- Open the cursor and initialize the active set
  OPEN c_HistoryStudents;

  -- Retrieve the first row, to set up for the WHILE loop
  FETCH c_HistoryStudents INTO v_StudentData;
```

```
-- Continue looping while there are more rows to fetch
WHILE c_HistoryStudents%FOUND LOOP
   -- Process the fetched rows, in this case sign up each
   -- student for History 101 by inserting them into the
   -- registered_students table. Record the first and last
   -- names in temp_table as well.
   INSERT INTO registered_students (student_id, department, course)
      VALUES (v_StudentData.ID, 'HIS', 101);

   INSERT INTO temp_table (num_col, char_col)
      VALUES (v_StudentData.ID,
              v_StudentData.first_name || ' ' ||
              v_StudentData.last_name);

   -- Retrieve the next row. The %FOUND condition will be checked
   -- before the loop continues again.
   FETCH c_HistoryStudents INTO v_StudentData;
END LOOP;

-- Free resources used by the cursor
CLOSE c_HistoryStudents;

-- Commit our work
COMMIT;
END;
```

This fetch loop behaves the same as the LOOP..END LOOP example in the previous section. Note that the FETCH statement appears twice—once before the loop and once after the loop processing. This is necessary so that the loop condition (**c_HistoryStudents%FOUND**) will be evaluated for each iteration of the loop.

Cursor FOR Loops

Both of the FETCH loops just described require explicit processing of the cursor, via the OPEN, FETCH, and CLOSE statements. PL/SQL provides a shortcut for this, via the cursor FOR loop, which implicitly handles the cursor processing. A cursor FOR loop, which again is equivalent to the previous two examples, is illustrated here:

```
DECLARE
   -- Cursor to retrieve the information about History students
   CURSOR c_HistoryStudents IS
      SELECT id, first_name, last_name
```

```
      FROM students
      WHERE major = 'History';
BEGIN
  -- Begin the loop. An implicit OPEN of c_HistoryStudents
  -- is done here.
  FOR v_StudentData IN c_HistoryStudents LOOP
    -- An implicit FETCH is done here.

    -- Process the fetched rows, in this case sign up each
    -- student for History 101 by inserting them into the
    -- registered_students table. Record the first and last
    -- names in temp_table as well.
    INSERT INTO registered_students (student_id, department, course)
      VALUES (v_StudentData.ID, 'HIS', 101);

    INSERT INTO temp_table (num_col, char_col)
      VALUES (v_StudentData.ID,
              v_StudentData.first_name || ' ' ||
              v_StudentData.last_name);

    -- Before the loop will continue, an implicit check of
    -- c_HistoryStudents is done here.
  END LOOP;
  -- Now that the loop is finished, an implicit CLOSE of
  -- c_HistoryStudents is done.

  -- Commit our work.
  COMMIT;
END;
```

There are two important things to note about this example. First, the record
v_StudentData is *not* declared in the declarative section of the block. This variable
is *implicitly* declared by the PL/SQL compiler, similar to the loop index for a
numeric FOR loop. The type of this variable is **c_HistoryStudents%ROWTYPE**, and
the scope of **v_StudentData** is only the FOR loop itself. The implicit declaration of
the loop index, and the scope of this declaration, are the same behavior as seen in
a numeric FOR loop, as described in Chapter 2. Because of this, you can not assign
to a loop variable inside a cursor FOR loop.

Second, **c_HistoryStudents** is implicitly opened, fetched from, and closed by
the loop at the places indicated by the comments. Before the loop starts, the cursor
is opened. Before each loop iteration, the %FOUND attribute is checked to make
sure there are remaining rows in the active set. When the active set is completely
fetched, the cursor is closed as the loop ends.

Cursor FOR loops have the advantage of providing the functionality of a cursor fetch loop simply and cleanly, with a minimum of syntax.

NO_DATA_FOUND vs. %NOTFOUND

The NO_DATA_FOUND exception is raised only for SELECT..INTO statements, when the WHERE clause of the query does not match any rows. When the WHERE clause of an explicit cursor does not match any rows, the %NOTFOUND attribute is set to TRUE instead. If the WHERE clause of an UPDATE or DELETE statement does not match any rows, SQL%NOTFOUND is set to TRUE, rather than raising NO_DATA_FOUND. Because of this, all of the fetch loops shown so far use %NOTFOUND or %FOUND to determine the exit condition for the loop, rather than the NO_DATA_FOUND exception.

SELECT FOR UPDATE Cursors

Very often, the processing done in a fetch loop modifies the rows that have been retrieved by the cursor. PL/SQL provides a convenient syntax for doing this. This method consists of two parts—the FOR UPDATE clause in the cursor declaration and the WHERE CURRENT OF clause in an UPDATE or DELETE statement.

FOR UPDATE
The FOR UPDATE clause is part of a SELECT statement. It is legal as the last clause of the statement, after the ORDER BY clause (if it is present). The syntax is

    SELECT ... FROM ... FOR UPDATE [OF *column_reference*] [NOWAIT]

where *column_reference* is a column in the table against which the query is performed. A list of columns can also be used. For example, the following declarative section defines two cursors that are both legal forms of the SELECT..FOR UPDATE syntax.

```
DECLARE
  -- This cursor lists two columns for the UPDATE clause.
  CURSOR c_AllStudents IS
    SELECT *
      FROM students
      FOR UPDATE OF first_name, last_name;

  -- This cursor does not list any columns.
  CURSOR c_LargeClasses IS
```

```
SELECT department, course
  FROM classes
  WHERE max_students > 50
  FOR UPDATE;
```

Normally, a SELECT operation will not take any locks on the rows being accessed. This allows other sessions connected to the database to change the data being selected. At OPEN time, when the active set is determined, Oracle takes a snapshot of the table. Any changes that have been committed prior to this point are reflected in the active set. Any changes made after this point, even if they are committed, are not reflected unless the cursor is reopened, which will evaluate the active set again. This is the read-consistency process mentioned at the beginning of the chapter. However, if the FOR UPDATE clause is present, exclusive row locks are taken on the rows in the active set before the OPEN returns. These locks prevent other sessions from changing the rows in the active set until the transaction is committed.

If another session already has locks on the rows in the active set, then the SELECT FOR UPDATE operation will wait for these locks to be released by the other session. There is no time-out for this waiting period—the SELECT FOR UPDATE will hang until the other session releases the lock. To handle this situation, the NOWAIT clause is available. If the rows are locked by another session, then the OPEN will return immediately with the Oracle error

```
ORA-54: resource busy and acquire with NOWAIT specified
```

In this case, you may want to retry the OPEN later or change the active set to fetch unlocked rows.

WHERE CURRENT OF

If the cursor is declared with the FOR UPDATE clause, the WHERE CURRENT OF clause can be used in an UPDATE or DELETE statement. The syntax for this clause is

WHERE CURRENT OF *cursor*

where *cursor* is the name of a cursor that has been declared with a FOR UPDATE clause. The WHERE CURRENT OF clause evaluates to the row that was just retrieved by the cursor. For example, the following block will update the current credits for all registered students in HIS 101.

```
DECLARE
  -- Number of credits to add to each student's total
  v_NumCredits  classes.num_credits%TYPE;
```

```
-- This cursor will select only those students who are currently
-- registered for HIS 101.
CURSOR c_RegisteredStudents IS
  SELECT *
    FROM students
    WHERE id IN (SELECT student_id
                   FROM registered_students
                   WHERE department= 'HIS'
                   AND course = 101)
  FOR UPDATE OF current_credits;

BEGIN
  -- Set up the cursor fetch loop.
  FOR v_StudentInfo IN c_RegisteredStudents LOOP
  -- Determine the number of credits for HIS 101.
  SELECT num_credits
    INTO v_NumCredits
    FROM classes
    WHERE department = 'HIS'
    AND course = 101;

  -- Update the row we just retrieved from the cursor.
  UPDATE students
    SET current_credits = current_credits + v_NumCredits
    WHERE CURRENT OF c_RegisteredStudents;
  END LOOP;

  -- Commit our work.
  COMMIT;
END;
```

NOTE

Note that the UPDATE statement updates only the column listed in the FOR UPDATE clause of the cursor declaration. If no columns are listed, then any column can be updated.

It is legal to execute a query with a FOR UPDATE clause, but not reference the rows fetched via WHERE CURRENT OF. In this case, the rows are still locked and thus can only be modified by the current session (which holds the lock). UPDATE and DELETE statements that modify these rows will not block if they are executed by the session holding the lock.

Fetching Across Commits

Note that the COMMIT in the example in the previous section is done after the fetch loop is complete. This is done because a COMMIT will release any locks held by the session. Since the FOR UPDATE clause acquires locks, these will be released by the COMMIT. When this happens, the cursor is invalidated. Any subsequent fetches will return the Oracle error

```
ORA-1002: fetch out of sequence
```

Consider the following example, which raises this error.

```
DECLARE
  -- Cursor to retrieve all students, and lock the rows as well.
  CURSOR c_AllStudents IS
    SELECT *
      FROM students
      FOR UPDATE;

  -- Variable for retrieved data.
  v_StudentInfo  c_AllStudents%ROWTYPE;
BEGIN
  -- Open the cursor. This will acquire the locks.
  OPEN c_AllStudents;

  -- Retrieve the first record.
  FETCH c_AllStudents INTO v_StudentInfo;

  -- Issue a COMMIT. This will release the locks, invalidating the
  -- cursor.
  COMMIT WORK;

  -- This FETCH will raise the ORA-1002 error.
  FETCH c_AllStudents INTO v_StudentInfo;
END;
```

Thus, if there is a COMMIT inside a SELECT FOR UPDATE fetch loop, any fetches done after the COMMIT will fail. So it is not advisable to use a COMMIT inside the loop. If the cursor is not defined as a SELECT FOR UPDATE, there is no problem.

What do you do if you want to update the row just fetched from the cursor and use a COMMIT inside the fetch loop? The WHERE CURRENT OF clause isn't available, since the cursor can't be defined with a FOR UPDATE clause. However, you can use the primary key of the table in the WHERE clause of the UPDATE, as illustrated by the following example:

```
DECLARE
  -- Number of credits to add to each student's total
  v_NumCredits  classes.num_credits%TYPE;

  -- This cursor will select only those students who are currently
  -- registered for HIS 101.
  CURSOR c_RegisteredStudents IS
    SELECT *
      FROM students
      WHERE id IN (SELECT student_id
                     FROM registered_students
                     WHERE department= 'HIS'
                     AND course = 101);

BEGIN
  -- Set up the cursor fetch loop.
  FOR v_StudentInfo IN c_RegisteredStudents LOOP
  -- Determine the number of credits for HIS 101.
  SELECT num_credits
    INTO v_NumCredits
    FROM classes
    WHERE department = 'HIS'
    AND course = 101;

  -- Update the row we just retrieved from the cursor.
  UPDATE students
    SET current_credits = current_credits + v_NumCredits
    WHERE id = v_Studentinfo.id;

  -- We can commit inside the loop, since the cursor is
  -- not declared FOR UPDATE.
  COMMIT;
  END LOOP;
END;
```

This example essentially simulates the WHERE CURRENT OF clause, but does not create locks on the rows in the active set. As a result, it may not perform as expected if other sessions are accessing the data concurrently.

Cursor Variables

All of the explicit cursor examples we have seen so far are examples of *static cursors*—the cursor is associated with one SQL statement, and this statement is known when the block is compiled. A *cursor variable*, on the other hand, can be associated with different statements at run time. Cursor variables are analogous to PL/SQL variables, which can hold different values at run time. Static cursors are analogous to PL/SQL constants, since they can only be associated with one run-time query.

PL/SQL 2.2 ...and HIGHER Cursor variables are not available in PL/SQL versions prior to 2.2. They were introduced in version 2.2, and their functionality has been enhanced for PL/SQL 2.3. This section describes the features available in both versions. All of the examples in this section will work with 2.2 and, where indicated, with 2.3.

In order to use a cursor variable, you must first declare it. Storage for it must then be allocated at run time, since a cursor variable is a REF type. The variable will then be opened, fetched, and closed similar to a static cursor.

Declaring a Cursor Variable

A cursor variable is a reference type. With versions 2.2 and 2.3 of PL/SQL, it is the only reference type available. As discussed in Chapter 2, a reference type is the same as a pointer in C or Pascal. It can name different storage locations as the program runs. In order to use a reference type, first the variable has to be declared, and then the storage has to be allocated. Reference types in PL/SQL are declared using the syntax

> REF *type*

where *type* is an already defined type. The REF keyword indicates that the new type will be a pointer to the defined type. The type of a cursor variable is therefore REF CURSOR. This is the only legal REF type up to version 2.3 of PL/SQL. The complete syntax for defining a cursor variable type is

> TYPE *type_name* IS REF CURSOR RETURN *return_type*;

where *type_name* is the name of the new reference type, and *return_type* is a record type indicating the types of the select list that will eventually be returned by the cursor variable.

The return type for a cursor variable must be a record type. It can be declared explicitly as a user-defined record, or %ROWTYPE can be used. Once the reference type is defined, the variable can be declared. The following declarative section shows different declarations for cursor variables.

```
DECLARE
  -- Definition using %ROWTYPE.
  TYPE t_StudentsRef IS REF CURSOR
    RETURN students%ROWTYPE;

  -- Define a new record type,
  TYPE t_NameRecord IS RECORD (
    first_name   students.first_name%TYPE,
    last_name    students.last_name%TYPE);

  -- a variable of this type,
  v_NameRecord   t_NameRecord;

  -- And a cursor variable using the record type.
  TYPE t_NamesRef IS REF CURSOR
    RETURN t_NameRecord;

  -- We can define another type, using %TYPE for the previously
  -- defined record.
  TYPE t_NamesRef2 IS REF CURSOR
    RETURN v_NameRecord%TYPE;

  -- Declare cursor variables using the above types.
  v_StudentCV t_StudentsRef;
  v_NameCV    t_NamesRef;
```

Constrained and Unconstrained Cursor Variables

The cursor variables in the prior section are *constrained*—they are declared for a specific return type only. When the variable is later opened, it must be opened for a query whose select list matches the return type of the cursor. If not, the predefined exception ROWTYPE_MISMATCH is raised.

 PL/SQL 2.3 ...and HIGHER PL/SQL 2.3, however, allows the declaration of *unconstrained* cursor variables. An unconstrained cursor variable does not have a RETURN clause. When an unconstrained cursor variable is later opened, it can be opened for any query. The following declarative section declares some unconstrained cursor variables.

```
DECLARE
  -- Define an unconstrained reference type.
  TYPE t_FlexibleRef IS REF CURSOR;
```

```
-- and a variable of that type.
v_CursorVar t_FlexibleRef;
```

Allocating Storage for Cursor Variables

Since a cursor variable is a reference type, no storage is allocated for it when it is declared. Before it can be used, it needs to point to a valid area of memory. This memory can be created in two ways—by allocating it in an OCI or precompiler program, or automatically by the PL/SQL engine.

NOTE:
PL/SQL 2.2 cannot allocate storage for reference variables automatically. Therefore, in order to use cursor variables with release 2.2, either OCI or a precompiler is *required,* since they are the only tools that can allocate the necessary memory. PL/SQL 2.3 can allocate storage for cursor variables, and thus the precompiler or OCI is no longer necessary.

Using EXEC SQL ALLOCATE

In order to allocate storage when using Pro*C, you need to declare a variable of type SQL_CURSOR. This variable should be declared in the declare section of the Pro*C program, since it is a host variable. It is then allocated with the EXEC SQL ALLOCATE command. For example, the following Pro*C fragment declares and allocates a cursor variable:

```
EXEC SQL BEGIN DECLARE SECTION;
  SQL_CURSOR v_CursorVar;
EXEC SQL END DECLARE SECTION;

EXEC SQL ALLOCATE :v_CursorVar;
```

The use of PL/SQL in Pro*C and other precompilers is discussed in more detail in Chapter 7. A host cursor variable is unconstrained, since it has no return type associated with it. This is the only way to declare an unconstrained cursor variable in PL/SQL 2.2. EXEC SQL ALLOCATE is available with Pro*C 2.1 or higher.

Automatic Allocation

PL/SQL 2.3 ...and HIGHER With PL/SQL 2.3, cursor variables are automatically allocated when necessary. When the variable goes out of scope and thus no longer references the storage, it is de-allocated.

Opening a Cursor Variable for a Query

In order to associate a cursor variable with a particular SELECT statement, the OPEN syntax is extended to allow the query to be specified. This is done with the OPEN FOR syntax,

OPEN *cursor variable* FOR *select_statement*;

where *cursor_variable* is a previously declared cursor variable, and *select_statement* is the desired query. If the cursor variable is constrained, then the select list must match the return type of the cursor. If it does not, the error

```
ORA-6504: PL/SQL: return types of result set variables or query
          do not match
```

is returned. (See Chapter 6 for more information on PL/SQL errors and how to handle them.) For example, given a cursor variable declaration like

```
DECLARE
   TYPE t_ClassesRef IS REF CURSOR RETURN classes%ROWTYPE;
   v_ClassesCV t_ClassesRef;
```

we can open **v_ClassesCV** with

```
OPEN v_ClassesCV FOR
   SELECT * FROM CLASSES;
```

If, on the other hand, we attempt to open **v_ClassesCV** with

```
OPEN v_ClassesCV FOR
   SELECT department, course FROM CLASSES
```

we would receive ORA-6504 since the select list of the query does not match the return type of the cursor variable.

OPEN..FOR behaves the same way as OPEN—any bind variables in the query are examined and the active set is determined. Following the OPEN..FOR, the cursor variable is fetched from using the FETCH statement. The fetch must be done on the client with version 2.2, or can be done on the server with version 2.3.

Closing Cursor Variables

Cursor variables are closed just like static cursors—with the CLOSE statement. This frees the resources used for the query. It does not necessarily free the storage for the cursor itself, however. It is illegal to close a cursor or cursor variable that is already closed. Cursor variables can be closed on either the client or the server.

Cursor Variable Example 1

The following is a complete Pro*C program which demonstrates the use of cursor variables. It uses an embedded PL/SQL block to select from either the **classes** or the **rooms** table, depending on user input. For the benefit of those who may not be familiar with C, the code is more heavily commented than usual. This program will work with PL/SQL 2.2 and Pro*C 2.1, and higher.

```
/* Include C and SQL header files. */
#include <stdio.h>
EXEC SQL INCLUDE SQLCA;

/* SQL Declare section. All host variables must be declared
   here. */
EXEC SQL BEGIN DECLARE SECTION;
  /* Character string to hold the username and password. */
  char *v_Username = "example/example";

  /* SQL Cursor variable */
  SQL_CURSOR v_CursorVar;

  /* Integer variable used to control table selection. */
  int v_Table;

  /* Output variables for rooms. */
  int v_RoomID;
  VARCHAR v_Description[2001];

  /* Output variables for classes. */
  VARCHAR v_Department[4];
  int v_Course;
EXEC SQL END DECLARE SECTION;


/* Error handling routine. Print out the error, and exit. */
void handle_error() {
  printf("SQL Error occurred!\n");
  printf("%.*s\n", sqlca.sqlerrm.sqlerrml, sqlca.sqlerrm.sqlerrmc);
  EXEC SQL ROLLBACK WORK RELEASE;
```

```
    exit(1);
}

int main() {
  /* Character string to hold user input. */
  char v_Choice[20];

  /* Set up the error handling. Whenever an SQL error occurs, we
     will call the handle_error() routine. */
  EXEC SQL WHENEVER SQLERROR DO handle_error();

  /* Connect to the database. */
  EXEC SQL CONNECT :v_Username;
  printf("Connected to Oracle.\n");

  /* Allocate the cursor variable. */
  EXEC SQL ALLOCATE :v_CursorVar;

  /* Print a message asking the user for input, and retreive their
     selection into v_Choice. */
  printf("Choose from (C)lasses or (R)omms. Enter c or r: ");
  gets(v_Choice);

  /* Determine the correct table. */
  if (v_Choice[0] == 'c')
    v_Table = 1;
  else
    v_Table = 2;

  /* Open the cursor variable using an embedded PL/SQL block. */
  EXEC SQL EXECUTE
    BEGIN
      IF :v_Table = 1 THEN
        /* Open variable for the classes table. */
        OPEN :v_CursorVar FOR
          SELECT department, course
            FROM classes;
      ELSE
        /* Open variable for the rooms table. */
        OPEN :v_CursorVar FOR
          SELECT room_id, description
            FROM rooms;
```

```
        END IF;
      END;
END-EXEC;

/* Exit the loop when we are done fetching. */
EXEC SQL WHENEVER NOT FOUND DO BREAK;

/* Begin the fetch loop. */
for (;;) {
  if (v_Table == 1) {
    /* Fetch class info. */
    EXEC SQL FETCH :v_CursorVar
      INTO :v_Department, :v_Course;

    /* Display it to the screen. Since v_Department is a
       VARCHAR, use the .len field for the actual length
       and the .arr field for the data. */
    printf("%.*s %d\n", v_Department.len, v_Department.arr,
                      v_Course);
  }
  else {
    /* Fetch room info. */
    EXEC SQL FETCH :v_CursorVar
      INTO :v_RoomID, v_Description;

    /* Display it to the screen. Since v_Description is a
       VARCHAR, use the .len field for the actual length
       and the .arr field for the data. */
    printf("%d %.*s\n", v_RoomID, v_Description.len,
                      v_Description.arr);
  }
}

/* Close the cursor. */
EXEC SQL CLOSE :v_CursorVar;

/* Disconnect from the database. */
EXEC SQL COMMIT WORK RELEASE;
}
```

In the above program, the cursor is opened on the server (via the embedded anonymous block), and fetched from and closed back on the client. Since the cursor variable is declared as a host variable, it is unconstrained. Thus, we are able to use the same variable for selecting both from **classes** and from **rooms**.

Cursor Variable Example 2

PL/SQL 2.3 ...and HIGHER The following example is similar to the Pro*C example in the previous section, but is written entirely in PL/SQL. It is a stored procedure which selects from **classes** or **rooms** depending on its input. Since the fetch is done in the procedure and therefore on the server, it will only work in PL/SQL 2.3. For more information on stored procedures, see Chapter 5.

```
CREATE OR REPLACE PROCEDURE ShowCursorVariable
  /* Demonstrates the use of a cursor variable on the server.
     If p_Table is 'classes', then information from the classes
     table is inserted into temp_table. If p_Table is 'rooms'
     then information from rooms is inserted. */
  (p_Table IN VARCHAR2) AS

  /* Define the cursor variable type */
  TYPE t_ClassesRooms IS REF CURSOR;

  /* and the variable itself. */
  v_CursorVar t_ClassesRooms;

  /* Variables to hold the output. */
  v_Department  classes.department%TYPE;
  v_Course      classes.course%TYPE;
  v_RoomID      rooms.room_id%TYPE;
  v_Description rooms.description%TYPE;
BEGIN
  -- Based on the input parameter, open the cursor variable.
  IF p_Table = 'classes' THEN
    OPEN v_CursorVar FOR
      SELECT department, course
        FROM classes;
  ELSIF p_table = 'rooms' THEN
    OPEN v_CursorVar FOR
      SELECT room_id, description
        FROM rooms;
  ELSE
    /* Wrong value passed as input - raise an error */
    RAISE_APPLICATION_ERROR(-20000,
      'Input must be ''classes'' or ''rooms''');
  END IF;
```

```
/* Fetch loop. Note the EXIT WHEN clause after the FETCH -
   with PL/SQL 2.3 we can use cursor attributes with cursor
   variables. */
LOOP
  IF p_Table = 'classes' THEN
    FETCH v_CursorVar INTO
      v_Department, v_Course;
    EXIT WHEN v_CursorVar%NOTFOUND;

    INSERT INTO temp_table (num_col, char_col)
      VALUES (v_Course, v_Department);
  ELSE
    FETCH v_CursorVar INTO
      v_RoomID, v_Description;
    EXIT WHEN v_CursorVAR%NOTFOUND;

    INSERT INTO temp_table (num_col, char_col)
      VALUES (v_RoomID, SUBSTR(v_Description, 1, 60));
  END IF;
END LOOP;

/* Close the cursor. */
CLOSE v_CursorVar;

COMMIT;
END ShowCursorVariable;
```

Restrictions on Using Cursor Variables

Cursor variables are a powerful feature, and they can greatly simplify processing, since they allow different kinds of data to be returned in the same variable. However, there are a number of restrictions associated with their use; these are listed here. Some of the restrictions have been lifted in version 2.3, and it is likely that the remainder will be lifted in future versions of PL/SQL and the precompilers.

- In PL/SQL 2.2, cursor variables cannot be declared in a package. This is because the storage for a cursor variable has to be allocated using Pro*C or OCI. With version 2.2, the only means of passing a cursor variable to a PL/SQL block is via a bind variable or a procedure parameter. This restriction has been lifted in PL/SQL 2.3.

- Remote subprograms cannot return the value of a cursor variable. This restriction still exists between database servers in 2.3, but cursor variables can be passed between client- and server-side PL/SQL.

- Cursor attributes cannot be used with cursor variables in PL/SQL 2.2. This reatriction has been lifted for version 2.3; however, the %ROWTYPE attribute cannot be applied to a cursor variable in either version.

- In version 2.2, all fetches from cursor variables have to be done on the client, written in Pro*C or OCI. In version 2.3, cursor variables can be fetched from on the server.

- PL/SQL tables cannot store cursor variables in either version.

- Cursor variables cannot be used with dynamic SQL in Pro*C.

- The query associated with a cursor variable in the OPEN..FOR statement cannot be FOR UPDATE.

Summary

In this chapter, we've covered the steps necessary for processing cursors, which allow explicit control of SQL statement processing. For explicit cursors, the steps include declaring, opening, fetching, and closing the cursor. Cursor attributes are used to determine the current state of a cursor, and thus how to manipulate it. In addition, we discussed different kinds of fetch loops. The chapter concluded with a discussion of cursor variables and the difference between their implementation

in PL/SQL 2.2 and 2.3. In the next chapter, we will continue with the basics of PL/SQL by examining procedures, functions, packages, and triggers.

CHAPTER 5

Procedures, Functions, Packages, and Triggers

The PL/SQL blocks that we have seen so far have been anonymous ones. One of the main properties of an anonymous block is that it is compiled and run each time it is loaded. In addition, an anonymous block is not stored in the database, and it cannot be called directly from other PL/SQL blocks. The constructs that we will look at in this chapter—procedures, functions, packages, and triggers—do not have these restrictions. They can be stored in the database and run when appropriate.

Procedures and Functions

PL/SQL procedures and functions behave very much like procedures and functions in other third-generation languages. They share many of the same properties. Collectively, procedures and functions are also known as *subprograms.* As an example, the following creates a procedure in the database:

```
CREATE OR REPLACE PROCEDURE AddNewStudent (
  p_FirstName   students.first_name%TYPE,
  p_LastName    students.last_name%TYPE,
  p_Major       students.major%TYPE) AS
BEGIN
  -- Insert a new row in the students table. Use
  -- student_sequence to generate the new student ID, and
  -- 0 for current_credits.
  INSERT INTO students (ID, first_name, last_name,
                        current_credits,  major)
    VALUES (student_sequence.nextval, p_FirstName, p_LastName,
            p_Major, 0);

  COMMIT;
END AddNewStudent;
```

Once this procedure is created, we can call it from another PL/SQL block, as in this example:

```
BEGIN
  AddNewStudent('David', 'Dinsmore', 'Music');
END;
```

This example illustrates several notable points:

- The **AddNewStudent** procedure is created first, via the CREATE OR REPLACE PROCEDURE statement. When a procedure is created, it is compiled and stored in the database in compiled form. This compiled code can then be run later, from another PL/SQL block.

- When the procedure is called, parameters can be passed. In the preceding example, the new student's first name, last name, and major are passed to the procedure at run time. Inside the procedure, the parameter **p_FirstName** will have the value 'David', **p_LastName** will have the value 'Dinsmore', and **p_Major** will have the value 'Music', since these literals are passed to the procedure when it is called.

■   A procedure call is a PL/SQL statement by itself. It is not called as part of an expression. When a procedure is called, control passes to the first executable statement inside the procedure. When the procedure finishes, control resumes at the statement following the procedure call.

■   A procedure is a PL/SQL block, with a declarative section, executable section, and exception-handling section. As in an anonymous block, only the executable section is required. **AddNewStudent** only has an executable section.

Creating a Procedure

The syntax for the CREATE OR REPLACE PROCEDURE statement is

```
CREATE [OR REPLACE] PROCEDURE procedure_name
    [(argument [{IN | OUT | IN OUT}] type,
    ...
    argument[{IN | OUT | IN OUT}] type)] {IS | AS}
    procedure_body
```

where *procedure_name* is the name of the procedure to be created, *argument* is the name of a procedure parameter, *type* is the type of the associated parameter, and *procedure_body* is a PL/SQL block that makes up the code of the procedure.

In order to change the code of a procedure, the procedure must be dropped and then re-created. Since this is a common operation while the procedure is under development, the OR REPLACE keywords allow this to be done in one operation. If the procedure exists, it is dropped first, without a warning message. To drop a procedure, use the DROP PROCEDURE command, described in the "Dropping Procedures and Functions" section later in this chapter. If the procedure does not already exist, then it is simply created. If the procedure exists and the OR REPLACE keywords are not present, the CREATE statement will return this Oracle error:

```
ORA-00955: name is already used by an existing object
```

As in other CREATE statements, creating a procedure is a DDL operation, so an implicit COMMIT is done both before and after the procedure is created. Either the IS or the AS keyword can be used—they are equivalent.

Parameters and Modes

Given the **AddNewStudent** procedure shown earlier, we can call this procedure from the following anonymous PL/SQL block:

```
DECLARE
  -- Variables describing the new student
  v_NewFirstName  students.first_name%TYPE := 'Margaret';
  v_NewLastName   students.last_name%TYPE := 'Mason';
  v_NewMajor      students.major%TYPE := 'History';
BEGIN
  -- Add Margaret Mason to the database.
  AddNewStudent(v_NewFirstName, v_NewLastName, v_NewMajor);
END;
```

The variables declared in the above block (**v_NewFirstName**, **v_NewLastName**, **v_NewMajor**) are passed as arguments to **AddNewStudent**. In this context, they are known as *actual parameters*, while the parameters in the procedure declaration (**p_FirstName**, **p_LastName**, **p_Major**) are known as *formal parameters*. Actual parameters contain the values that are passed to a procedure when it is called, and they receive results from the procedure when it returns. The values of the actual parameters are the ones that will be used in the procedure. The formal parameters are the placeholders for the values of the actual parameters. When the procedure is called, the formal parameters are assigned the values of the actual parameters. Inside the procedure, they are referred to by the formal parameters. When the procedure returns, the actual parameters are assigned the value of the formal parameters. These assignments follow the normal rules for PL/SQL assignment, including type conversion if necessary.

Formal parameters can have three modes—IN, OUT, or IN OUT. If the mode is not specified for a formal parameter, it defaults to IN. The differences between each mode are described in Table 5-1 and illustrated in the following example:

```
CREATE OR REPLACE PROCEDURE ModeTest (
  p_InParameter    IN NUMBER,
  p_OutParameter   OUT NUMBER,
  p_InOutParameter IN OUT NUMBER) IS

  v_LocalVariable  NUMBER;
BEGIN
  /* Assign p_InParameter to v_LocalVariable. This is legal,
     since we are reading from an IN parameter and not writing
     to it. */
  v_LocalVariable := p_InParameter;  -- Legal

  /* Assign 7 to p_InParameter. This is ILLEGAL, since we
     are writing to a IN parameter. */
  p_InParameter := 7;  -- Illegal
```

```
    /* Assign 7 to p_OutParameter. This is legal, since we
       are writing to an OUT parameter and not reading from
       it. */
    p_OutParameter := 7;   -- Legal

    /* Assign p_OutParameter to v_LocalVariable. This is
       ILLEGAL, since we are reading from an OUT parameter. */
    v_LocalVariable := p_outParameter;   -- Illegal

    /* Assign p_InOutParameter to v_LocalVariable. This is legal,
       since we are reading from an IN OUT parameter. */
    v_LocalVariable := p_InOutParameter;   -- Legal

    /* Assign 7 to p_InOutParameter. This is legal, since we
       are writing to an IN OUT parameter. */
    p_InOutParameter := 7;   -- Legal
END ModeTest;
```

Mode	Description
IN	The value of the actual parameter is passed into the procedure when the procedure is invoked. Inside the procedure, the formal parameter is considered *read-only*—it cannot be changed. When the procedure finishes and control returns to the calling environment, the actual parameter is not changed.
OUT	Any value the actual parameter has when the procedure is called is ignored. Inside the procedure, the formal parameter is considered *write-only*—it can only be assigned to and cannot be read from. When the procedure finishes and control returns to the calling environment, the contents of the formal parameter are assigned to the actual parameter.
IN OUT	This mode is a combination of IN and OUT. The value of the actual parameter is passed into the procedure when the procedure is invoked. Inside the procedure, the formal parameter can be read from and written to. When the procedure finishes and control returns to the calling environment, the contents of the formal parameter are assigned to the actual parameter.

TABLE 5-1.   *Parameter Modes*

NOTE
The **ModeTest** example shows legal and illegal PL/SQL assignments.
A SELECT..INTO or a FETCH..INTO statement also assigns to the
variables in the INTO clause, and these variables are subject to the
same restrictions.

PL/SQL will check for legal assignments when the procedure is created. For
example, **ModeTest** generates the following errors if we attempt to compile it, since
it does contain illegal assignments:

```
PLS-363: expression 'P_INPARAMETER' cannot be used as an
         assignment target
PLS-365: 'P_OUTPARAMETER' is an OUT parameter and cannot be read
```

An IN parameter is an rvalue inside a procedure; it can only appear on the
right-hand side of an assignment statement. An OUT parameter is an lvalue; it can
only appear on the left-hand side of an assignment statement. (See Chapter 2 for
more information on lvalues and rvalues.) An IN OUT parameter is both an rvalue
and an lvalue, since it can appear on either side of an assignment statement.

If a parameter is OUT or IN OUT, the actual parameter will be written into
by the procedure. When the procedure finishes, the contents of the formal
parameters are written to their corresponding actual parameters. Because of this,
the actual parameter must be an lvalue. A literal is an rvalue and thus cannot be
used for OUT or IN OUT parameters, since there is no permanent memory
allocated for a literal. For example, the following would be a legal call to
ModeTest, since the actual parameters for **p_OutParameter** and **p_InOutParameter**
are variable declarations:

```
DECLARE
  v_Variable1 NUMBER;
  v_Variable2 NUMBER;
BEGIN
  ModeTest(12, v_Variable1, v_Variable2);
END;
```

If we were to replace **v_Variable2** with a literal, however, we would get the
following illegal example:

```
DECLARE
  v_Variable1 NUMBER;
BEGIN
  ModeTest(12, v_Variable1, 11);
END;
```

This block produces the following errors:

```
ERROR at line 4:
ORA-06550: line 4, column 29:
PLS-00363: expression '11' cannot be used as an assignment target
ORA-06550: line 4, column 3:
PL/SQL: Statement ignored
```

If there are no parameters for a procedure, there are no parentheses in either the procedure declaration or the procedure call.

The Procedure Body

The body of a procedure is a PL/SQL block with declarative, executable, and exception sections. The declarative section is located between the IS or AS keyword and the BEGIN keyword. The executable section (the only one that is required) is located between the BEGIN and EXCEPTION keywords. The exception section is located between the EXCEPTION and END keywords.

NOTE
There is no DECLARE keyword in a procedure or function declaration. The IS or AS keyword is used instead. This is similar to the Ada syntax.

Here is the structure of a procedure:

CREATE OR REPLACE PROCEDURE *procedure_name* **AS**
   Declarative section
   Executable section
EXCEPTION
   Exception section
END [*procedure_name*];

The procedure name can optionally be included after the final END statement in the procedure declaration. If there is an identifier after the END, it must match the name of the procedure. It is good style to include this, since it emphasizes the END statement, which matches the CREATE statement.

Constraints on Formal Parameters

When a procedure is called, the values of the actual parameters are passed in, and they are referred to using the formal parameters inside the procedure. Not only the values are passed, but the constraints on the variables are passed as well, as part of the parameter passing mechanism. In a procedure declaration, it is illegal to constrain CHAR and VARCHAR2 parameters with a length and NUMBER parameters with a precision and/or scale. For example, the following procedure declaration is illegal and will generate a compile error:

```
CREATE OR REPLACE PROCEDURE ParameterLength (
  p_Parameter1 IN OUT VARCHAR2(10),
  p_Parameter2 IN OUT NUMBER(3,2)) AS
BEGIN
  p_Parameter1 := 'abcdefghijklm';
  p_Parameter2 := 12.3;
END ParameterLength;
```

The correct declaration for this procedure would be

```
CREATE OR REPLACE PROCEDURE ParameterLength (
  p_Parameter1 IN OUT VARCHAR2,
  p_Parameter2 IN OUT NUMBER) AS
BEGIN
  p_Parameter1 := 'abcdefghijklmno';
  p_Parameter2 := 12.3;
END ParameterLength;
```

So, what are the constraints on **p_Parameter1** and **p_Parameter2**? They come from the actual parameters. If we call **ParameterLength** with

```
DECLARE
  v_Variable1 VARCHAR2(40);
  v_Variable2 NUMBER(3,4);
BEGIN
  ParameterLength(v_Variable1, v_Variable2);
END;
```

then **p_Parameter1** will have a maximum length of 40 (coming from the actual parameter **v_Variable1**) and **p_Parameter2** will have precision 3 and scale 4 (coming from the actual parameter **v_Variable2**). It is important to be aware of this. Consider the following block, which also calls **ParameterLength**:

```
DECLARE
  v_Variable1 VARCHAR2(10);
  v_Variable2 NUMBER(3,4);
BEGIN
  ParameterLength(v_Variable1, v_Variable2);
END;
```

The only difference between this block and the prior one is that **v_Variable1**, and hence **p_Parameter1**, has a length of 10 rather than 40. Since **ParameterLength** assigns a character string of length 15 to **p_Parameter1** (and hence **v_Variable1**), there is not enough room in the string. This will result in the following Oracle error when the procedure is called:

```
ORA-6502: numeric or value error
```

The source of the error is not in the procedure, it is in the code that calls the procedure.

TIP

In order to avoid errors such as ORA-6502, document any constraint requirements of the actual parameters when the procedure is created. This documentation should consist of comments stored with the procedure.

%TYPE and Procedure Parameters   The only way to get constraints on a formal parameter is to use %TYPE. If a formal parameter is declared using %TYPE, and the underlying type is constrained, then the constraint will be on the formal parameter rather than the actual parameter. If we declare **ParameterLength** with

```
CREATE OR REPLACE PROCEDURE ParameterLength (
  p_Parameter1 IN OUT VARCHAR2,
  p_Parameter2 IN OUT students.current_credits%TYPE) AS
BEGIN
  p_Parameter2 := 12345;
END ParameterLength;
```

p_Parameter2 will be constrained with precision of 3, since that is the precision of the **current_credits** column. Even if we call **ParameterLength** with an actual parameter of enough precision, the formal precision is taken. The following example will generate the ORA-6502 error:

```
DECLARE
  v_Variable1 VARCHAR2(1);
```

```
   v_Variable2 NUMBER; -- Declare v_Variable2 with no constraints
BEGIN
   -- Even though the actual parameter has room for 12345, the
   -- constraint on the formal parameter is taken and we get
   -- ORA-6502 on this procedure call.
   ParameterLength(v_Variable1, v_Variable2);
END;
```

Positional and Named Notation

In all of the examples shown so far in this chapter, the actual arguments are associated with the formal arguments by position. Given a procedure declaration such as

```
CREATE OR REPLACE PROCEDURE CallMe (
   p_ParameterA VARCHAR2,
   p_ParameterB NUMBER,
   p_ParameterC BOOLEAN,
   p_ParameterD DATE) AS
BEGIN
   ...
END CallMe;
```

and a calling block such as

```
DECLARE
   v_Variable1 VARCHAR2(10);
   v_Variable2 NUMBER(7,6);
   v_Variable3 BOOLEAN;
   v_Variable4 DATE;
BEGIN
   CallMe(v_Variable1, v_Variable2, v_Variable3, v_Variable4);
END;
```

the actual parameters are associated with the formal parameters by position: **v_Variable1** is associated with **p_ParameterA**, **v_Variable2** is associated with **p_ParameterB**, and so on. This is known as *positional notation*. Positional notation is more commonly used, and it is also the notation used in other third-generation languages such as C.

Alternatively, we can call the procedure using *named notation*:

```
DECLARE
  v_Variable1 VARCHAR2(10);
  v_Variable2 NUMBER(7,6);
  v_Variable3 BOOLEAN;
  v_Variable4 DATE;
BEGIN
  CallMe(p_ParameterA => v_Variable1,
         p_ParameterB => v_Variable2,
         p_ParameterC => v_Variable3,
         p_ParameterD => v_Variable4);
END;
```

In named notation, the formal parameter and the actual parameter are both included for each argument. This allows us to rearrange the order of the arguments, if desired. For example, the following block also calls **CallMe**, with the same arguments:

```
DECLARE
  v_Variable1 VARCHAR2(10);
  v_Variable2 NUMBER(7,6);
  v_Variable3 BOOLEAN;
  v_Variable4 DATE;
BEGIN
  CallMe(p_ParameterB => v_Variable2,
         p_ParameterC => v_Variable3,
         p_ParameterD => v_Variable4,
         p_ParameterA => v_Variable1);
END;
```

Positional and named notation can be mixed in the same call as well, if desired. The first arguments must be specified positionally, and the remaining arguments can be specified by name. The following block illustrates this method:

```
DECLARE
  v_Variable1 VARCHAR2(10);
  v_Variable2 NUMBER(7,6);
  v_Variable3 BOOLEAN;
  v_Variable4 DATE;
BEGIN
  -- First 2 parameters passed positionally, the second 2 are
```

```
  -- passed by name.
  CallMe(v_Variable1, v_Variable2,
         p_ParameterC => v_Variable3,
         p_ParameterD => v_Variable4);
END;
```

Named notation is another feature of PL/SQL that comes from Ada. When should you use positional notation, and when should you use named notation? Neither is more efficient than the other, so the only preference is one of style. Some of the style differences are illustrated in Table 5-2.

I generally use positional notation, as I prefer to write succinct code. It is important to use good names for the actual parameters, however. On the other hand, if the procedure takes a large number of arguments (more than ten is a good measure), then named notation is desirable, since it is easier to match the formal

Positional Notation	Named Notation
Clearly illustrates the association between the actual and formal parameters.	Relies more on good names for the actual parameters to illustrate what each is used for.
Names used for the formal and actual parameters are independent; one can be changed without modifying the other.	Can be more difficult to maintain because all calls to the procedure using named notation must be changed if the names of the formal parameters are changed.
If the order of the formal parameters is changed, calls to the procedure using positional notation will not have to be changed.	On the other hand, if the order of the formal parameters is changed, calls to the procedure using named notation will not have to be changed.
More succinct than named notation.	Requires more coding, since both the formal and actual parameters are included in the procedure call.
Parameters with default values must be at the end of the argument list.	Allows default values[1] for formal parameters to be used, regardless of which parameter has the default.

TABLE 5-2.   *Positional vs. Named Notation*

[1] Default parameters are discussed in the next section.

and actual parameters. Procedures with this many arguments are fairly rare, however.

TIP
The more parameters a procedure has, the more difficult it is to call and make sure that all of the required parameters are present. If you have a significant number of parameters that you would like to pass to or from a procedure, consider defining a record type with the parameters as fields within the record. Then you can use a single parameter of the record type. PL/SQL has no explicit limit on the number of parameters you can use in a procedure.

Parameter Default Values

Similar to variable declarations, the formal parameters to a procedure or function can have default values. If a parameter has a default value, it does not have to be passed from the calling environment. If it is passed, the value of the actual parameter will be used instead of the default. A default value for a parameter is included using the syntax

parameter_name [*mode*] *parameter_type* {:= | DEFAULT} *initial_value*

where *parameter_name* is the name of the formal parameter, *mode* is the parameter mode (IN, OUT, or IN OUT), *parameter_type* is the parameter type (either predefined or user-defined), and *initial_value* is the value to be assigned to the formal parameter by default. Either := or the DEFAULT keyword can be used. For example, we can rewrite the **AddNewStudent** procedure to assign the economics major by default to all new students, unless overridden by an explicit argument:

```
CREATE OR REPLACE PROCEDURE AddNewStudent (
  p_FirstName   students.first_name%TYPE,
  p_LastName    students.last_name%TYPE,
  p_Major       students.major%TYPE DEFAULT 'Economics') AS
BEGIN
  -- Insert a new row in the students table. Use
  -- student_sequence to generate the new student ID, and
  -- 0 for current_credits.
  INSERT INTO students VALUES (student_sequence.nextval,
    p_FirstName, p_LastName, p_Major, 0);

  COMMIT;
END AddNewStudent;
```

The default value will be used if the **p_Major** formal parameter does not have an actual parameter associated with it in the procedure call. We can do this with positional notation,

```
BEGIN
  AddNewStudent('Barbara', 'Blues');
END;
```

or with named notation:

```
BEGIN
  AddNewStudent(p_FirstName => 'Barbara',
                p_LastName => 'Blues');
END;
```

If positional notation is used, all parameters with default values that don't have an associated actual parameter must be at the end of the parameter list. Consider the following example:

```
CREATE OR REPLACE PROCEDURE DefaultTest (
  p_ParameterA NUMBER DEFAULT 10,
  p_ParameterB VARCHAR2 DEFAULT 'abcdef',
  p_ParameterC DATE DEFAULT SYSDATE) AS
BEGIN
  ...
END DefaultTest;
```

All three parameters to **DefaultTest** take default arguments. If we wanted to take the default value for **p_ParameterB** only, but specify values for **p_ParameterA** and **p_ParameterC**, we would have to use named notation, as follows:

```
BEGIN
  DefaultTest(p_ParameterA => 7, p_ParameterC => '30-DEC-95');
END;
```

If we wanted to use the default value for **p_ParameterB** when using positional notation, we would also have to use the default value for **p_ParameterC**. With positional notation, all default parameters for which there are no associated actual parameters must be at the end of the parameter list, as in the following example:

```
BEGIN
  /* Uses the default value for both p_ParameterB and
     p_ParameterC. */
  DefaultTest(7);
END;
```

TIP
When using default values, make them the last parameters in the
argument list if possible. This way, either positional or named
notation can be used.

Creating a Function

A function is very similar to a procedure. Both take arguments, which can be of
different modes. Both are different forms of PL/SQL blocks, with a declarative,
executable, and exception section. Both can be stored in the database or declared
within a block. (Procedures and functions not stored in the database are discussed
later in this chapter, in the section "Subprogram Locations.") However, a procedure
call is a PL/SQL statement by itself, while a function call is called as part of an
expression.

A function call is an rvalue. For example, the following function returns TRUE if
the specified class is more than 90% full and FALSE otherwise:

```
CREATE OR REPLACE FUNCTION AlmostFull (
  p_Department classes.department%TYPE,
  p_Course     classes.course%TYPE)
  RETURN BOOLEAN IS

  v_CurrentStudents NUMBER;
  v_MaxStudents     NUMBER;
  v_ReturnValue     BOOLEAN;
  v_FullPercent     CONSTANT NUMBER := 90;
BEGIN
  -- Get the current and maximum students for the requested
  -- course.
  SELECT current_students, max_students
    INTO v_CurrentStudents, v_MaxStudents
    FROM classes
    WHERE department = p_Department
    AND course = p_Course;

  -- If the class is more full than the percentage given by
```

```
   -- v_FullPercent, return TRUE. Otherwise, return FALSE.
   IF (v_CurrentStudents / v_MaxStudents * 100) > v_FullPercent THEN
     v_ReturnValue := TRUE;
   ELSE
     v_ReturnValue := FALSE;
   END IF;

   RETURN v_ReturnValue;
END AlmostFull;
```

The **AlmostFull** function returns a BOOLEAN value. It can be called from the following PL/SQL block. Note that the function call is not a statement by itself—it is used as part of the IF statement inside the loop.

```
DECLARE
   CURSOR c_Classes IS
     SELECT department, course
       FROM classes;
BEGIN
   FOR v_ClassRecord IN c_Classes LOOP
     -- Record all classes which don't have very much room left
     -- in temp_table.
     IF AlmostFull(v_ClassRecord.department, v_ClassRecord.course) THEN
       INSERT INTO temp_table (char_col) VALUES
         (v_ClassRecord.department || ' ' || v_ClassRecord.course ||
          ' is almost full!');
     END IF;
   END LOOP;
END;
```

Function Syntax

The syntax for creating a stored function is very similar to the syntax for a procedure. It is

```
CREATE [OR REPLACE] FUNCTION function_name
    [(argument [{IN | OUT | IN OUT}] type,
     ...
      argument [{IN | OUT | IN OUT}] type)]
    RETURN return_type {IS | AS}
    function_body
```

where *function_name* is the name of the function, *argument* and *type* are the same as for procedures, *return_type* is the type of the value that the function returns, and *function_body* is a PL/SQL block containing the code for the function.

Similar to procedures, the argument list is optional. In this case, there are no parentheses either in the function declaration or in the function call. However, the function return type is required, since the function call is part of an expression. The type of the function is used to determine the type of the expression containing the function call.

The RETURN Statement

Inside the body of the function, the RETURN statement is used to return control to the calling environment with a value. The general syntax of the RETURN statement is

    RETURN *expression*;

where *expression* is the value to be returned. The value *expression* will be converted to the type specified in the RETURN clause of the function definition, if it is not already of that type. When the RETURN statement is executed, control immediately returns to the calling environment.

There can be more than one RETURN statement in a function, although only one of them will be executed. It is an error for a function to end without executing a RETURN. The following example illustrates multiple RETURN statements in one function. Even though there are five different RETURN statements in the function, only one of them is executed. Which one is executed depends on how full the class specified by **p_Department** and **p_Course** is.

```
CREATE OR REPLACE FUNCTION ClassInfo (
   /* Returns 'Full' if the class is completely full,
      'Some Room' if the class is over 80% full,
      'More Room' if the class is over 60% full,
      'Lots of Room' if the class is less than 60% full, and
      'Empty' if there are no students registered. */
   p_Department classes.department%TYPE,
   p_Course     classes.course%TYPE)
   RETURN VARCHAR2 IS

   v_CurrentStudents NUMBER;
   v_MaxStudents     NUMBER;
   v_PercentFull     NUMBER;
BEGIN
   -- Get the current and maximum students for the requested
```

```
-- course.
SELECT current_students, max_students
  INTO v_CurrentStudents, v_MaxStudents
  FROM classes
  WHERE department = p_Department
  AND course = p_Course;

-- Calculate the current percentage.
v_PercentFull := v_CurrentStudents / v_MaxStudents * 100;

IF v_PercentFull = 100 THEN
  RETURN 'Full';
ELSIF v_PercentFull > 80 THEN
  RETURN 'Some Room';
ELSIF v_PercentFull > 60 THEN
  RETURN 'More Room';
ELSIF v_PercentFull > 0 THEN
  RETURN 'Lots of Room';
ELSE
  RETURN 'Empty';
END IF;
END ClassInfo;
```

When used in a function, the RETURN statement must have an expression associated with it. RETURN can also be used in a procedure, however. In this case, it has no arguments, which causes control to pass back to the calling environment immediately. The current values of the formal parameters declared as OUT or IN OUT are passed back to the actual parameters, and execution continues from the statement following the procedure call.

Function Style
Functions share many of the same features as procedures:

■ Functions can return more than one value via OUT parameters.

■ Function code has declarative, executable, and exception-handling sections.

■ Functions can accept default values.

■ Functions can be called using positional or named notation.

So when is a function appropriate, and when is a procedure appropriate? It generally depends on how many values the subprogram is expected to return and how those values will be used. The general rule of thumb is that if there is more than one return value, use a procedure. If there is only one return value, a function can be used. Although it is legal for a function to have OUT parameters (and thus return more than one value) it is poor style, and I don't recommend it.

Exceptions Raised Inside Procedures and Functions

If an error occurs inside a procedure, an exception is raised. This exception may be user-defined or predefined. If the procedure has no exception handler for this error, control immediately passes out of the procedure to the calling environment, in accordance with the exception propagation rules. (Exceptions and propagation rules are discussed in detail in Chapter 6.) However, in this case, the values of OUT and IN OUT formal parameters are *not* returned to the actual parameters. The actual parameters will have the same values as they would had the procedure not been called. For example, suppose we create the following procedure:

```
CREATE OR REPLACE PROCEDURE RaiseError (
  /* Illustrates the behavior of unhandled exceptions and
     OUT variables. If p_Raise is TRUE, then an unhandled
     error is raised. If p_Raise is FALSE, the procedure
     completes successfully. */
  p_Raise IN BOOLEAN := TRUE,
  p_ParameterA OUT NUMBER) AS
BEGIN
  p_ParameterA := 7;

  IF p_Raise THEN
    /* Even though we have assigned 7 to p_ParameterA, this
       unhandled exception causes control to return immediately
       without returning 7 to the actual parameter associated
       with p_ParameterA. */
    RAISE DUP_VAL_ON_INDEX;
  ELSE
    /* Simply return with no error. This will return 7 to the
       actual parameter. */
    RETURN;
  END IF;
END RaiseError;
```

If we call **RaiseError** with the following block,

```
DECLARE
  v_TempVar NUMBER := 1;
BEGIN
  INSERT INTO temp_table (num_col, char_col)
    VALUES (v_TempVar, 'Initial value');
  RaiseError(FALSE, v_TempVar);

  INSERT INTO temp_table (num_col, char_col)
    VALUES (v_TempVar, 'Value after successful call');

  v_TempVar := 2;
  INSERT INTO temp_table (num_col, char_col)
    VALUES (v_TempVar, 'Value before 2nd call');
  RaiseError(TRUE, v_TempVar);
EXCEPTION
  WHEN OTHERS THEN
    INSERT INTO temp_table (num_col, char_col)
      VALUES (v_TempVar, 'Value after unsuccessful call');
END;
```

and select from **temp_table**, we get the following results:

```
SQL> SELECT * FROM temp_table;

  NUM_COL CHAR_COL
--------- -------------------------------
        1 Initial value
        7 Value after successful call
        2 Value before 2nd call
        2 Value after unsuccessful call
```

Before the first call to **RaiseError**, **v_TempVar** contained 1. The first call was successful, and **v_TempVar** was assigned the value 7. The block then changed **v_TempVar** to 2 before the second call to **RaiseError**. This second call did not complete successfully, and **v_TempVar** was unchanged at 2 (rather than being changed to 7 again).

Dropping Procedures and Functions

Similar to dropping a table, procedures and functions can also be dropped. This removes the procedure or function from the data dictionary. The syntax for dropping a procedure is

DROP PROCEDURE *procedure_name*;

and the syntax for dropping a function is

DROP FUNCTION *function_name*;

where *procedure_name* is the name of an existing procedure, and *function_name* is the name of an existing function. For example, the following statement drops the **AddNewStudent** procedure:

```
DROP PROCEDURE AddNewStudent;
```

If the object to be dropped is a function, you must use DROP FUNCTION, and if the object is a procedure, you must use DROP PROCEDURE. DROP is a DDL command, so an implicit COMMIT is done both before and after the statement.

Subprogram Locations

Subprograms can be stored in the data dictionary, as all of the examples in this chapter have shown. The subprogram is created first via the CREATE OR REPLACE command, and then it is called from another PL/SQL block. A subprogram can also be defined within the declarative section of a block, in which case, it is known as a *local subprogram*.

Stored Subprograms and the Data Dictionary

When a subprogram is created via the CREATE OR REPLACE command, it is stored in the database. The subprogram is stored in compiled form, which is known as *p-code*. The p-code has all of the references in the subprogram evaluated, and the source code is translated into a form that is easily readable by the PL/SQL engine. When the subprogram is called, the p-code is read from disk, if necessary, and executed. P-code is analogous to the object code generated by other 3GL (third-generation language) compilers. Since the p-code has the object references in the subprogram evaluated (this is a property of early binding, as defined in Chapter 3), executing the p-code is a comparatively inexpensive operation.

Information about the subprogram is accessible through various data dictionary views. The **user_objects** view contains information about all objects, including stored subprograms. This information includes when the object was created and last modified, the type of the object (table, sequence, function, and so on), and the validity of the object. The **user_source** view contains the original source code for the object. The **user_errors** view contains information about compile errors.

Consider the following simple procedure:

```
CREATE OR REPLACE PROCEDURE Simple AS
  v_Counter NUMBER;
BEGIN
  v_Counter := 7;
END Simple;
```

After this procedure is created, **user_objects** shows it as valid, and **user_source** contains the source code for it. **User_errors** has no rows, since the procedure was compiled successfully. This is illustrated in Figure 5-1.

If, however, we change the code of **Simple** so that it has a compile error (note the missing semicolon), such as

```
CREATE OR REPLACE PROCEDURE Simple AS
  v_Counter NUMBER;
BEGIN
  v_Counter := 7
END Simple;
```

and examine the same three data dictionary views (as shown in Figure 5-2), we see several differences. **User_source** still shows the source code for the procedure.

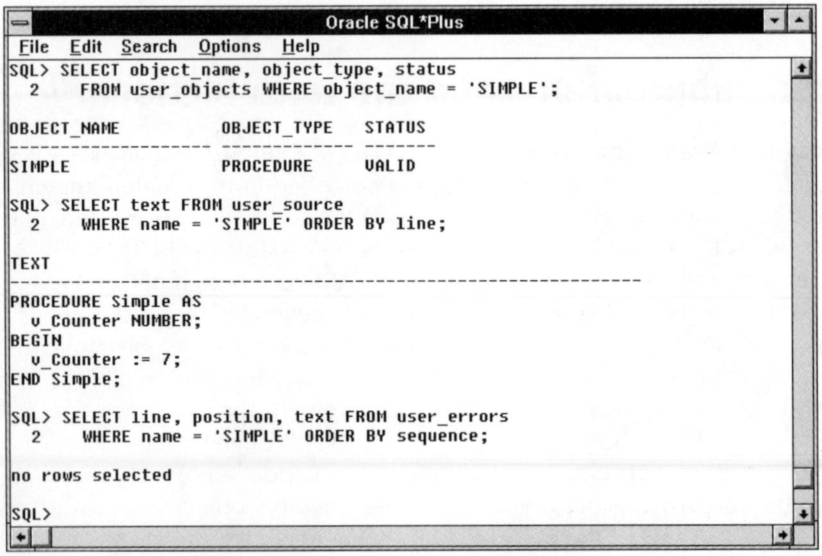

FIGURE 5-1. *Data dictionary views after successful compilation*

```
┌─────────────────────────────────────────────────────────────┐
│ ─                    Oracle SQL*Plus                    ▼ ▲   │
├─────────────────────────────────────────────────────────────┤
│ File   Edit   Search   Options   Help                         │
├─────────────────────────────────────────────────────────────┤
│SQL>                                                        ▲  │
│SQL> SELECT object_name, object_type, status                  │
│  2     FROM user_objects WHERE object_name = 'SIMPLE';        │
│                                                               │
│OBJECT_NAME            OBJECT_TYPE    STATUS                    │
│-------------------    -------------  -------                   │
│SIMPLE                 PROCEDURE      INVALID                   │
│                                                               │
│SQL> SELECT text FROM user_source                              │
│  2     WHERE name = 'SIMPLE' ORDER BY line;                   │
│                                                               │
│TEXT                                                           │
│---------------------------------------------------------------│
│PROCEDURE Simple AS                                            │
│  v_Counter NUMBER;                                            │
│BEGIN                                                          │
│  v_Counter := 7                                               │
│END Simple;                                                    │
│                                                               │
│SQL> SELECT line, position, text FROM user_errors              │
│  2     WHERE name = 'SIMPLE' ORDER BY sequence;               │
│                                                               │
│LINE POSITION TEXT                                             │
│---- -------- ------------------------------------------------ │
│   5        1 PLS-00103: Encountered the symbol "END" when expecting one of │
│              the following:                                   │
│              * & = - + ; < / > in mod not rem an exponent (**)│
│              <> or != or ~= >= <= <> and or like between is null etc. ▼ │
│ ←│ ├────────────────────────────────────────────────────────→│ │
└─────────────────────────────────────────────────────────────┘
```

FIGURE 5-2.   *Data dictionary views after unsuccessful compilation*

However, in **user_objects** the status is listed as 'INVALID' rather than 'VALID'. And **user_errors** contains the compilation error PLS-103.

> **TIP**
> In SQL*Plus, the SHOW ERRORS command will query **user_errors** for you and format the output for readability. You can use SHOW ERRORS after receiving the message "Warning: Procedure created with compilation errors." For more information, see Chapter 7.

A stored subprogram that is invalid is still stored in the database. However, it cannot be called successfully until the error is fixed. If an invalid procedure is called, the following error is returned:

```
PLS-905: object is invalid
```

The data dictionary is discussed in more detail in Appendix D.

Local Subprograms

A local subprogram, declared in the declarative section of a PL/SQL block, is illustrated in the following example:

```
DECLARE
  CURSOR c_AllStudents IS
    SELECT first_name, last_name
      FROM students;

  v_FormattedName VARCHAR2(50);

  /* Function which will return the first and last name
     concatenated together, separated by a space. */
  FUNCTION FormatName(p_FirstName IN VARCHAR2,
                      p_LastName IN VARCHAR2)
    RETURN VARCHAR2 IS
  BEGIN
    RETURN p_FirstName || ' ' || p_LastName;
  END FormatName;

-- Begin main block.
BEGIN
  FOR v_StudentRecord IN c_AllStudents LOOP
    v_FormattedName :=
      FormatName(v_StudentRecord.first_name,
                 v_StudentRecord.last_name);
    INSERT INTO temp_table (char_col)
      VALUES (v_FormattedName);
  END LOOP;

  COMMIT;
END;
```

The **FormatName** function is declared in the declarative section of the anonymous block. The function name is a PL/SQL identifier and thus follows the same scoping and visibility rules as any other PL/SQL identifier. Specifically, it is only visible in the block in which it is declared. Its scope extends from the point of declaration until the end of the block. No other block can call **FormatName**, since it would not be visible from another block. The scope and visibility rules are discussed in Chapter 2.

Any local subprogram must be declared at the end of the declarative section. If we were to move **FormatName** above the declaration for **c_AllStudents**, as the following illegal example illustrates, we would get a compile error.

```
DECLARE
  /* Declare FormatName first. This will generate a compile
     error, since all other declarations have to be before
```

```
      any local subprograms. */
  FUNCTION FormatName(p_FirstName IN VARCHAR2,
                      p_LastName IN VARCHAR2)
    RETURN VARCHAR2 IS
  BEGIN
    RETURN p_FirstName || ' ' || p_LastName;
  END FormatName;

  CURSOR c_AllStudents IS
    SELECT first_name, last_name
      FROM students;

  v_FormattedName VARCHAR2(50);
-- Begin main block
BEGIN
  NULL;
END;
```

Forward Declarations

Since the names of local PL/SQL subprograms are identifiers, they must be declared before they are referenced. This is normally not a problem. However, in the case of mutually referential subprograms, this does present a difficulty. Consider the following example:

```
DECLARE
  v_TempVal BINARY_INTEGER := 5;

  -- Local procedure A. Note that the code of A calls procedure B.
  PROCEDURE A(p_Counter IN OUT BINARY_INTEGER) IS
  BEGIN
    IF p_Counter > 0 THEN
      B(p_Counter);
      p_Counter := p_Counter - 1;
    END IF;
  END A;

  -- Local procedure B. Note that the code of B calls procedure A.
  PROCEDURE B(p_Counter IN OUT BINARY_INTEGER) IS
  BEGIN
    p_Counter := p_Counter - 1;
    A(p_Counter);
  END B;
```

```
BEGIN
  B(v_TempVal);
END;
```

This example is impossible to compile. Since procedure **A** calls procedure **B**, **B** must be declared prior to **A** so that the reference to **B** can be resolved. Since procedure **B** calls procedure **A**, **A** must be declared prior to **B** so that the reference to **A** can be resolved. Both of these can't be true at the same time. In order to rectify this, we can use a *forward declaration*. This is simply a procedure name and its formal parameters, which allow mutually referential procedures to exist. The following example illustrates this technique:

```
DECLARE
  v_TempVal BINARY_INTEGER := 5;

  -- Forward declaration of procedure B.
  PROCEDURE B(p_Counter IN OUT BINARY_INTEGER);

  PROCEDURE A(p_Counter IN OUT BINARY_INTEGER) IS
  BEGIN
    IF p_Counter > 0 THEN
      B(p_Counter);
      p_Counter := p_Counter - 1;
    END IF;
  END A;

  PROCEDURE B(p_Counter IN OUT BINARY_INTEGER) IS
  BEGIN
    p_Counter := p_Counter - 1;
    A(p_Counter);
  END B;
BEGIN
  B(v_TempVal);
END;
```

Stored vs. Local Subprograms

Stored subprograms and local subprograms behave differently, and they have different properties. When should they each be used? I generally prefer to use stored subprograms. If you develop a useful subprogram, chances are that you will want to call it from more than one block. In order to do this, the subprogram must be stored in the database. The size and complexity benefits are also usually a factor. The only procedures and functions that I would declare local to a block would tend to be short ones, which are only called from one specific section of the

program (their containing block). Table 5-3 summarizes the differences between
stored and local subprograms.

Subprogram Dependencies

When a procedure or function is compiled, all of the Oracle objects that it
references are recorded in the data dictionary. The procedure is *dependent* on
these objects. We have seen that a subprogram that has compile errors is marked as
invalid in the data dictionary. A stored subprogram can also become invalid if a
DDL operation is performed on one of its dependent objects. The best way to
illustrate this is by example. The **AlmostFull** function (defined earlier in this
chapter) queries the **classes** table. The dependencies of **AlmostFull** are illustrated in
Figure 5-3. **AlmostFull** depends on only one object—**classes**. This is indicated by
the arrow in the figure.

Stored Subprograms	Local Subprograms
Stored in compiled p-code in the database; when the procedure is called, it does not have to be compiled.	The local subprogram is compiled as part of its containing block. If the block is run multiple times, the subprogram has to be compiled each time.
Can be called from any block submitted by a user who has EXECUTE privileges on the subprogram.	Can be called only from the block containing the subprogram.
By keeping the subprogram code separate from the calling block, the calling block is shorter and easier to understand. The subprogram and calling block can also be maintained separately, if desired.	The subprogram and the calling block are one and the same, which can lead to confusion. If a change to the calling block is made, the subprogram has to be recompiled.
The compiled p-code can be pinned in the shared pool using the DBMS_SHARED_POOL.KEEP packaged procedure.[1] This can improve performance.	Local subprograms cannot be pinned in the shared pool by themselves.

TABLE 5-3. *Stored vs. Local Subprograms*

[1] The shared pool and the DBMS_SHARED_POOL package are discussed in Chapter 12.

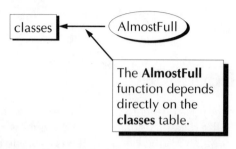

FIGURE 5-3. *AlmostFull dependencies*

Now suppose we create a procedure that calls **AlmostFull** and inserts the results into **temp_table**. This procedure is **RecordFullClasses**:

```
CREATE OR REPLACE PROCEDURE RecordFullClasses AS
  CURSOR c_Classes IS
    SELECT department, course
      FROM classes;
BEGIN
  FOR v_ClassRecord IN c_Classes LOOP
    -- Record all classes which don't have very much room left
    -- in temp_table.
    IF AlmostFull(v_ClassRecord.department, v_ClassRecord.course) THEN
      INSERT INTO temp_table (char_col) VALUES
        (v_ClassRecord.department || ' ' || v_ClassRecord.course ||
         ' is almost full!');
    END IF;
  END LOOP;
END RecordFullClasses;
```

The dependency information is illustrated by the arrows in Figure 5-4. **RecordFullClasses** depends both on **AlmostFull** and on **temp_table**. These are *direct* dependencies, since **RecordFullClasses** refers directly to both **AlmostFull** and **temp_table**. **AlmostFull** depends on **classes**, so **RecordFullClasses** has an *indirect* dependency on **classes**.

If a DDL operation is performed on **classes**, all objects that depend on **classes** (directly or indirectly) are invalidated. Suppose we alter the **classes** table in our example by adding an extra column:

```
ALTER TABLE classes ADD (
  student_rating  NUMBER(2)); -- Difficulty rating from 1 to 10
```

This will cause both **AlmostFull** and **RecordFullClasses** to become invalid, since they depend on **classes**. This is illustrated by the SQL*Plus session in Figure 5-5.

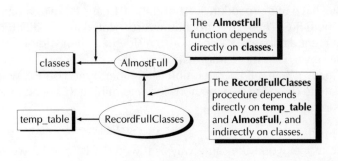

FIGURE 5-4. *RecordFullClasses dependencies*

How Dependencies Are Determined

To determine when objects should be evaluated, PL/SQL compares the timestamps of their last modifications. The LAST_DDL_TIME field of USER_OBJECTS contains this timestamp. This method works fine when comparing two objects on the same database, but it raises some issues when the objects reside in different PL/SQL engines.

```
                        Oracle SQL*Plus
 File  Edit  Search  Options  Help
SQL> SELECT object_name, object_type, status
  2    FROM user_objects
  3    WHERE object_name IN ('ALMOSTFULL', 'RECORDFULLCLASSES');

OBJECT_NAME          OBJECT_TYPE    STATUS
-------------------- -------------- -------
RECORDFULLCLASSES    PROCEDURE      VALID
ALMOSTFULL           FUNCTION       VALID

SQL> ALTER TABLE classes ADD (
  2    student_rating  NUMBER(2)   -- Difficulty rating from 1 to 10
  3    );

Table altered.

SQL> SELECT object_name, object_type, status
  2    FROM user_objects
  3    WHERE object_name IN ('ALMOSTFULL', 'RECORDFULLCLASSES');

OBJECT_NAME          OBJECT_TYPE    STATUS
-------------------- -------------- -------
RECORDFULLCLASSES    PROCEDURE      INVALID
ALMOSTFULL           FUNCTION       INVALID

SQL>
```

FIGURE 5-5. *Invalidation as a result of a DDL operation*

Suppose we have two procedures, **P1** and **P2**. **P1** calls **P2** over a database link, as shown in Figure 5-6. These two procedures are located in two different PL/SQL engines, in different databases. **P1** could also reside in a client-side PL/SQL engine, with **P2** on the server. (For more information on client-side versus server-side PL/SQL, see Chapter 7.) If a DDL operation is then performed on **P2**, when should **P1** get invalidated? There are two methods for determining this—the timestamp and signature methods.

Timestamp Model

The timestamp model works the same way as it would if **P1** and **P2** were in the same PL/SQL engine. When **P2** is altered, **P1** is invalidated the next time it is called. This can cause unnecessary compilations, however. If only the body of **P2** is altered, and not its specification, then **P1** doesn't really have to be recompiled, since the call

```
P2(...)@DBLINK
```

in **P1** wouldn't have to change. However, with the timestamp model, **P1** would be recompiled.

Slightly more serious is when **P1** is contained in a client-side PL/SQL engine, such as Oracle Forms. In this case, it may not be possible to recompile **P1**, since the source for it may not be included with the run-time version of Forms.

Signature Model

PL/SQL 2.3 ...and HIGHER PL/SQL 2.3 provides a different method for determining when remote dependent objects need to be recompiled, called the signature model. When a procedure is created, a *signature* is stored as well. The signature encodes the procedure specification, including the types and order of the parameters. With this model, the signature of **P2** will change only when the specification changes.

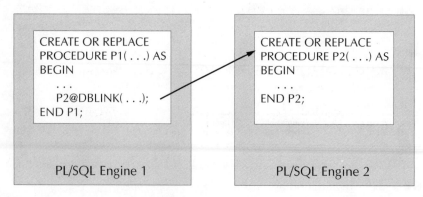

FIGURE 5-6. *A remote procedure call*

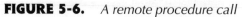

When **P1** is compiled, the signature of **P2** is included (rather than the timestamp). Thus **P1** only needs to be recompiled when the signature of **P2** changes.

In order to use the signature model, the parameter REMOTE_DEPENDENCIES_MODE must be set to SIGNATURE. This is a parameter in the database initialization file, which is usually called INIT.ORA. It can also be set interactively. There are three ways of setting this mode:

1. Add the line REMOTE_DEPENDENCIES_MODE=SIGNATURE to the INIT.ORA file. The next time the database is started, the mode will be set to SIGNATURE for all sessions.

2. Issue the command

   ```
   ALTER SYSTEM SET REMOTE_DEPENDENCIES_MODE = SIGNATURE;
   ```

   This will affect the entire database (all sessions) from the time the statement is issued. You must have the ALTER SYSTEM system privilege to issue this command.

3. Issue the command

   ```
   ALTER SESSION SET REMOTE_DEPENDENCIES_MODE = SIGNATURE;
   ```

   This will only affect your session. Objects created after this point in the current session will use the signature method.

In all of these options, TIMESTAMP can be used instead of SIGNATURE to get the 2.2 and earlier behavior. TIMESTAMP is the default, so if you don't change REMOTE_DEPENDENCIES_MODE, the system will behave as it does in version 2.2.

There are several things to be aware of when using the signature method:

■ Signatures don't get modified if the default values of formal parameters are changed. Suppose **P2** has a default value for one of its parameters, and **P1** is using this default value. If the default value in the specification for **P2** is changed, **P1** will not be recompiled by default. The old value for the default parameter will still be used until **P1** is manually recompiled. This applies for IN parameters only.

■ If **P1** is calling a packaged procedure **P2**, and a new overloaded version of **P2** is added to the remote package, the signature is not changed. **P1** will still use the old version (not the new overloaded one) until **P1** is recompiled manually. (Packages and overloading are dicsussed later in this chapter.)

■ To manually recompile a procedure, use the command

```
ALTER PROCEDURE procedure_name COMPILE;
```

where *procedure_name* is the name of the procedure to be compiled. For functions, use

```
ALTER FUNCTION function_name COMPILE;
```

For more information on the signature model, see the *Oracle7 Server Application Developer's Guide*, release 7.3 or later.

Packages

Another Ada feature included with PL/SQL is the *package*. Packages are PL/SQL constructs that allow related objects to be stored together. A package has two separate parts—the specification and the body. Each of them is stored separately in the data dictionary. Unlike procedures and functions, which can be contained locally in a block or stored in the database, a package can only be stored; it cannot be local. Besides allowing related objects to be grouped together, packages are useful because they are less restrictive with respect to dependencies. They also have a number of performance advantages, which are discussed in Chapter 12.

A package is essentially a named declarative section. Anything that can go in the declarative part of a block can go in a package. This includes procedures, functions, cursors, types, and variables. One advantage of putting these objects into a package is the ability to reference them from other PL/SQL blocks, so packages also provide global variables to PL/SQL.

Package Specification

The *package specification* (also known as the *package header*) contains information about the contents of the package. However, it does not contain the code for any procedures. Consider the following example:

```
CREATE OR REPLACE PACKAGE ClassPackage AS
  -- Add a new student into the specified class.
  PROCEDURE AddStudent(p_StudentID  IN students.id%TYPE,
                       p_Department IN classes.department%TYPE,
                       p_Course     IN classes.course%TYPE);

  -- Removes the specified student from the specified class.
  PROCEDURE RemoveStudent(p_StudentID  IN students.id%TYPE,
                          p_Department IN classes.department%TYPE,
```

```
                         p_Course      IN classes.course%TYPE);

  -- Exception raised by RemoveStudent.
  e_StudentNotRegistered EXCEPTION;

  -- Table type used to hold student info.
  TYPE t_StudentIDTable IS TABLE OF students.id%TYPE
    INDEX BY BINARY_INTEGER;

  -- Returns a PL/SQL table containing the students currently
  -- in the specified class.
  PROCEDURE ClassList(p_Department  IN  classes.department%TYPE,
                      p_Course      IN  classes.course%TYPE,
                      p_IDs         OUT t_StudentIDTable,
                      p_NumStudents IN OUT BINARY_INTEGER);
END ClassPackage;
```

ClassPackage contains three procedures, a type, and an exception. (Exceptions are used for PL/SQL error handling and are discussed in more detail in Chapter 6.) The general syntax for creating a package header is

```
CREATE [OR REPLACE] PACKAGE package_name {IS | AS}
    procedure_specification |
    function_specification |
    variable_declaration |
    type_definition |
    exception_declaration |
    cursor_declaration
END [package_name];
```

where *package_name* is the name of the package. The *elements* within the package (procedure and function specifications, variables, and so on) are the same as they would be in the declarative section of an anonymous block. The same syntax rules apply for a package header as for a declarative section, except for procedure and function declarations. These rules are as follows:

■   Package elements can appear in any order. However, as in a declarative section, an object must be declared before it is referenced. If a cursor contains a variable as part of the WHERE clause, for example, the variable must be declared before the cursor declaration.

■ All elements do not have to be present. A package can contain only procedure and function specifications, for example, without declaring any exceptions or types.

■ Any declarations for procedures and functions must be forward declarations. This is different from the declarative section of a block, where both forward declarations and the actual code for procedures or functions may be found. The code for packaged procedures and functions is found in the package body.

Package Body

The *package body* is a separate data dictionary object from the package header. It cannot be successfully compiled without the header, however. The body contains the code for the forward subprogram declarations in the package header. The following example shows the package body for **ClassPackage**:

```
CREATE OR REPLACE PACKAGE BODY ClassPackage AS
  -- Add a new student for the specified class.
  PROCEDURE AddStudent(p_StudentID  IN students.id%TYPE,
                       p_Department IN classes.department%TYPE,
                       p_Course     IN classes.course%TYPE) IS
  BEGIN
    INSERT INTO registered_students (student_id, department, course)
      VALUES (p_StudentID, p_Department, p_Course);
    COMMIT;
  END AddStudent;


  -- Removes the specified student from the specified class.
  PROCEDURE RemoveStudent(p_StudentID  IN students.id%TYPE,
                          p_Department IN classes.department%TYPE,
                          p_Course     IN classes.course%TYPE) IS
  BEGIN
    DELETE FROM registered_students
      WHERE student_id = p_StudentID
      AND department = p_Department
      AND course = p_Course;

    -- Check to see if the DELETE operation was successful. If
```

```
    -- it didn't match any rows, raise an error.
    IF SQL%NOTFOUND THEN
      RAISE e_StudentNotRegistered;
    END IF;

    COMMIT;
  END RemoveStudent;


  -- Returns a PL/SQL table containing the students currently
  -- in the specified class.
  PROCEDURE ClassList(p_Department  IN  classes.department%TYPE,
                      p_Course      IN  classes.course%TYPE,
                      p_IDs         OUT t_StudentIDTable,
                      p_NumStudents IN OUT BINARY_INTEGER) IS

    v_StudentID  registered_students.student_id%TYPE;

    -- Local cursor to fetch the registered students.
    CURSOR c_RegisteredStudents IS
      SELECT student_id
        FROM registered_students
        WHERE department = p_Department
        AND course = p_Course;
  BEGIN
    /* p_NumStudents will be the table index. It will start at
       0, and be incremented each time through the fetch loop.
       At the end of the loop, it will have the number of rows
       fetched, and therefore the number of rows returned in
       p_IDs. */
    p_NumStudents := 0;

    OPEN c_RegisteredStudents;
    LOOP
      FETCH c_RegisteredStudents INTO v_StudentID;
      EXIT WHEN c_RegisteredStudents%NOTFOUND;

      p_NumStudents := p_NumStudents + 1;
      p_IDs(p_NumStudents) := v_StudentID;
    END LOOP;
  END ClassList;
END ClassPackage;
```

The package body contains the code for the forward declarations in the package header. Objects in the header that are not forward declarations (such as the **e_StudentNotRegistered** exception) can be referenced in the package body without being redeclared.

The package body is optional. If the package header does not contain any procedures or functions (only variable declarations, cursors, types, and so on), then the body does not have to be present. This technique is valuable for declaring global variables, since all objects in a package are visible outside the package. (Scope and visibility are discussed in the next section.)

Any forward declaration in the package header must be fleshed out in the package body. The specification for the procedure or function must be the same in both. This includes the name of the subprogram, the names of its parameters, and the mode of the parameters. For example, the following package header does not match the package body, since the body uses a different parameter list for **FunctionA**:

```
CREATE OR REPLACE PACKAGE PackageA AS
   FUNCTION FunctionA(p_Parameter1 IN NUMBER,
                      p_Parameter2 IN DATE)
     RETURN VARCHAR2;
END PackageA;

CREATE OR REPLACE PACKAGE BODY PackageA AS
   FUNCTION FunctionA(p_Parameter1 IN CHAR)
     RETURN VARCHAR2;
END PackageA;
```

If we try to create **PackageA**, we get the following errors:

```
PLS-00328: A subprogram body must be defined for the forward
declaration of FUNCTIONA.

PLS-00323: subprogram or cursor 'FUNCTIONA' is declared in a
package specification and must be defined in the package body.
```

Packages and Scope

Any object declared in a package header is in scope and is visible outside the package, by qualifying the object with the package name. For example, we can call **ClassPackage.RemoveStudent** from the following PL/SQL block:

```
BEGIN
  ClassPackage.RemoveStudent(10006, 'HIS', 101);
END;
```

The procedure call is the same as it would be for a stand-alone procedure. The only difference is that it is prefixed by the package name. Packaged procedures can have default parameters, and they can be called using either positional or named notation, just like stand-alone stored procedures.

This also applies to user-defined types defined in the package. In order to call **ClassList**, for example, we need to declare a variable of **ClassPackage.t_StudentIDTable**:

```
DECLARE
  v_HistoryStudents  ClassPackage.t_StudentIDTable;
  v_NumStudents      BINARY_INTEGER := 20;
BEGIN
  -- Fill the PL/SQL table with the first 20 History 101
  -- students.
  ClassPackage.ClassList('HIS', 101, v_HistoryStudents,
                         v_NumStudents);

  -- Insert these students into temp_table.
  FOR v_LoopCounter IN 1..v_NumStudents LOOP
    INSERT INTO temp_table (num_col, char_col)
      VALUES (v_HistoryStudents(v_LoopCounter),
              'In History 101');
  END LOOP;
END;
```

Inside the package body, objects in the header can be referenced without the package name. For example, the **RemoveStudent** procedure can simply reference the exception with **e_StudentNotRegistered**, not **ClassPackage.e_StudentNotRegistered**.

Overloading Subprograms

Inside a package, procedures and functions can be *overloaded*. This means that there is more than one procedure or function with the same name, but with different parameters. This is a very useful feature, since it allows the same operation to be applied to objects of different types. For example, suppose we want to add a student to a class either by specifying the student ID or by specifying the first and last names. We could do this by modifying **ClassPackage** as follows:

```
CREATE OR REPLACE PACKAGE ClassPackage AS
  -- Add a new student into the specified class.
  PROCEDURE AddStudent(p_StudentID  IN students.id%TYPE,
                       p_Department IN classes.department%TYPE,
                       p_Course     IN classes.course%TYPE);

  -- Also adds a new student, by specifying the first and last
  -- names, rather than ID number.
  PROCEDURE AddStudent(p_FirstName IN students.first_name%TYPE,
                       p_LastName  IN students.last_name%TYPE,
                       p_Department IN classes.department%TYPE,
                       p_Course     IN classes.course%TYPE);
  ...
END ClassPackage;

CREATE OR REPLACE PACKAGE BODY ClassPackage AS
  -- Add a new student for the specified class.
  PROCEDURE AddStudent(p_StudentID  IN students.id%TYPE,
                       p_Department IN classes.department%TYPE,
                       p_Course     IN classes.course%TYPE) IS
  BEGIN
    INSERT INTO registered_students (student_id, department, course)
      VALUES (p_StudentID, p_Department, p_Course);
    COMMIT;
  END AddStudent;

  -- Add a new student by name, rather than ID.
  PROCEDURE AddStudent(p_FirstName IN students.first_name%TYPE,
                       p_LastName  IN students.last_name%TYPE,
                       p_Department IN classes.department%TYPE,
                       p_Course     IN classes.course%TYPE) IS
    v_StudentID students.ID%TYPE;
  BEGIN
    /* First we need to get the ID from the students table. */
    SELECT ID
      INTO v_StudentID
      FROM students
      WHERE first_name = p_FirstName
      AND last_name = p_LastName;

    -- Now we can add the student by ID.
    INSERT INTO registered_students (student_id, department, course)
```

```
      VALUES (v_StudentID, p_Department, p_Course);
    COMMIT;
  END AddStudent;
  ...
END ClassPackage;
```

We can now add a student to Music 410 with either

```
BEGIN
  ClassPackage.AddStudent(10000, 'MUS', 410);
END;
```

or

```
BEGIN
  ClassPackage.AddStudent('Barbara', 'Blues', 'MUS', 410);
END;
```

Package Initialization

The first time a package is called, it is *instantiated*. This means that the package is read from disk into memory, and the p-code is run. At this point, memory is allocated for any variables defined in the package. Each session will have its own copy of packaged variables. Thus there is no worry about two simultaneous sessions accessing the same memory locations.

In many cases, initialization code needs to be run the first time the package is instantiated. This can be done by adding an initialization section to the package body, after any other objects, with the syntax

```
CREATE OR REPLACE PACKAGE BODY package_name {IS | AS}
   ...
BEGIN
   initialization_code;
END [package_name];
```

where *package_name* is the name of the package, and *initialization_code* is the code to be run. For example, the following package implements a random number function:

```
CREATE OR REPLACE PACKAGE Random AS
/* Random number generator. Uses the same algorithm as the
```

```
 rand() function in C. */

-- Used to change the seed. From a given seed, the same
-- sequence of random numbers will be generated.
PROCEDURE ChangeSeed(p_NewSeed IN NUMBER);

-- Returns a random integer between 1 and 32767.
FUNCTION Rand RETURN NUMBER;
PRAGMA RESTRICT_REFERENCES(rand, WNDS );

-- Same as Rand, but with a procedural interface.
PROCEDURE GetRand(p_RandomNumber OUT NUMBER);

-- Returns a random integer between 1 and p_MaxVal.
FUNCTION RandMax(p_MaxVal IN NUMBER) RETURN NUMBER;
PRAGMA RESTRICT_REFERENCES(RandMax, WNDS);

-- Same as RandMax, but with a procedural interface.
PROCEDURE GetRandMax(p_RandomNumber OUT NUMBER,
                     p_MaxVal IN NUMBER);
END Random;

CREATE OR REPLACE PACKAGE BODY Random AS

  /* Used for calculating the next number. */
  v_Multiplier  CONSTANT NUMBER := 22695477;
  v_Increment   CONSTANT NUMBER := 1;

  /* Seed used to generate random sequence. */
  v_Seed        number := 1;

  PROCEDURE ChangeSeed(p_NewSeed IN NUMBER) IS
  BEGIN
    v_Seed := p_NewSeed;
  END ChangeSeed;

  FUNCTION Rand RETURN NUMBER IS
  BEGIN
    v_Seed := MOD(v_Multiplier * v_Seed + v_Increment,
                  (2 ** 32));
    RETURN BITAND(v_Seed/(2 ** 16), 32767);
  END Rand;
```

```
PROCEDURE GetRand(p_RandomNumber OUT NUMBER) IS
BEGIN
  -- Simply call Rand and return the value.
  p_RandomNumber := Rand;
END GetRand;

FUNCTION RandMax(p_MaxVal IN NUMBER) RETURN NUMBER IS
BEGIN
  RETURN MOD(Rand, p_MaxVal) + 1;
END RandMax;

PROCEDURE GetRandMax(p_RandomNumber OUT NUMBER,
                     p_MaxVal IN NUMBER) IS
BEGIN
  -- Simply call RandMax and return the value.
  p_RandomNumber := RandMax(p_MaxVal);
END GetRandMax;

BEGIN
  /* Package initialization. Initialize the seed to the current
     time in seconds. */
  ChangeSeed(TO_NUMBER(TO_CHAR(SYSDATE, 'SSSSS')));
END Random;
```

In order to retrieve a random number, you can simply call **Random.Rand**. The sequence of random numbers is controlled by the initial seed—the same sequence is generated for a given seed. Thus, in order to provide more random values, we need to initialize the seed to a different value each time the package is instantiated. This is accomplished with a call to the **ChangeSeed** procedure from the package initialization section. The Debug package, which we'll examine in Chapter 8, also contains an initialization section.

NOTE
The Random package also uses the RESTRICT_REFERENCES pragma, so that Random.Rand can be called from within SQL statements. This pragma is discussed later in this chapter, in the section "Using Stored Functions in SQL Statements."

Packages and Dependencies

The dependency picture for **ClassPackage** is shown in Figure 5-7. The package body depends on **registered_students** and the package header. The package header does *not* depend on anything. This is the advantage of packages: We can change the package body without having to change the header. Therefore, other objects that depend on the header won't have to be recompiled at all, since they never get invalidated. If the header is changed, this automatically invalidates the body, since the body depends on the header.

Triggers

Triggers are similar to procedures, in that they are named PL/SQL blocks with declarative, executable, and exception-handling sections. However, a procedure is executed explicitly from another block via a procedure call, which can also pass arguments. A trigger is executed implicitly whenever the triggering event happens, and a trigger doesn't accept arguments. The act of executing a trigger is known as *firing* the trigger. The triggering event is a DML (INSERT, UPDATE, or DELETE) operation on a database table.

Triggers can be used for many things, including

- Maintaining complex integrity constraints not possible through declarative constraints enabled at table creation

- Auditing information in a table by recording the changes made and who made them

- Automatically signaling other programs that action needs to take place when changes are made to a table

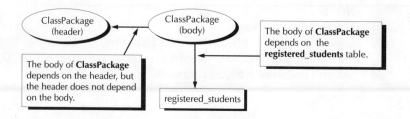

FIGURE 5-7. *ClassPackage dependencies*

As an example, suppose we want to track statistics about different majors, including the number of students registered and the total credits taken. We are going to store these results in the **major_stats** table:

```
CREATE TABLE major_stats (
  major            VARCHAR2(30),
  total_credits    NUMBER,
  total_students NUMBER);
```

In order to keep **major_stats** up-to-date, we can create a trigger on **students** that will update **major_stats** every time **students** is modified. The **UpdateMajorStats** trigger, shown next, does this. The trigger will execute after any DML operation on **students**. The body of the trigger queries **students** and updates **major_stats** with the current statistics.

```
CREATE OR REPLACE TRIGGER UpdateMajorStats
  /* Keeps the major_stats table up-to-date with changes made
     to the students table. */
  AFTER INSERT OR DELETE OR UPDATE ON students
DECLARE
  CURSOR c_Statistics IS
    SELECT major, COUNT(*) total_students,
           SUM(current_credits) total_credits
      FROM students
      GROUP BY major;
BEGIN
  /* Loop through each major. Attempt to update the statistics
     in major_stats corresponding to this major. If the row
     doesn't exist, create it. */
  FOR v_StatsRecord in c_Statistics LOOP
    UPDATE major_stats
      SET total_credits = v_StatsRecord.total_credits,
          total_students = v_StatsRecord.total_students
      WHERE major = v_StatsRecord.major;
    /* Check to see if the row exists. */
    IF SQL%NOTFOUND THEN
      INSERT INTO major_stats (major, total_credits, total_students)
        VALUES (v_StatsRecord.major, v_StatsRecord.total_credits,
                v_StatsRecord.total_students);
    END IF;
  END LOOP;
END UpdateMajorStats;
```

The general syntax for creating a trigger is

```
CREATE [OR REPLACE] TRIGGER trigger_name
    {BEFORE | AFTER} triggering_event ON table_reference
    [FOR EACH ROW [WHEN trigger_condition]]
    trigger_body;
```

where *trigger_name* is the name of the trigger, *triggering_event* specifies when the trigger fires (in the case of **UpdateMajorStats**, after any DML operation), *table_reference* is the table for which the trigger is defined, and *trigger_body* is the main code for the trigger. The *trigger_condition* in the WHEN clause, if present, is evaluated first. The body of the trigger is executed only when this condition evaluates to TRUE.

Trigger Components

The required components of a trigger are the trigger name, triggering event, and the body. The WHEN clause is optional.

Trigger Names

The namespace for trigger names is different from that of other subprograms. A *namespace* is the set of legal identifiers available for use as the names of an object. Procedures, packages, and tables all share the same namespace. This means that, within one database schema, all objects in the same namespace must have unique names. For example, it is illegal to give the same name to a procedure and a package.

Triggers, however, exist in a separate namespace. This means that a trigger can have the same name as a table or procedure. Within one schema, however, a given name can be used for only one trigger. Trigger names are database identifiers, and as such, they follow the same rules as other identifiers. (See Chapter 2.)

TIP

Although it is possible to use the same name for a trigger and a table, I don't recommend it. It is better to give each trigger a unique name that identifies its function as well as the table on which it is defined.

Types of Triggers

The triggering event determines the type of the trigger. Triggers can be defined for INSERT, UPDATE, or DELETE operations. They can be fired before or after the operation, and they can also fire on row or statement operations. Table 5-4 summarizes the various options.

Category	Values	Comments
Statement	INSERT, DELETE, UPDATE	Defines which kind of DML statement causes the trigger to fire.
Timing	BEFORE or AFTER	Defines whether the trigger fires before the statement is executed, or after the statement is executed.
Level	Row or statement	If the trigger is a row-level trigger, it fires once for each row affected by the triggering statement. If the trigger is a statement-level trigger, it fires once, either before or after the statement. A row-level trigger is identified by the FOR EACH ROW clause in the trigger definition.

TABLE 5-4. *Types of Triggers*

The values for the statement, timing, and level determine the type of the trigger. There are a total of 12 possible types: 3 statements × 2 timing × 2 levels. For example, all of the following are valid trigger types:

- Before update statement level

- After insert row level

- Before delete row level

 A table can have up to 12 triggers defined on it—one of each type. Starting with PL/SQL 2.1 (Oracle7 release 7.1), however, a table can have more than one trigger of each type. This capability allows you to define as many triggers as you want for one table. The order in which the triggers are fired is described in the "Order of Trigger Firing" section later in this chapter.

A trigger can also be fired for more than one type of triggering statement. For example, the **UpdateMajorStats** trigger is fired on INSERT, UPDATE, and DELETE statements. The triggering event specifies one or more of the DML operations that should fire the trigger.

Restrictions on Triggers

The body of a trigger is a PL/SQL block. Any statement that is legal in a PL/SQL block is legal in a trigger body, subject to the following restrictions:

- A trigger may not issue any transaction control statements—COMMIT, ROLLBACK, or SAVEPOINT. The trigger is fired as part of the execution of the triggering statement and is in the same transaction as the triggering statement. When the triggering statement is committed or rolled back, the work in the trigger is committed or rolled back as well.

■ Similar to the first restriction, any procedures or functions that are called by the trigger body cannot issue any transaction control statements.

■ The trigger body cannot declare any LONG or LONG RAW variables. Also, :new and :old (described later) cannot refer to a LONG or LONG RAW column in the table for which the trigger is defined.

■ There are restrictions on which tables a trigger body may access. Depending on the type of trigger and the constraints on the tables, tables may be mutating. This situation is discussed in detail in the section "Mutating Tables" later in this chapter.

Triggers and the Data Dictionary

Triggers interact with the data dictionary in much the same way as procedures or functions. Certain data dictionary views contain information about triggers and their status.

Data Dictionary Views

When a trigger is created, its source code is stored in the data dictionary view **user_triggers**. This view includes the trigger body, WHEN clause, triggering table, and the trigger type. For example, the following query returns information about **UpdateMajorStats**:

```
SQL> SELECT trigger_type, table_name, triggering_event
  2    FROM user_triggers
  3    WHERE trigger_name = 'UPDATEMAJORSTATS';

TRIGGER_TYPE     TABLE_NAME      TRIGGERING_EVENT
---------------- --------------- ---------------------------
AFTER STATEMENT  STUDENTS        INSERT OR UPDATE OR DELETE
```

For more information on data dictionary views, see Appendix D.

Dropping and Disabling Triggers

Similar to procedures and packages, triggers can be dropped. The command to do this has the syntax

DROP TRIGGER *triggername*;

where *triggername* is the name of the trigger to be dropped. This permanently removes the trigger from the data dictionary. Similar to subprograms, the OR REPLACE clause can be specified in the trigger CREATE statement. In this case, the trigger is dropped first, if it already exists.

Unlike procedures and packages, however, a trigger can be disabled without dropping it. When a trigger is disabled, it still exists in the data dictionary but is never fired. To disable a trigger, use the ALTER TRIGGER statement

ALTER TRIGGER *triggername* {DISABLE | ENABLE};

where *triggername* is the name of the trigger. By default, all triggers are enabled when they are created. ALTER TRIGGER can disable, and then reenable, any trigger. For example, the following sequence disables and then reenables **UpdateMajorStats**:

```
SQL> ALTER TRIGGER UpdateMajorStats DISABLE
Trigger altered.


SQL> ALTER TRIGGER UpdateMajorStats ENABLE;
Trigger altered.
```

All triggers for a particular table can be enabled or disabled using the ALTER TABLE command as well, by adding the ENABLE ALL TRIGGERS or the DISABLE ALL TRIGGERS clause. For example:

```
SQL> ALTER TABLE students
  2     ENABLE ALL TRIGGERS;
Table altered.


SQL> ALTER TABLE students
  2     DISABLE ALL TRIGGERS;
Table altered.
```

The **status** column of **user_triggers** contains either 'ENABLED' or 'DISABLED', indicating the current status of a trigger. Disabling a trigger does not remove it from the data dictionary, like dropping it would do.

Trigger P-Code
When a package or subprogram is stored in the data dictionary, the compiled p-code is stored in addition to the source code for the object. This is not the case for triggers, however. The only item stored in the data dictionary is the source code for the trigger, not the p-code. As a result, the trigger must be compiled each time it is read from the dictionary. This doesn't have any effect on the way triggers are

defined and used, but it can have an effect on trigger performance. For more information on performance and tuning, see Chapter 12.

PL/SQL 2.3 ...and HIGHER PL/SQL 2.3, with Oracle7 Release 7.3, stores triggers in compiled form, like procedures, functions, and packages. This allows triggers to be called without recompilation. However, since triggers are stored objects just like packages and subprograms, they do have dependency information stored as well. Thus they can be automatically invalidated in the same manner as packages and subprograms.

Order of Trigger Firing

Triggers are fired as the DML statement is executed. The algorithm for executing a DML statement is given here.

1. Execute the before statement-level trigger, if present.

2. For each row affected by the statement:

   a. Execute the before row-level trigger, if present.

   b. Execute the statement itself.

   c. Execute the after row-level trigger, if present.

3. Execute the after statement-level trigger, if present.

To illustrate this, suppose we have all four kinds of UPDATE triggers defined on the **classes** table—before and after, statement and row level. Suppose we then issue the following UPDATE statement:

```
UPDATE classes
  SET num_credits = 4
  WHERE department IN ('HIS', 'CS');
```

This statement affects four rows. The before and after statement-level triggers are each executed once, and the before and after row-level triggers are each executed four times. As each trigger is fired, it will see the changes made by the earlier triggers, as well as any database changes made by the statement so far.

The order in which triggers of the same type are fired is not defined. If the order is important, combine all of the operations into one trigger.

Using :old and :new in Row-Level Triggers

A row-level trigger fires once per row processed by the triggering statement. Inside the trigger, you can access the row that is currently being processed. This is accomplished through two *pseudorecords*—:old and :new. :old and :new are not true records. Although syntactically they are treated as records, in reality they are not (as you will soon see). Thus they are known as pseudorecords, with meanings as described in Table 5-5. Note that :old is undefined for INSERT statements, and :new is undefined for DELETE statements. Therefore, :old is not generally used for INSERT, and :new is not generally used for DELETE. The type of both is

   triggering_table%ROWTYPE;

where *triggering_table* is the table for which the trigger is defined.

The colon in front of :new and :old is required. This is the only place within PL/SQL where colons are used. The reason is that :new and :old are actually implemented as bind variables. Like other bind variables, the colon delimits them from regular PL/SQL variables. Bind variables are used in different PL/SQL execution environments (see Chapter 7 for more information). A reference such as

   :new.*field*

will be valid only if *field* is a field in the triggering table.

CAUTION
Operations that would normally be valid on records are not valid for :new and :old. For example, they cannot be assigned as entire records. Only the individual fields within them may be assigned. The following example illustrates this:

```
CREATE OR REPLACE TRIGGER TempDelete
BEFORE DELETE ON temp_table
FOR EACH ROW
DECLARE
  v_TempRec temp_table%ROWTYPE;
BEGIN
  /* This is not a legal assignment, since :old is not truly
     a record. */
  v_TempRec := :old;

  /* We can accomplish the same thing, however, by assigning
     the fields individually. */
  v_TempRec.char_col := :old.char_col;
```

```
      v_TempRec.num_col := :old.num_col;
   END TempDelete;
```

Likewise, :old and :new cannot be passed to procedures or functions that take arguments of *triggering_table*%ROWTYPE, since the actual parameter is assigned to the formal parameter in the same way as a standard assignment.

The **GenerateStudentID** trigger shown next uses :new. It is a before INSERT or UPDATE trigger, and its purpose is to fill in the **ID** field of **students** with a value generated from the **student_sequence** sequence.

```
CREATE OR REPLACE TRIGGER GenerateStudentID
  BEFORE INSERT OR UPDATE ON students
  FOR EACH ROW
BEGIN
  /* Fill in the ID field of students with the next value from
     student_sequence. Since ID is a column in students, :new.ID
     is a valid reference. */
  SELECT student_sequence.nextval
    INTO :new.ID
    FROM dual;
END GenerateStudentID;
```

GenerateStudentID actually modifies the value of **:new.ID**. This is one of the useful features of :new—when the statement is actually executed, whatever values

Triggering Statement	:old	:new
INSERT	Undefined—all fields are NULL.	Values that will be inserted when the statement is complete.
UPDATE	Original values for the row before the update.	New values that will be updated when the statement is complete.
DELETE	Original values before the row is deleted.	Undefined—all fields are NULL.

TABLE 5-5. *:old and :new*

are in :new will be used. With **GenerateStudentID**, we can issue an INSERT statement such as

```
INSERT INTO students (first_name, last_name)
  VALUES ('Lolita', 'Lazarus');
```

without generating an error. Even though we haven't specified a value for the primary key column **ID** (which is required), the trigger will supply it. In fact, if we do specify a value for **ID**, it will be ignored, since the trigger changes it. If we issue

```
INSERT INTO students (ID, first_name, last_name)
  VALUES (-7, 'Lolita', 'Lazarus');
```

we get the same behavior. In either case, **student_sequence.nextval** will be used for the **ID** column.

As a result of this, you cannot change :new in an after row-level trigger, since the statement has already been processed. In general, :new is modified only in a before row-level trigger, and :old is never modified, only read from.

The :new and :old records are only valid inside row-level triggers. If you try to reference either inside a statement-level trigger, you will get a compile error. Since a statement-level trigger executes once—even if there are many rows processed by the statement—:old and :new have no meaning. Which row would they refer to?

The WHEN Clause

The WHEN clause is valid for row-level triggers only. If present, the trigger body will be executed only for those rows that meet the condition specified by the WHEN clause. The WHEN clause looks like

WHEN *condition*

where *condition* is a boolean expression. It will be evaluated for each row. The :new and :old records can be referenced inside *condition* as well, but the colon is *not* used there. The colon is only valid in the trigger body. For example, the body of the **CheckCredits** trigger is only executed if the current credits being taken by a student are more than 20:

```
CREATE OR REPLACE TRIGGER CheckCredits
  BEFORE INSERT OR UPDATE OF current_credits ON students
  FOR EACH ROW
  WHEN (new.current_credits > 20)
BEGIN
  /* Trigger body goes here. */
END;
```

CheckCredits could also be written as follows:

```
CREATE OR REPLACE TRIGGER CheckCredits
  BEFORE INSERT OR UPDATE OF current_credits ON students
  FOR EACH ROW
BEGIN
  IF :new.current_credits > 20 THEN
    /* Trigger body goes here. */
  END IF;
END;
```

Using Trigger Predicates: INSERTING, UPDATING, and DELETING

The **UpdateMajorStats** trigger earlier in this chapter is an INSERT, UPDATE, and a DELETE trigger. Inside a trigger of this type (that will fire for different kinds of DML statements) there are three boolean functions that you can use to determine what the operation is. These predicates are INSERTING, UPDATING, and DELETING. Their behavior is described in the following table:

Predicate	Behavior
INSERTING	TRUE if the triggering statement is an INSERT; FALSE otherwise.
UPDATING	TRUE if the triggering statement is an UPDATE; FALSE otherwise.
DELETING	TRUE if the triggering statement is a DELETE; FALSE otherwise.

The **LogRSChanges** trigger uses these predicates to record all changes made to the **registered_students** table. In addition to the change, it records the user who makes the change. The records are kept in the **RS_audit** table, which looks like:

```
CREATE TABLE RS_audit (
  old_student_id NUMBER(5),
  old_department CHAR(3),
  old_course     NUMBER(3),
  old_grade      CHAR(1),
  new_student_id NUMBER(5),
  new_department CHAR(3),
  new_course     NUMBER(3),
  new_grade      CHAR(1),
  changed_by     VARCHAR2(8),
```

```
timestamp       DATE
);
```

LogRSChanges is created with:

```
CREATE OR REPLACE TRIGGER LogRSChanges
  BEFORE INSERT OR DELETE OR UPDATE ON registered_students
  FOR EACH ROW
DECLARE
  v_ChangeType CHAR(1);
BEGIN
  /* Use 'I' for an INSERT, 'D' for DELETE, and 'U' for UPDATE. */
  IF INSERTING THEN
    v_ChangeType := 'I';
  ELSIF UPDATING THEN
    v_ChangeType := 'U';
  ELSE
    v_ChangeType := 'D';
  END IF;

  /* Record all the changes made to registered_students in
     RS_audit. Use SYSDATE to generate the timestamp, and
     USER to return the userid of the current user. */
  INSERT INTO RS_audit
    (change_type, changed_by, timestamp,
     old_student_id, old_department, old_course, old_grade,
     new_student_id, new_department, new_course, new_grade)
  VALUES
    (v_ChangeType, USER, SYSDATE,
     :old.student_id, :old.department, :old.course, :old.grade,
     :new.student_id, :new.department, :new.course, :new.grade);
END LogRSChanges;
```

Triggers are commonly used for auditing, as in **LogRSChanges**. Oracle provides auditing as part of the database, but triggers allow for more flexible auditing. **LogRSChanges** could be modified, for example, to record changes only made by certain people. It could also check to see if users have permission to make changes and raise an error (with RAISE_APPLICATION_ERROR) if they don't.

Mutating Tables

There are restrictions on the tables and columns that a trigger body may access. In order to define these restrictions, it is necessary to understand mutating and constraining tables. A *mutating table* is a table that is currently being modified by a DML statement. For a trigger, this is the table on which the trigger is defined. Tables that may need to be updated as a result of DELETE CASCADE referential integrity constraints are also mutating. (For more information on referential integrity constraints, see the *Oracle7 Server Reference*.) A *constraining table* is a table that might need to be read from for a referential integrity constraint. To illustrate these definitions, consider the **registered_students** table, which is created with

```
CREATE TABLE registered_students (
  student_id NUMBER(5) NOT NULL,
  department CHAR(3)   NOT NULL,
  course     NUMBER(3) NOT NULL,
  grade      CHAR(1),
  CONSTRAINT rs_grade
    CHECK (grade IN ('A', 'B', 'C', 'D', 'E')),
  CONSTRAINT rs_student_id
    FOREIGN KEY (student_id) REFERENCES students (id),
  CONSTRAINT rs_department_course
    FOREIGN KEY (department, course)
    REFERENCES classes (department, course)
);
```

Registered_students has two declarative referential integrity constraints. Thus, both **students** and **classes** are constraining tables for **registered_students**. **Registered_students** itself is mutating during execution of a DML statement against it. Because of the constraints, **classes** and **students** also need to be modified and/or queried by the DML statement.

SQL statements in a trigger body may not:

- Read from or modify any mutating table of the triggering statement. This includes the triggering table itself.

- Read from or modify the primary, unique, or foreign key columns of a constraining table of the triggering table. They may, however, modify the other columns if desired.

These restrictions apply to all row-level triggers. They apply for statement triggers only when the statement trigger would be fired as a result of a DELETE CASCADE operation.

NOTE
If an INSERT statement affects only one row, then the before and after row triggers for that row do not treat the triggering table as mutating. This is the only case where a row-level trigger may read from or modify the triggering table. Statements such as

```
INSERT INTO table SELECT ...
```

always treat the triggering table as mutating, even if the subquery returns only one row.

As an example, consider the **CascadeRSInserts** trigger shown next. Even though it modifies both **students** and **classes**, it is legal because the columns in **students** and **classes** that are modified are not key columns. In the next section, we will examine an illegal trigger.

```
CREATE OR REPLACE TRIGGER CascadeRSInserts
  /* Keep the registered_students, students, and classes
     tables in synch. */
  BEFORE INSERT ON registered_students
  FOR EACH ROW
DECLARE
  v_Credits classes.num_credits%TYPE;
BEGIN
  -- Determine the number of credits for this class.
  SELECT num_credits
    INTO v_Credits
    FROM classes
    WHERE department = :new.department
    AND course = :new.course;

  -- Modify the current credits for this student.
  UPDATE students
    SET current_credits = current_credits + v_Credits
    WHERE ID = :new.student_id;

  -- Add one to the number of students in the class.
  UPDATE classes
    SET current_students = current_students + 1
    WHERE department = :new.department
    AND course = :new.course;
END CascadeRSInserts;
```

To make the procedure more complete, triggers should also be written that update **students** and **classes** when **registered_students** is deleted from or updated. These triggers would be very similar to **CascadeRSInserts**.

Mutating Table Example

Suppose we want to limit the number of students in each major to 5. We could accomplish this with a before insert or update row-level trigger on **students**, given here:

```
CREATE OR REPLACE TRIGGER LimitMajors
  /* Limits the number of students in each major to 5.
     If this limit is exceeded, an error is raised with
     RAISE_APPLICATION_ERROR. */
  BEFORE INSERT OR UPDATE OF major ON students
  FOR EACH ROW
DECLARE
  v_MaxStudents CONSTANT NUMBER := 5;
  v_CurrentStudents NUMBER;
BEGIN
  -- Determine the current number of students in this
  -- major.
  SELECT COUNT(*)
    INTO v_CurrentStudents
    FROM students
    WHERE major = :new.major;

  -- If there isn't room, raise an error.
  IF v_CurrentStudents + 1 > v_MaxStudents THEN
    RAISE_APPLICATION_ERROR(-20000,
      'Too many students in major ' || :new.major);
  END IF;
END LimitMajors;
```

The RAISE_APPLICATION_ERROR procedure is a standard procedure, which is discussed in more detail in Chapter 6. At first glance, this trigger seems to accomplish the desired result. However, if we update **students** and fire the trigger, we get

```
SQL> UPDATE students
  2    SET major = 'History'
  3    WHERE ID = 10003;
UPDATE students
  *
```

```
ERROR at line 1:
ORA-04091: table EXAMPLE.STUDENTS is mutating, trigger/function
           may not see it
ORA-06512: at line 7
ORA-04088: error during execution of trigger 'EXAMPLE.LIMITMAJORS'
```

The ORA-4091 error results because **LimitMajors** queries its own triggering table, which is mutating. ORA-4091 is raised when the trigger is fired, not when it is created.

A Workaround for the Mutating Table Error

Students is mutating only for a row-level trigger. This means that we cannot query it in a row-level trigger, but we can in a statement-level trigger. However, we can't simply make **LimitMajors** into a statement trigger, since we need to use the value of **:new.major** in the trigger body. The solution for this is to create two triggers—a row and a statement level. In the row-level trigger, we record the value of **:new.major**, but we don't query **students**. The query is done in the statement level trigger and uses the value recorded in the row-level trigger.

How do we record this value? The best way is to use a PL/SQL table inside a package. This way, we can save multiple values per update. Also, each session gets its own instantiation of packaged variables, so we don't have to worry about simultaneous updates by different sessions. This solution is implemented with the **student_data** package and the **RLimitMajors** and **SLimitMajors** triggers:

```
CREATE OR REPLACE PACKAGE StudentData AS
  TYPE t_Majors IS TABLE OF students.major%TYPE
    INDEX BY BINARY_INTEGER;
  TYPE t_IDs IS TABLE OF students.ID%TYPE
    INDEX BY BINARY_INTEGER;

  v_StudentMajors t_Majors;
  v_StudentIDs    t_IDs;
  v_NumEntries    BINARY_INTEGER := 0;
END StudentData;


CREATE OR REPLACE TRIGGER RLimitMajors
  BEFORE INSERT OR UPDATE OF major ON students
  FOR EACH ROW
BEGIN
  /* Record the new data in StudentData. We don't make any
     changes to students, to avoid the ORA-4091 error. */
  StudentData.v_NumEntries := StudentData.v_NumEntries + 1;
  StudentData.v_StudentMajors(StudentData.v_NumEntries) :=
```

```
      :new.major;
    StudentData.v_StudentIDs(StudentData.v_NumEntries) := :new.id;
END RLimitMajors;

CREATE OR REPLACE TRIGGER SLimitMajors
  AFTER INSERT OR UPDATE OF major ON students
DECLARE
  v_MaxStudents     CONSTANT NUMBER := 5;
  v_CurrentStudents NUMBER;
  v_StudentID       students.ID%TYPE;
  v_Major           students.major%TYPE;
BEGIN
  /* Loop through each student inserted or updated, and verify
     that we are still within the limit. */
  FOR v_LoopIndex IN 1..StudentData.v_NumEntries LOOP
    v_StudentID := StudentData.v_StudentIDs(v_LoopIndex);
    v_Major := StudentData.v_StudentMajors(v_LoopIndex);

    -- Determine the current number of students in this major.
    SELECT COUNT(*)
      INTO v_CurrentStudents
      FROM students
      WHERE major = v_Major;

    -- If there isn't room, raise an error.
    IF v_CurrentStudents > v_MaxStudents THEN
      RAISE_APPLICATION_ERROR(-20000,
        'Too many students for major ' || v_Major ||
        ' because of student ' || v_StudentID);
    END IF;
  END LOOP;

  -- Reset the counter so the next execution will use new data.
  StudentData.v_NumEntries := 0;
END LimitMajors;
```

We can now test this series of triggers by updating **students** until we have too many history majors:

```
SQL> UPDATE students
  2    SET major = 'History'
  3    WHERE ID = 10003;
1 row updated.
```

```
SQL> UPDATE students
  2    SET major = 'History'
  3    WHERE ID = 10002;
1 row updated.

SQL> UPDATE students
  2    SET major = 'History'
  3    WHERE ID = 10009;
UPDATE students
       *
ERROR at line 1:
ORA-20000: Too many students for major History because of student 10009
ORA-06512: at line 20
ORA-04088: error during execution of trigger 'EXAMPLE.SLIMITMAJORS'
```

This is the desired behavior. This technique can be applied to occurrences of
ORA-4091 when a row-level trigger reads from or modifies a mutating table.
Instead of doing the illegal processing in the row-level trigger, we defer the
processing to an after statement-level trigger, where it is legal. The packaged
PL/SQL tables are used to store the rows that have been changed.

There are several things to note about this technique:

- The PL/SQL tables are contained in a package so that they will be visible
  to both the row- and the statement-level trigger. The only way to ensure
  that variables are global is to put them in a package.

- A counter variable, **StudentData.v_NumEntries**, is used. This is initialized
  to zero when the package is created. It is incremented by the row-level
  trigger. The statement-level trigger references it and then resets it to zero
  after processing. This is necessary so that the next UPDATE statement
  issued by this session will have the correct value.

- The check in **SLimitMajors** for the maximum number of students had to be
  changed slightly. Since this is now an after statement trigger,
  v_CurrentStudents will hold the number of students in the major after the
  insert or update, not before. Thus the check for **v_CurrentStudents + 1**,
  which we did in **LimitMajors**, is replaced by **v_CurrentStudents**.

- A database table could have been used instead of PL/SQL tables. I don't
  recommend this technique, since simultaneous sessions issuing an
  UPDATE would interfere with each other. Packaged PL/SQL tables are
  unique among sessions, which avoids the problem.

Privileges and Stored Subprograms

Stored subprograms and packages are objects in the data dictionary, and as such, they are owned by a particular database user, or schema. Other users can access these objects, if they are granted the correct privileges for them. Privileges and roles also come into play when creating a stored object, with regard to the access available inside the subprogram.

EXECUTE Privilege

In order to allow access to a table, the SELECT, INSERT, UPDATE, and DELETE object privileges are used. The GRANT statement gives these privileges to a database user or a role (see Chapter 3 for more information on GRANT). For stored subprograms and packages, the relevant privilege is EXECUTE. Consider the **RecordFullClasses** procedure, which we examined earlier in this chapter:

```
CREATE OR REPLACE PROCEDURE RecordFullClasses AS
  CURSOR c_Classes IS
    SELECT department, course
      FROM classes;
BEGIN
  FOR v_ClassRecord IN c_Classes LOOP
    -- Record all classes which don't have very much room left
    -- in temp_table.
    IF AlmostFull(v_ClassRecord.department, v_ClassRecord.course) THEN
      INSERT INTO temp_table (char_col) VALUES
        (v_ClassRecord.department || ' ' || v_ClassRecord.course ||
         ' is almost full!');
    END IF;
  END LOOP;
END RecordFullClasses;
```

Suppose that the objects on which **RecordFullClasses** depends (the function **AlmostFull** and tables **classes** and **temp_table**) are all owned by the database user **UserA**. **RecordFullClasses** is owned by **UserA** as well. If we grant the EXECUTE privilege on **RecordFullClasses** to another database user, say **UserB**, with

```
GRANT EXECUTE on RecordFullClasses TO UserB;
```

then **UserB** can execute **RecordFullClasses** with the following block:

```
BEGIN
  UserA.RecordFullClasses;
END;
```

In this scenario, all of the database objects are owned by **UserA**. This situation is illustrated in Figure 5-8. The dotted line signifies the GRANT statement from **UserA** to **UserB**, while the solid lines signify object dependencies.

Now suppose that **UserB** has another table, also called **temp_table**, as illustrated in Figure 5-9. If **UserB** calls **UserA.RecordFullClasses**, which table gets modified? The table in **UserA** does. This concept can be expressed as:

■ A subprogram executes under the privilege set of its owner.

Even though **UserB** is calling **RecordFullClasses**, **RecordFullClasses** is owned by **UserA**. Thus the identifier **temp_table** will evaluate to the table belonging to **UserA**, *not* **UserB**.

Stored Subprograms and Roles

Let's modify the situation in Figure 5-9 slightly. Suppose that **UserA** does not own **temp_table** or **RecordFullClasses**, and these are owned by **UserB**. Furthermore,

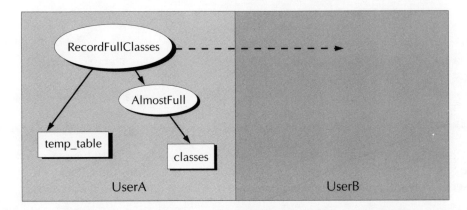

FIGURE 5-8. *Database objects owned by UserA*

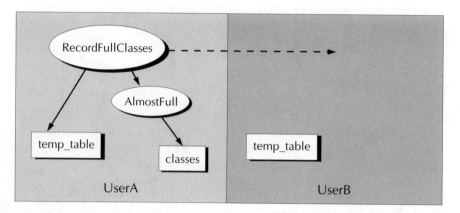

FIGURE 5-9. *Temp_table owned by UserB and UserA*

suppose we have modified **RecordFullClasses** to explicitly refer to the objects in **UserA**. This is illustrated both by the following listing and by Figure 5-10.

```
CREATE OR REPLACE PROCEDURE RecordFullClasses AS
  CURSOR c_Classes IS
    SELECT department, course
      FROM UserA.classes;
BEGIN
  FOR v_ClassRecord IN c_Classes LOOP
    -- Record all classes which don't have very much room left
    -- in temp_table.
    IF UserA.AlmostFull(v_ClassRecord.department,
                        v_ClassRecord.course) THEN
      INSERT INTO temp_table (char_col) VALUES
        (v_ClassRecord.department || ' ' || v_ClassRecord.course ||
        ' is almost full!');
    END IF;
  END LOOP;
END RecordFullClasses;
```

In order for **RecordFullClasses** to compile correctly, **UserA** must have granted the SELECT privilege on **classes** and the EXECUTE privilege on **AlmostFull** to **UserB**. The dotted lines in Figure 5-10 show this. Furthermore, this grant must be

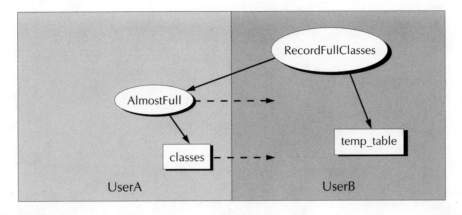

FIGURE 5-10. *RecordFullClasses owned by UserB*

done explicitly and *not* through a role. The following grants, executed by **UserA**, would allow a successful compilation of **UserB.RecordFullClasses**:

```
GRANT SELECT ON classes TO UserB;
GRANT EXECUTE ON AlmostFull TO UserB;
```

A grant done through an intermediate role, as in

```
CREATE ROLE UserA_Role;
GRANT SELECT ON classes TO UserA_Role;
GRANT EXECUTE ON AlmostFull TO UserA_Role;
GRANT UserA_Role to UserB;
```

will not work. The role is illustrated in Figure 5-11.

So we can clarify the rule in the previous section as:

■ A subprogram executes under the privileges that have been granted explicitly to its owner, not via a role.

If the grants had been done via a role, we would have received PLS-201 errors when we tried to compile **RecordFullClasses**:

```
PLS-201: identifier 'CLASSES' must be declared
PLS-201: identifier 'ALMOSTFULL' must be declared
```

This rule also applies for triggers. Essentially, *the only objects available inside a stored subprogram or trigger are the ones owned by the owner of the subprogram, or explicitly granted to the owner.*

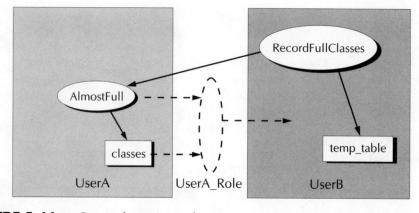

FIGURE 5-11. *Grants done via a role*

Why is this? To explain this restriction, we need to examine binding again. Recall that PL/SQL uses early binding—references are evaluated when a subprogram is compiled, not when it is run. GRANT and REVOKE are both DDL statements. They take effect immediately, and the new privileges are recorded in the data dictionary. All database sessions will see the new privilege set. However, this is not necessarily true for roles. A role can be granted to a user, and that user can then choose to disable the role with the SET ROLE command. The distinction is that SET ROLE applies to one database session only, while GRANT and REVOKE apply to all sessions. A role can be disabled in one session but enabled in other sessions.

In order to allow privileges granted via a role to be used inside stored subprograms and triggers, the privileges would have to be checked every time the procedure is run. The privileges are checked as part of the binding process. But early binding means that the privileges are checked at compile time, not run time. In order to maintain early binding, *all roles are disabled inside stored procedures and triggers.*

Using Stored Functions in SQL Statements

PL/SQL 2.1 ...and HIGHER A procedure call is a procedural, not a SQL, statement. The function calls that we have seen in this chapter so far are procedural as well. As such, procedure and function calls cannot be made from within SQL statements. PL/SQL 2.1, however, lifts this restriction for stored functions. If a stand-alone or packaged function meets certain restrictions, it can be called during execution of a SQL statement. This feature is available with PL/SQL 2.1 (Oracle7 Release 7.1) and higher.

The user-defined function is called the same way as the built-in functions we examined in Chapter 3, such as TO_CHAR, UPPER, or ADD_MONTHS. A function must meet different restrictions depending on where it is used. These restrictions are defined in terms of purity levels.

Purity Levels

There are four different *purity levels* for functions. A purity level defines what kinds of data structures the function reads or modifies. The available levels are listed in Table 5-6. Depending on the purity level of a function, it is subject to the following restrictions:

- Any function called from a SQL statement cannot modify any database tables (WNDS).

- In order to be executed remotely (via a database link) or in parallel, a function must not read or write the value of packaged variables (RNPS and WNPS).

- Functions called from the SELECT, VALUES, or SET clauses can write packaged variables. Functions in all other clauses must have the WNPS purity level.

- A function is only as pure as the subprograms it calls. If a function calls a stored procedure that does an UPDATE, for example, the function does not have the WNDS purity level and thus cannot be used inside a SQL statement.

- Regardless of their purity level, stored PL/SQL functions cannot be called from a CHECK constraint clause of a CREATE TABLE or ALTER TABLE command, or be used to specify a default value for a column, because each of these situations requires an unchanging definition.

In addition to the above restrictions, a user-defined function must also meet the following requirements before it can be called from a SQL statement. (All of the predefined functions meet these requirements as well.)

- The function has to be stored in the database, either alone or as part of a package. It must not be local to another block.

- The function can take only IN parameters, not IN OUT or OUT.

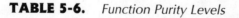

The formal parameters must use only database types, not PL/SQL types such as BOOLEAN or RECORD. Database types are NUMBER, CHAR, VARCHAR2, ROWID, LONG, LONG RAW, and DATE.

The return type of the function must also be a database type.

As an example, the **FullName** function takes a student ID number as input and returns the concatenated first and last names:

```
CREATE OR REPLACE FUNCTION FullName (
  p_StudentID  students.ID%TYPE)
  RETURN VARCHAR2 IS

  v_Result  VARCHAR2(100);
BEGIN
  SELECT first_name || ' ' || last_name
    INTO v_Result
    FROM students
    WHERE ID = p_StudentID;

  RETURN v_Result;
END FullName;
```

Purity Level	Meaning	Description
WNDS	Writes no database state	The function does not modify any database tables (using DML statements).
RNDS	Reads no database state	The function does not read any database tables (using the SELECT statement).
WNPS	Writes no package state	The function does not modify any packaged variables (no packaged variables are used on the left side of an assignment, or in a FETCH statement).
RNPS	Reads no package state	The function does not examine any packaged variables (no packaged variables appear on the right side of an assignment, or as part of a procedural or SQL expression).

TABLE 5-6. *Function Purity Levels*

FullName meets all of the restrictions, so we can call it from SQL statements, as follows:

```
SQL> SELECT ID, FullName(ID) "Full Name"
  2    FROM students;

       ID Full Name
--------- -------------------------------
    10000 Scott Smith
    10001 Margaret Mason
    10002 Joanne Junebug
    10003 Manish Murgratroid
    10004 Patrick Poll
    10005 Timothy Taller
    10006 Barbara Blues
    10007 David Dinsmore
    10008 Ester Elegant
    10009 Rose Riznit
    10010 Rita Razmataz

11 rows selected.
SQL> INSERT INTO temp_table (char_col)
  2    VALUES (FullName(10010));

1 row created.
```

RESTRICT_REFERENCES

The PL/SQL engine can determine the purity level of stand-alone functions. When the function is called from a SQL statement, the purity level is checked. If it does not meet the restrictions, an error is returned. For packaged functions, however, the RESTRICT_REFERENCES pragma is required. This pragma specifies the purity level of a given function, with the syntax

```
    PRAGMA RESTRICT_REFERENCES(function_name,
        WNDS [, WNPS] [, RNDS] [, RNPS]);
```

where *function_name* is the name of a packaged function. Since WNDS is required for all functions used in SQL statements, it is also required for the pragma. The other purity levels can be specified in any order. The pragma goes in the package header, with the specification for the function. For example, the **StudentOps** package uses RESTRICT_REFERENCES twice:

```
CREATE OR REPLACE PACKAGE StudentOps AS
  FUNCTION FullName(p_StudentID IN students.ID%TYPE)
    RETURN VARCHAR2;
  PRAGMA RESTRICT_REFERENCES(FullName, WNDS, WNPS, RNPS);

  /* Returns the number of History majors. */
  FUNCTION NumHistoryMajors
    RETURN NUMBER;
  PRAGMA RESTRICT_REFERENCES(NumHistoryMajors, WNDS, WNPS, RNPS);
END StudentOps;

CREATE OR REPLACE PACKAGE BODY StudentOps AS

  -- Packaged variable to hold the number of history majors.
  v_NumHist NUMBER;

  FUNCTION FullName(p_StudentID IN students.ID%TYPE)
    RETURN VARCHAR2 IS
    v_Result  VARCHAR2(100);
  BEGIN
    SELECT first_name || ' ' || last_name
      INTO v_Result
      FROM students
      WHERE ID = p_StudentID;

    RETURN v_Result;
  END FullName;

  FUNCTION NumHistoryMajors RETURN NUMBER IS
    v_Result NUMBER;
  BEGIN
    IF v_NumHist IS NULL THEN
      /* Determine the answer. */
      SELECT COUNT(*)
        INTO v_Result
        FROM students
        WHERE major = 'History';
      /* And save it for future use. */
      v_NumHist := v_Result;
    ELSE
      v_Result := v_NumHist;
    END IF;
```

```
      RETURN v_Result;
   END NumHistoryMajors;
END StudentOps;
```

NOTE

The WNPS and RNPS purity levels apply to variables in *other* packages. **NumHistoryMajors** does modify the **v_NumHist** packaged variable, but **v_NumHist** is contained in the same package as **StudentOps**. So we can still assert the WNPS and RNPS purity levels for **NumHistoryMajors**.

Initialization Section   The code in the initialization section of a package can have a purity level as well. The first time any function in the package is called, the initialization section is run. Thus a packaged function is only as pure as its initialization section. The purity level for a package is also done with RESTRICT_REFERENCES, but with the package name rather than a function name:

```
CREATE OR REPLACE PACKAGE StudentOps AS
   PRAGMA RESTRICT_REFERENCES (StudentOps, WNDS, WNPS, RNPS);
   ...
END StudentOps;
```

Overloaded Functions   RESTRICT_REFERENCES can appear anywhere in the package specification, after the function declaration. It can apply to only one function definition, however. Thus, for overloaded functions, the pragma applies to the nearest definition prior to the pragma. In the following example, the function applies to the second declaration of **F**:

```
CREATE OR REPLACE PACKAGE TestPackage AS
   FUNCTION F(p_ParameterOne IN NUMBER) RETURN VARCHAR2;
   FUNCTION F RETURN DATE;
   PRAGMA RESTRICT_REFERENCES(F, WNDS, RNDS);
END TestPackage;
```

Built-in Packages   Packages supplied with PL/SQL are not considered pure as of PL/SQL 2.3; these include DBMS_OUTPUT, DBMS_PIPE, DBMS_ALERT, DBMS_SQL, and UTL_FILE. Consequently, any function that uses these packages is also not pure, and thus can't be used in SQL statements. These packages are discussed in more detail in later chapters.

Default Parameters

When calling a function from a procedural statement, you can use the default values for formal parameters, if they are present. When calling a function from an SQL statement, however, all parameters must be specified. Furthermore, you have to use positional notation and not named notation. The following call to **FullName** is illegal:

```
SELECT FullName(p_StudentID => 10000) FROM dual;
```

Summary

This chapter has covered a lot of material. Subprograms (procedures, functions, packages, and triggers) are essential to PL/SQL development. We discussed the differences between these subprograms, including how each is created, and how they are called. We also discussed how dependencies between PL/SQL objects are maintained, and examined their effects on subprogram development. We concluded with a discussion of roles and procedures, and the use of stored functions in SQL statements. In Chapter 6, we will examine PL/SQL error handling, and in Chapter 7 we'll continue exploring the advanced features of PL/SQL.

CHAPTER 6

Error Handling

Any well-written program must have the ability to handle errors intelligently and recover from them if possible. PL/SQL implements error handling via *exceptions* and *exception handlers.* Exceptions can be associated with Oracle errors or with your own user-defined errors. In this chapter, we will discuss the syntax of exceptions and exception handlers, how exceptions are raised and handled, and the rules of exception propagation. The chapter closes with guidelines on using exceptions.

What Is an Exception?

In Chapter 1 we discussed how PL/SQL is based on the Ada language. One of the features of Ada that is also incorporated into PL/SQL is the exception mechanism. By using exceptions and exception handlers, you can make your PL/SQL programs robust and able to deal with both unexpected and expected errors during execution. **275**

What kinds of errors can occur in a PL/SQL program? Errors can be classified according to Table 6-1. Exceptions are designed for run-time error handling, rather than compile-time error handling. Errors that occur during the compilation phase are detected by the PL/SQL engine and reported back to the user. The program cannot handle these, since it has yet to run. Exceptions and exception handlers are how the program responds to run-time errors. Run-time errors include SQL errors such as

```
ORA-1: unique constraint violated
```

and procedural errors such as

```
ORA-06502: PL/SQL: numeric or value error
```

When an error occurs, an exception is *raised*. When this happens, control is passed to the exception handler, which is a separate section of the program. This separates the error handling from the rest of the program, which makes the logic of the program easier to understand. This also ensures that all errors will be trapped.

In a language (such as C) that doesn't use the exception model for error handling, you must explicitly insert error-handling code in order to ensure that your program can handle errors in all cases. For example:

```
int x, y, z;
f(x);   /* Function call, passing x as an argument. */
if <an error occurred>
   handle_error(...);
y = 1 / z;
if <an error occurred>
   handle_error(...);
z = x + y;
if <an error occurred>
   handle_error(...);
```

CAUTION
A check for errors must occur after each statement in the program. If you forget to insert the check, the program will not properly handle an error situation. In addition, the error handling can clutter up the program, making it difficult to understand the program's logic.

Compare the preceding example to the similar example in PL/SQL:

```
DECLARE
   x NUMBER;
   y NUMBER;
   z NUMBER;
```

```
BEGIN
  f(x);
  y := 1 / z;
  z := x + y;
EXCEPTION
  WHEN OTHERS THEN
    /* Handler to execute for all errors */
    handle_error(...);
END;
```

Note that the error handling is separated from the program logic. This solves both problems with the C example:

- Program logic is easier to understand, since it is clearly visible.

- No matter which statement fails, the program will detect and handle the error.

Declaring Exceptions

Exceptions are declared in the declarative section of the block, raised in the executable section, and handled in the exception section. There are two types of exceptions—*predefined* and *user-defined*.

User-Defined Exceptions

A user-defined exception is an error that is defined by the program. The error that it signifies is not necessarily an Oracle error—it could be an error with the data, for example. Predefined exceptions, on the other hand, correspond to common SQL errors.

Error Type	When Reported	How Handled
Compile-time	PL/SQL compiler	Interactively—compiler reports errors, and you have to correct them.
Run-time	PL/SQL run-time engine	Pragmatically—exceptions are raised and caught by exception handlers.

TABLE 6-1. *Types of PL/SQL Errors*

User-defined exceptions are declared in the declarative section of a PL/SQL block. Just like variables, exceptions have a type (EXCEPTION) and scope. For example:

```
DECLARE
  e_TooManyStudents EXCEPTION;
```

e_TooManyStudents is an identifier that will be visible until the end of this block. Note that the scope of an exception is the same as the scope of any other variable or cursor in the same declarative section. See Chapter 2 for information on the scope and visibility rules for PL/SQL identifiers.

Predefined Exceptions

Oracle has predefined several exceptions that correspond to the most common Oracle errors. Like the predefined types (NUMBER, VARCHAR2, and so on), the identifiers for these exceptions are defined in package STANDARD. (See Chapter 2 for more information on predefined types and package STANDARD.) Because of this, they are already available to the program—it is not necessary to declare them in the declarative section like a user-defined exception. These predefined exceptions are described in Table 6-2.

Short descriptions of some of the predefined exceptions follow. For more information on these errors, see Appendix C.

INVALID_CURSOR   This error is raised when an illegal cursor operation is performed, such as attempting to close a cursor that is already closed. The analogous situation of attempting to open a cursor that is already open causes CURSOR_ALREADY_OPEN to be raised.

NO_DATA_FOUND   This exception can be raised in two different situations. The first is when a SELECT..INTO statement does not return any rows. If the statement returns more than one row, TOO_MANY_ROWS is raised. The second situation is an attempt to reference a PL/SQL table element that has not been assigned a value. For example, the following anonymous block will raise NO_DATA_FOUND because **v_NumberTable(1)** has not been assigned a value.

```
DECLARE
  TYPE t_NumberTableType IS TABLE OF NUMBER
    INDEX BY BINARY_INTEGER;
  v_NumberTable t_NumberTableType;
  v_TempVar NUMBER;
BEGIN
  v_TempVar := v_NumberTable(1);
END;
```

Oracle Error	Equivalent Exception	Description
ORA-0001	DUP_VAL_ON_INDEX	Unique constraint violated.
ORA-0051	TIMEOUT_ON_RESOURCE	Time-out occurred while waiting for resource.
ORA-0061	TRANSACTION_BACKED_OUT[1]	The transaction was rolled back due to deadlock.
ORA-1001	INVALID_CURSOR	Illegal cursor operation.
ORA-1012	NOT_LOGGED_ON	Not connected to Oracle.
ORA-1017	LOGIN_DENIED	Invalid user name/password.
ORA-1403	NO_DATA_FOUND	No data found.
ORA-1422	TOO_MANY_ROWS	A SELECT..INTO statement matches more than one row.
ORA-1476	ZERO_DIVIDE	Division by zero.
ORA-1722	INVALID_NUMBER	Conversion to a number failed—for example, '1A' is not valid.
ORA-6500	STORAGE_ERROR	Internal PL/SQL error raised if PL/SQL runs out of memory.
ORA-6501	PROGRAM_ERROR	Internal PL/SQL error.
ORA-6502	VALUE_ERROR	Truncation, arithmetic, or conversion error.
ORA-6504	ROWTYPE_MISMATCH[2]	Host cursor variable and PL/SQL cursor variable have incompatible row types.
ORA-6511	CURSOR_ALREADY_OPEN	Attempt to open a cursor that is already open.

TABLE 6-2. *Predefined Oracle Exceptions*

[1] This exception is predefined only in PL/SQL 2.0 and 2.1.
[2] This exception is predefined in PL/SQL 2.2 and higher.

INVALID_NUMBER   This exception is raised in an SQL statement when an attempted conversion from a character string to a number fails. In a procedural statement, VALUE_ERROR is raised instead. For example, the following statement raises INVALID_NUMBER since 'X' is not a valid number:

```
INSERT INTO students (id, first_name, last_name)
  VALUES ('X', 'Scott', 'Smith');
```

STORAGE_ERROR and PROGRAM_ERROR   These are internal exceptions, which are not normally raised. If they occur, either your machine has run out of memory (STORAGE_ERROR) or a PL/SQL internal error has occurred (PROGRAM_ERROR). Internal errors are often caused by bugs in the PL/SQL engine and should be reported to Oracle Technical Support.

VALUE_ERROR   This exception is raised when an arithmetic, conversion, truncation, or constraint error occurs in a procedural statement. If the error occurs in an SQL statement, an error such as INVALID_NUMBER is raised instead. The error can occur either as a result of an assignment statement or a SELECT..INTO statement. Both of the following examples will raise VALUE_ERROR:

```
DECLARE
  v_TempVar VARCHAR2(3);
BEGIN
  v_TempVar := 'ABCD';
END;
```

```
DECLARE
  v_TempVar NUMBER(2);
BEGIN
  SELECT id
    INTO v_TempVar
    FROM students
    WHERE last_name = 'Smith';
END;
```

PL/SQL 2.2
...and HIGHER

ROWTYPE MISMATCH   This exception is raised when the types of a host cursor variable and a PL/SQL cursor variable do not match. For example, if the actual and formal return types don't match for a procedure that takes a cursor variable as an argument, ROWTYPE_MISMATCH is raised. See Chapter 4 for more information on cursor variables and an example that raises this exception.

Raising Exceptions

When the error associated with an exception occurs, the exception is raised. User-defined exceptions are raised explicitly via the RAISE statement, while predefined exceptions are raised implicitly when their associated Oracle error occurs. Continuing the example started earlier in the "User-Defined Exceptions" section, we have:

```
DECLARE
  e_TooManyStudents EXCEPTION;    -- Exception to indicate an
                                  -- error condition
  v_CurrentStudents NUMBER(3);    -- Current number of students
                                  -- registered for HIS-101
  v_MaxStudents NUMBER(3);        -- Maximum number of students
                                  -- allowed for HIS-101
BEGIN
  /* Find the current number of registered students,
     and the maximum number of students allowed. */
  SELECT current_students, max_students
    INTO v_CurrentStudents, v_MaxStudents
    FROM classes
    WHERE department = 'HIS' AND course = 101;
  /* Check the number of students in this class. */
  IF v_CurrentStudents > v_MaxStudents THEN
    /* Too many students registered -- raise exception. */
    RAISE e_TooManyStudents;
  END IF;
END;
```

When an exception is raised, control immediately passes to the exception section of the block. If there is no exception section, the exception is propagated to the enclosing block (see the section "Exception Propagation" later in this chapter for more information). Once control passes to the exception handler, there is *no* way to return to the executable section of the block. This is illustrated in Figure 6-1.

Predefined exceptions are automatically raised when the associated Oracle error occurs. For example, the following PL/SQL block will raise the DUP_VAL_ON_INDEX exception:

```
BEGIN
  INSERT INTO students (id, first_name, last_name)
    VALUES (10001, 'John', 'Smith');
  INSERT INTO students (id, first_name, last_name)
    VALUES (10001, 'Susan', 'Ryan');
END;
```

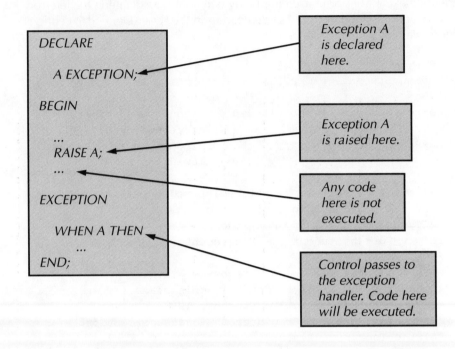

FIGURE 6-1. *Control passing to exception handler*

The exception is raised because the **id** column of the students table is a primary key and therefore has a unique constraint defined on it. When the second INSERT statement attempts to insert 10001 into this column, the error

```
ORA-0001: unique constraint violated
```

is raised. This corresponds to the DUP_VAL_ON_INDEX exception.

Handling Exceptions

When an exception is raised, control passes to the exception section of the block, as illustrated in Figure 6-1. The exception section consists of *handlers* for all the exceptions. An exception handler contains the code that is executed when the error associated with the exception occurs, and the exception is raised. The syntax for the exception section is as follows:

EXCEPTION
> **WHEN** *exception_name* **THEN**
> > *sequence_of_statements1*;
> **WHEN** *exception_name* **THEN**
> > *sequence_of_statements2*;
> **WHEN OTHERS THEN**
> > *sequence_of_statements3*;

END;

Each exception handler consists of the WHEN clause and statements to execute when the exception is raised. The WHEN clause identifies which exception this handler is for. Continuing the example started earlier, we have:

```
DECLARE
  e_TooManyStudents EXCEPTION;    -- Exception to indicate an
                                  -- error condition
  v_CurrentStudents NUMBER(3);    -- Current number of students
                                  -- registered for HIS-101
  v_MaxStudents NUMBER(3);        -- Maximum number of students
                                  -- allowed for HIS-101
BEGIN
  /* Find the current number of registered students,
     and the maximum number of students allowed. */
  SELECT current_students, max_students
    INTO v_CurrentStudents, v_MaxStudents
    FROM classes
    WHERE department = 'HIS' AND course = 101;
  /* Check the number of students in this class. */
  IF v_CurrentStudents > v_MaxStudents THEN
    /* Too many students registered - raise exception. */
    RAISE e_TooManyStudents;
  END IF;
EXCEPTION
  WHEN e_TooManyStudents THEN
    /* Handler which executes when there are too many students
       registered for HIS-101. We will insert a log message
       explaining what has happened. */
    INSERT INTO log_table (info)
      VALUES ('History 101 has ' || v_CurrentStudents ||
      'students: max allowed is ' || v_Max_Students);
END;
```

A single handler can also be executed for more than one exception. Simply list the exception names in the WHEN clause separated by the keyword OR:

```
EXCEPTION
  WHEN NO_DATA_FOUND OR TOO_MANY_ROWS THEN
    INSERT INTO log_table (info) VALUES ('A select error occurred.');
END;
```

The OTHERS Exception Handler

The OTHERS handler will execute for all raised exceptions. It should always be the last handler in the block. It is good programming practice to have an OTHERS handler at the top level of your program (the outermost block) to ensure that no errors go undetected. The next listing continues the previous example by adding an OTHERS handler:

```
DECLARE
  e_TooManyStudents EXCEPTION;    -- Exception to indicate an
                                  -- error condition
  v_CurrentStudents NUMBER(3);    -- Current number of students
                                  -- registered for HIS-101
  v_MaxStudents NUMBER(3);        -- Maximum number of students
                                  -- allowed for HIS-101
BEGIN
  /* Find the current number of registered students,
     and the maximum number of students allowed. */
  SELECT current_students, max_students
    INTO v_CurrentStudents, v_MaxStudents
    FROM classes
    WHERE department = 'HIS' AND course = 101;
  /* Check the number of students in this class. */
  IF v_CurrentStudents > v_MaxStudents THEN
    /* Too many students registered - raise exception. */
    RAISE e_TooManyStudents;
  END IF;
EXCEPTION
  WHEN e_TooManyStudents THEN
    /* Handler which executes when there are too many students
       registered for HIS-101. We will insert a log message
       explaining what has happened. */
    INSERT INTO log_table (info)
      VALUES ('History 101 has ' || v_CurrentStudents ||
              'students: max allowed is ' || v_Max_Students);
  WHEN OTHERS THEN
    /* Handler which executes for all other errors. */
```

```
      INSERT INTO log_table (info) VALUES ('Another error occurred');
END;
```

The OTHERS exception handler in this example simply records the fact that an error occurred. However, it doesn't record which error. We can determine which error raised the exception that is being handled by an OTHERS handler through the predefined functions SQLCODE and SQLERRM, described next.

SQLCODE and SQLERRM   Inside an OTHERS handler, it is often useful to know which Oracle error raised the exception. One reason would be to log which error occurred, rather than the fact that an error happened. PL/SQL provides this via two built-in functions, SQLCODE and SQLERRM. SQLCODE returns the current error code, and SQLERRM returns the current error message text.

Here is the complete PL/SQL block that we have developed so far, with a complete OTHERS exception handler:

```
DECLARE
  e_TooManyStudents EXCEPTION;    -- Exception to indicate an
                                  -- error condition
  v_CurrentStudents NUMBER(3);    -- Current number of students
                                  -- registered for HIS-101
  v_MaxStudents NUMBER(3);        -- Maximum number of students
                                  -- allowed for HIS-101
  v_ErrorCode NUMBER;             -- Variable to hold the error
                                  -- message code
  v_ErrorText VARCHAR2(200);      -- Variable to hold the error
                                  -- message text

BEGIN
  /* Find the current number of registered students,
     and the
     maximum number of students allowed. */
  SELECT current_students, max_students
    INTO v_CurrentStudents, v_MaxStudents
    FROM classes
    WHERE department = 'HIS' AND course = 101;
  /* Check the number of students in this class. */
  IF v_CurrentStudents > v_MaxStudents THEN
    /* Too many students registered - raise exception. */
    RAISE e_TooManyStudents;
  END IF;
EXCEPTION
  WHEN e_TooManyStudents THEN
    /* Handler which executes when there are too many students
```

```
        registered for HIS-101. We will insert a log message
        explaining what has happened. */
    INSERT INTO log_table (info)
      VALUES ('History 101 has ' || v_CurrentStudents ||
             'students: max allowed is ' || v_Max_Students);
   WHEN OTHERS THEN
    /* Handler which executes for all other errors. */
    v_ErrorCode := SQLCODE;
    v_ErrorText := SUBSTR(SQLERRM, 1, 200);  -- Note the use of
    SUBSTR here. INSERT INTO log_table (code, message, info) VALUES
       (v_ErrorCode, v_ErrorText, 'Oracle error occurred');
END;
```

The maximum length of an Oracle error message is 512 characters. In the preceding listing, **v_ErrorText** is only 200 characters (to match the **code** field of the log_table table). If the error message text is longer than 200 characters, the assignment

```
v_ErrorText := SQLERRM;
```

will itself raise the predefined exception VALUE_ERROR. To prevent this, we use the SUBSTR built-in function to ensure that at most 200 characters of the error message text are assigned to **v_ErrorText**. For more information on SUBSTR and other predefined PL/SQL functions, see Chapter 2.

NOTE
The values of SQLCODE and SQLERRM are assigned to local variables first; then these variables are used in an SQL statement. Because these functions are procedural, they cannot be used directly inside an SQL statement.

SQLERRM can also be called with a single number argument. In this case, it returns the text associated with the number. This argument should always be negative. If SQLERRM is called with zero, the message

```
ORA-0000: normal, successful completion
```

is returned. If SQLERRM is called with any positive value other than +100, the message

```
User-Defined Exception
```

is returned. SQLERRM(100) returns

```
ORA-1403: no data found
```

When called from an exception handler, SQLCODE will return a negative value indicating the Oracle error. The only exception to this is the error "ORA-1403: no data found," in which case SQLCODE returns +100.

If SQLERRM (with no arguments) is called from the executable section of a block, it always returns

```
ORA-0000: normal, successful completion
```

and SQLCODE returns 0. All of these situations are shown in the following listing.

```
DECLARE
  v_ErrorText    log_table.message%TYPE;   -- Variable to hold
                                           -- error message text
BEGIN
  /* SQLERRM(0) */
  v_ErrorText := SUBSTR(SQLERRM(0), 1, 200);
  INSERT INTO log_table (code, message, info)
    VALUES (0, v_ErrorText, 'SQLERRM(0)');

  /* SQLERRM(100) */
  v_ErrorText := SUBSTR(SQLERRM(100), 1, 200);
  INSERT INTO log_table (code, message, info)
    VALUES (100, v_ErrorText, 'SQLERRM(100)');

  /* SQLERRM(10) */
  v_ErrorText := SUBSTR(SQLERRM(10), 1, 200);
  INSERT INTO log_table (code, message, info)
    VALUES (10, v_ErrorText, 'SQLERRM(10)');

  /* SQLERRM with no argument */
  v_ErrorText := SUBSTR(SQLERRM, 1, 200);
  INSERT INTO log_table (code, message, info)
    VALUES (NULL, v_ErrorText, 'SQLERRM with no argument');

  /* SQLERRM(-1) */
  v_ErrorText := SUBSTR(SQLERRM(-1), 1, 200);
  INSERT INTO log_table (code, message, info)
    VALUES (-1, v_ErrorText, 'SQLERRM(-1)');

  /* SQLERRM(-54) */
  v_ErrorText := SUBSTR(SQLERRM(-54), 1, 200);
  INSERT INTO log_table (code, message, info)
    VALUES (-54, v_ErrorText, 'SQLERRM(-54)');

END;
```

If we were to run the preceding example, the **log_table** table would contain the values in Table 6-3.

The EXCEPTION_INIT Pragma

You can associate a named exception with a particular Oracle error. This gives you the ability to trap this error specifically, rather than via an OTHERS handler. This is done via the EXCEPTION_INIT pragma. For more information on pragmas and how they are used, see Chapter 2. The EXCEPTION_INIT pragma is used as follows:

PRAGMA EXCEPTION_INIT (*exception_name, Oracle error number*);

where *exception name* is the name of an exception declared prior to the pragma, and *Oracle error number* is the desired error code to be associated with this named exception. This pragma must be in the declarative section. The following example will raise the **e_MissingNull** user-defined exception if the "ORA-1400: mandatory NOT NULL column missing or NULL during insert" error is encountered at run time:

```
DECLARE
  e_MissingNull EXCEPTION;
  PRAGMA EXCEPTION_INIT(e_MissingNull, -1400);
BEGIN
  INSERT INTO students (id) VALUES (NULL);
EXCEPTION
  WHEN e_MissingNull then
    INSERT INTO log_table (info) VALUES ('ORA-1400 occurred');
END;
```

Using RAISE_APPLICATION_ERROR

You can use the built-in function RAISE_APPLICATION_ERROR to create your own error messages, which can be more descriptive than named exceptions. User-defined errors are passed out of the block the same way as Oracle errors to the calling environment. The syntax of RAISE_APPLICATION_ERROR is

RAISE_APPLICATION_ERROR(*error number, error message,* [*keep errors*]);

where *error number* is a parameter between –20,000 and –20,999, *error message* is the text associated with this error, and *keep errors* is a boolean value.

Code	Message	SQLERRM Function Used
0	ORA-0000: normal, successful completion	SQLERRM(0)
100	ORA-01403: no data found	SQLERRM(100)
10	User-Defined Exception	SQLERRM(10)
NULL	ORA-0000: normal, successful completion	SQLERRM with no argument
−1	ORA-00001: unique constraint (.) violated	SQLERRM(−1)
−54	ORA-00054: resource busy and acquire with NOWAIT specified	SQLERRM(−54)

TABLE 6-3. *Log_table Contents*

The *error_message* parameter must be less than 512 characters. The boolean parameter *keep_errors,* is optional. If *keep_errors* is TRUE, the new error is added to the list of errors already raised (if one exists). If it is FALSE, which is the default, the new error will replace the current list of errors. For example, the following procedure checks to see if there is enough room in a class before registering a student:

```
CREATE OR REPLACE PROCEDURE Register (
  /* Registers the student identified by the p_StudentID
     parameter in the classidentified by the p_Department and
     p_Course parameters. Before calling ClassPackage.AddStudent,
     which actually adds the student to the class, this
     procedure verifies that there is room in the class,
     and that the class exists. */
  p_StudentID IN students.id%TYPE,
  p_Department IN classes.department%TYPE,
  p_Course IN classes.course%TYPE) AS

  v_CurrentStudents NUMBER;  -- Current number of students in the class
  v_MaxStudents NUMBER;      -- Maximum number of students in the class
```

```
BEGIN
  /* Determine the current number of students registered, and the
     maximum number of students allowed to register. */
  SELECT current_students, max_students
    INTO v_CurrentStudents, v_MaxStudents
    FROM classes
    WHERE course = p_Course
    AND department = p_Department;

  /* Make sure there is enough room for this additional student. */
  IF v_CurrentStudents + 1 > v_MaxStudents THEN
    RAISE_APPLICATION_ERROR(-20000, 'Can''t add more students to
                            ' || p_Department || ' ' || p_Course);
  END IF;

  /* Add the student to the class. */
  ClassPackage.AddStudent(p_StudentID, p_Department, p_Course);

EXCEPTION
  WHEN NO_DATA_FOUND THEN
    /* Class information passed to this procedure doesn't exist.
       Raise an error to let the calling program know of this. */
    RAISE_APPLICATION_ERROR(-20001, p_Department || ' ' ||
                            p_Course || ' doesn''t exist!');
END Register;
```

The **Register** procedure uses RAISE_APPLICATION_ERROR in two different places. The first thing the procedure does is to determine the current number of students registered for the class. This is done via the SELECT..INTO statement. If this statement returns NO_DATA_FOUND, control passes to the exception handler, and RAISE_APPLICATION_ERROR is used to notify the user that the class doesn't exist. If the class does exist, the procedure then verifies that there is room for the new student. If there isn't, RAISE_APPLICATION_ERROR is again used to notify the user that there isn't enough room. Finally, if there is enough room, the student is actually added to the class. The packaged procedure **ClassPackage.AddStudent**, described in Chapter 5, does this.

Figure 6-2 shows the output when we call the **Register** procedure from SQL*Plus. Note the select statement in the figure—this shows that History 101 is full. So when the procedure is called, we should get an error indicating that there is no more room. This is in fact what happens, and the error is returned as follows:

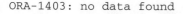
ORA-20000: Can't add more students to HIS 101

Compare the output in Figure 6-2 to the output shown in Figure 6-3, which illustrates an anonymous block executed via SQL*Plus. This block simply raises the NO_DATA_FOUND exception. Note that predefined exceptions can also be raised explicitly, if desired. The error is returned to the screen as follows:

ORA-1403: no data found

The format of both outputs is the same—an Oracle error number and text associated with it. Note that both also include an ORA-6512 statement indicating the line that caused the error. So RAISE_APPLICATION_ERROR can be used to return error conditions to the user in a manner consistent with other Oracle errors. This is very useful, because no special error handling is necessary for user-defined errors versus predefined ones.

Exception Propagation

Exceptions can occur in the declarative, executable, or the exception section of a PL/SQL block. We have seen in the previous section what happens when

```
┌────────────────────────────────────────────────────────────┐
│ ═                        Oracle SQL*Plus              ▼ ▲    │
├────────────────────────────────────────────────────────────┤
│ File  Edit  Search  Options  Help                        ▲  │
│ SQL> select department, course, max_students, current_students │
│   2  from classes;                                           │
│                                                              │
│ DEP    COURSE MAX_STUDENTS CURRENT_STUDENTS                  │
│ ---    ------ ------------ ----------------                  │
│ HIS    101         30              30                        │
│                                                              │
│ SQL> exec Register(10000, 'HIS', 101);                       │
│ begin Register(10000, 'HIS', 101); end;                      │
│                                                              │
│ *                                                            │
│ ERROR at line 1:                                             │
│ ORA-20000: Can't add more students to HIS-101                │
│ ORA-06512: at "EXAMPLE.REGISTER", line 16                    │
│ ORA-06512: at line 1                                         │
│                                                              │
│                                                              │
│ SQL>                                                      ▼  │
│ ◄                                                         ►  │
└────────────────────────────────────────────────────────────┘
```

FIGURE 6-2.   *Results of calling the Register procedure*

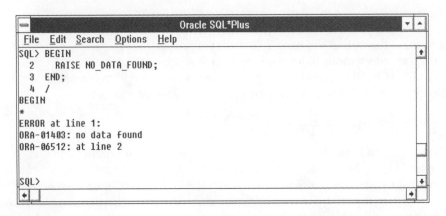

FIGURE 6-3. *Results of an anonymous block that raises NO_DATA_FOUND*

exceptions are raised in the executable portion of the block, and there is a handler for the exception. But what if there isn't a handler, or the exception is raised from a different section of the block? The process that governs this is known as *exception propagation*.

Exceptions Raised in the Executable Section

When an exception is raised in the executable section of a block, PL/SQL uses the following algorithm to determine which exception handler to invoke.

1. If the current block has a handler for the exception, execute it and complete the block successfully. Control then passes to the enclosing block.

2. If there is no handler for the current exception, propagate the exception by raising it in the enclosing block. Step 1 will then be executed for the enclosing block.

Before we can examine this algorithm in detail, we need to define an *enclosing block*. A block can be embedded inside another block. In this case, the outer block encloses the inner block. For example:

```
DECLARE
  -- Begin outer block.
  ...
BEGIN
  ...
  DECLARE
    -- Begin inner block 1. This is embedded in the outer block.
  ...
  BEGIN
    ...
  END;
  ...
  BEGIN
    -- Begin inner block 2. This is also embedded in the outer
block.
    -- Note that this block doesn't have a declarative part.
    ...
  END;
  ...
  -- End outer block.
END;
```

In the preceding listing, inner blocks 1 and 2 are both enclosed by the outer block. Any unhandled exceptions in blocks 1 and 2 will be propagated to the outer block.

A procedure call will also create an enclosing block, and is illustrated in the following example.

```
BEGIN
  -- Begin outer block.
  -- Call a procedure. The procedure will be enclosed by
  -- this outer block.
  F(...);
END;
```

If procedure **F** raises an unhandled exception, it will be propagated to the outer block, since it encloses the procedure.

Different cases for the exception propagation algorithm are illustrated in examples 1, 2, and 3, in the following sections.

Propagation Example 1
The example shown here illustrates application of rule 1. Exception A is raised and handled in the sub-block. Control then returns to the outer block.

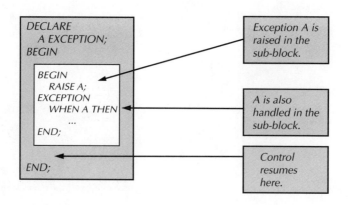

Propagation Example 2

In this example, rule 2 is applied for the sub-block. The exception is propagated to the enclosing block, where rule 1 is applied. The enclosing block then completes successfully.

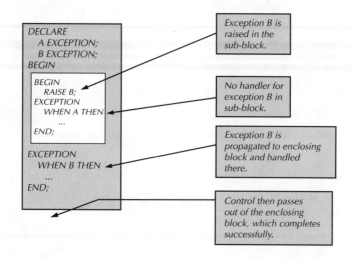

Propagation Example 3

Here, rule 2 is applied for the sub-block. The exception is propagated to the enclosing block, where there is still no handler for it. Rule 2 is applied again, and the enclosing block completes unsuccessfully with an unhandled exception.

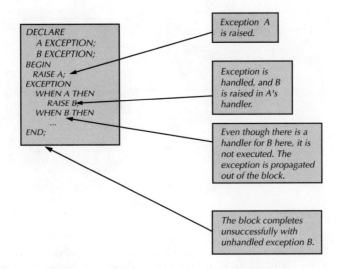

| ```
DECLARE
    A EXCEPTION;
    B EXCEPTION;
BEGIN
    RAISE A;
EXCEPTION
    WHEN A THEN
        RAISE B;
    WHEN B THEN
        ...
END;
``` | *Exception A is raised.* |
	Exception is handled, and B is raised in A's handler.
	Even though there is a handler for B here, it is not executed. The exception is propagated out of the block.
	The block completes unsuccessfully with unhandled exception B.

Exceptions Raised in the Declarative Section

If an assignment in the declarative section raises an exception, the exception
is immediately propagated to the enclosing block. Once there, the rules
given in the previous section are applied to propagate the exception further.
Even if there is a handler in the current block, it is *not* executed. Examples 4 and 5
illustrate this.

Propagation Example 4

In this example, the VALUE_ERROR exception is raised by the declaration

```
v_Number NUMBER(3) := 'ABC';
```

This exception is immediately propagated to the enclosing block. Even though
there is an OTHERS exception, it is not executed. If this block had been enclosed
in an outer block, the outer block would have been able to catch this exception.
(Example 5 illustrates this scenario.)
```

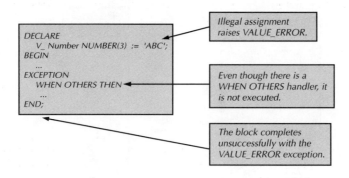

Propagation Example 5

Similar to example 4, the VALUE_ERROR exception is raised in the declarative section of the inner block. The exception is immediately propagated to the outer block. Since the outer block has an OTHERS exception handler, the exception is handled and the outer block completes successfully.

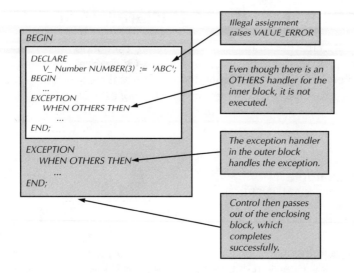

Exceptions Raised in the Exception Section

Exceptions can also be raised while in an exception handler, either explicitly via the RAISE statement or implicitly via a run-time error. In either case, the exception is propagated immediately to the enclosing block, like exceptions raised in the declarative section. This is done because only one exception can be "active" at a time in the exception section. As soon as one is handled, another can be raised. But there cannot be more than one exception raised simultaneously. Examples 6, 7, and 8 illustrate this scenario.

Propagation Example 6

In this example, exception A is raised and then handled. But in the exception handler for A, exception B is raised. This exception is immediately propagated to the outer block, bypassing the handler for B. Similar to example 5, if this block had been enclosed in an outer block, this outer block could have caught exception B. (Example 7 illustrates the latter case.)

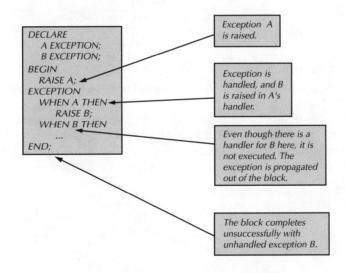

Propagation Example 7

Similar to example 6, exception B is raised in the handler for exception A. This exception is immediately propagated to the enclosing block, bypassing the inner handler for B. However, in example 7 we have an outer block that handles exception B and completes successfully.

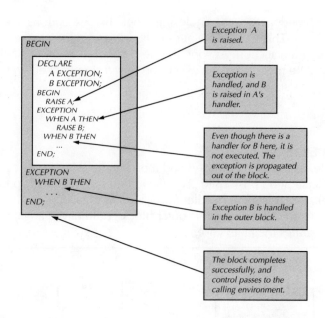

Propagation Example 8

As examples 6 and 7 illustrate, RAISE can be used to raise another exception inside a handler. In an exception handler, RAISE can also be used without an argument. If RAISE doesn't have an argument, the current exception is propagated to the enclosing block. This technique is useful for logging the error and/or doing any necessary cleanup because of it, and then notifying the enclosing block that it occurred. We will see this technique again in Chapter 10. Example 8 illustrates this final scenario.

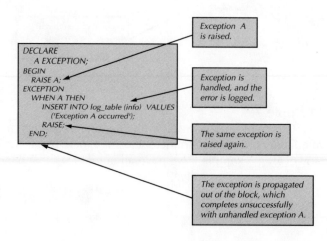

Exception Guidelines

This section contains guidelines and tips on how best to use exceptions in your programs. These guidelines include the scope of exceptions, avoiding unhandled exceptions, and how to identify which statement raised a given exception. These guidelines should help you use exceptions more effectively in your own programs, and avoid some common pitfalls.

Scope of Exceptions

Exceptions are scoped just like variables. If a user-defined exception is propagated out of its scope, it can no longer be referenced by name. The next listing illustrates this.

```
DECLARE
  ...
BEGIN
  ...
  DECLARE
    e_UserDefinedException EXCEPTION;
  BEGIN
    RAISE e_UserDefinedException;
  END;
EXCEPTION
  /* e_UserDefinedException is out of scope here - can only be
     handled by an OTHERS handler */
  WHEN OTHERS THEN
    /* Handle error */
END;
```

In general, if a user-defined error is to be propagated out of a block, it is best to define the exception in a package so that it will still be visible outside the block, or to use RAISE_APPLICATION_ERROR instead. See the section "Using RAISE_APPLICATION_ERROR" earlier in this chapter for more information. If we create a package called **Globals** and define **e_UserDefinedException** in this package, the exception will still be visible in the outer block. For example:

```
CREATE OR REPLACE PACKAGE Globals
  /* This package contains global declarations. Objects declared
     here will be visible via qualified references for any other
     blocks or procedures. Note that this package does not have
     a package body. */

  /* A user defined exception. */
  e_UserDefinedException EXCEPTION;
END Globals;
```

Given package **Globals**, we can rewrite the preceding listing as:

```
DECLARE
  ...
BEGIN
  ...
  BEGIN
    /* Note that we must qualify e_UserDefinedException with the
       package name */
    RAISE Globals.e_UserDefinedException;
  END;
EXCEPTION
  /* Since e_UserDefinedException is still visible, we can handle
     it explicitly */
  WHEN Globals.e_UserDefinedException THEN
    /* Handle error */
END;
```

Package **Globals** can also be used for common PL/SQL tables, variables, and types, in addition to exceptions. See Chapter 5 for more information on packages.

Avoiding Unhandled Exceptions

It is good programming practice to avoid unhandled exceptions. This can be done via an OTHERS handler at the topmost level of your program. This handler may simply log the error and where it occurred. This way, you ensure that no error will go undetected. For example:

```
DECLARE
  v_ErrorNumber NUMBER;      -- Variable to hold the error number
  v_ErrorText VARCHAR2(200); -- Variable to hold the error message text
BEGIN
  /* Normal PL/SQL processing */
  ...
EXCEPTION
  WHEN OTHERS THEN
    /* Log all exceptions so we complete successfully */
    v_ErrorNumber := SQLCODE;
    v_ErrorText := SUBSTR(SQLERRM, 1, 200);
    INSERT INTO log_table (code, message, info) VALUES
      (v_ErrorNumber, v_ErrorText, 'Oracle error occurred');
END;
```

Masking Location of the Error

Since the same exception section is examined for the entire block, it can be
difficult to determine which SQL statement caused the error. Consider the
following example:

```
BEGIN
  SELECT ...
  SELECT ...
  SELECT ...
EXCEPTION
  WHEN NO_DATA_FOUND THEN
    -- Which select statement raised the exception?
END;
```

There are two methods to solve this. The first is to increment a counter
identifying the SQL statement:

```
DECLARE
  v_SelectCounter NUMBER := 1;  -- Variable to hold the select
                                -- statement number
BEGIN
  SELECT ...
  v_SelectCounter := 2;
  SELECT ...
  v_SelectCounter := 3;
  SELECT ...
```

```
EXCEPTION
   WHEN NO_DATA_FOUND THEN
      INSERT INTO log_table (info) VALUES ('No data found in select
                                    ' || v_SelectCounter);
END;
```

The second method is to put each statement into its own sub-block:

```
BEGIN
   BEGIN
      SELECT ...
   EXCEPTION
      WHEN NO_DATA_FOUND THEN
         INSERT INTO log_table (info) VALUES ('No data found
                                    in select 1');
   END;
   BEGIN
      SELECT ...
   EXCEPTION
      WHEN NO_DATA_FOUND THEN
         INSERT INTO log_table (info) VALUES ('No data found
                                    in select 2');
   END;
   BEGIN
      SELECT ...
   EXCEPTION
      WHEN NO_DATA_FOUND THEN
         INSERT INTO log_table (info) VALUES ('No data found
                                    in select 3');
   END;
END;
```

Summary

This chapter explained how PL/SQL programs can detect and react intelligently to run-time errors. The mechanism provided by PL/SQL to do this includes exceptions and exception handlers. We have seen how exceptions are defined and how they correspond to either user-defined errors or predefined Oracle errors. We have also discussed the rules for exception propagation, including exceptions raised in all parts of a PL/SQL block. The chapter concluded with guidelines on using exceptions.

CHAPTER 7

PL/SQL Execution Environments

In Chapters 2 through 6, we covered the basics of PL/SQL. Chapters 7 through 12 explain how PL/SQL is used and present some of the advanced features of the language. This chapter includes a discussion of PL/SQL execution environments. PL/SQL blocks can be run entirely on the client, without interacting with the database server. They can also be submitted from a client program to run on the server. Depending on the environment, different features are available for the control of the PL/SQL block.

Different PL/SQL Engines

PL/SQL has been available in the database server since version 6 of Oracle. This means that both SQL statements and PL/SQL blocks can be sent to the database and processed. As described in Chapter 1, Oracle7 contains version 2 of PL/SQL. A client application, written using either Oracle's development tools or tools by another vendor, can issue both SQL statements and PL/SQL blocks to the server. SQL*Plus is an example of such a client application in which SQL statements and PL/SQL blocks entered interactively at the SQL prompt are sent to the server for execution.

Figure 7-1 illustrates this scenario. As you can see, both the PL/SQL block and the SQL statement are sent over the network to the server. Once there, the SQL statement is sent directly to the SQL statement executor contained in the server. The PL/SQL block is parsed and executed by the PL/SQL engine. Any SQL statements inside the block (such as the SELECT statement) are sent to the same SQL statement executor. The procedural statements (such as the assignment) are processed within the PL/SQL engine itself.

In addition to the PL/SQL engine on the server, several of Oracle's tools contain a PL/SQL engine. The development tool itself runs on the client, not the server. The PL/SQL engine also runs on the client. With client-side PL/SQL, procedural statements within PL/SQL blocks are run on the client and not sent to the server. As an example, Oracle Forms (bundled as part of the Developer 2000 suite of Oracle products) contains a separate PL/SQL engine. Other tools in this suite, such as Oracle Reports or Oracle Graphics, also contain a PL/SQL engine. This engine is different from the PL/SQL on the server. PL/SQL blocks are contained within a client-side application written using these tools. An Oracle Forms application, for example, contains triggers and procedures. These are executed on the client, and only the SQL statements within them are sent to the server for processing. The local PL/SQL engine on the client processes the procedural statements, as illustrated in Figure 7-2.

SQL statements issued by the application (the UPDATE statement) are sent directly over the network to the SQL statement executor on the server, as before. However, the client processes PL/SQL blocks locally. Any procedural statements can be processed without network traffic. SQL statements within PL/SQL blocks (such as SELECT) are also sent to the server. The rationale for this situation is discussed later in this chapter, in the section "Client-side PL/SQL."

Implications of Client-side PL/SQL

In this scenario, there are two separate PL/SQL engines, which communicate between each other. For example, a trigger within a form (running in client-side

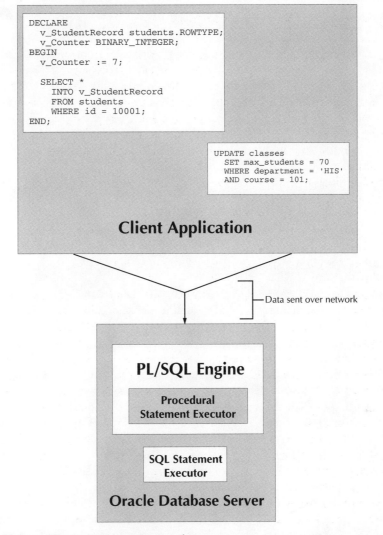

```
DECLARE
  v_StudentRecord students.ROWTYPE;
  v_Counter BINARY_INTEGER;
BEGIN
  v_Counter := 7;

  SELECT *
    INTO v_StudentRecord
    FROM students
    WHERE id = 10001;
END;
```

```
UPDATE classes
  SET max_students = 70
  WHERE department = 'HIS'
  AND course = 101;
```

Client Application

Data sent over network

PL/SQL Engine

Procedural Statement Executor

SQL Statement Executor

Oracle Database Server

FIGURE 7-1. *The PL/SQL engine on the server*

PL/SQL) can call a procedure that is stored within the database (running in server-side PL/SQL). Communications such as these take place through remote procedure calls. A similar mechanism is used to communicate between PL/SQL engines in two different servers, through database links. The dependencies between the various PL/SQL objects are discussed in Chapter 5.

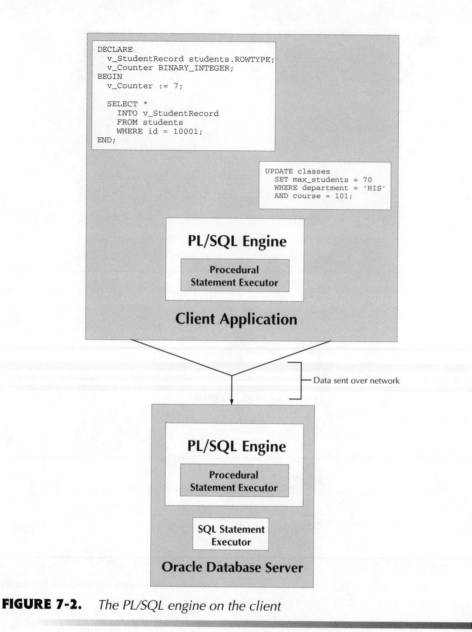

```
DECLARE
  v_StudentRecord students.ROWTYPE;
  v_Counter BINARY_INTEGER;
BEGIN
  v_Counter := 7;

  SELECT *
    INTO v_StudentRecord
    FROM students
    WHERE id = 10001;
END;
```

```
UPDATE classes
  SET max_students = 70
  WHERE department = 'HIS'
  AND course = 101;
```

PL/SQL Engine

**Procedural
Statement Executor**

Client Application

Data sent over network

PL/SQL Engine

**Procedural
Statement Executor**

**SQL Statement
Executor**

Oracle Database Server

FIGURE 7-2. *The PL/SQL engine on the client*

In general, the two PL/SQL engines may be different versions. The current versions of Oracle's client-side tools (Developer 2000 version 1.2, for example) use PL/SQL version 1, while the server uses PL/SQL version 2. This implies that features contained in PL/SQL version 2, such as user-defined tables and records and fixed-length CHAR datatypes, among others, can't be used in client-side PL/SQL.

> **TIP**
> When PL/SQL 2 becomes available for client-side applications, the PL/SQL blocks contained within these applications will have to be migrated to version 2 syntax and semantics. One of the main differences is the behavior of the CHAR datatype. In version 1 of PL/SQL, both CHAR and VARCHAR2 variables are variable length strings. In version 2, CHAR variables are fixed length, and VARCHAR2 variables are variable length. In order to make migration easier, avoid using CHAR variables in client-side PL/SQL, and use VARCHAR or VARCHAR2 instead.

Server-side PL/SQL

This section covers PL/SQL blocks that run on the server. They can be submitted to the server from various client tools, including SQL*Plus, the Oracle precompilers, and OCI. Applications written in tools that contain a PL/SQL engine, such as Oracle Forms, can also make calls to server-side PL/SQL.

SQL*Plus

SQL*Plus allows the user to enter SQL statements and PL/SQL blocks interactively from a prompt. These statements are sent directly to the database, and the results are returned to the screen. Because of its interactive nature, SQL*Plus is perhaps the most convenient way to manipulate PL/SQL on the server. For more information on SQL*Plus and its commands not covered in this section, see the *SQL*Plus User's Guide and Reference.*

SQL*Plus commands are not case-sensitive. For example, all of the following commands declare bind variables:

```
SQL> VARIABLE v_Num NUMBER
SQL> variable v_Char char(3)
SQL> vaRIAbLe v_Varchar VarCHAR2(5)
```

Manipulating Blocks in SQL*Plus

When you execute an SQL statement in SQL*Plus, the semicolon terminates the statement. The semicolon is not part of the statement itself—it is the statement terminator. When SQL*Plus reads the semicolon, it knows that the statement is complete and sends it to the database. On the other hand, with a PL/SQL block, the semicolon is a syntactic part of the block itself—it is not a statement terminator. When you enter the DECLARE or BEGIN keyword, SQL*Plus detects this and knows that you are running a PL/SQL block, rather than a SQL statement. But SQL*Plus still needs to know when the block has ended. This is done with a forward slash, which is short for the SQL*Plus RUN command.

Notice the slash after the PL/SQL block that updates the **registered_students** table in Figure 7-3. The SELECT statement after the block does not need the slash because the semicolon is present.

Substitution Variables
PL/SQL doesn't really have any capabilities for input from the user and output from the screen. There is a built-in package, DBMS_OUTPUT, which remedies PL/SQL output. This package is discussed in detail in Chapter 8. PL/SQL 2.3 also has a built-in package, UTL_FILE (discussed in Chapter 11), which allows input from and output to operating system files. However, SQL*Plus itself has a mechanism for accepting input from the user. Input is accomplished through *substitution variables*. A textual substitution of the variable is done by SQL*Plus before the PL/SQL block

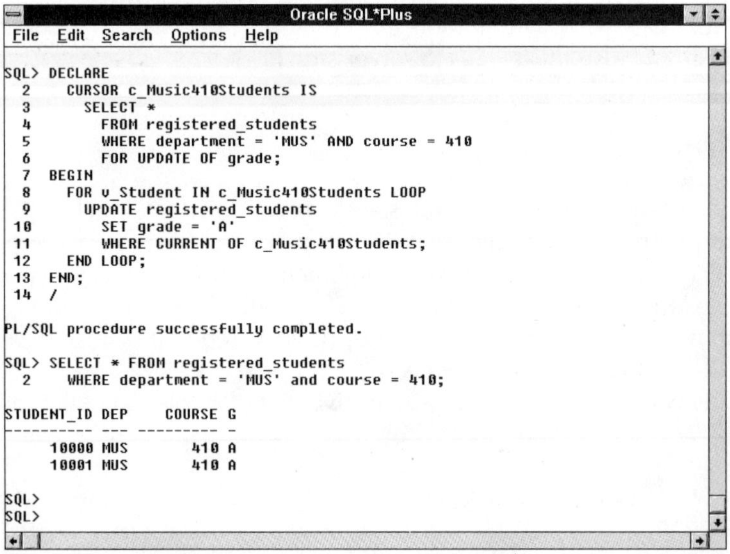

FIGURE 7-3. *PL/SQL in SQL*Plus*

or SQL statement is sent to the server, similar to the behavior of C macros. Substitution variables are delineated by the ampersand (&) character.

Figure 7-4 illustrates the use of substitution variables. The same block is run twice, each time initializing **v_StudentID** to a different value. The user inputs the values 10004 and 10005, and they are textually replaced in the block for **&student_id**.

> **NOTE**
> No memory is actually allocated for substitution variables. SQL*Plus replaces the substitution variable with the value you input before the block is sent to the database for execution. Because of this, substitution variables can be used for input only. Bind variables, however, can be used for input or output.

Although substitution variables can be used for input only, they can be used anywhere in the SQL statement or PL/SQL block. Figure 7-5 illustrates this. The substitution variables **&columns** and **&where_clause** are used for structural parts of the statements themselves—table and column names, for example. The only way to

```
                        Oracle SQL*Plus
 File  Edit  Search  Options  Help
SQL> DECLARE
  2      v_StudentID students.id%TYPE := &student_id;
  3   BEGIN
  4      Register(v_StudentID, 'CS', 102);
  5   END;
  6   /
Enter value for student_id: 10004
old    2:    v_StudentID students.id%TYPE := &student_id;
new    2:    v_StudentID students.id%TYPE := 10004;

PL/SQL procedure successfully completed.

SQL> DECLARE
  2      v_StudentID students.id%TYPE := &student_id;
  3   BEGIN
  4      Register(v_StudentID, 'CS', 102);
  5   END;
  6   /
Enter value for student_id: 10005
old    2:    v_StudentID students.id%TYPE := &student_id;
new    2:    v_StudentID students.id%TYPE := 10005;

PL/SQL procedure successfully completed.

SQL>
```

FIGURE 7-4. *SQL*Plus substitution variables*

```
━                          Oracle SQL*Plus                          ▾ ↕
 File  Edit  Search  Options  Help
SQL> SELECT &columns FROM CLASSES;                                  ↑
Enter value for columns: department, course
old   1: SELECT &columns FROM CLASSES
new   1: SELECT department, course FROM CLASSES

DEP   COURSE
---   --------
HIS      101
HIS      301
CS       101
ECN      203
CS       102
MUS      410
ECN      101
NUT      307

8 rows selected.

SQL> SELECT first_name, last_name
  2     FROM students
  3     WHERE &where_clause;
Enter value for where_clause: ID = 10000
old   3:    WHERE &where_clause
new   3:    WHERE ID = 10000

FIRST_NAME           LAST_NAME
-------------------- --------------------
Scott                Smith                                          ↓
 ◄                                                                  ►
```

FIGURE 7-5. *More substitution variables*

accomplish this in pure PL/SQL is to use the DBMS_SQL package, explained in Chapter 10.

SQL*Plus Bind Variables

SQL*Plus can also allocate memory. This storage can be used inside PL/SQL blocks and SQL statements. Because this storage is allocated outside the block, it can be used for more than one block in succession, and it can be printed after a block completes. This storage is known as a *bind variable*, illustrated in Figure 7-6. The **v_Count** bind variable is allocated using the SQL*Plus command VARIABLE.

NOTE
The SQL*Plus VARIABLE command is valid only from the SQL prompt, and not inside a PL/SQL block. Inside the block, the bind variable is delimited by the leading colon rather than an ampersand. After the block, the PRINT command shows the value of the variable. The only types valid for SQL*Plus bind variables are VARCHAR2, CHAR, and NUMBER. If the length isn't specified for bind variables of type VARCHAR2 or CHAR, the length defaults to 1. NUMBER bind variables *cannot* be constrained by a precision or scale.

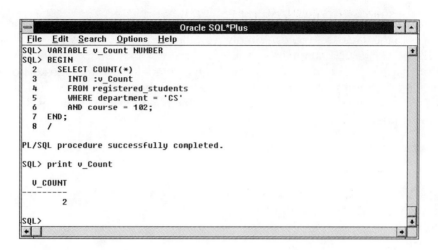

```
                          Oracle SQL*Plus
 File   Edit   Search   Options   Help
SQL> VARIABLE v_Count NUMBER
SQL> BEGIN
  2      SELECT COUNT(*)
  3         INTO :v_Count
  4         FROM registered_students
  5         WHERE department = 'CS'
  6         AND course = 102;
  7  END;
  8  /

PL/SQL procedure successfully completed.

SQL> print v_Count

  V_COUNT
---------
        2

SQL>
```

FIGURE 7-6. *SQL*Plus bind variables*

Calling Stored Procedures with EXECUTE

A stored procedure call must be made from the executable or exception-handling
section of a PL/SQL block. SQL*Plus provides a useful shorthand for this
syntax—the EXECUTE command. All that EXECUTE does is to take its arguments,
put BEGIN before them, and END; after. The resulting block is then submitted to
the database. For example, if we enter

```
SQL> EXECUTE Register(10006, 'CS', 102)
```

from the SQL prompt, the PL/SQL block

```
BEGIN Register(10006, 'CS', 102); END;
```

would actually be sent to the database. A semicolon is optional after the EXECUTE
command. This is true of all the SQL*Plus commands—if a semicolon is present, it
is ignored. Like PRINT or VARIABLE, EXECUTE is a SQL*Plus command and thus is
not valid inside a PL/SQL block.

Using Files

SQL*Plus can save the current PL/SQL block or SQL statement to a file, and this
file can then be read back in and executed. This useful feature is valuable both
during development of a PL/SQL program and during the later execution of it. For
example, you can store a CREATE OR REPLACE command in a file. This way,

any modifications to the procedure can be done to the file. In order to save the changes in the database, you can simply read the file into SQL*Plus.

The SQL*Plus GET command reads a file from disk into the local buffer. A forward slash will then run it, as if it had been entered directly from the keyboard. If the file contains a slash at the end, however, it can be read in and run using the at sign (@) shortcut. For example, assume that the file register.sql contains the following lines:

```
VARIABLE v_Count NUMBER

BEGIN
  Register(&student_id, 'CS', 102);
  SELECT COUNT(*)
    INTO :v_Count
    FROM registered_students
    WHERE department = 'CS'
    AND course = 102;
END;
/

PRINT v_Count
```

We can now execute this file from the SQL prompt with

```
SQL> @register
```

The output from this is shown in Figure 7-7. The SET ECHO ON command tells SQL*Plus to echo the contents of the file to the screen as they are read from the file.

Using the SHOW ERRORS Command

As discussed in Chapter 5, when a stored subprogram is created, information about it is stored in the data dictionary. Specifically, any compile errors are stored in the **user_errors** data dictionary view. SQL*Plus provides a useful command, SHOW ERRORS, which will query this view and report the errors. Figure 7-8 illustrates this. SHOW ERRORS can be used after SQL*Plus reports this message:

```
Warning: Procedure created with compilation errors.
```

Oracle Precompilers

Using the Oracle precompilers, SQL statements and PL/SQL blocks can be contained inside 3GL programs written in C, C++, Cobol, Pascal, Fortran, PL/1, and

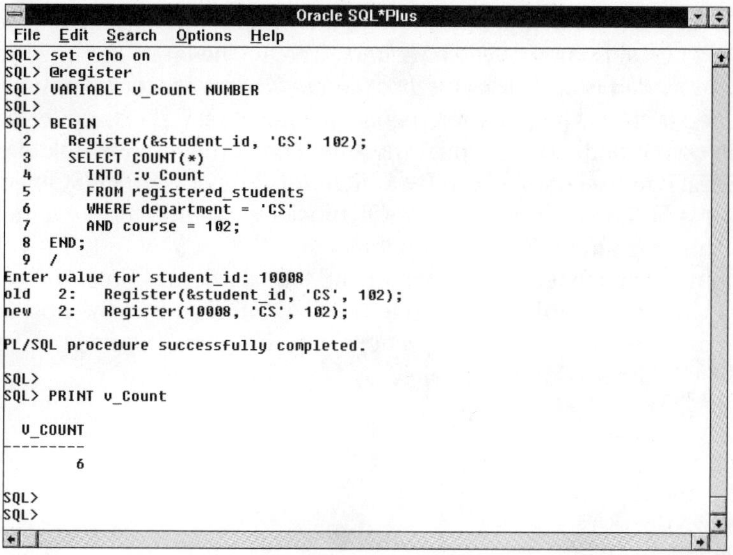

```
⊟                          Oracle SQL*Plus                          ▼ ◆
 File   Edit  Search  Options  Help
SQL> set echo on                                                        ▲
SQL> @register
SQL> VARIABLE v_Count NUMBER
SQL>
SQL> BEGIN
  2     Register(&student_id, 'CS', 102);
  3     SELECT COUNT(*)
  4       INTO :v_Count
  5       FROM registered_students
  6       WHERE department = 'CS'
  7       AND course = 102;
  8  END;
  9  /
Enter value for student_id: 10008
old   2:    Register(&student_id, 'CS', 102);
new   2:    Register(10008, 'CS', 102);

PL/SQL procedure successfully completed.

SQL>
SQL> PRINT v_Count

  V_COUNT
---------
        6

SQL>                                                                    ▼
SQL>
◆                                                                     ◆
```

FIGURE 7-7.   *Using a file in SQL*Plus*

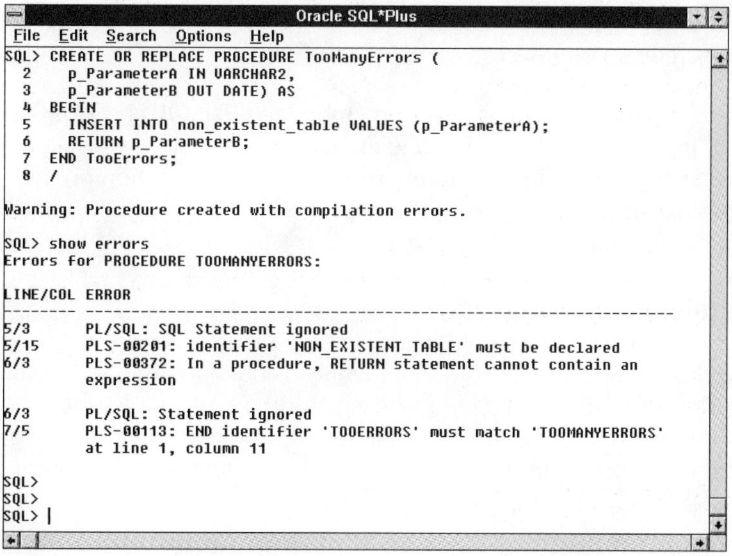

```
⊟                          Oracle SQL*Plus                          ▼ ◆
 File   Edit  Search  Options  Help
SQL> CREATE OR REPLACE PROCEDURE TooManyErrors (                        ▲
  2     p_ParameterA IN VARCHAR2,
  3     p_ParameterB OUT DATE) AS
  4  BEGIN
  5     INSERT INTO non_existent_table VALUES (p_ParameterA);
  6     RETURN p_ParameterB;
  7  END TooErrors;
  8  /

Warning: Procedure created with compilation errors.

SQL> show errors
Errors for PROCEDURE TOOMANYERRORS:

LINE/COL ERROR
-------- ------------------------------------------------------------
5/3      PL/SQL: SQL Statement ignored
5/15     PLS-00201: identifier 'NON_EXISTENT_TABLE' must be declared
6/3      PLS-00372: In a procedure, RETURN statement cannot contain an
         expression

6/3      PL/SQL: Statement ignored
7/5      PLS-00113: END identifier 'TOOERRORS' must match 'TOOMANYERRORS'
         at line 1, column 11

SQL>
SQL>
SQL> |                                                                  ▼
◆                                                                     ◆
```

FIGURE 7-8.   *Using SHOW ERRORS*

Ada. The precompilers are known as Pro*C, Pro*Cobol, Pro*Pascal, and so on. This form of PL/SQL is known as *embedded PL/SQL*. The language in which PL/SQL is embedded is known as the *host language*. The precompiler will translate the embedded SQL and PL/SQL statements into calls to the precompiler's run time library. The output of the precompiler must then be compiled and linked with this library to create an executable. Similar to SQL*Plus, there is no PL/SQL engine on the client—the SQL statements and PL/SQL blocks are sent to the server to be executed. The program itself resides on the client.

Communication between the program and the database is done through *host variables*. These are variables declared according to the rules of the host language, except that they are inside a special section of the program known as the declare section. The declare section is delimited by

```
EXEC SQL BEGIN DECLARE SECTION;
```

and

```
EXEC SQL END DECLARE SECTION;
```

in the source code.

NOTE
With version 2.0 and higher of Pro*C/C++, the declare section is no longer required. Any host variable can be used in an embedded SQL statement or PL/SQL block whether or not it is declared in a declare section.

There are several differences between embedded PL/SQL and PL/SQL entered interactively in SQL*Plus. These include the use of bind variables, statement terminators, and precompiler requirements. For more information on the Oracle precompilers, see the *Programmer's Guide to the Pro*C/C++ Precompiler*, or the *Programmer's Guide to the Oracle Precompilers*.

Bind Variables in Precompilers
Variables that are declared in the declare section are legal to use inside embedded PL/SQL blocks and embedded SQL statements. Inside of an embedded statement, the bind variables are delimited by a leading colon. For example, the following Pro*C program fragment calls the **Register** stored procedure. For the benefit of readers who may not be familiar with C, this code is more heavily commented than usual.

```
EXEC SQL BEGIN DECLARE SECTION;
  /* Declare C variables. */
  VARCHAR v_Department[4]; /* The VARCHAR pseudo-type is
                              available only in Pro*C, and is
                              converted into a record type with
                              two fields - .arr and .len */
  int v_Course;           /* v_Course is an integer. */
  int v_StudentID;        /* So is v_StudentID. */
EXEC SQL END DECLARE SECTION;


  /* Initialize the host variables. Here we are just assigning
     to them, but they could be read from a file, accepted from
     user input, etc. For the VARCHAR variables, the string is
     copied into the .arr field, and the length of the string (3
     in this case) is assigned to the .len field. */
  strcpy(v_Department.arr, "ECN");
  v_Department.len = 3;
  v_Course = 101;
  v_StudentID = 10006;


  /* Begin the embedded PL/SQL block. Note the EXEC SQL EXECUTE
     and END-EXEC; keywords, which delimit the block for the
     precompiler. */
EXEC SQL EXECUTE
  BEGIN
    Register(:v_Department, :v_Course, :v_StudentID);
  END;
END-EXEC;
```

Inside the embedded block, the host variables **v_Department**, **v_Course**, and **v_StudentID** are prefixed by colons. If they were not, the program would not precompile and would return this error:

```
PLS-201: identifier must be declared
```

Embedding a Block
Notice how the PL/SQL block itself is delimited in the preceding program fragment. An embedded PL/SQL block starts with the keywords

```
EXEC SQL EXECUTE
```

and ends with

```
END-EXEC;
```

The semicolon after the END-EXEC is required. Between these two keywords, place an entire PL/SQL block, including the trailing semicolon following the END. The embedded block can have declarative and exception-handling sections as well.

Indicator Variables

PL/SQL variables, like database columns, can have either a value or the non-value NULL. However, 3GLs, like C, have no concept of NULL. C can simulate NULLs for strings with the empty string, but there is no way to have a NULL integer, for example. In order to remedy this, an *indicator variable* is used. An indicator variable is simply a 2-byte integer that is appended to the host variable reference in the embedded block or SQL statement. For example, the following embedded block selects from the **registered_students** table. The grade column in this table can have a NULL value, so we need the indicator variable to detect this.

```
EXEC SQL BEGIN DECLARE SECTION;
   char v_Grade;     /* v_Grade is a single character. */
   short i_Grade;  /* Note that the indicator is declared as a
                      short, which is a 2-byte integer. */
EXEC SQL END DECLARE SECTION;

EXEC SQL EXECUTE
   BEGIN
     SELECT grade
       INTO :v_Grade INDICATOR :i_Grade
       FROM registered_students
       WHERE student_id = 10006
       AND department = 'ECN'
       AND course = 101;
   END;
END-EXEC;

   if (i_Grade != 0)
     printf("No grade recorded for this student\n");
   else
     printf("The grade recorded is %c\n", v_Grade);
```

Between the host variable and the indicator variable, the keyword INDICATOR can be used, as in the preceding example. This keyword is optional, so we could have written the block with

```
EXEC SQL EXECUTE
  BEGIN
    SELECT grade
      INTO :v_Grade:i_Grade
      FROM registered_students
      WHERE student_id = 10006
      AND department = 'ECN'
      AND course = 101;
  END;
END-EXEC;
```

The **v_Grade** variable in the preceding example is an *output variable*—the variable is assigned to by the block. For output variables, the indicators have the meanings described in the following table:

Value of Indicator Variable	Meaning
0	The host variable was retrieved successfully.
−1	The host variable was assigned a NULL value.
>0	The host variable was not large enough to hold the returned value and was truncated. The indicator variable contains the original length of the result.
−2	The host variable was not large enough to hold the returned value and was truncated. However, the original length was too large to fit in 2 bytes.

An *input variable* is read from inside the embedded block. Indicator variables can also be used for input variables. Their meanings are similar to those of the indicators used for output variables, and are described as follows:

Value of Indicator Variable	Meaning
0	The associated host variable should be used.
−1	A NULL should be used.

Error Handling

Error handling in a Pro*C program is done with either the sqlca structure, or the SQLCODE and/or SQLSTATE status variables. After each executable embedded SQL statement, the status variables will contain the error code from the statement, or zero if the statement is successful. This behavior is the same for embedded PL/SQL blocks. If the block exits with an unhandled exception, the error code is returned to the status variable. If the block handles any exceptions that are raised, then the entire block completes successfully, and the status variable would contain zero, indicating successful completion. The complete rules for exception propagation are described in Chapter 6.

For example, the following Pro*C fragment contains an embedded block that calls the **RecordFullClasses** procedure, defined in Chapter 5. After the block completes, the program checks the sqlca.sqlcode status variable to see if the block was successful. If not, the error message is printed.

```
EXEC SQL INCLUDE SQLCA; /* This statement includes the SQLCA
                           structure. This structure contains
                           fields used for error handling. */
EXEC SQL EXECUTE
  BEGIN
    RecordFullClasses;
  END;
END-EXEC;
/* sqlca.sqlcode will be zero if the statement was successful,
   and will contain the error code if the statement completed
   with an error. If an error occurs, sqlca.sqlerrm.sqlerrmc
   will contain the error message text, and sqlca.sqlerrm.sqlerrml
   will contain the length of the message. */
if (sqlca.sqlcode != 0) {
  printf("Error during execution of RecordFullClasses.\n");
  printf("%.70s\n", sqlca.sqlerrm.sqlerrml, sqlca.sqlerrm.sqlerrmc);
  }
else
  printf("Execution successful.\n");
```

Necessary Precompiler Options

In order to precompile a program with an embedded PL/SQL block, the precompiler option SQLCHECK must be set to SEMANTICS. When SQLCHECK=SEMANTICS, the precompiler will attempt to connect to the database during precompile time to verify the syntax and semantics of the database objects referenced by the program. In order to do this, the precompiler needs a user name and password. This is provided through the USERID precompiler option. The same username and password that the program uses at run time should be used at precompile time. For example, if your program connects to the database as the Oracle user example, with password example, the precompiler options would have to include the following:

```
SQLCHECK=SEMANTICS USERID=example/example
```

The USERID parameter can accept both a username and a password as in the above example, or just the username. If the password is not specified, then the precompiler will prompt you for it.

If the USERID option is not specified, you must supply embedded DECLARE TABLE statements to identify the structure of tables referenced. However, there is no DECLARE PROCEDURE statement, so if your program calls stored procedures, USERID is required along with SQLCHECK=SEMANTICS.

NOTE
If USERID is not specified and there are no DECLARE TABLE statements for the tables referenced by the program, the precompiler will return errors such as

```
PLS-201: identifier must be declared
```

which can be confusing. The table does exist and the user does have permission to access it, but the error seems to imply otherwise. This error is a result of the missing USERID parameter, rather than a missing table. As a general rule, whenever SQLCHECK=SEMANTICS, USERID should also be specified to avoid confusion.

OCI

The Oracle Call Interface (OCI) provides another method of accessing the database from a 3GL program. Rather than embedding PL/SQL and SQL statements, however, a function library is used. The OCI library provides functions to parse SQL statements, bind input variables, define output variables, execute statements, and fetch the results. The source program is written entirely in the third generation language, and no precompiler is required. For more information on OCI, see the *Programmer's Guide to the Oracle Call Interface.*

Using PL/SQL with OCI is straightforward. Rather than parsing a SQL statement, simply parse an anonymous PL/SQL block. For example, the following program fragment parses an anonymous block.

```
char *plsql_block =
  "BEGIN \
     Register(:v_StudentID, :v_Department, :v_Course); \
   END;";
int return_val;
Cda_Def cda;

return_val = oparse(&cda, plsql_block, -1, 1, 2);
```

Guidelines for PL/SQL Blocks in OCI

The **oparse** call expects a string containing the SQL statement that you want to execute. In order to execute a PL/SQL block, this string should contain the entire block, including the trailing semicolon, as in the preceding example.

CAUTION
Beware of comments inside the block. Newlines are not significant inside a string passed to **oparse**, so a -- comment will comment out the entire remaining portion of the block, rather than to the return character. Use the C-style comments /* and */ instead, to ensure the correct behavior.

OCI Calling Structure

PL/SQL blocks are executed like other DML statements. Notably, it is illegal to fetch from a PL/SQL block. Here are the required steps:

1. Parse the block using **oparse**.

2. Bind any placeholders using **obndrv** or **obndra**.

3. Execute the block with **oexec**.

It is illegal to use **odefin** or **ofetch** for a PL/SQL block; they are valid only for SELECT statements. In addition, all placeholders must be bound by name using **obndrv** or **obndra**—**obndrn** is not allowed.

The following is a complete OCI example that calls the Register procedure. It is written for a Unix system, and thus won't necessarily compile on other platforms.

```
/* Include the standard header files, plus the OCI headers. */
#include <stdio.h>
#include <oratypes.h>
#include <ocidfn.h>
#include <ociapr.h>
```

```c
/* Declare an LDA, HDA and CDA for use in later statements. */
Lda_Def lda;
ub1 HDA[512];
Cda_Def cda;

/* Declare the variables that will be used for input. */
char v_Department[4] = "ECN";
int v_Course = 101;
int v_StudentID = 10006;

/* String that contains the block calling Register.
   Note that the return characters are escaped with a
   backslash to keep this all in one C string. The trailing
   semicolon is included in the string, since it is a
   syntactic part of the block. */
char *plsqlBlock =
  "BEGIN \
      Register(:v_StudentID, :v_Department, :v_Course); \
  END;";

/* Username and password to connect the database. */
char *username = "example";
char *password = "example";


/* Error reporting function. Uses oerhms to get the full
   error, and prints it to the screen. */
void print_error(Lda_Def *lda, Cda_Def *cda) {
  int v_ReturnChars;
  char v_Buffer[1000];

  v_ReturnChars = oerhms(lda, cda->rc, (text *) v_Buffer,
                         (sword) sizeof(v_Buffer));
  printf("Oracle error occurred!\n");
  printf("%s\n", v_Buffer);
}


main() {
  /* Connect to the database. */
  if (orlon(&lda, HDA, (text *) username, -1,
```

```
              (text *) password, -1, 0)) {
    print_error(&lda, &lda);
    exit(-1);
}
printf("Connected to Oracle\n");

/* Open a cursor for later use. */
if (oopen(&cda, &lda, (text *) 0, -1, -1,
            (text *) 0, -1)) {
    print_error(&lda, &cda);
    exit(-1);
}

/* Parse the PL/SQL block. */
if (oparse(&cda, (text *) plsqlBlock,
            (sb4) -1, 1, (ub4) 2)) {
    print_error(&lda, &cda);
    exit(-1);
}

/* Bind the department using type 5, STRING. */
if (obndrv(&cda, (text *) ":v_Department", -1,
            (ub1 *) v_Department, sizeof(v_Department),
            5, -1, (sb2 *) 0, 0, -1, -1)) {
    print_error(&lda, &cda);
    exit(-1);
}

/* Bind the course using type 3, INTEGER. */
if (obndrv(&cda, (text *) ":v_Course", -1,
            (ub1 *) &v_Course, sizeof(v_Course),
            3, -1, (sb2 *) 0, 0, -1, -1)) {
    print_error(&lda, &cda);
    exit(-1);
}

/* Bind the student ID using type 3, INTEGER. */
if (obndrv(&cda, (text *) ":v_StudentID", -1,
            (ub1 *) &v_StudentID, sizeof(v_StudentID),
            3, -1, (sb2 *) 0, 0, -1, -1)) {
    print_error(&lda, &cda);
    exit(-1);
```

```
}

/* Execute the statement. */
if (oexec(&cda)) {
  print_error(&lda, &cda);
  exit(-1);
}

/* Commit our work. */
if (ocom(&lda)) {
  print_error(&lda, &cda);
  exit(-1);
}

/* Close the cursor. */
if (oclose(&cda)) {
  print_error(&lda, &cda);
  exit(-1);
}

/* Log off from the database. */
if (ologof(&lda)) {
  print_error(&lda, &cda);
  exit(-1);
}
}
```

Client-side PL/SQL

The Oracle tools that contain a PL/SQL engine on the client include the Developer 2000, Designer 2000, and Discoverer 2000 suites. Each suite consists of several development or query tools bundled together. All of them contain a PL/SQL engine locally on the client. This PL/SQL engine is used to control the processing of the application, as illustrated in Figure 7-2.

If a PL/SQL object is created within client-side PL/SQL, it is accessible only within the object that creates it. For example, a Forms procedure is accessible only from within one form. It is not accessible from other database procedures or other forms. Table 7-1 compares stored procedures and client procedures, and Table 7-2 compares database triggers and client triggers. Stored procedures and database triggers are discussed in Chapter 5.

Stored Procedure	Client Procedure
Stored in the data dictionary as a database object.	Stored as part of the client application; does not exist as a database object.
Can be executed by any session connecting to a user who has EXECUTE privilege on the procedure.	Can only be executed from the application that defines the procedure.
Can call other stored procedures.	Can call client procedures within the same application and stored procedures in the database.
Can manipulate data stored in Oracle tables via SQL statements.	Can manipulate data stored in Oracle tables, as well as variables in the application.

TABLE 7-1.　*Stored Procedures vs. Client Procedures*

Why a Client-side Engine Is Provided

Most of the work in applications developed using the Developer, Designer, and Discoverer 2000 tools is very suitable for PL/SQL. Oracle Forms, especially, uses PL/SQL constructs heavily. Every form trigger is a PL/SQL block, for example. Fields within the form are treated as bind variables.

Database Trigger	Form Trigger
Fired when a DML operation is performed on a database table.	Fired when the user presses a key or navigates between fields on the screen.
Can be row level or statement level.	No distinction between row and statement level.
Can manipulate data stored in Oracle tables via SQL.	Can manipulate data in Oracle tables as well as variables in forms.
Can be fired from any session executing the triggering DML statement.	Can be fired only from the form that defines the trigger.
Can cause other database triggers to fire.	Can cause database triggers to fire, but not other form triggers.

TABLE 7-2.　*Database Triggers vs. Form Triggers*

At first glance, it may seem that having a PL/SQL engine on the client removes the benefit of PL/SQL. After all, one of the purposes of the language is to reduce network traffic, as described in Chapter 1. With a client-side PL/SQL engine, the SQL statements go over the network while the procedural statements are processed on the client. This appears to generate more network traffic and thus cause the application to run slower.

However, the majority of the work done in a Forms application is procedural in nature. As the user navigates between fields and blocks in the form, or presses a key, triggers automatically fire, and the form's fields get different values. These are all procedural actions and thus should be done on the client for best performance.

All of these suites of tools behave the same with regard to PL/SQL. In this chapter, we will look at Oracle Forms and Procedure Builder.

Oracle Forms

The Forms Designer is a GUI environment. As such, it has several different windows available to you. The windows that are relevant to PL/SQL are the Object Navigator and the PL/SQL Editor. For more information on Oracle Forms and how it is used, see the *Oracle Forms User's Guide*.

PL/SQL Editor

The PL/SQL Editor can be used to modify procedures and functions both on the client and on the server. The Editor looks different depending on the location of the object being modified. Figure 7-9 shows a PL/SQL Editor with the **Register** procedure. This procedure is stored on the server. The Save button in the Editor is the equivalent of the CREATE OR REPLACE PROCEDURE command; when it is pressed the procedure is created in the data dictionary. The Drop button is the equivalent of the DROP PROCEDURE command; pressing this button drops the object from the data dictionary.

Compare Figure 7-9 with Figure 7-10. Figure 7-10 shows the PL/SQL Editor with a local procedure. The Save button has been replaced by Compile. Compile will save the procedure to the PL/SQL engine on the client, not the server. The data dictionary in the database will not be modified. Likewise, the Delete button will remove the procedure from the local PL/SQL engine. The New button allows creation of a new form procedure, function, or trigger.

Object Navigator

The Object Navigator is used to manipulate all of the objects within the form. By clicking on each object icon, the properties of that object can be edited. Objects can also be moved around by dragging and dropping. This includes moving procedures from the client to the server and vice versa. Figure 7-11 shows the Object Navigator.

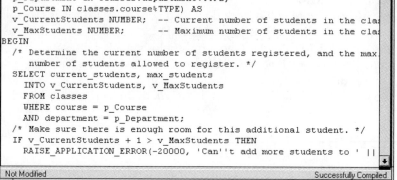

FIGURE 7-9. *The PL/SQL Editor with a stored procedure*

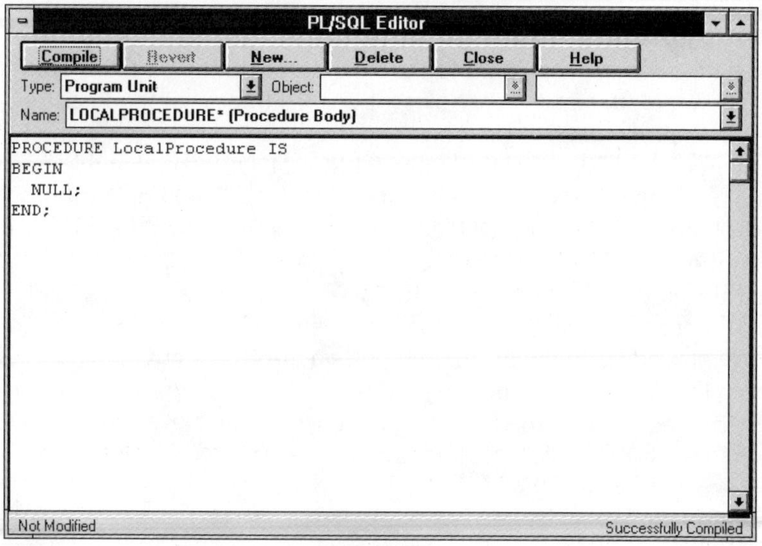

FIGURE 7-10. *The PL/SQL Editor with a local procedure*

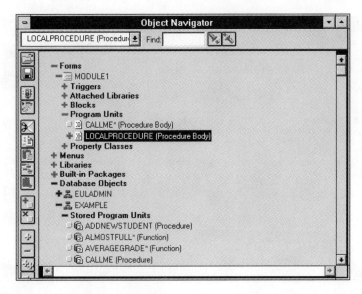

FIGURE 7-11. *The Object Navigator*

Procedure Builder

Procedure Builder is part of the Developer 2000 toolset, along with Oracle Forms, Oracle Reports, and Oracle Graphics. It extends the PL/SQL manipulation tools of Forms by adding the PL/SQL Interpreter. This window is the main part of Procedure Builder, and it is what makes it unique among the Oracle products. The Interpreter allows you to step through client-side PL/SQL line-by-line, examining the values of local variables as you go. This capability is very similar to the debuggers available for other third generation languages such as C.

The Interpreter, illustrated in Figure 7-12, is divided into two panes—the viewer and the command prompt.

The Viewer

The viewer pane of the Interpreter shows the block, procedure, or function that is currently being executed. It shows the entire block, with line numbers. The buttons at the top of the window are used for stepping line-by-line through the code. By double-clicking on a line number, a breakpoint can be set as well. Figure 7-13 shows the same block shown in Figure 7-12, but with a breakpoint set at line 9.

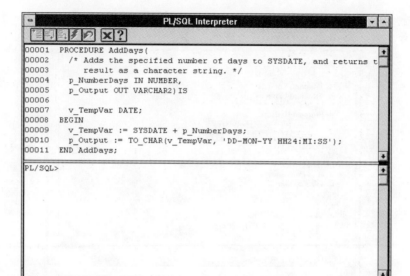

FIGURE 7-12. *The PL/SQL Interpreter*

FIGURE 7-13. *Debugging a PL/SQL block*

The Command Prompt

The command prompt section of the Interpreter allows execution of individual PL/SQL statements on-the-fly. This prompt is similar to the SQL prompt in SQL*Plus, in that SQL statements can be typed in and executed. However, PL/SQL procedural statements can also be entered, including variable assignments and procedure calls. This is also shown in Figure 7-13.

Interactive PL/SQL Debugging

Because Procedure Builder allows interactive debugging of PL/SQL code, it is invaluable during development. As of this writing, I don't know of any other tool, made by Oracle or a third-party vendor, that allows interactive PL/SQL debugging. The benefits of having this feature are discussed in more detail in Chapter 8, but here are a few of them:

- The ability to examine the values of local variables while the block is running. Without this ability, the variables would have to be inserted into a database table and queried after the block is finished, or echoed using the DBMS_OUTPUT package.

- The ability to modify local variables while the block is running. During execution of **AddDays**, for example, we can change **p_NumberDays** to test different results. No other debugging tools available for PL/SQL have this capability.

- The ability to run PL/SQL commands and stored procedures on-the-fly from the command prompt in the Interpreter. Although SQL*Plus can do this to a certain extent, Procedure Builder greatly enhances this feature.

The PL/SQL Wrapper

When a procedure, function, or package is stored in the database, the source for this object is available in the **user_source** data dictionary view. This can be very useful during development, since it provides a current view of the contents of the procedure. Procedure Builder and the other client tools use this view for manipulating stored procedures as well. However, this is not always desired. If you are developing an application written in PL/SQL, the only way to ship the application to your customers would be by providing the source code, which is then loaded into the database and compiled at the customer's site. This is not always desirable, since the source code may contain proprietary algorithms and data structures.

PL/SQL 2.2 ...and HIGHER Oracle provides a solution for this, available with PL/SQL 2.2 and higher—the PL/SQL wrapper. This utility encodes PL/SQL source code into a hexadecimal format that customers cannot read. However, the database can decode the wrapped procedure and store it in the database.

Running the Wrapper

The wrapper is an operating system executable. The location and name of the executable is system dependent, but on most systems it is named WRAP. The format for executing the wrapper is

WRAP INAME=*input_file* [ONAME=*output_file*]

where *input_file* is the name of a file containing a CREATE OR REPLACE statement. The filename can have any extension, but by default it is assumed to be .sql. If specified, *output_file* is the name of the output file. If no output file is specified, *output_file* defaults to the name of the input file with extension .plb.

The following listing shows some legal WRAP command lines. All of them take a file called **register.sql** as input and create **register.plb** as output.

```
WRAP INAME=register.sql
WRAP INAME=register
WRAP INAME=register.sql ONAME=register.plb
```

The options INAME and ONAME are not case-sensitive, but your operating system may be. If so, the name of the WRAP executable itself, as well as the filenames, may be case-sensitive.

Input and Output Files

The input file for the wrapper can contain only the following SQL commands (in addition to comments):

```
CREATE [OR REPLACE] PROCEDURE
CREATE [OR REPLACE] PACKAGE
CREATE [OR REPLACE] PACKAGE BODY
CREATE [OR REPLACE] FUNCTION
```

Given an input file that looks like this,

```
CREATE OR REPLACE PROCEDURE Register(...) AS
  ...
BEGIN
  ...
END Register;
```

the output of the wrapper would look like this:

```
CREATE OR REPLACE PROCEDURE Register WRAPPED
  012ba779f...
```

All of the source code for the procedure has been converted into hexadecimal digits. The **.plb** file can be loaded from SQL*Plus like any other **.sql** file and the **Register** procedure created. However, the **user_source** view will hold the wrapped version of the code, preventing exposure of the actual algorithm.

The size of the output file is usually significantly longer than the size of the input file. However, the size of the compiled p-code is the same, since it does not change.

Checking Syntax and Semantics

The wrapper will check the syntax of the input file, but it will not check the semantics. This means that if any objects referenced in the file don't exist, the errors won't be reported until run time. For example, if we wrap an input file that looks like this,

```
CREATE OR REPLACE PROCEDURE CountStudents
  (p_Major IN students.major%TYPE,
   p_TotalNumber OUT NUMBER) AS
BEGIN
  SELECT COUNT(*)
    INTO p_TotalNumber
    FROM student
    WHERE major = p_Major;
END CountStudents;
/
```

we don't get any errors, even though the **student** table doesn't exist (it should be **students**). We will get the following error if we try to run the output **.plb** file, however.

```
PLS-201: identifier 'student' must be declared
```

In this case, the **.plb** file can't be edited to fix the error since the source is not available. The original **.sql** file would have to be modified, then wrapped again.

Guidelines for the Wrapper

Once a procedure, function, or package is wrapped, the output file cannot be edited. The contents are not readable and thus can't be changed. The only way to change a wrapped object is to modify the original source file. So, don't wrap an object until it is completely developed.

The package bodies for Oracle-supplied packages (DBMS_OUTPUT, DBMS_PIPE, and so on) are shipped in wrapped form. (These packages are described in the following chapters and in Appendix B.) However, the package headers are shipped in clear text. This is a good guideline to follow for your own packages as well. The public portions of the package—namely the package header—should be visible so that users will know the names of the procedures and their parameters. Only the package body needs to be wrapped. This neatly hides the actual implementation while allowing the interface to be visible.

Summary

In this chapter, we have discussed various envrionments from which PL/SQL can be run. These can be divided into client and server-side PL/SQL. Server PL/SQL environments include SQL*Plus, the Oracle Precompilers, and OCI. Client-side PL/SQL is available through tools such as Oracle Forms and Procedure Builder. Procedure Builder also provides an interactive PL/SQL debugging and testing environment. Finally, the PL/SQL wrapper allows procedures to be packaged into a binary equivalent for shipment to end users. Chapter 8 continues the PL/SQL development process with tips and techniques for testing and debugging.

CHAPTER 8

Testing and Debugging

Very few programs perform correctly the first time they are written. Plus, the requirements for a program often change during development, and the program must be rewritten. In either case, the program needs to be tested thoroughly to make sure that it is working properly and performing as expected. This chapter describes three techniques for testing and debugging PL/SQL programs: inserting into a test table, the DBMS_OUTPUT package, and Procedure Builder. It also discusses programming strategies that can help avoid errors in the first place.

Problem Diagnosis

Every bug is different from the last, which is what makes debugging and testing a challenge. We can reduce the occurrences of bugs by testing and QA analysis during development, but if you do program development for a while you will almost certainly have to find the bugs and errors in your own or somebody else's code.

Debugging Guidelines

Even though every bug is different, and there could be many fixes for any given bug, the process of finding and fixing bugs can be defined. I have developed several guidelines for determining the cause of a problem over the past few years of debugging both my own and other programmers' code. These guidelines can be applied to development in any programming language, not just PL/SQL.

Find the Place Where the Error Occurs

This may seem like an obvious idea, but it is crucial to fixing coding problems. If you have a large, complicated program that simply fails, the first step is to determine exactly where the failure is occurring. This is not necessarily an easy task, depending on the complexity of the code. The easiest way to find the source of an error is to trace the program as it runs, examining the values of the data structures to determine what went wrong.

Define Exactly What Is Wrong

Once you know where the problem happens, you need to define exactly what the problem is. Is an Oracle error returned? Does a calculation return the wrong result? Does the wrong data get inserted into the database? In order to fix a bug, it is necessary to know how the bug manifests itself.

Reduce the Program to a Simple Test Case

This is a good strategy to follow when you don't know where the error is occurring. Start cutting out parts of the code, and rerun the program. If the error still occurs, you know that the section you removed did not cause the error. If the error goes away, examine the section that was removed.

Remember that one area of your code may have the bug, but the problem may manifest itself in another part of the code. For example, a procedure may return an incorrect value, but the returned value is not actually used until later in the main program. The problem here is not the main program (where the error appears to be), but in the procedure. Cutting out the procedure call and replacing it with a direct assignment to the returned value would reveal the source of the problem. We will examine this particular case later in this chapter.

Establish a Testing Environment

Ideally, testing and debugging are not done in a production environment. It is a good idea to maintain a testing environment that duplicates production as much as possible—the same database structure but with less data, for example. This way you can develop and test newer versions of your application without affecting the production version that is already running. If a problem occurs in production, try reproducing the problem in test first. This follows the previous principle of reducing the problem to a smaller test case. A test case may involve more than just the code—PL/SQL is very dependent on the database structure and the contents of the data, and these should be reduced as well.

The Debug Package

PL/SQL is designed primarily for manipulation of data stored in an Oracle database. The structure of the language is based on this use, and it performs admirably. For practical purposes, however, we need some additional tools to help write and debug programs.

The rest of this chapter examines in detail several methods of debugging PL/SQL code. Each section focuses on a different problem and uses a different method to isolate the problem following the guidelines just given. Each section will first describe the general debugging method, then give a description of the problem to be solved. In the course of solving each problem, we will develop different versions of a debugging package, Debug, which you can use in your own programs. Depending on your environment and needs, the different capabilities of each package will be useful.

Inserting into a Test Table

The simplest method of debugging is to insert the values of local variables into a temporary table as the program is running. When the program has completed, you can query the table to determine the values of the variables. This method requires the least effort to implement and will work regardless of the execution environment.

Problem 1

Suppose we want to write a function that will return the average grade for each class, based on currently registered students. We could write this function as follows:

```
CREATE OR REPLACE FUNCTION AverageGrade (
/* Determines the average grade for the class specified. Grades
   are stored in the registered_students table as single characters
   A through E. This function will return the average grade,
   again as a single letter. If there are no students registered for
   the class, an error is raised. */
p_Department IN VARCHAR2,
p_Course IN NUMBER) RETURN VARCHAR2 AS

v_AverageGrade VARCHAR2(1);
v_NumericGrade NUMBER;
v_NumberStudents NUMBER;

CURSOR c_Grades IS
  SELECT grade
    FROM registered_students
    WHERE department = p_Department
    AND course = p_Course;
BEGIN
  /* First we need to see how many students there are for
     this class. If there aren't any, we need to raise an error. */
  SELECT COUNT(*)
    INTO v_NumberStudents
    FROM registered_students
    WHERE department = p_Department
      AND course = p_Course;

  IF v_NumberStudents = 0 THEN
    RAISE_APPLICATION_ERROR(-20001, 'No students registered for ' ||
      p_Department || ' ' || p_Course);
  END IF;

  /* Since grades are stored as letters, we can't use the AVG
     function directly on them. Instead, we can use the DECODE
     function to convert the letter grades to numeric values,
     and take the average of those. */
```

```
SELECT AVG(DECODE(grade, 'A', 5,
                         'B', 4,
                         'C', 3,
                         'D', 2,
                         'E', 1))
   INTO v_NumericGrade
   FROM registered_students
   WHERE department = p_Department
   AND course = p_Course;

/* v_NumericGrade now contains the average grade, as a number
   from 1 to 5. We need to convert this back into a letter. The
   DECODE function can be used here as well. Note that we are
   SELECTing the result into v_AverageGrade rather than assigning
   to it,because the DECODE function is only legal in an SQL
   statement.*/
SELECT DECODE(ROUND(v_NumericGrade), 5, 'A',
                                     4, 'B',
                                     3, 'C',
                                     2, 'D',
                                     1, 'E')
   INTO v_AverageGrade
   FROM dual;

   RETURN v_AverageGrade;
END AverageGrade;
```

Let's suppose that the content of **registered_students** looks like this:

```
SQL> select * from registered_students;

STUDENT_ID DEP   COURSE G
---------- ---   --------- -
     10000 CS       102 A
     10002 CS       102 B
     10003 CS       102 C
     10000 HIS      101 A
     10001 HIS      101 B
     10002 HIS      101 B
     10003 HIS      101 A
     10004 HIS      101 C
     10005 HIS      101 C
     10006 HIS      101 E
```

```
10007 HIS      101 B
10008 HIS      101 A
10009 HIS      101 D
10010 HIS      101 A
10008 NUT      307 A
10010 NUT      307 A
10009 MUS      410 B
10006 MUS      410 E
```

```
18 rows selected.
```

Four classes have students registered in them: Computer Science 102, History 101, Nutrition 307, and Music 410. So we can call **AverageGrade** with these four classes. Any other classes should raise the error "No students registered." A sample SQL*Plus output is shown here:

```
SQL> VARIABLE v_AveGrade VARCHAR2(1)
SQL> exec :v_AveGrade := AverageGrade('HIS', 101)

PL/SQL procedure successfully completed.

SQL> print v_AveGrade

V_AVEGRADE
-------------------------------
B

SQL> exec :v_AveGrade := AverageGrade('NUT', 307)

PL/SQL procedure successfully completed.

SQL> print v_AveGrade

V_AVEGRADE
-------------------------------
A

SQL> exec :v_AveGrade := AverageGrade('MUS', 410)

PL/SQL procedure successfully completed.

SQL> print v_AveGrade

V_AVEGRADE
-------------------------------
```

C

```
SQL> exec :v_AveGrade := AverageGrade('CS', 102)
begin :v_AveGrade := AverageGrade('CS', 102); end;

  *
ERROR at line 1:
ORA-20001: No students registered for CS 102
ORA-06512: at "EXAMPLE.AVERAGEGRADE", line 21
```

The last call illustrates the bug. The ORA-20001 error is returned even though students are registered for Computer Science 102.

Problem 1: The Debug Package

The version of Debug that we will use to find this bug is shown next. The **Debug.Debug** procedure is the main procedure in the package. It takes two parameters—a description and a variable. These are concatenated and inserted into the **debug_table** table. The **Debug.Reset** procedure should be called at the start of the program, to initialize the table and the internal line counter. The line counter is necessary to ensure that the rows in **debug_table** will be selected in the order in which they were inserted.

```
CREATE OR REPLACE PACKAGE Debug AS
  /* First version of the debug package. This package works
     by inserting into the debug_table table. In order to see
     the output, select from debug_table in SQL*Plus with:
  SELECT debug_str FROM debug_table ORDER BY linecount; */

  /* This is the main debug procedure. p_Description will be
     concatenated with p_Value, and inserted into debug_table. */
  PROCEDURE Debug(p_Description IN VARCHAR2, p_Value IN VARCHAR2);

  /* Resets the Debug environment. Reset is called when the
     package is instantiated for the first time, and should be
     called to delete the contents of debug_table for a new
     session. */
  PROCEDURE Reset;
END Debug;

CREATE OR REPLACE PACKAGE BODY Debug AS
  /* v_LineCount is used to order the rows in debug_table. */
```

```
v_LineCount NUMBER;

PROCEDURE Debug(p_Description IN VARCHAR2, p_Value IN VARCHAR2) IS
BEGIN
  INSERT INTO debug_table (linecount, debug_str)
    VALUES (v_LineCount, p_Description || ': ' || p_Value);
  COMMIT;
  v_LineCount := v_LineCount + 1;
END Debug;

PROCEDURE Reset IS
BEGIN
  v_LineCount := 1;
  DELETE FROM debug_table;
END Reset;

BEGIN /* Package initialization code */
  Reset;
END Debug;
```

Problem 1: Using the Debug Package

In order to determine the problem with **AverageGrade**, we need to look at the value of the variables used by the procedure. We do this by inserting debugging statements in the code. With this version of Debug, we need to call **Debug.Reset** at the start of **AverageGrade**, and **Debug.Debug** whenever we want to look at a variable. The modified version is given next. Some of the comments have been removed for brevity.

```
CREATE OR REPLACE FUNCTION AverageGrade (
  p_Department IN VARCHAR2,
  p_Course IN NUMBER) RETURN VARCHAR2 AS

  v_AverageGrade VARCHAR2(1);
  v_NumericGrade NUMBER;
  v_NumberStudents NUMBER;

  CURSOR c_Grades IS
    SELECT grade
      FROM registered_students
      WHERE department = p_Department
      AND course = p_Course;
BEGIN
```

```
Debug.Reset;
Debug.Debug('p_Department', p_Department);
Debug.Debug('p_Course', p_Course);

/* First we need to see how many students there are for
   this class. If there aren't any, we need to raise an
   error. */
SELECT COUNT(*)
  INTO v_NumberStudents
  FROM registered_students
  WHERE department = p_Department
  AND course = p_Course;

Debug.Debug('After select, v_NumberStudents', v_NumberStudents);
IF v_NumberStudents = 0 THEN
  RAISE_APPLICATION_ERROR(-20001, 'No students registered for ' ||
    p_Department || ' ' || p_Course);
END IF;

SELECT AVG(DECODE(grade, 'A', 5,
                         'B', 4,
                         'C', 3,
                         'D', 2,
                         'E', 1))
  INTO v_NumericGrade
  FROM registered_students
  WHERE department = p_Department
    AND course = p_Course;

SELECT DECODE(ROUND(v_NumericGrade), 5, 'A',
                                     4, 'B',
                                     3, 'C',
                                     2, 'D',
                                     1, 'E')
  INTO v_AverageGrade
  FROM dual;

  RETURN v_AverageGrade;
END AverageGrade;
```

Now we can call **AverageGrade** again and select from the **debug_table** afterwards to see the results:

```
SQL> EXEC :v_AveGrade := AverageGrade('CS', 102)
begin :v_AveGrade := AverageGrade('CS', 102); end;

 *
ERROR at line 1:
ORA-20001: No students registered for CS 102
ORA-06512: at "EXAMPLE.AVERAGEGRADE", line 25
ORA-06512: at line 1


SQL> SELECT debug_str FROM debug_table ORDER BY linecount;

DEBUG_STR
------------------------------------------------------------
p_Department: CS
p_Course: 102
After select, v_NumberStudents: 0
```

We have verified that **v_NumberStudents** is in fact 0, which explains why we are getting the ORA-20001 error. This narrows the problem down to the SELECT statement, which isn't matching any rows. We therefore need to examine the WHERE clause of this statement in more detail:

```
SELECT COUNT(*)
    INTO v_NumberStudents
    FROM registered_students
    WHERE department = p_Department
    AND course = p_Course;
```

The Debug output seems to show the correct values for **p_Department** and **p_Course**, but SQL*Plus pads the output with spaces, so this output may be deceiving. Let's change the calls to **Debug.Debug** to put quotes around **p_Department** and **p_Course**. This will reveal any leading or trailing spaces.

```
CREATE OR REPLACE FUNCTION AverageGrade
  ...
BEGIN
  Debug.Reset;
  Debug.Debug('p_Department', '''' || p_Department || '''');
  Debug.Debug('p_Course', '''' || p_Course || '''');

  /* First we need to see how many students there are for this
     class. If there aren't any, we need to raise an error. */
```

```
SELECT COUNT(*)
  INTO v_NumberStudents
  FROM registered_students
  WHERE department = p_Department
    AND course = p_Course;

Debug.Debug('After select, v_NumberStudents', v_NumberStudents);
...
```

Now when we run **AverageGrade** and query **debug_table**, we get the following result:

```
SQL> exec :v_AveGrade := AverageGrade('CS', 102)
begin :v_AveGrade := AverageGrade('CS', 102); end;


 *

ERROR at line 1:
ORA-20001: No students registered for CS 102
ORA-06512: at "EXAMPLE.AVERAGEGRADE", line 25
ORA-06512: at line 1



SQL> SELECT debug_str FROM debug_table ORDER BY linecount;

DEBUG_STR
------------------------------------------------------------
p_Department: 'CS'
p_Course: '102'
After select, v_NumberStudents: 0
```

We can see that **p_Department** doesn't have a trailing space. This is the problem. The **department** column of **registered_students** is CHAR(3), and **p_Department** is VARCHAR2. This means that the database column contains 'CS ' (with a trailing space), which explains why the SELECT statement doesn't return any rows. Thus **v_NumberStudents** is assigned 0.

TIP
The built-in function DUMP can be used to examine the exact contents of a database column. For example, we can determine the contents of the **department** column in **registered_students** with:

```
SQL> SELECT DISTINCT DUMP(department)
  2    FROM registered_students
```

```
  3     WHERE department = 'CS';

DUMP(DEPARTMENT)
--------------------------------------
Typ=96 Len=3: 67,83,32
```

The type is 96, indicating CHAR, and the last byte in the column is 32, which is the ASCII code for a space. This tells us that the column is blank-padded. For more information on DUMP and other built-in functions, see Chapter 3.

One fix for the problem with **AverageGrade** is to change the type of **p_Department** to CHAR:

```
CREATE OR REPLACE FUNCTION AverageGrade (
  p_Department IN CHAR,
  p_Course IN NUMBER) RETURN VARCHAR2 AS
  ...
BEGIN
  ...
END AverageGrade;
```

After doing this, we get the correct result for **AverageGrade**:

```
SQL> exec :v_AveGrade := AverageGrade('CS', 102)

PL/SQL procedure successfully completed.

SQL> print v_AveGrade

V_AVEGRADE
--------------------------------
B
```

This works because both values in the WHERE clause are now CHAR, and blank-padded character comparison semantics are used, resulting in the match. See Chapter 2 for more information on the semantics of character comparison.

TIP
Had we used the %TYPE attribute in the function declaration, the type of **p_Department** would have been correct. This is another reason why %TYPE is advisable. Also, since the return value of **AverageGrade** is a character string of length 1, and it will always be 1, we can use

the fixed-length type CHAR for the RETURN clause as well. The declaration of **AverageGrade** therefore looks like this:

```
CREATE OR REPLACE FUNCTION AverageGrade (
  p_Department IN registered_students.department%TYPE,
  p_Course IN registered_students.course%TYPE) RETURN CHAR AS

  v_AverageGrade CHAR(1);
  v_NumericGrade NUMBER;
  v_NumberStudents NUMBER;
...
BEGIN
  ...
END AverageGrade;
```

Problem 1: Comments

This version of Debug is very simple. All it does is insert into **debug_table**. But we were still able to use it to find the bug in **AverageGrade**. There are some advantages to this technique:

- ■ Since Debug doesn't rely on anything but SQL, it can be used from any environment. The SELECT statement that shows the output can be run from SQL*Plus or another tool.

- ■ Debug is simple, so it doesn't add too much overhead to the procedure being debugged.

There are also disadvantages:

- ■ **AverageGrade** raised an exception in the preceding example. This causes any SQL done by the program to be rolled back, which requires the COMMIT in **Debug.Debug**. This can cause a problem if other work in the procedure being debugged shouldn't be committed. This commit will also invalidate any SELECT FOR UPDATE cursors that may be open.

- ■ As currently written, Debug won't work properly if more than one session is using it simultaneously. The SELECT statement will return the results from both sessions. This can be fixed by modifying both the Debug package and **debug_table** to include a column uniquely identifying the session.

The disadvantages of this version of Debug will be resolved by using the DBMS_OUTPUT package, described in the next section.

DBMS_OUTPUT

The first version of Debug, which we saw in the last section, essentially implemented a limited version of I/O. PL/SQL has no input/output capability built into the language. This was an intentional design decision, since the ability to print out the values of variables and data structures is not required to manipulate data stored in the database. It is, however, a very useful debugging tool. As a result, output capability was added to PL/SQL 2.0 through the built-in package DBMS_OUTPUT. We will use DBMS_OUTPUT in the second version of Debug, described in this section.

PL/SQL still doesn't have input capability built into the language, but SQL*Plus substitution variables (described in Chapter 7) can be used to overcome this. PL/SQL 2.3 has a new package, UTL_FILE, which is used to read from and write to operating system files. Chapter 11 will examine UTL_FILE in detail.

The DBMS_OUTPUT Package

Before we discuss the debugging problem for this section, we need to examine DBMS_OUTPUT in some detail. This package, like other DBMS packages, is owned by the Oracle user SYS. When DBMS_OUTPUT is installed, a public synonym DBMS_OUTPUT is created for the package, and EXECUTE permission on the package is granted to PUBLIC. This means that any Oracle user can call the routines in DBMS_OUTPUT without having to prefix the package name with SYS.

How does DBMS_OUTPUT work? Two basic operations, GET and PUT, are implemented through procedures in the package. A PUT operation takes its argument and places it into an internal buffer for storage. A GET operation reads from this buffer and returns the contents as an argument to the procedure. There is also an ENABLE procedure that sets the size of the buffer.

Procedures in DBMS_OUTPUT
The PUT routines in the package are PUT, PUT_LINE, and NEW_LINE. The GET routines are GET_LINE and GET_LINES. ENABLE and DISABLE control the buffer.

PUT and PUT_LINE   The syntax for the PUT and PUT_LINE calls is

```
PROCEDURE PUT(a NUMBER);
PROCEDURE PUT(a DATE);

PROCEDURE PUT_LINE(a VARCHAR2);
PROCEDURE PUT_LINE(a NUMBER);
PROCEDURE PUT_LINE(a DATE);
```

where *a* is the argument to be placed in the buffer. Keep in mind that these procedures are overloaded by the type of the parameter (overloading is discussed in Chapter 5). Because of the three different versions of PUT and PUT_LINE, the buffer can contain values of types VARCHAR2, NUMBER, and DATE. They are stored in the buffer in their original format. However, GET_LINE and GET_LINES retrieve from the buffer and return character strings only. When a GET operation is performed, the contents of the buffer will be converted to a character string according to the default datatype conversion rules. If you want to specify a format for the conversion, use an explicit TO_CHAR call on the PUT, rather than the GET.

The buffer is organized into lines, each of which can have a maximum of 255 bytes. PUT_LINE appends a newline character after its argument, signaling the end of a line. PUT does not. PUT_LINE is equivalent to calling PUT and then calling NEW_LINE.

NEW_LINE   The syntax for the NEW_LINE call is

    PROCEDURE NEW_LINE;

NEW_LINE puts a newline character into the buffer, signaling the end of a line. There is no limit to the number of lines in the buffer. The total size of the buffer is limited to the value specified in ENABLE, however.

GET_LINE   The syntax for GET_LINE is

    PROCEDURE GET_LINE(*line* OUT VARCHAR2, *status* OUT INTEGER);

where *line* is a character string that will contain one line of the buffer, and *status* indicates whether the line was retrieved successfully. The maximum length of a line is 255 bytes. If the line was retrieved, *status* will be 0; if there are no more lines, it will be 1.

NOTE
Although the maximum size of a buffer line is 255 bytes, the output variable **line** can be more than 255 characters. The buffer line can consist of DATE values, for example. These take up 7 bytes of storage in the buffer but are usually converted to character strings with length greater than 7.

GET_LINES   The GET_LINES procedure has an argument that is a PL/SQL table. The table type and the syntax are

```
TYPE CHARARR IS TABLE OF VARCHAR2(255)
  INDEX BY BINARY_INTEGER;
PROCEDURE GET_LINES(lines OUT CHARARR,
                    numlines IN OUT INTEGER);
```

where *lines* is a PL/SQL table that will contain multiple lines from the buffer, and *numlines* indicates how many lines are requested. On input to GET_LINES, *numlines* specifies the requested number of lines. On output, *numlines* will contain the actual number of lines returned, which will be less than or equal to the number requested. GET_LINES is designed to replace multiple calls to GET_LINE.

The **chararr** type is also defined in DBMS_OUTPUT. Therefore, if you want to call GET_LINES explicitly in your code, you need to declare a variable of type DBMS_OUTPUT.CHARARR. For example:

```
DECLARE
  /* Demonstrates using PUT_LINE and GET_LINE. */
  v_Data      DBMS_OUTPUT.CHARARR;
  v_NumLines  NUMBER;
BEGIN
  -- Enable the buffer first.
  DBMS_OUTPUT.ENABLE(1000000);

  -- Put some data in the buffer first, so GET_LINES will
  -- retrieve something.
  DBMS_OUTPUT.PUT_LINE('Line One');
  DBMS_OUTPUT.PUT_LINE('Line Two');
  DBMS_OUTPUT.PUT_LINE('Line Three');

  -- Set the maximum number of lines which we want to retrieve.
  v_NumLines := 3;

  /* Get the contents of the buffer back. Note that v_Data is
     declared of type DBMS_OUTPUT.CHARARR, so that it matches
     the declaration of DBMS_OUTPUT.GET_LINES. */
  DBMS_OUTPUT.GET_LINES(v_Data, v_NumLines);

  /* Loop through the returned buffer, and insert the contents
     into temp_table. */
  FOR v_Counter IN 1..v_NumLines LOOP
    INSERT INTO temp_table (char_col)
      VALUES (v_Data(v_Counter));
  END LOOP;
END;
```

ENABLE and DISABLE   The forms for the ENABLE and DISABLE calls are

   PROCEDURE ENABLE (*buffer_size* IN INTEGER DEFAULT 20000);

and

   PROCEDURE DISABLE;

where *buffer_size* is the initial size of the internal buffer, in bytes. The default size is 20,000 bytes, and the maximum size is 1,000,000 bytes. Later arguments to PUT or PUT_LINE will be placed in this buffer. They are stored in their internal format, taking up as much space in the buffer as their structure dictates. If DISABLE is called, the contents of the buffer are purged, and subsequent calls to PUT and PUT_LINE have no effect.

Using DBMS_OUTPUT

The DBMS_OUTPUT package itself does not contain any mechanism for printing. Essentially, it simply implements a first in, first out data structure. Having said that, how can we use DBMS_OUTPUT for printing? SQL*Plus, SQL*DBA, and Server Manager all have an option known as SERVEROUTPUT. With this option on, SQL*Plus will automatically call DBMS_OUTPUT.GET_LINES when a PL/SQL block concludes and print the results, if any, to the screen. This is illustrated by Figure 8-1.

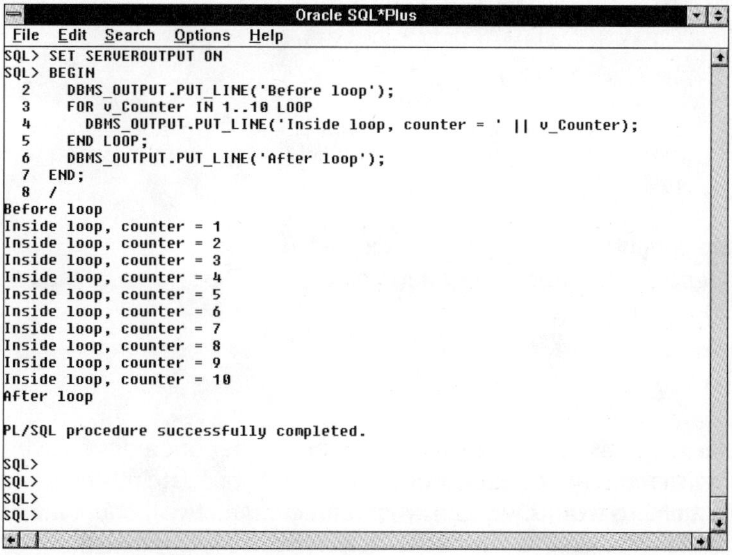

FIGURE 8-1. *Using SERVEROUTPUT and PUT_LINE*

The SQL*Plus command SET SERVEROUTPUT ON implicitly calls DBMS_OUTPUT.ENABLE, which sets up the internal buffer. Optionally, you can specify a size with

SET SERVEROUTPUT ON SIZE *buffer_size*

where *buffer_size* will be used as the initial size of the buffer (the argument to DBMS_OUTPUT.ENABLE). With SERVEROUTPUT on, SQL*Plus will call DBMS_OUTPUT.GET_LINES *after* the PL/SQL block has completed. This means that the output will be echoed to the screen when the block has finished, and *not* during execution of the block. This is normally not a problem when DBMS_OUTPUT is used for debugging.

> **CAUTION**
> DBMS_OUTPUT is designed to be used primarily for debugging. It is not meant for general reporting. If you need to customize the output from your queries, it is better to use tools such as Oracle Reports than DBMS_OUTPUT and SQL*Plus.

The internal buffer does have a maximum size (specified in DBMS_OUTPUT .ENABLE), and each line has a maximum length of 255 bytes. As a result, calls to DBMS_OUTPUT.PUT, DBMS_OUTPUT.PUT_LINE, and DBMS_OUTPUT.NEW_LINE can raise either

```
ORA-20000: ORU-10027: buffer overflow,
          limit of <buf_limit> bytes.
```

or

```
ORA-20000: ORU-10028: line length overflow,
          limit of 255 bytes per line.
```

The message depends on which limit is exceeded.

See Appendix B for more information on DBMS_OUTPUT and the other supplied DBMS packages.

Problem 2

The **students** table has a column for the current number of credits for which the student is registered. The **Register** procedure does not update this column as it is currently written. To fix this, we can write a function that will count the total credits for which a student is registered. **Register** can then update the

current_credits column of the **students** table. We could write function
CountCredits with:

```
CREATE OR REPLACE FUNCTION CountCredits (
  /* Returns the number of credits for which the student
     identified by p_StudentID is currently registered */
  p_StudentID IN students.ID%TYPE)
  RETURN NUMBER AS

  v_TotalCredits NUMBER;   -- Total number of credits
  v_CourseCredits NUMBER;  -- Credits for one course
  CURSOR c_RegisteredCourses IS
    SELECT department, course
      FROM registered_students
      WHERE student_id = p_StudentID;
BEGIN
  FOR v_CourseRec IN c_RegisteredCourses LOOP
    -- Determine the credits for this class.
    SELECT num_credits
      INTO v_CourseCredits
      FROM classes
      WHERE department = v_CourseRec.department
      AND course = v_CourseRec.course;

    -- Add it to the total so far.
    v_TotalCredits := v_TotalCredits + v_CourseCredits;
  END LOOP;

  RETURN v_TotalCredits;
END CountCredits;
```

Since **CountCredits** doesn't modify any database or package state, we can call
it directly from a SQL statement (with PL/SQL 2.1 or higher). (Calling functions
from SQL statements is discussed in Chapter 5.) We can therefore determine the
current number of credits for all students by selecting from the **students** table. We
get the following result:

```
SQL> SELECT ID, CountCredits(ID) "Total Credits"
  2    FROM students;

     ID Total Credits
--------- -------------
```

```
10000
10001
10002
10003
10004
10005
10006
10007
10008
10009
10010
```

```
11 rows selected.
```

There is no output for **CurrentCredits**, which means that the function is returning NULL. This is not the correct result.

Problem 2: The Debug Package

We will use the DBMS_OUTPUT package to find the bug in **CountCredits**. To do this, we can use the following version of Debug. It has the same interface as the first version of Debug, which we saw in the previous section, so we only have to change the package body.

```
CREATE OR REPLACE PACKAGE BODY Debug AS
  PROCEDURE Debug(p_Description IN VARCHAR2,
                  p_Value IN VARCHAR2) IS
  BEGIN
    DBMS_OUTPUT.PUT_LINE(p_Description || ': ' || p_Value);
  END Debug;

  PROCEDURE Reset IS
  BEGIN
      /* Disable the buffer first, then enable it with the
      maximum size. Since DISABLE purges the buffer, this
      ensures that we will have a fresh buffer whenever
      Reset is called. */
    DBMS_OUTPUT.DISABLE;
    DBMS_OUTPUT.ENABLE(1000000);
  END Reset;
BEGIN /* Package initialization code */
  Reset;
END Debug;
```

We no longer use **debug_table**; instead we use DBMS_OUTPUT. As a result, the version of Debug will work only in SQL*Plus, SQL*DBA, or Server Manager because these tools automatically call DBMS_OUTPUT.GET_LINES and print the buffer contents. SERVEROUTPUT also needs to be on before using Debug.

Problem 2: Using the Debug Package

CountCredits is returning a NULL result. Let's verify this, as well as what value we are adding to **v_TotalCredits** in the loop. We do this by adding Debug calls, as shown here:

```
CREATE OR REPLACE FUNCTION CountCredits (
  /* Returns the number of credits for which the student
     identified by p_StudentID is currently registered */
  p_StudentID IN students.ID%TYPE)
  RETURN NUMBER AS

  v_TotalCredits NUMBER;  -- Total number of credits
  v_CourseCredits NUMBER; -- Credits for one course
  CURSOR c_RegisteredCourses IS
    SELECT department, course
      FROM registered_students
      WHERE student_id = p_StudentID;
BEGIN
  Debug.Reset;
  FOR v_CourseRec IN c_RegisteredCourses LOOP
    -- Determine the credits for this class.
    SELECT num_credits
      INTO v_CourseCredits
      FROM classes
      WHERE department = v_CourseRec.department
      AND course = v_CourseRec.course;

    Debug.Debug('Inside loop, v_CourseCredits', v_CourseCredits);
    -- Add it to the total so far.
    v_TotalCredits := v_TotalCredits + v_CourseCredits;
  END LOOP;

  Debug.Debug('After loop, returning', v_TotalCredits);
  RETURN v_TotalCredits;
END CountCredits;
```

We now get the following output:

```
SQL> VARIABLE v_Total NUMBER
SQL> SET SERVEROUTPUT ON
SQL> exec :v_Total := CountCredits(10006);
Inside loop, v_CourseCredits: 4
Inside loop, v_CourseCredits: 3
After loop, returning:

PL/SQL procedure successfully completed.

SQL> print v_Total

  V_TOTAL
---------


SQL>
```

NOTE
We are testing **CountCredits** with a SQL*Plus bind variable, rather than selecting the value of the function from the **students** table. This is because **CountCredits** now calls DBMS_OUTPUT, which is not considered to be a pure function. If we were to use **CountCredits** inside a SQL statement, we would get the ORA-6571 error. See Chapter 5 for more information on this error and calling stored functions from SQL statements.

Based on this Debug output, it looks like the number of credits calculated for each class is correct: the loop was executed twice, with 4 and 3 credits returned each time. But clearly, this isn't being added to the total properly. Let's add some more debugging statements:

```
CREATE OR REPLACE FUNCTION CountCredits (
  /* Returns the number of credits for which the student
     identified by p_StudentID is currently registered */
  p_StudentID IN students.ID%TYPE)
  RETURN NUMBER AS

  v_TotalCredits NUMBER;  -- Total number of credits
  v_CourseCredits NUMBER; -- Credits for one course
  CURSOR c_RegisteredCourses IS
    SELECT department, course
```

```
       FROM registered_students
       WHERE student_id = p_StudentID;
BEGIN
  Debug.Reset;
  Debug.Debug('Before loop, v_TotalCredits', v_TotalCredits);
  FOR v_CourseRec IN c_RegisteredCourses LOOP
    -- Determine the credits for this class.
    SELECT num_credits
      INTO v_CourseCredits
      FROM classes
      WHERE department = v_CourseRec.department
      AND course = v_CourseRec.course;

    Debug.Debug('Inside loop, v_CourseCredits', v_CourseCredits);
    -- Add it to the total so far.
    v_TotalCredits := v_TotalCredits + v_CourseCredits;
    Debug.Debug('Inside loop, v_TotalCredits', v_TotalCredits);
  END LOOP;

  Debug.Debug('After loop, returning', v_TotalCredits);
  RETURN v_TotalCredits;
END CountCredits;
```

The output from this latest version of **CountCredits** is

```
SQL> exec :v_Total := CountCredits(10006);
Before loop, v_TotalCredits:
Inside loop, v_CourseCredits: 4
Inside loop, v_TotalCredits:
Inside loop, v_CourseCredits: 3
Inside loop, v_TotalCredits:
After loop, returning:

PL/SQL procedure successfully completed.
```

We can see the problem from this output. Notice that **v_TotalCredits** is NULL before the loop starts and remains NULL during the loop. This is because we didn't initialize **v_TotalCredits** in the declaration. We can fix this with the final version of **CountCredits**, which also has the debugging statements removed:

```
CREATE OR REPLACE FUNCTION CountCredits (
  /* Returns the number of credits for which the student
     identified by p_StudentID is currently registered */
```

```
    p_StudentID IN students.ID%TYPE)
    RETURN NUMBER AS

    v_TotalCredits NUMBER := 0;   -- Total number of credits
    v_CourseCredits NUMBER;       -- Credits for one course
    CURSOR c_RegisteredCourses IS
      SELECT department, course
        FROM registered_students
        WHERE student_id = p_StudentID;
BEGIN
  FOR v_CourseRec IN c_RegisteredCourses LOOP
    -- Determine the credits for this class.
    SELECT num_credits
      INTO v_CourseCredits
      FROM classes
      WHERE department = v_CourseRec.department
      AND course = v_CourseRec.course;

    -- Add it to the total so far.
    v_TotalCredits := v_TotalCredits + v_CourseCredits;
  END LOOP;

  RETURN v_TotalCredits;
END CountCredits;
```

The output from this is as follows:

```
SQL> exec :v_Total := CountCredits(10006);

PL/SQL procedure successfully completed.

SQL> print v_Total

  V_TOTAL
---------
        7

SQL> SELECT ID, CountCredits(ID) "Total Credits"
  2    FROM students;

       ID Total Credits
--------- -------------
    10000             8
```

```
10001            4
10002            8
10003            8
10004            4
10005            4
10006            7
10007            4
10008            8
10009            7
10010            8
```

We can see that **CountCredits** is working properly now, both for the single student example and for the entire table. If a variable is not initialized when it is declared, it is assigned the non-value NULL. The NULL value is maintained throughout the addition operation, according to the rules for evaluating NULL expressions, as described in Chapter 2.

Problem 2: Comments

This version of Debug has different features than the first version. Namely, we have eliminated the dependency on **debug_table**. This gives us several advantages:

- There is no need to worry about multiple database sessions interfering with each other, since each session will have its own DBMS_OUTPUT internal buffer.

- We no longer have to issue a COMMIT inside **Debug.Debug**.

- As long as SERVEROUTPUT is on, no additional SELECT statement is necessary to see the output. Also, we can turn off debugging by simply setting SERVEROUTPUT off.

On the other hand, there are still some things to be aware of with this version:

- If we are not using SQL*Plus, SQL*DBA, or Server Manager, the debugging output will not be printed to the screen automatically. The package can still be used from other PL/SQL execution environments, but you may have to call DBMS_OUTPUT.GET_LINE or DBMS_OUTPUT.GET_LINES explicitly and display the results yourself.

- The amount of debugging output is limited by the size of the DBMS_OUTPUT buffer. This affects both the size of each line and the total size of the buffer. If you find that there is too much output and the buffer is not large enough, the first version of Debug may be a better option.

Procedure Builder

Procedure Builder is a PL/SQL development environment that is part of the Developer 2000 series of products. Procedure Builder allows us to step through PL/SQL code line-by-line, examining variables as we go. As with debuggers for other languages, we can also set breakpoints and modify the value of variables while the program is running. We examined Procedure Builder in Chapter 7, but in this section we will focus on the debugging aspects. We won't develop a Debug package in this section because Procedure Builder incorporates the debugging features we need.

Problem 3

Consider the following procedure:

```
CREATE OR REPLACE PROCEDURE CreditLoop AS
  /* Inserts the student ID numbers and their current credit
     values into temp_table. */
  v_StudentID students.ID%TYPE;
  v_Credits   students.current_credits%TYPE;
  CURSOR c_Students IS
    SELECT ID
      FROM students;
BEGIN
  OPEN c_Students;
  LOOP
    FETCH c_Students INTO v_StudentID;
    v_Credits := CountCredits(v_StudentID);
    INSERT INTO temp_table (num_col, char_col)
      VALUES (v_StudentID, 'Credits = ' || TO_CHAR(v_Credits));
    EXIT WHEN c_Students%NOTFOUND;
  END LOOP;
  CLOSE c_Students;
END CreditLoop;
```

CreditLoop simply records the number of credits for each student in **temp_table**. When running **CreditLoop** and querying **temp_table** in SQL*Plus, we get

```
SQL> exec CreditLoop;
PL/SQL procedure successfully completed.
SQL> SELECT * FROM temp_table
  2    ORDER BY num_col;
```

```
NUM_COL CHAR_COL
-------- --------------------
   10000 Credits = 8
   10001 Credits = 4
   10002 Credits = 8
   10003 Credits = 8
   10004 Credits = 4
   10005 Credits = 4
   10006 Credits = 7
   10007 Credits = 4
   10008 Credits = 8
   10009 Credits = 7
   10010 Credits = 8
   10010 Credits = 8
```

```
12 rows selected.
```

The problem is that the last two rows are inserted twice—there are two rows for student ID 100010 and one row for all the others.

Problem 3: Using Procedure Builder

The first step is to copy **CreditLoop** into the client-side PL/SQL engine. (Procedure Builder can call server-side stored procedures, but it can't debug them.) We do this by dragging the procedure from "Stored Program Units" to "Program Units" in the Object Navigator window, as shown in Figure 8-2.

Once **CreditLoop** is on the client side, we can view it in the PL/SQL Interpreter window. This is where we will control the execution of the procedure. First, we should set a breakpoint. When we run the procedure, execution will stop at the breakpoint, and we can look at the values of the local variables in the Object Navigator. One way of setting breakpoints is to double-click on the line number at the desired place. For **CreditLoop**, this is at line 13, which is immediately after the FETCH statement. We want to examine **v_StudentID** to see where the duplicate value is coming from. Figure 8-3 shows the Interpreter with the breakpoint set.

We are now ready to run **CreditLoop**. We do this by entering

```
CreditLoop;
```

at the PL/SQL prompt in the Interpreter. This will start the procedure and stop at the breakpoint that we set. This situation is shown in Figure 8-4.

At this point, we have several options. We can continue execution of the procedure by using the buttons at the top of the Interpreter. These allow us to step through the code in various ways (the first three buttons), or allow the procedure to

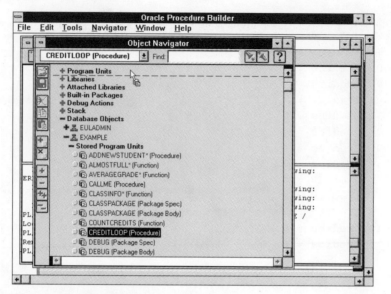

FIGURE 8-2. *Copying CreditLoop to the client*

```
00008        FROM students;
00009   BEGIN
00010     OPEN c_Students;
00011     LOOP
00012       FETCH c_Students INTO v_StudentID;
B(01)       v_Credits := CountCredits(v_StudentID);
00014       INSERT INTO temp_table (num_col, char_col)
00015         VALUES (v_StudentID, 'Credits = ' || TO_CHAR(v_Credits));
00016       EXIT WHEN c_Students%NOTFOUND;
00017     END LOOP;
00018     CLOSE c_Students;
00019   END CreditLoop;

PL/SQL> .break .
Breakpoint #1 installed at line 13 of CREDITLOOP
PL/SQL>
```

FIGURE 8-3. *Setting a breakpoint*

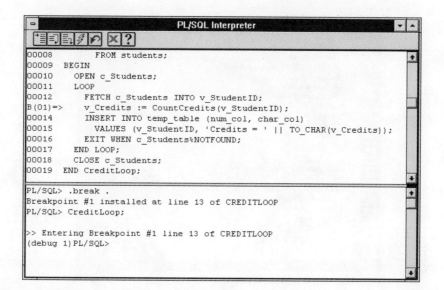

```
                    PL/SQL Interpreter
00008        FROM students;
00009   BEGIN
00010     OPEN c_Students;
00011     LOOP
00012       FETCH c_Students INTO v_StudentID;
B(01)=>     v_Credits := CountCredits(v_StudentID);
00014       INSERT INTO temp_table (num_col, char_col)
00015         VALUES (v_StudentID, 'Credits = ' || TO_CHAR(v_Credits));
00016       EXIT WHEN c_Students%NOTFOUND;
00017     END LOOP;
00018     CLOSE c_Students;
00019   END CreditLoop;

PL/SQL> .break .
Breakpoint #1 installed at line 13 of CREDITLOOP
PL/SQL> CreditLoop;

>> Entering Breakpoint #1 line 13 of CREDITLOOP
(debug 1)PL/SQL>
```

FIGURE 8-4. *Stopped at the breakpoint*

run until completion (the fourth button, with the lightning bolt). We can also look at the value of local variables. This is done by looking at the "Stack" section in the Object Navigator. Figure 8-5 shows the values of the two local variables visible at the breakpoint: **v_StudentID** and **v_Credits**. We can see that **v_StudentID** contains the first ID, resulting from the FETCH statement, and that **v_Credits** is NULL. This is what we expect.

From here, we can step through the code and examine **v_StudentID** after each FETCH. As we do this, we can see **v_StudentID** changing, as it should. This continues until the last FETCH, which happens to return student ID 10010. We insert this value into **temp_table**, and then loop again. The next FETCH doesn't change the value of **v_StudentID**—it is still 10010. Thus it gets inserted twice. After the second INSERT, the loop exits because **c_Students%NOTFOUND** becomes TRUE. This points out the problem, which is that the EXIT statement should be immediately after the FETCH. We can modify **CreditLoop** in the Program Unit Editor, and then test it. The correct version is shown in Figure 8-6.

Now that we have fixed the problem, we need to copy **CreditLoop** back to the server so it can be called from other sessions as well. Similar to the procedure that we followed to copy it to the client, we simply drag the procedure from the "Program Units" section of the Object Navigator to the "Stored Program Units" section, as shown in Figure 8-7. After doing this, we can test the procedure again from SQL*Plus. The output is shown here:

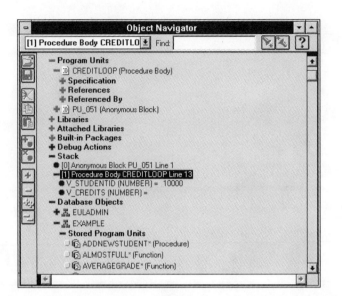

FIGURE 8-5. *Examining local variables in the Object Navigator*

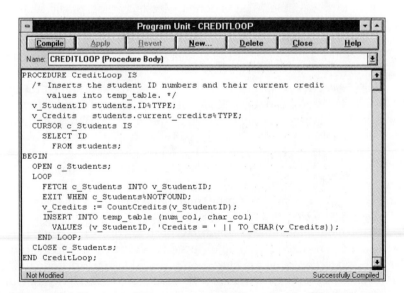

FIGURE 8-6. *The correct version of CreditLoop*

```
SQL> exec CreditLoop
PL/SQL procedure successfully completed.

SQL> SELECT * FROM temp_table
  2    ORDER BY num_col;

  NUM_COL CHAR_COL
--------- --------------------------------
    10000 Credits = 8
    10001 Credits = 4
    10002 Credits = 8
    10003 Credits = 8
    10004 Credits = 4
    10005 Credits = 4
    10006 Credits = 7
    10007 Credits = 4
    10008 Credits = 8
    10009 Credits = 7
    10010 Credits = 8

11 rows selected.
```

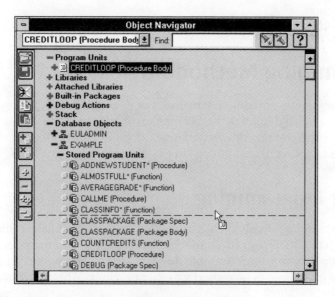

FIGURE 8-7.   *Copying CreditLoop back to the server*

Problem 3: Comments

Using Procedure Builder has several advantages:

- We don't need to add any debugging code to the procedure; we simply run the procedure in a controlled debugging environment.

- Since the code doesn't have to be changed, then recompiled, then run to see different variables, we have much more flexibility in what we can debug.

- Procedure Builder provides an integrated development environment, including the PL/SQL Editor and the Object Navigator. No other tool is necessary to develop PL/SQL.

However, there are still some concerns:

- The current version of Procedure Builder (1.5) can only debug client-side PL/SQL. The version of PL/SQL on the client is still version 1.0, as opposed to PL/SQL 2.0 or higher on the server. This means that you can't debug any code that uses version 2 features, such as PL/SQL tables and user-defined records.

- In order to use Procedure Builder, you must have a system capable of running it. This requires a windowing environment at the minimum. The Debug packages that we examined earlier in this chapter did not have this restriction.

Programming Methodologies

We have examined several different methods of debugging PL/SQL programs in this chapter. You can also minimize the occurrence of bugs in the first place if you practice good programming design and methodologies. The following concepts can be applied to other programming languages as well, not just PL/SQL.

Modular Programming

Modular programming simply means separating your program into distinct parts, or modules, each of which performs a specific function. You can then develop and test each module in turn, and assemble them into the final program. In addition, the individual modules can be reused for other programs. This concept is best illustrated by example. Suppose we want to write a program that will print student transcripts. We can divide this task into steps, which constitute the algorithm for the program:

1. Determine the student ID whose transcript we want to output.

2. Determine the classes for which this student is registered.

3. For each class, output the department, course, course description, and grade.

4. Determine the grade point average (GPA) for the student and output it.

Each of these steps can be accomplished by a different PL/SQL construct. We then combine all of the constructs to get the final program. For example, we can implement each of the steps as follows:

1. The student ID can be passed to the procedure as a parameter.

2. The classes for this student are determined by selecting from **registered_students**.

3. The information about each class is selected from the **classes** table.

4. Calculating the GPA for the student can be done by another procedure, **CalculateGPA**.

Now that we have decided on the basic design for the procedure, we can sketch the procedure out as follows:

```
CREATE OR REPLACE PROCEDURE PrintTranscript(
  /* Outputs a transcript for the indicated student. The
     transcript will consist of the classes for which the
     student is currently registered and the grade received
     for each class. At the end of the transcript, the student's
     GPA is output. */
  p_StudentID IN students.ID%TYPE) AS

  v_StudentGPA  NUMBER;  -- Grade point average for this student.
  CURSOR CurrentClasses IS
    SELECT *
      FROM registered_students
      WHERE student_id = p_StudentID;
BEGIN
  --Output some header information about the student such
```

```
    -- as first and last name, major, etc.

    FOR v_ClassesRecord IN CurrentClasses LOOP
      -- Output information about each class.
    END LOOP;

    -- Determine the GPA.
    CalculateGPA(p_StudentID, v_StudentGPA);

    -- Output the GPA.
END PrintTranscript;
```

We now have the basic structure of **PrintTranscript**. We can implement the individual sections of the procedure one by one, ensuring that each is correct before proceeding. We will do this in Chapter 11.

Top-Down Design

Top-down design complements modular programming. This means that we develop the basic shell of the program first, and then implement the details. This way, we can define exactly what each subprogram will have to do before implementing it. PL/SQL allows us to do this through procedure stubs. Consider the **CalculateGPA** procedure. We will need this for **PrintTranscript**. Without having to develop the actual algorithm for **CalculateGPA**, we can still write the stub of the procedure:

```
CREATE OR REPLACE PROCEDURE CalculateGPA(
  /* Returns the grade point average for the student identified
     by p_StudentID in p_GPA. */
  p_StudentID IN students.ID%TYPE,
  p_GPA OUT NUMBER) AS
BEGIN
  NULL;
END CalculateGPA;
```

This procedure can be compiled, which allows the skeleton of **PrintTranscript** to be compiled as well. The NULL statement by itself serves as a placeholder for the actual code of the procedure. By creating this stub first, we can now continue with the development of **PrintTranscript** without worrying about the details of **CalculateGPA**.

We have worked from the top of the program first, then developed the details. This is the principle of top-down design. If we had chosen *bottom-up design* instead, we would have implemented **CalculateGPA** before **PrintTranscript**. Top-down design allows more flexibility. As we develop **PrintTranscript**, for example, we may determine that **CalculateGPA** works better as a function. Or, it might need to take additional parameters. We can simply modify the stub of **CalculateGPA** to continue our development of **PrintTranscript**, and then complete **CalculateGPA** once we are sure of its interface and requirements.

Data Abstraction

Data abstraction is another good programming technique. This means that we can hide some of the implementation details for a particular algorithm, and just present the interface to it. **CalculateGPA** is a good example of this. **PrintTranscript** doesn't need to know how the GPA is determined, only that it is determined, and **CalculateGPA** determines it. We are free to change the contents of **CalculateGPA**, as long as we don't change how it is called.

The fact that objects within a package body are private to that package also can be used to implement data abstraction. The package header documents the external interface to the data, and the package body actually does the manipulation. The DBMS_OUTPUT package itself uses this technique. The interface to GET_LINES, for example, is documented with the declaration of the procedure and the CHARARR type in the package header. The body of GET_LINES would have to loop through the buffer in some way and return the contents in the **lines** parameter. But we don't know how this is done, or even how the buffer is implemented. We don't need to know how the buffer is implemented (perhaps it uses a PL/SQL table, perhaps a database table, or some other data structure) to use DBMS_OUTPUT.

Summary

In this chapter, we have examined three different methods for debugging PL/SQL code—inserting into an output table, using the DBMS_OUTPUT package, and Procedure Builder. Depending on your environment and needs, different methods may be appropriate. As we examined each of these debugging methods, we also discussed three common PL/SQL errors and how to resolve them. These were incorrect character comparison, uninitialized variables, and an improper exit condition for a loop. Finally, we introduced several principles of good programming methodology, which can be applied to program development in general, not just PL/SQL.

CHAPTER 9

Intersession
Communication

In addition to reading and writing into database tables, PL/SQL provides two built-in packages for intersession communication. These packages are DBMS_PIPE and DBMS_ALERT. They can be used to send messages between sessions connected to the same database instance. As such, they provide an extremely useful facility which has many applications. In this chapter, we will examine DBMS_PIPE and DBMS_ALERT in detail, and compare their behavior so you can choose the appropriate package for your needs.

DBMS_PIPE

The DBMS_PIPE package implements *database pipes.* A database pipe is similar to a Unix pipe. Different sessions connected to the same Oracle instance can send and receive messages over a pipe. Pipes can have multiple *readers* (sessions that receive the message) and *writers* (sessions that send the message). Readers and writers can reside on different machines, or can be written using different PL/SQL execution environments. All that is required is that they connect to the same Oracle instance, and that they both have the ability to execute PL/SQL blocks.

Pipes are *asynchronous*—they operate independent of transactions. Once a message is sent along a pipe, there is no way of retrieving it, even if the transaction that sent it issues a ROLLBACK.

The writer packs a series of data items into a local message buffer. This buffer is sent over the pipe into the message buffer of the reader process, and the reader then unpacks its buffer into the data. For example, the **LogRSInserts** trigger records the inserts into **registered_students**. The changes are sent over a pipe, so the trigger is the writer in this case:

```
CREATE OR REPLACE TRIGGER LogRSInserts
  BEFORE INSERT ON registered_students
  FOR EACH ROW
DECLARE
  v_Status    INTEGER;
BEGIN

  /* Pack the description into the buffer first. */
  DBMS_PIPE.PACK_MESSAGE('I');

  /* Pack the current user and the timestamp. */
  DBMS_PIPE.PACK_MESSAGE(user);
  DBMS_PIPE.PACK_MESSAGE(sysdate);

  /* Pack the new values. */
  DBMS_PIPE.PACK_MESSAGE(:new.student_ID);
  DBMS_PIPE.PACK_MESSAGE(:new.department);
  DBMS_PIPE.PACK_MESSAGE(:new.course);
  DBMS_PIPE.PACK_MESSAGE(:new.grade);

  /* Send the message over the 'RSInserts' pipe. */
  v_Status := DBMS_PIPE.SEND_MESSAGE('RSInserts');

  /* If the send is unsuccessful, raise an error so the change
```

```
      doesn't go through. */
   IF v_Status != 0 THEN
     RAISE_APPLICATION_ERROR(-20010, 'LogRSInserts trigger ' ||
       'couldn''t send the message, status = ' || v_Status);
   END IF;

END LogRSChanges;
```

The trigger is only one component of a logging system, however. It is the writer
on the **RSInserts** pipe. We still need a reader. This can be done by the following
Pro*C program, which reads from the pipe and writes the changes to an operating
system file:

```
/* RSInsert.pc
   This program receives messages from the RSInserts pipe, and logs
   them to a file. */

/* C and SQL header files */
#include <stdio.h>
EXEC SQL INCLUDE sqlca;

EXEC SQL BEGIN DECLARE SECTION;
  /* Username and password to connect to the database */
  char *v_Connect = "example/example";

  /* Status variables used in the calls to DBMS_PIPE */
  int v_Status;
  VARCHAR v_Code[5];

  /* Variables sent over the pipe - these will be logged. */
  VARCHAR v_Userid[9];
  VARCHAR v_Changedate[10];
  int v_StudentID;
  VARCHAR v_Department[4];
  int v_Course;
  VARCHAR v_Grade[2];
  short v_Grade_ind;
EXEC SQL END DECLARE SECTION;

/* File pointer to log file */
FILE *outfile;

void sqlerror();
```

```c
int main() {

  /* Set up the error handling. */
  EXEC SQL WHENEVER SQLERROR DO sqlerror();

  /* Connect to the database. */
  EXEC SQL CONNECT :v_Connect;

  /* Open the log file. */
  outfile = fopen("rs.log", "w");

  /* Main loop. The only way we'll break out of the loop is if we
     receive the 'STOP' message or if an error occurs. */
  for (;;) {
    /* Sleep until a message is received over the 'RSInserts' pipe.
       The timeout is not specified, so the default will be used. */
    EXEC SQL EXECUTE
      BEGIN
        :v_Status := DBMS_PIPE.RECEIVE_MESSAGE('RSInserts');
      END;
    END-EXEC;

    if (v_Status == 0) {
      /* Successful retreival of the message. We now need to get
         the first data element, to decide what to do with it. */
      v_Code.len = 5;
      EXEC SQL EXECUTE
        BEGIN
          DBMS_PIPE.UNPACK_MESSAGE(:v_Code);
        END;
      END-EXEC;
      v_Code.arr[v_Code.len] = '\0';

      if (!strcmp(v_Code.arr, "STOP")) {
        /* Stop message received. Break out of the loop. */
        break;
      }

      /* Retreive the rest of the message, which consists of the
         userid, date, and new values. */
      v_Userid.len = 9;
      v_Changedate.len = 10;
```

```
   v_Department.len = 4;
   v_Grade.len = 2;
   EXEC SQL EXECUTE
     DECLARE
       v_ChangeDate DATE;
     BEGIN
       DBMS_PIPE.UNPACK_MESSAGE(:v_Userid);
       DBMS_PIPE.UNPACK_MESSAGE(v_ChangeDate);
       :v_Changedate := TO_CHAR(v_ChangeDate, 'DD-MON-YY');
       DBMS_PIPE.UNPACK_MESSAGE(:v_StudentID);
       DBMS_PIPE.UNPACK_MESSAGE(:v_Department);
       DBMS_PIPE.UNPACK_MESSAGE(:v_Course);
       DBMS_PIPE.UNPACK_MESSAGE(:v_Grade:v_Grade_ind);
     END;
   END-EXEC;

   /* Null terminate the character strings */
   v_Userid.arr[v_Userid.len] = '\0';
   v_Changedate.arr[v_Changedate.len] = '\0';
   v_Department.arr[v_Department.len] = '\0';

   if (v_Grade_ind == -1)
     v_Grade.arr[0] = '\0';
   else
     v_Grade.arr[v_Grade.len] = '\0';

   /* Print the data to the log file. */
   fprintf(outfile, "User: %s Timestamp: %s",
     v_Userid.arr, v_Changedate.arr);
   fprintf(outfile, " ID: %d Course: %s %d Grade: %s\n",
     v_StudentID, v_Department.arr, v_Course, v_Grade.arr);

}
else if (v_Status == 1) {
  /* The RECEIVE_MESSAGE call timed out. Loop back to wait again. */
  continue;
}
else {
  /* The RECEIVE_MESSAGE call exited with an error. Print it, and
     exit. */
  printf("RECEIVE_MESSAGE Error!  Status = %d\n", v_Status);
  EXEC SQL ROLLBACK WORK RELEASE;
```

```
      exit(1);
    }

  }  /* End of main loop */

  /* Close the file */
  fclose(outfile);

  /* Disconnect from the database. */
  EXEC SQL COMMIT WORK RELEASE;
}


/* Error handling function. Print the error to the screen,
   and exit. */
void sqlerror() {

  printf("SQL Error!\n");
  printf("%.*s\n", sqlca.sqlerrm.sqlerrml, sqlca.sqlerrm.sqlerrmc);

  EXEC SQL WHENEVER SQLERROR CONTINUE;

  EXEC SQL ROLLBACK RELEASE;
}
```

Since the write to the pipe is asynchronous, the insert into **registered_students** will be logged, even if the transaction rolls back. This trigger will thus log both attempted and actual changes to the database.

Sending a Message

Messages are sent in two steps. First the data is packed into the local message buffer, and then the buffer is sent along the pipe. Data is packed using the PACK_MESSAGE procedure, and the SEND_MESSAGE function sends the buffer along the pipe.

PACK_MESSAGE
The PACK_MESSAGE procedure is overloaded to accept different types of data items. On the receiving end of the pipe, the UNPACK_MESSAGE procedure is similarly overloaded to retrieve the different types. The procedure is defined with

```
PROCEDURE PACK_MESSAGE(item IN VARCHAR2);
PROCEDURE PACK_MESSAGE(item IN NUMBER);
PROCEDURE PACK_MESSAGE(item IN DATE);
PROCEDURE PACK_MESSAGE_RAW(item IN RAW);
PROCEDURE PACK_MESSAGE_ROWID(item IN ROWID);
```

The size of the buffer is 4096 bytes. If the total size of the packed data exceeds this value, ORA-6558 is generated. Each item in the buffer takes one byte to represent the datatype, two bytes to represent the length, and the size of the data itself. One additional byte is needed to terminate the message. Because the buffer size is limited, there is no way to send LONG or LONG RAW data along a pipe.

SEND_MESSAGE
Once the local message buffer is filled with one or more calls to PACK_MESSAGE, the contents of the buffer are sent along the pipe with SEND_MESSAGE:

```
FUNCTION SEND_MESSAGE(pipename IN VARCHAR2,
                      timeout IN INTEGER DEFAULT MAXWAIT,
                      maxpipesize IN INTEGER DEFAULT 8192)
    RETURN INTEGER;
```

If the pipe does not yet exist, SEND_MESSAGE will create it. Pipes can also be created with the CREATE_PIPE procedure, which is available in PL/SQL 2.2 and higher and described in the "Creating and Managing Pipes" section later in this chapter. The parameters for SEND_MESSAGE are listed here:

Parameter	Type	Description
pipename	VARCHAR2	Name of the pipe. Pipe names are limited to 30 characters and are not case-sensitive. Names beginning with ORA$ are reserved for use by the database.
timeout	INTEGER	Time-out in seconds. If the message can't be sent for some reason (seethe next table for reasons), then the call will return after timeout seconds. The default value is DBMS_PIPE.MAXWAIT, which is defined as 86400000 seconds (1000 days).

Parameter	Type	Description
maxpipesize	INTEGER	Total size of the pipe, in bytes. Defaults to 8192 bytes (two messages of the maximum size). The sum of the sizes of all the messages in the pipe cannot exceed this value. (As a message is retrieved with RECEIVE_MESSAGE, it is removed from the pipe.) Once the pipe is created, its maximum size is part of the pipe definition, and it persists as long as the pipe itself persists. Different calls to SEND_MESSAGE can provide different *maxpipesize* values. If the new value provided is larger than the existing size, the pipe size is increased. If the new value provided is smaller, the existing larger value is kept.

The return codes for SEND_MESSAGE are listed here:

Return Value	Meaning
0	The message was sent successfully. A call to RECEIVE_MESSAGE will retrieve it.
1	The call timed out. This can happen if the pipe is too full for the message, or if a lock on the pipe could not be obtained.
3	The call was interrupted because of an internal error.

Receiving a Message

Three calls in DBMS_PIPE can be used to receive messages sent along a pipe and to unpack the messages into the original data items. They are RECEIVE_MESSAGE, NEXT_ITEM_TYPE, and UNPACK_MESSAGE.

RECEIVE_MESSAGE
RECEIVE_MESSAGE is the counterpart to SEND_MESSAGE. It retrieves a message from a pipe and places it into the local message buffer. UNPACK_MESSAGE is then used to retrieve the data from the buffer. RECEIVE_MESSAGE is defined as

```
FUNCTION RECEIVE_MESSAGE(pipename IN VARCHAR2,
                         timeout IN INTEGER DEFAULT MAXWAIT)
          RETURN INTEGER;
```

Typically, the receiving program issues a RECEIVE_MESSAGE call. If there is no message waiting, RECEIVE_MESSAGE will block until a message is retrieved. This causes the receiving session to sleep until the message is sent along the pipe. The receiving program is very similar to a Unix daemon, in that it sleeps until a message is received along the pipe to wake it up. The parameters for RECEIVE_MESSAGE are described here:

Parameter	Type	Description
pipename	VARCHAR2	Name of the pipe. This should be the same pipe name as used in SEND_MESSAGE, subject to the same restrictions (<30 characters, case insensitive).
timeout	INTEGER	Maximum time, in seconds, to wait for a message. Similar to SEND_MESSAGE, the time-out defaults to MAXWAIT (100 days). If *timeout* is 0, RECEIVE_MESSAGE returns immediately with a status of 0 (message retrieved) or 1 (time-out).

The return codes are described here:

Return Value	Meaning
0	Success. The message was retrieved into the local buffer and can be unpacked with UNPACK_MESSAGE.
1	Time-out. No message was sent along the pipe during the time that RECEIVE_MESSAGE was waiting.
2	The message in the pipe was too large for the buffer. This is an internal error, which should not normally occur.
3	The call was interrupted because of an internal error.

NEXT_ITEM_TYPE

This function returns the datatype of the next item in the buffer. Based on this value, you can determine which variable should receive the data. If you know this in advance, you don't have to use NEXT_ITEM_TYPE. For more information on how this can be set up, see the section "Establishing a Communications Protocol" later in this chapter. NEXT_ITEM_TYPE is defined with

```
FUNCTION NEXT_ITEM_TYPE RETURN INTEGER;
```

The return codes are described here:

Return Value	Meaning
0	No more items
6	NUMBER
9	VARCHAR2
11	ROWID
12	DATE
23	RAW

UNPACK_MESSAGE
UNPACK_MESSAGE is the counterpart to PACK_MESSAGE. Like PACK_MESSAGE, it is overloaded on the type of the item to retrieve.

```
PROCEDURE UNPACK_MESSAGE(item OUT VARCHAR2);
PROCEDURE UNPACK_MESSAGE(item OUT NUMBER);
PROCEDURE UNPACK_MESSAGE(item OUT DATE);
PROCEDURE UNPACK_MESSAGE_RAW(item OUT RAW);
PROCEDURE UNPACK_MESSAGE_ROWID(item OUT ROWID);
```

The *item* parameter will receive the data item in the buffer. If there are no more items in the buffer, or if the next item in the buffer is not of the same type as requested, the Oracle error ORA-6556 or ORA-6559 is raised. Before raising the error, PL/SQL will try to convert the next item to the requested type, using the default conversion format as described in Chapter 2.

Creating and Managing Pipes

The first time a pipe name is referenced in a SEND_MESSAGE call, the pipe is created implicitly, if it does not already exist. With PL/SQL 2.2 and higher, pipes can be created and dropped explicitly with the CREATE_PIPE and REMOVE_PIPE procedures.

Pipes and the Shared Pool
A pipe itself consists of a data structure in the shared pool area of the SGA (system global area). As such, it does take up space that could be used by other database objects as they are read from disk. Because of this, pipes are automatically purged from the shared pool when the space is required. A pipe will only be purged if it has no waiting messages. The algorithm for doing this is the LRU (least recently

used) algorithm—at any given point, the pipe that will be purged is the one that hasn't been used for the longest amount of time. For more information on the shared pool and how it affects performance, see Chapter 12.

The maximum size of a pipe, and hence the size of the data structure in the shared pool, is given by the **maxpipesize** parameter in SEND_MESSAGE and CREATE_PIPE.

Public vs. Private Pipes

PL/SQL **2.2** ...and HIGHER Pipes that are created implicitly with SEND_MESSAGE are known as *public* pipes. Any user with EXECUTE permission on the DBMS_PIPE package, and who knows the pipe name, can read and write to a public pipe. *Private* pipes, on the other hand, have restricted access. Access to a private pipe is restricted to the user who created the pipe, to stored procedures running under the privilege set of the pipe owner, or to users connected as SYSDBA or INTERNAL.

PL/SQL 2.0 and 2.1 have only public pipes, created implicitly. With PL/SQL 2.2 and higher, private pipes can be created explicitly with the CREATE_PIPE function. This function is the only way to create a private pipe. It can also be used to create a public pipe, if desired. Pipes created with CREATE_PIPE remain in the shared pool until they are explicitly dropped with REMOVE_PIPE, or until the instance is shut down. They are never purged automatically from the SGA. The syntax for CREATE_PIPE is

```
FUNCTION CREATE_PIPE(pipename IN VARCHAR2,
                     maxpipesize IN INTEGER DEFAULT 8192,
                     private IN BOOLEAN DEFAULT TRUE)
    RETURN INTEGER;
```

The parameters for CREATE_PIPE are listed here:

Parameter	Type	Description
pipename	VARCHAR2	Name of the pipe to be created. Pipe names are restricted to 30 characters and less. Names beginning with ORA$ are reserved for internal use.
maxpipesize	INTEGER	Maximum pipe size in bytes. This is the same parameter as in SEND_MESSAGE for implicitly created pipes. The default value is 8192 bytes. If SEND_MESSAGE is called with a higher value for *maxpipesize*, the pipe size is increased to the new larger value. If SEND_MESSAGE is called with a lower value, the existing higher value is retained.

Parameter	Type	Description
private	BOOLEAN	TRUE if the pipe should be private, FALSE otherwise. The default is TRUE. Since public pipes are created implicitly by CREATE_MESSAGE, there is normally little reason to set *private* to FALSE.

CREATE_PIPE will return zero if the pipe is successfully created. If the pipe already exists, and the current user has privileges to access it, a zero is returned and any data already in the pipe remains. If a public pipe exists with the same name, or a private pipe exists with the same name owned by another user, the error "ORA-23322: insufficient privilege to access pipe" is raised and the function does not succeed.

Pipes created explicitly with CREATE_PIPE are dropped with the REMOVE_PIPE function. If any messages still exist in the pipe when it is removed, they are deleted. This is the only way to drop pipes created explicitly other than shutting the instance down. The syntax for REMOVE_PIPE is

```
FUNCTION REMOVE_PIPE(pipename IN VARCHAR)
    RETURN INTEGER;
```

The only parameter is the name of the pipe to be removed. If the pipe exists and the current user has privileges on the pipe, the pipe is removed and the function returns zero. If the pipe does not exist, zero is also returned. If the pipe exists but the current user does not have privileges to access it, ORA-23322 is raised (similar to CREATE_PIPE).

The PURGE Procedure

PURGE will remove the contents of a pipe. The pipe itself will still exist. If it is an implicitly created pipe, since it is now empty, it is eligible to be aged out of the shared pool according to the LRU algorithm. PURGE calls RECEIVE_MESSAGE repeatedly, so the contents of the local message buffer may be overwritten. PURGE is defined with

```
PROCEDURE PURGE(pipename IN VARCHAR2);
```

Privileges and Security

There are three different levels of security implemented with the DBMS_PIPE package. The first is the EXECUTE privilege on the package itself. By default, when the package is created, the privilege is not granted to any user. Therefore, only users with the EXECUTE ANY PROCEDURE system privilege will be able to access the DBMS_PIPE package. In order to allow other database users to utilize the package, use GRANT to assign them EXECUTE privileges on the package.

NOTE
The DBA role includes the EXECUTE ANY PROCEDURE system privilege. Consequently, users with the DBA role granted to them (such as SYSTEM) will be able to access DBMS_PIPE from anonymous PL/SQL blocks by default. Since this privilege is granted via a role, they will not be able to access DBMS_PIPE from stored procedures and triggers, since roles are disabled there. For more information on roles and their interaction with stored subprograms, see Chapter 5.

A good method for using this security is to grant the EXECUTE privilege only to certain database users. Then you can design your own package to control access to the underlying pipes. The EXECUTE privilege on this package can then be granted to other users.

The second security method is the pipe name itself. Unless users know the name of a pipe, they cannot send or receive messages along it. You can take advantage of this feature by using randomly generated pipe names, or by making the pipe names specific to the two sessions communicating over the pipe. The latter method can be accomplished with the UNIQUE_SESSION_NAME function and is described in the following section, "Establishing a Communications Protocol."

Private Pipes

PL/SQL 2.2 ...and HIGHER The most reliable security method is the private pipes available with PL/SQL 2.2. Since a private pipe is available only to the user who created it and users connected as SYSDBA or INTERNAL, access is significantly limited. Even if another user has EXECUTE privileges on the DBMS_PIPE package and knows the name of the pipe, he or she will receive the Oracle error

```
ORA-23322: Insufficient privilege to access pipe
```

This error is raised in the situations identified in Table 9-1. Notice that the error is raised only when a user is creating or dropping a pipe, or trying to send or receive a message. The other calls in DBMS_PIPE do not actually access pipes themselves.

Again, the best way to use private pipes is to create stored procedures or packages that in turn call DBMS_PIPE. Since stored subprograms run under the privilege set of the user who owns them, private pipes can be accessed from stored subprograms.

Procedure or Function	When ORA-23322 Is Raised
CREATE_PIPE	A private pipe with the same name already exists, and the current user does not have privileges to access it. If the current user does have privileges, CREATE_PIPE returns 0 and the pipe ownership is not changed.
SEND_MESSAGE	The current user does not have privileges to access the pipe.
RECEIVE_MESSAGE	The current user does not have privileges to access the pipe.
REMOVE_PIPE	The current user does not have privileges to access the pipe. The pipe will still exist, including any messages currently in it.

TABLE 9-1. *Situations in Which ORA-23322 Is Raised*

Establishing a Communications Protocol

Using pipes is similar to using other low-level communications packages, such as TCP/IP. You have the flexibility of deciding how the data will be formatted and how it will be sent. In addition, you can decide who will receive the message. In order to use this flexibility properly, however, you should keep in mind the suggestions in this section.

Data Formatting

Each message sent over a pipe consists of one or more data items. The data items are inserted into the message buffer using PACK_MESSAGE, and the entire buffer is then sent with SEND_MESSAGE. At the receiving end, the buffer is received with RECEIVE_MESSAGE and the data items retrieved with NEXT_ITEM_TYPE and UNPACK_MESSAGE.

Typically, the receiving program can do different things based on the contents of the message received. For example, the Pro*C program, which implements the back end of the **LogRSChanges** trigger (described earlier in this chapter), uses the first data item to format the message logged to the data file. Essentially, the first data item is an opcode, or instruction, which tells the receiving program how to interpret the remainder of the data. Depending on the type of information, there may be different datatypes in the message, or different numbers of data elements.

TIP
It is a good idea to include a STOP instruction in addition to other instructions that you may need. You can use STOP to cause the waiting program to disconnect from the database and exit cleanly. Without a message such as this, the waiting program would have to be killed from the operating system and/or database level, which is not as clean. We will see an example of this in the following section.

Data Addressing

There can be multiple readers and writers for the same pipe. Only one reader will receive the message, however. Furthermore, it is not defined which reader will actually get it. Because of this, it is best to address your messages to a specific reader program. This can be accomplished by generating a unique pipe name that will be used only by the two sessions involved—one reader and one writer. The UNIQUE_SESSION_NAME function can be used for this. It is defined with

    FUNCTION UNIQUE_SESSION_NAME RETURN VARCHAR2;

Each call to UNIQUE_SESSION_NAME will return a string with a maximum length of 30 characters. Every call from the same database session will return the same string. This string will be unique among all sessions currently connected to the database. If a session disconnects, however, its name can be used by another session at a later point.

UNIQUE_SESSION_NAME can be used as the pipe name, which ensures that the message will go to only one recipient. One method of setting this up is to send the initial message over a pipe with a predefined name. Part of the initial message is the name of the pipe over which to send the response. The receiving program then decodes the initial message and sends the response over this new pipe, which will be used only by these two sessions. Since there is only one reader and one writer, there is no ambiguity about which session will receive the information. We will see an example of this technique in the following section.

Example

This is another version of the Debug package, which we saw in Chapter 8. Similar to the example at the beginning of this chapter, one of the two sessions communicating is a Pro*C program. The Debug package itself communicates with this program.

debug.pc

The program (debug.pc) is shown here:

```
/* debug.pc
   This program is the back end of the DBMS_PIPE version of the
   Debug package. It should be running in another window from
   the PL/SQL session which you are trying to debug. */

/* C and SQL header files */
#include <stdio.h>
EXEC SQL INCLUDE sqlca;

EXEC SQL BEGIN DECLARE SECTION;
  /* Username and password to connect to the database */
  char *v_Connect = "example/example";

  /* Status variables used in the calls to DBMS_PIPE */
  int v_Status;
  VARCHAR v_Code[6];

  /* Variables send and received along pipes. */
  VARCHAR v_ReturnPipeName[31];
  VARCHAR v_Description[100];
  VARCHAR v_Value[100];
EXEC SQL END DECLARE SECTION;

/* Error handling function. */
void sqlerror();

int main() {

  /* Set up the error handling. */
  EXEC SQL WHENEVER SQLERROR DO sqlerror();

  /* Connect to the database. */
  EXEC SQL CONNECT :v_Connect;

  printf("Debug ready for input.\n");

  /* Main loop. The only way we'll break out of the loop is if
     we receive the 'STOP' message or if an error occurs. */
  for (;;) {
    /* Sleep until a message is received over the 'Debug' pipe.
       The timeout is not specified, so the default will be
       used. */
```

```
EXEC SQL EXECUTE
  BEGIN
    :v_Status := DBMS_PIPE.RECEIVE_MESSAGE('DebugPipe');
  END;
END-EXEC;

if (v_Status == 0) {
  /* Successful retrieval of the message. We now need to get
     the first data element, to decide what to do with it. */
  v_Code.len = 6;
  EXEC SQL EXECUTE
    BEGIN
      DBMS_PIPE.UNPACK_MESSAGE(:v_Code);
    END;
  END-EXEC;
  v_Code.arr[v_Code.len] = '\0';

  if (!strcmp(v_Code.arr, "STOP")) {
    /* STOP message received. Break out of the loop. */
    break;
  } /* End of STOP processing */

  else if (!strcmp(v_Code.arr, "TEST")) {
    /* TEST message received. Send back a handshake over the
       same pipe. */
    EXEC SQL EXECUTE
      BEGIN
        DBMS_PIPE.PACK_MESSAGE('Handshake');
        :v_Status := DBMS_PIPE.SEND_MESSAGE('DebugPipe');
      END;
    END-EXEC;

    if (v_Status != 0) {
      /* Error message. Print it out. */
      printf("Error %d while responding to TEST message\n",
          v_Status);
    }
  } /* End of TEST processing */

  else if (!strcmp(v_Code.arr, "DEBUG")) {
    /* DEBUG message received. Unpack the return pipe,
       description, and output value. */
```

```
        v_ReturnPipeName.len = 30;
        v_Description.len = 100;
        v_Value.len = 100;
        EXEC SQL EXECUTE
          BEGIN
            DBMS_PIPE.UNPACK_MESSAGE(:v_ReturnPipeName);
            DBMS_PIPE.UNPACK_MESSAGE(:v_Description);
            DBMS_PIPE.UNPACK_MESSAGE(:v_Value);
          END;
        END-EXEC;

        /* Null-terminate the output variables. */
        v_Description.arr[v_Description.len] = '\0';
        v_Value.arr[v_Value.len] = '\0';

        /* Echo the debugging info to the screen. */
        printf("%s: %s\n", v_Description.arr, v_Value.arr);

        /* Send the handshake message back. */
        EXEC SQL EXECUTE
          BEGIN
            DBMS_PIPE.PACK_MESSAGE('Processed');
            :v_Status := DBMS_PIPE.SEND_MESSAGE(:v_ReturnPipeName);
          END;
        END-EXEC;

        if (v_Status != 0) {
          /* Error message. Print it out. */
          printf("Error %d while sending handshake message\n",
              v_Status);
        }
      } /* End of DEBUG processing */
    } /* End of successful retreive of a message */

  else if (v_Status == 1) {
    /* The RECEIVE_MESSAGE call timed out. Loop back to
       wait again. */
    continue;
  }

  else {
    /* The RECEIVE_MESSAGE call exited with an error.
```

```
          Print it, and exit. */
       printf("Main loop RECEIVE_MESSAGE Error. Status = %d\n",
               v_Status);
       EXEC SQL ROLLBACK WORK RELEASE;
       exit(1);
     }

  }  /* End of main loop */

  /* Disconnect from the database. */
  EXEC SQL COMMIT WORK RELEASE;
}


/* Error handling function. Print the error to the screen,
   and exit. */
void sqlerror() {

  printf("SQL Error!\n");
  printf("%.*s\n", sqlca.sqlerrm.sqlerrml,
                   sqlca.sqlerrm.sqlerrmc);

  EXEC SQL WHENEVER SQLERROR CONTINUE;

  EXEC SQL ROLLBACK RELEASE;
}
```

Debug Package
The Debug package itself is defined with

```
CREATE OR REPLACE PACKAGE Debug AS
  -- Maximum number of seconds to wait for a handshake message.
  v_TimeOut NUMBER := 10;

  -- Main Debug procedure.
  PROCEDURE Debug(p_Description IN VARCHAR2, p_Value IN VARCHAR2);

  -- Sets up the Debug environment.
  PROCEDURE Reset;

  -- Causes the daemon to exit.
```

```
    PROCEDURE Exit;
END Debug;

CREATE OR REPLACE PACKAGE BODY Debug as

  v_CurrentPipeName VARCHAR2(30);

  PROCEDURE Debug(p_Description IN VARCHAR2, p_Value IN
VARCHAR2) IS
    v_ReturnCode NUMBER;
    v_Handshake  VARCHAR2(10);
  BEGIN
    /* If we don't already have a pipe name, determine one. */
    IF v_CurrentPipeName IS NULL THEN
      v_CurrentPipeName := DBMS_PIPE.UNIQUE_SESSION_NAME;
    END IF;

    /* Send the 'DEBUG' message, along with:
         - pipe name for the handshake
         - description
         - value
    */
    DBMS_PIPE.PACK_MESSAGE('DEBUG');
    DBMS_PIPE.PACK_MESSAGE(v_CurrentPipeName);
    DBMS_PIPE.PACK_MESSAGE(p_Description);
    DBMS_PIPE.PACK_MESSAGE(p_Value);
    v_ReturnCode := DBMS_PIPE.SEND_MESSAGE('DebugPipe');

    IF v_ReturnCode != 0 THEN
      RAISE_APPLICATION_ERROR(-20210,
        'Debug.Debug: SEND_MESSAGE failed with ' || v_ReturnCode);
    END IF;

    /* Wait for the handshake message on the return pipe. */
    v_ReturnCode := DBMS_PIPE.RECEIVE_MESSAGE(v_CurrentPipeName);

    IF v_ReturnCode = 1 THEN
      -- Timeout
      RAISE_APPLICATION_ERROR(-20211,
        'Debug.Debug: No handshake message received');
    ELSIF v_ReturnCode != 0 THEN
      -- Other error
```

```
      RAISE_APPLICATION_ERROR(-20212,
        'Debug.Debug: RECEIVE_MESSAGE failed with ' ||
      v_ReturnCode);
  ELSE
    -- Check for the handshake message.
    DBMS_PIPE.UNPACK_MESSAGE(v_Handshake);
    IF v_Handshake = 'Processed' THEN
      -- Output processed.
      NULL;
    ELSE
      -- No handshake
      RAISE_APPLICATION_ERROR(-20213,
        'Debug.Debug: Incorrect handshake message received');
    END IF;
  END IF;
END Debug;


PROCEDURE Reset IS
  /* Check to make sure the daemon is running by sending the
     test message over the pipe. If not, raise an error. */
  v_ReturnCode NUMBER;
BEGIN
  DBMS_PIPE.PACK_MESSAGE('TEST');
  v_ReturnCode := DBMS_PIPE.SEND_MESSAGE('DebugPipe');

  IF v_ReturnCode != 0 THEN
    RAISE_APPLICATION_ERROR(-20200,
      'Debug.Reset: SEND_MESSAGE failed with ' || v_ReturnCode);
  END IF;

  /* The daemon will respond over the same pipe. If this call
     times out, then the daemon isn't ready and we should raise
     an error. */
  v_ReturnCode := DBMS_PIPE.RECEIVE_MESSAGE('DebugPipe', v_TimeOut);
  IF v_ReturnCode = 1 THEN
    -- Timeout
    RAISE_APPLICATION_ERROR(-20201,
      'Debug.Reset: Daemon not ready');
  ELSIF v_ReturnCode != 0 THEN
    -- Other error
    RAISE_APPLICATION_ERROR(-20202,
      'Debug.Reset: RECEIVE_MESSAGE failed with ' ||
```

```
         v_ReturnCode);
    ELSE
      -- Daemon is ready.
      NULL;
    END IF;
  END Reset;

  PROCEDURE Exit IS
    v_ReturnCode NUMBER;
  BEGIN
    -- Send the 'STOP' message.
    DBMS_PIPE.PACK_MESSAGE('STOP');
    v_ReturnCode := DBMS_PIPE.SEND_MESSAGE('DebugPipe');

    IF v_ReturnCode != 0 THEN
      RAISE_APPLICATION_ERROR(-20230,
        'Debug.Exit: SEND_MESSAGE failed with ' || v_ReturnCode);
    END IF;
  END Exit;

END Debug;
```

Comments

There are several things to note about this version of Debug. First of all, the Pro*C program is necessary for the output. When you call **Debug.Debug**, the output will be printed to the screen by the Pro*C program, not by the PL/SQL session. Thus, you should run the program in a separate window from your PL/SQL session. The program is essentially functioning as a *daemon*—it spends most of its time sleeping, waiting for a message to be sent along the pipe.

Opcodes   The first message sent along "DebugPipe" is the opcode for the daemon. This can be either "STOP", "TEST", or "DEBUG". Depending on this opcode, the daemon will respond differently. This allows the daemon to function as a dispatcher. In a more complicated scenario, the daemon could then spawn other processes depending on the opcode, which would then process the data. The daemon itself would then wait for another message.

Communications Protocol   **Debug.Debug** passes a pipe name as part of the initial message. This pipe name is generated uniquely by UNIQUE_SESSION_NAME. After **Debug.Debug** sends the message, it then listens on this new pipe. This is a very useful technique, since it allows multiple daemons to run at the same time. The first message will be received by a waiting daemon. The return pipe name will be used by only one session, so it uniquely identifies the session which has sent the message. This neatly solves the problem of multiple readers on the same pipe. Once the unique pipe name is established, both sessions can send and receive messages along the new pipe, with the assurance that no other session will be listening.

Handshake Messages   Both the PL/SQL package and the Pro*C daemon are readers and writers. Consider the "TEST" message, which is sent by **Debug.Debug**, as an example. The Debug package sends a message, then waits for a reply. If the reply times out, we know that the initial message has not been received properly. Using handshake messages is a valuable part of a good communications protocol.

DBMS_ALERT

The DBMS_ALERT package implements database alerts. An *alert* is a message that is sent when a transaction commits. Unlike pipes, which are asynchronous, alerts are synchronized with transactions. Alerts are generally used for one-way communication, while pipes are used for two-way communication.

The sending session issues a SIGNAL call for a particular alert. This call records the fact that the alert has been signaled in the data dictionary, but does not actually send it. When the transaction containing the SIGNAL call commits, the alert is actually sent. If the transaction rolls back, the alert is not sent. The receiving session first registers interest in particular alerts using the REGISTER procedure. Only alerts that have been registered will be received. The receiving session then waits for alerts to be signaled by the WAITONE or WAITANY procedure.

Sending an Alert

Alerts are sent with the SIGNAL procedure, which records the alert information in the data dictionary. The syntax for SIGNAL is

```
PROCEDURE SIGNAL(name IN VARCHAR2,
                 message IN VARCHAR2);
```

SIGNAL takes only two parameters—the name of the alert to be signaled and a message. Alert names have a maximum length of 30 characters and are not case-sensitive. Similar to pipes, alert names beginning with ORA$ are reserved for use by Oracle and should not be used for user applications. The maximum message length is 1800 bytes.

A given alert can only be in one of two states—signaled or not signaled. The SIGNAL call changes the state of the alert to signaled. This change is recorded in the **dbms_alert_info** data dictionary table, described in the "Alerts and the Data Dictionary" section later in this chapter. Because of this, only one session can signal an alert at a time. Multiple sessions can signal the same alert. However, the first session will cause the later sessions to block.

When the alert is sent, all sessions that are currently waiting for that alert will receive the message. If no sessions are currently waiting, the next session to wait for it will receive it immediately.

Receiving an Alert

Receiving an alert involves two steps—registering interest in an alert and then waiting for it. A receiving session will only receive the alerts for which it has registered.

Registering
The REGISTER procedure is used to register interest in a particular alert. A database session can register for as many alerts as desired. The session will remain registered until it disconnects from the database, or until it calls the REMOVE procedure (described later in this chapter) to indicate that it is no longer interested. The REGISTER procedure is defined with

    PROCEDURE REGISTER(name IN VARCHAR2);

The only parameter is the name of the alert. Registering for an alert does not cause the session to block; it only records that this session is interested.

Waiting for One Alert
The WAITONE procedure is used to wait for a particular alert to occur. If this alert has already been signaled, WAITONE returns immediately with a status of 0, indicating that the alert has been received. If the alert is not signaled, then WAITONE will block until either the alert is signaled or it times out. WAITONE is defined with

    PROCEDURE WAITONE(name IN VARCHAR2,
                      message OUT VARCHAR2,
                      status OUT INTEGER,
                      timeout IN NUMBER DEFAULT MAXWAIT);

The parameters for WAITONE are described here:

Parameter	Type	Description
name	VARCHAR2	Name of the alert for which to wait. The session should have registered interest in this alert with REGISTER prior to calling WAITONE.
message	VARCHAR2	Message text included in the SIGNAL call by the sending session. If there were multiple SIGNAL calls for the same alert before the alert was received, only the latest message is retrieved. Earlier messages are discarded.
status	INTEGER	Returns an indicator as to whether the alert was received. A value of zero indicates that the alert was received, and a value of one indicates that the call timed out.
timeout	NUMBER	Maximum time to wait before returning, in seconds. If *timeout* is not specified, it defaults to DBMS_ALERT.MAXWAIT, which is defined as 1000 days. If the alert is not received within *timeout* seconds, the call returns with status one.

Similar to RECEIVE_MESSAGE, WAITONE will cause the receiving session to sleep until the alert is signaled.

The same session can both signal an alert and then wait for it. In this case, be sure to issue a commit between the SIGNAL and the WAITONE call. Otherwise, the WAITONE call will always time out, since the alert would never have been sent.

Waiting for Any Alert

A session can also wait for any alerts for which it has registered interest to be signaled. This is done with the WAITANY procedure. Unlike WAITONE, WAITANY will return successfully if any of the alerts is signaled, rather than just one particular alert. WAITANY is defined with

```
PROCEDURE WAITANY(name OUT VARCHAR2,
                  message OUT VARCHAR2,
                  status OUT INTEGER,
                  timeout IN NUMBER DEFAULT MAXWAIT);
```

The parameters are described here:

Parameter	Type	Description
name	VARCHAR2	Name of the alert that was signaled. The session will only receive alerts for which it has registered interest prior to WAITONE.
message	VARCHAR2	Message text included in the SIGNAL call by the sending session. If there were multiple SIGNAL calls for the same alert before the alert was received, only the latest message is retrieved. Earlier messages are discarded.
status	INTEGER	Returns an indicator as to whether the alert was received. A value of zero indicates that the alert was received, and a value of one indicates that the call timed out.
timeout	NUMBER	Maximum time to wait before returning, in seconds. If *timeout* is not specified, it defaults to DBMS_ALERT.MAXWAIT, which is defined as 1000 days. If the alert is not received within *timeout* seconds, the call returns with status one.

These parameters are the same as for WAITONE, with the same meanings. The only difference is that *name* is an OUT parameter and will indicate which alert has actually been signaled.

Again, the same session can both signal an alert and then wait for it with WAITANY. If a COMMIT is not issued between the time the alert is signaled and the WAITANY call, WAITANY will always time out, since the alert will never have been actually sent.

Other Procedures

Two additional procedures are used to manage alerts: REMOVE and SET_DEFAULTS.

"Unregistering" for an Alert

When a session is no longer interested in an alert, it should unregister for it. This helps free the resources used to signal and receive the alert. Unregistering is accomplished with the REMOVE procedure:

    PROCEDURE REMOVE(*name* IN VARCHAR2);

The only parameter is the name of the alert. REMOVE is the counterpart to REGISTER.

Polling Intervals

In most cases, Oracle is event driven. This means that a session waiting for something will be notified when that event occurs, rather than having to check in a loop for the event. If a loop is required, it is known as a *polling loop*. The amount of time between each check is known as the *polling interval*. There are two cases in which polling is required for the implementation of alerts:

1. If the database is running in shared mode, polling is required to check for alerts signaled by another instance. The polling interval for this loop can be set by the SET_DEFAULTS procedure.

2. If no registered alerts have been signaled for the WAITANY call, a polling loop is required to check for the signaled alerts. The polling interval starts at 1 second and exponentially increases to a maximum of 30 seconds. This interval is not user configurable.

The SET_DEFAULTS procedure is defined with

    PROCEDURE SET_DEFAULTS(*polling_interval* IN NUMBER);

The only parameter is the polling interval, in seconds. The default is 5 seconds.

Alerts and the Data Dictionary

Alerts are implemented using a data dictionary view, **dbms_alert_info**. A row gets inserted into this table for each alert that a session registers interest in. If more than one session registers interest in the same alert, a row is inserted for each session. The **dbms_alert_info** view has four columns, with the structure indicated as follows:

Column	Datatype	Null?	Description
name	VARCHAR2(30)	NOT NULL	Name of the alert that was registered.
SID	VARCHAR2(30)	NOT NULL	Session identifier for the session that registered interest.
changed	VARCHAR2(1)		Y if the alert is signaled, N if not.
message	VARCHAR2(1800)		Message passed with the signal call.

We can see how this view works, and the implications it has, by examining the scenario illustrated in Figure 9-1. This figure shows three database sessions and the commands they issue over time. The contents of **dbms_alert_info** are shown at each time as well.

Here is a description of events:

Time T1:	Session B registers interest in the alert. At this point, a row is inserted into **dbms_alert_info**, recording this. Note that the **changed** field reads N, indicating that the alert has not yet been signaled.
Time T2:	Session A signals the alert, with message 'Message A'. Since session A hasn't issued a commit, **dbms_alert_info** is unchanged.
Time T3:	Session C signals the same alert, with message 'Message C'. Session A hasn't yet committed. Only one session can signal an alert at a time, so the SIGNAL call issued by session C will block.
Time T4:	Session A commits. Two things happen now. The SIGNAL issued by session C returns, and A's message is put into **dbms_alert_info**. The **changed** field is set to Y, indicating that the alert has been signaled.
Time T5:	Session C commits. This *replaces* the message in **dbms_alert_info**. Session A's message is lost.
Time T6:	Session B finally decides to wait for the alert. The WAITONE call returns immediately, with 'Message C'. The **changed** field is reset to N, indicating that the alert is not signaled anymore.

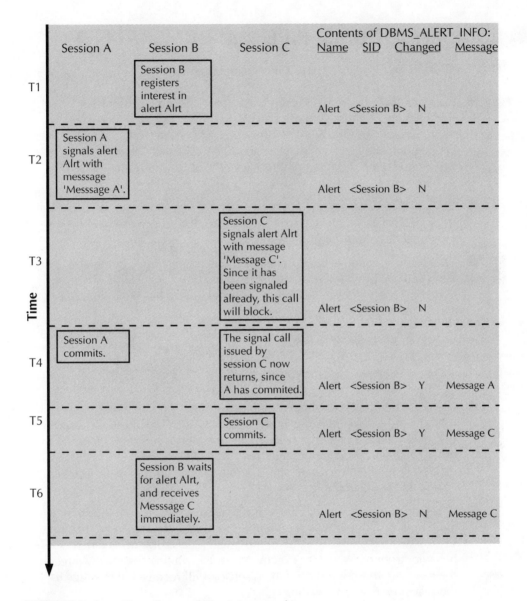

FIGURE 9-1.   *Signaling and receiving an alert*

Comparing DBMS_PIPE and DBMS_ALERT

DBMS_PIPE and DBMS_ALERT have several similarities:

- Both are implemented as PL/SQL packages. This means that the functionality of either package can be used from any PL/SQL execution environment. For DBMS_PIPE, we examined one such situation—the latest version of Debug sends the output to a Pro*C daemon. Both the calling program and the receiving program use PL/SQL, but from different environments.

- Both packages are designed to do the same thing—send messages between sessions that are connected to the same instance. In general, you can use either package for your application.

- PL/SQL does not have a direct means of interfacing with C programs. You can't call a C program from a PL/SQL stored procedure, for example. Currently, the only way around this restriction is to use a pipe or an alert to send a message to a waiting C daemon.

Although both packages accomplish very similar things, there are several important differences in their behavior. Review these differences, which are listed here, and use the package that best suits your needs.

- Alerts are transaction based, while pipes are not. An alert will not be sent until the transaction that contains the DBMS_ALERT.SIGNAL call issues a commit. If the transaction is rolled back, the alert is not sent. Pipes, on the other hand, are asynchronous. As soon as the DBMS_PIPE.SEND_MESSAGE call is issued, the message is sent. There is no way to retrieve it, even if the transaction is rolled back.

- When an alert is signaled, all sessions that have registered interest in the alert, and are waiting, will receive the message. If there is more than one session waiting on the alert, all of them will receive it. This is different behavior from pipes, where exactly one of the waiting sessions will receive the message. It is not defined which session will receive the message if there is more than one waiting.

- The methods of sending the information differ as well. An alert does not have the ability to pass more than a single character string in the message. When a message is sent along a pipe, however, the entire contents of the message buffer are sent. Thus the message can include several differing pieces of information, of different types.

■ Because the messages that can be sent with pipes are more complex than those sent with alerts, pipes can be easily used for two-way communication. A communications protocol is thus important for good pipe usage. Alerts, on the other hand, are generally used for single, one-way messages.

Summary

In this chapter, we have discussed two different mechanisms for intersession communication. Database pipes, implemented with the DBMS_PIPE package, allow two-way communication with complex messages. Database alerts, implemented with the DBMS_ALERT package, allow one-way, transaction-based messages. The packages behave differently, and are used for different types of applications. In Chapter 10 we will examine another built-in package, DBMS_SQL, which allows dynamic PL/SQL programming

CHAPTER 10

Dynamic PL/SQL

One of the design decisions for PL/SQL is the use of early binding, as we discussed in Chapter 2. The main consequence of this decision is that PL/SQL can contain DML statements only—no DDL. With PL/SQL 2.1 and higher, this restriction is lifted through the DBMS_SQL package. DBMS_SQL implements dynamic SQL and PL/SQL, called from other PL/SQL blocks. In this chapter, we will discuss how to use DBMS_SQL, and its implications. We will also compare DBMS_SQL to the dynamic methods available in other Oracle products, such as the precompilers and OCI.

Overview of DBMS_SQL

PL/SQL 2.1 ...and HIGHER The DBMS_SQL package is available with PL/SQL 2.1 (Oracle7 Release 7.1) and higher. Essentially, DBMS_SQL externalizes the normal process of executing SQL and PL/SQL and puts it under your control. Because the complete process is under programmatic control, we can use DBMS_SQL for both DDL and DML statements. The process consists of the following steps:

1. Put the SQL statement or PL/SQL block into a string.

2. Parse the string using DBMS_SQL.PARSE.

3. Bind any input variables using DBMS_SQL.BIND_VARIABLE.

4. If the statement is not a query, execute it using DBMS_SQL.EXECUTE and/or DBMS_SQL.VARIABLE_VALUE. If the statement is a query, continue with step 5.

5. If the statement is a query, define the output variables with DBMS_SQL.DEFINE_COLUMN.

6. Execute the query and fetch the results with DBMS_SQL.EXECUTE, DBMS_SQL.FETCH_ROWS, DBMS_SQL.COLUMN_VALUE, and DBMS_SQL.VARIABLE_VALUE.

As an example, the **RecreateTempTable** procedure first drops, then creates a table called **temp_table**, with the table description passed in to it.

```
CREATE OR REPLACE PROCEDURE RecreateTempTable (
  /* Drops temp_table and recreates it. The table description
     is passed in with p_Description, and should be the contents
     of the CREATE TABLE statement, after the table name. For
     example, the following is a legal call:

     RecreateTempTable('(num_col NUMBER, char_col VARCHAR2(50))');
  */
  p_Description IN VARCHAR2) IS

  v_Cursor        NUMBER;
  v_CreateString  VARCHAR2(100);
  v_DropString    VARCHAR2(100);
  v_NumRows       INTEGER;
BEGIN
  /* Open the cursor for processing. */
  v_Cursor := DBMS_SQL.OPEN_CURSOR;

  /* Drop the table first. */
  v_DropString := 'DROP TABLE temp_table';

  /* Parse and execute the 'DROP TABLE' command. Trap the
     ORA-942 error in case the table doesn't yet exist. */
  BEGIN
```

```
  -- DBMS_SQL.V7 is a constant defined in the package header.
  DBMS_SQL.PARSE(v_Cursor, v_DropString, DBMS_SQL.V7);
  v_NumRows := DBMS_SQL.EXECUTE(v_Cursor);
EXCEPTION
  WHEN OTHERS THEN
    IF SQLCODE != -942 THEN
      RAISE;
    END IF;
END;
/* Now recreate it. We need to create the CREATE TABLE
   string first, then parse and execute it. */
v_CreateString := 'CREATE TABLE temp_table ' || p_Description;
DBMS_SQL.PARSE(v_Cursor, v_CreateString, DBMS_SQL.V7);
v_NumRows := DBMS_SQL.EXECUTE(v_Cursor);

/* Close the cursor, now that we are finished. */
DBMS_SQL.CLOSE_CURSOR(v_Cursor);
EXCEPTION
  WHEN OTHERS THEN
    /* Close the cursor first, then reraise the error so it is
       propagated out. */
    DBMS_SQL.CLOSE_CURSOR(v_Cursor);
    RAISE;
END RecreateTempTable;
```

CAUTION
In order to run this example, you must have the CREATE TABLE and DROP TABLE system privileges granted directly, rather than via a role. See the section "Privileges and DBMS_SQL" later in this chapter for more information.

From this example, we can observe several things:

■ The string that is parsed can be a constant, such as **v_DropString**, or it can be created dynamically by the program using string functions such as concatenation (**v_CreateString** is done this way).

■ Error handling is very similar to the PL/SQL which we have been using so far in this book. The difference is that we can now get compile errors (such as ORA-942) at run time. With static PL/SQL, these would be caught during compile time, before the block starts to run.

■ We have control of cursor processing, including when cursors are opened and closed. It is necessary to close any cursors that we open. The call to DBMS_SQL.CLOSE_CURSOR in the exception handler guarantees this.

The flowchart in Figure 10-1 illustrates the order in which the calls to DBMS_SQL are typically made.

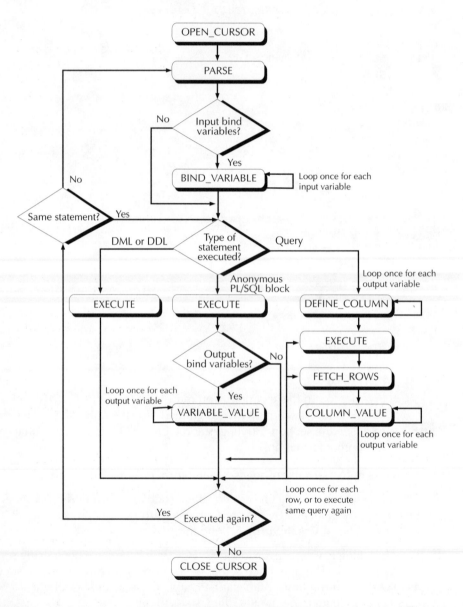

FIGURE 10-1. *Flow of execution in DBMS_SQL*

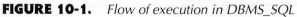

Three different types of statements can be processed with DBMS_SQL: DML and DDL statements, queries, and anonymous PL/SQL blocks. Each type is executed with different procedures. Brief descriptions of each of the procedures follow, with more detailed explanations later in this chapter.

OPEN_CURSOR   Like static PL/SQL, every SQL statement is executed within a cursor. For dynamic PL/SQL, you control the cursor processing. OPEN_CURSOR returns a cursor ID number that is used to identify the context area in which the statement will be processed. All subsequent calls will use this cursor ID number.

PARSE   Parsing a statement involves sending it to the server, where the syntax and semantics of the statement are identified. If the statement is a query, the execution plan is also determined at this point.

BIND_VARIABLE   Binding a variable to a placeholder is similar to the binding process PL/SQL uses for static SQL. A placeholder is a special identifier in the statement. Binding is the act of associating this placeholder with an actual variable. Binding is done for input variables.

DEFINE_COLUMN   Defining an output variable is similar to binding an input variable. The output variables in this case are the results of a query. DEFINE_COLUMN identifies the type and length of the PL/SQL variables that will receive the data when it is retrieved by FETCH_ROWS. DEFINE is used for output variables (the results of queries), while BIND is used for input variables (placeholders in statements).

EXECUTE   For a non-query, EXECUTE will execute the statement and return the number of rows processed. When a query is executed, the active set is determined by EXECUTE. The data is then fetched with FETCH_ROWS. For all statements, bind variables are examined at EXECUTE time.

FETCH_ROWS   Each call to FETCH_ROWS will return more data from the server. The data will be converted into the datatypes specified by the define. EXECUTE_AND_FETCH combines the execute and the fetch operations in one call.

VARIABLE_VALUE   This routine is used to determine the value of a bind variable if it is modified by the statement. This is only used when the statement is a PL/SQL block (perhaps calling a stored procedure).

COLUMN_VALUE   After calling FETCH_ROWS, COLUMN_VALUE is used to actually return the data. It takes variables of the same type specified by the define. COLUMN_VALUE should only be used for queries.

CLOSE_CURSOR   When processing is finished, the cursor is closed. This frees the resources used by the cursor.

Executing Non-Query DML and DDL Statements

This section discusses the steps necessary for executing INSERT, UPDATE, DELETE, and DDL statements. Processing for anonymous PL/SQL blocks is described in the "Executing PL/SQL" section later in this chapter.

The following steps are required for these types of statements:

1. Open the cursor (OPEN_CURSOR).

2. Parse the statement (PARSE).

3. Bind any input variables (BIND_VARIABLE).

4. Execute the statement (EXECUTE).

5. Close the cursor.

Open the Cursor

Every SQL statement or PL/SQL block (static or dynamic) is executed within a cursor. For static SQL, the PL/SQL engine handles the cursor processing for most statements. You can control the processing for queries with the OPEN and CLOSE commands, as discussed in Chapter 4.

Dynamic SQL is no different. Each call to OPEN_CURSOR returns an integer value, which is the cursor ID number. This ID number is used in subsequent calls. More than one SQL statement can be executed within the same cursor, or the same statement can be executed multiple times.

Every call to OPEN_CURSOR should be matched by a call to CLOSE_CURSOR, to free the resources used by the cursor. OPEN_CURSOR is defined with

    OPEN_CURSOR RETURN INTEGER;

It takes no parameters.

Parse the Statement

When the statement is parsed, it is sent to the server. The server checks the syntax and the semantics of the statement, and returns an error (via a raised exception) if the statement has a parse error. The execution plan for the statement is determined at PARSE time as well. The equivalent call in OCI, **oparse**, optionally allows the parse to be *deferred*. Deferring the parse reduces network traffic by buffering the statement until execute time. The statement is then parsed, resulting in only one network round-trip. However, DBMS_SQL does not currently support deferred parsing (up to version 2.3).

PARSE is defined with

```
PROCEDURE PARSE(c IN INTEGER,
               statement IN VARCHAR2,
               language_flag IN INTEGER);
```

The parameters for PARSE are described here:

Parameter	Type	Description
c	INTEGER	ID number for a cursor in which to parse the statement. The cursor must have already been opened with OPEN_CURSOR.
statement	VARCHAR2	SQL statement to be parsed. If the statement is a DML or DDL command, it should not include the final semicolon. If the statement is an anonymous PL/SQL block, it should include the semicolon after the final END.
language_flag	INTEGER	Determines how the statement is treated. SQL statements can be executed with version 6 or version 7 behavior. There are three possible values for this parameter: • V6: version 6 behavior • V7: Oracle7 behavior • NATIVE: behavior for the database to which the program is connected

The *language_flag* parameter specifies version 6 or version 7 behavior with the packaged constants DBMS_SQL.V6, DBMS_SQL.V7, or DBMS_SQL.NATIVE.

NOTE
The only way to use DBMS_SQL against a version 6 database would be if the statement involves a database link. DBMS_SQL itself is contained in PL/SQL 2.1 or higher, which requires Oracle7.

Bind Any Input Variables

Binding associates placeholders in the statement with actual PL/SQL variables. A placeholder is identified by a colon in front of the identifier. For example, the statement

```
INSERT INTO temp_table (num_col, char_col)
  VALUES (:number_value, :char_value);
```

has two placeholders—**:number_value** and **:char_value**. The names of the placeholders are not significant. If the same placeholder name is used more than once in the statement, the same value will be bound for both occurrences. If there are no placeholders in the statement, then no binds are necessary.

The BIND_VARIABLE procedure is used for the bind. It identifies placeholders by name. For example, we could bind the placeholders in the preceding INSERT statement with

```
DBMS_SQL.BIND_VARIABLE(v_CursorID, ':number_value', -7);
DBMS_SQL.BIND_VARIABLE(v_CursorID, ':char_value', 'Hello');
```

The length and datatype of the actual variable are also determined by BIND_VARIABLE, through a set of overloaded calls. The following call is used for binding NUMBERs:

```
PROCEDURE BIND_VARIABLE(c IN INTEGER,
                        name IN VARCHAR2,
                        value IN NUMBER);
```

These are used for binding VARCHAR2s:

```
PROCEDURE BIND_VARIABLE(c IN INTEGER,
                        name IN VARCHAR2,
                        value IN VARCHAR2);

PROCEDURE BIND_VARIABLE(c IN INTEGER,
                        name IN VARCHAR2,
```

```
                          value IN VARCHAR2,
                          out_value_size IN INTEGER);
```

This call is used for binding DATEs:

```
    PROCEDURE BIND_VARIABLE(c IN INTEGER,
                            name IN VARCHAR2,
                            value IN DATE);
```

The following are used for binding CHARs. Their names are different because
PL/SQL does not allow overloading on CHAR & VARCHAR2.

```
    PROCEDURE BIND_VARIABLE_CHAR(c IN INTEGER,
                                 name IN VARCHAR2,
                                 value IN CHAR);
```

```
    PROCEDURE BIND_VARIABLE_CHAR(c IN INTEGER,
                                 name IN VARCHAR2,
                                 value IN CHAR,
                                 out_value_size IN INTEGER);
```

These are used for binding RAWs:

```
    PROCEDURE BIND_VARIABLE_RAW(c IN INTEGER,
                                name IN VARCHAR2,
                                value IN RAW);
```

```
    PROCEDURE BIND_VARIABLE_RAW(c IN INTEGER,
                                name IN VARCHAR2,
                                value IN RAW,
                                out_value_size IN INTEGER);
```

This call is used for binding MLSLABELs:

```
    PROCEDURE BIND_VARIABLE(c IN INTEGER,
                            name IN VARCHAR2,
                            value IN MLSLABEL);
```

Finally, this call is used for binding ROWIDs:

```
    PROCEDURE BIND_VARIABLE_ROWID(c IN INTEGER,
                                  name IN VARCHAR2,
                                  value IN ROWID);
```

The various parameters for these calls are described as follows:

Parameter	Type	Description
c	INTEGER	ID number for a cursor. This cursor should have been previously opened with OPEN_CURSOR and have a statement parsed with PARSE.
name	VARCHAR	Name of the placeholder for which this variable will be bound. The colon should be included.
value	NUMBER, CHAR, VARCHAR2, DATE, ROWID, RAW	Data that will actually be bound. The type and the length of this variable are retrieved as well. The data in this variable will be converted if necessary.
out_value_size	INTEGER	Optional parameter. If specified, this is the maximum expected OUT value size, in bytes. If this parameter is not included, the size of *value* is used. *Out_value_size* should only be specified for anonymous PL/SQL blocks, when the bind variable could be written to. For input variables, the size of *value* won't change.

Execute the Statement

The EXECUTE function is used to execute the statement. It returns the number of rows processed. The return value is valid only for DML statements. For queries, DDL statements, and anonymous PL/SQL blocks, the value is undefined and should be ignored. However, EXECUTE is still a function, so it needs to be called from an expression. EXECUTE is defined as

    FUNCTION EXECUTE(c IN INTEGER) RETURN INTEGER;

The parameters and return value are described here:

Parameter	Type	Description
c	INTEGER	Cursor ID for the cursor containing the statement to be executed. The cursor should have already been opened, a statement parsed, and any placeholders bound.

return value	INTEGER	Number of rows processed by the statement. This is analogous to the %ROWCOUNT cursor attribute. Only defined when the statement executed is an INSERT, UPDATE, or DELETE.

Close the Cursor

The cursor should be closed when processing is complete. This frees the resources allocated by the cursor and signals that it will no longer be used. After a cursor is closed, it can no longer be used unless it is reopened. The syntax for CLOSE_CURSOR is

   PROCEDURE CLOSE_CURSOR(*c* IN OUT INTEGER);

The actual parameter passed into CLOSE_CURSOR should be a valid cursor ID. After the call, the actual parameter is set to NULL, meaning that the cursor is closed.

Example

The **DeleteMajor** procedure deletes all students with the specified major from **students**. Although this can be done with static SQL, this example illustrates the necessary steps for processing.

```
CREATE OR REPLACE PROCEDURE DeleteMajor(
  /* Uses DBMS_SQL to delete all students with the specified
     major from students. The number of rows deleted is
     returned in p_RowsDeleted. */
  p_Major       IN students.major%TYPE,
  p_RowsDeleted OUT INTEGER) AS

  v_CursorID   INTEGER;
  v_DeleteStmt VARCHAR2(100);
BEGIN
  -- Open the cursor for processing.
  v_ CursorID := DBMS_SQL.OPEN_CURSOR;

  -- Determine the SQL string.
  v_DeleteStmt := 'DELETE FROM students WHERE major = :m';

  -- Parse the statement.
```

```
    DBMS_SQL.PARSE(v_CursorID, v_DeleteStmt, DBMS_SQL.V7);

    -- Bind p_Major to the placeholder.
    DBMS_SQL.BIND_VARIABLE(v_CursorID, ':m', p_Major);

    -- Execute the statement.
    p_RowsDeleted := DBMS_SQL.EXECUTE(v_CursorID);

    -- Close the cursor.
    DBMS_SQL.CLOSE_CURSOR(v_CursorID);
EXCEPTION
  WHEN OTHERS THEN
    -- Close the cursor, then raise the error again.
    DBMS_SQL.CLOSE_CURSOR(v_CursorID);
    RAISE;
END DeleteMajor;
```

DeleteMajor can be called from SQL*Plus with

```
SQL> VARIABLE v_NumDeleted NUMBER
SQL> exec DeleteMajor('History', :v_NumDeleted)

PL/SQL procedure successfully completed.

SQL> print v_NumDeleted

V_NUMDELETED
------------
           5
```

Executing Queries

The process for executing queries with DBMS_SQL is much the same as executing
DML and DDL statements, until the call to EXECUTE. Before the execute, you need
to define the types and lengths of the output variables with DEFINE_COLUMN.
After the execute, call FETCH_ROWS and COLUMN_VALUE to retrieve the results.
The steps for queries are therefore:

1. Open a cursor (OPEN_CURSOR).
2. Parse the statement (PARSE).
3. Bind any input variables (BIND_VARIABLE).

4. Define the output variables (DEFINE_COLUMN).

5. Execute the query (EXECUTE).

6. Fetch the rows (FETCH_ROWS).

7. Return the results to PL/SQL variables (COLUMN_VALUE).

8. Close the cursor (CLOSE_CURSOR).

The steps that are the same as we've seen before (OPEN_CURSOR, PARSE, BIND_VARIABLE, EXECUTE, CLOSE_CURSOR) behave the same way as we've seen for DML and DDL statements. The remainder of this section examines in detail only those calls that we haven't seen yet.

Parse the Statement

PARSE behaves the same, but the string for a query needs to meet certain restrictions. It is important that the statement be a single SELECT, and not a SELECT embedded in a PL/SQL block. If the query is inside a block, it is processed according to the rules for PL/SQL blocks, described later in this chapter. In addition, the query should not have an INTO clause. Instead of this clause, we use the DEFINE_COLUMN and COLUMN_VALUE procedures. Finally, as for DML statements, the trailing semicolon should *not* be included. For example, all of the following queries are legal strings for use with DBMS_SQL:

```
SELECT * FROM students

SELECT COUNT(*) "Number of Students", department || course
  FROM registered_students
  WHERE department IN (:d1, :d2)
  GROUP BY department || course

SELECT FullName(ID), ID
  FROM students
  WHERE ID = :student_id
```

Define the Output Variables

The define process is very similar to the bind, except that define is used for output variables in a query. The DEFINE_COLUMN procedure specifies the type and length for the output variables. Each select list item will be converted into the type of its associated output variable.

Unlike BIND_VARIABLE placeholders, select list items are identified by position, not by name. The first position is number 1, the second is number 2, and so on. For example, if the query

```
SELECT first_name, last_name, num_credits
  FROM students
```

were parsed, the DEFINE_COLUMN calls could look like this:

```
DECLARE
  v_FirstName   VARCHAR2(30);
  v_LastName    VARCHAR2(40);
  v_NumCredits  NUMBER;
  v_CursorID    INTEGER;
BEGIN
  ...
  DBMS_SQL.DEFINE_COLUMN(v_CursorID, 1, v_FirstName);
  DBMS_SQL.DEFINE_COLUMN(v_CursorID, 2, v_LastName);
  DBMS_SQL.DEFINE_COLUMN(v_CursorID, 3, v_NumCredits);
  ...
END;
```

Similar to BIND_VARIABLE, DEFINE_COLUMN is overloaded as well. The following call is used for defining NUMBERs:

> PROCEDURE DEFINE_COLUMN(*c* IN INTEGER,
> *position* IN INTEGER,
> *column* IN **NUMBER**);

This call is used for defining VARCHAR2s:

> PROCEDURE DEFINE_COLUMN(*c* IN INTEGER,
> *position* IN INTEGER,
> *column* IN **VARCHAR2**,
> *column_size* IN INTEGER);

Here is the call for defining DATEs:

> PROCEDURE DEFINE_COLUMN(*c* IN INTEGER,
> *position* IN INTEGER,
> *column* IN **DATE**);

This call is used for defining CHARs:

```
PROCEDURE DEFINE_COLUMN_CHAR(c IN INTEGER,
                             position IN INTEGER,
                             column IN CHAR,
                             column_size IN INTEGER);
```

This is used for defining RAWs:

```
PROCEDURE DEFINE_COLUMN_RAW(c IN INTEGER,
                            position IN INTEGER,
                            column IN RAW,
                            column_size IN INTEGER);
```

The following call is used for defining MLSLABELs:

```
PROCEDURE DEFINE_COLUMN(c IN INTEGER,
                        position IN INTEGER,
                        column IN MLSLABEL);
```

And finally, here is the call used for for defining ROWIDs:

```
PROCEDURE DEFINE_COLUMN_ROWID(c IN INTEGER,
                              position IN INTEGER,
                              column IN ROWID);
```

The parameters for these calls are very similar to those for BIND_VARIABLE; they are listed here:

Parameter	Type	Description
c	INTEGER	Cursor ID number. The cursor should already have a query parsed and any input variables bound.
position	INTEGER	Relative position of the select list item. The first select list item starts at 1.
column	NUMBER, DATE, MLSLABEL, RAW, ROWID	Variable that defines the type and length of the output variable. The variable itself isn't necessarily important, but its type and length are. Usually, however, the same variables are used in DEFINE_COLUMN and COLUMN_VALUE.

| column_size | INTEGER | Maximum expected size of the output data. If this isn't specified, the length of *column* is used instead. |

Fetch the Rows

The rows that match the WHERE clause in the query are fetched into a buffer by use of FETCH_ROWS. COLUMN_VALUE is then called to retrieve from this buffer into PL/SQL variables. FETCH_ROWS looks like this:

    FUNCTION FETCH_ROWS(c IN INTEGER) RETURN INTEGER;

The only parameter is the cursor ID number. FETCH_ROWS returns the number of rows returned. Typically, FETCH_ROWS and COLUMN_VALUE are called repeatedly in a loop until FETCH_ROWS returns 0.

NOTE
The exit condition for the fetch loop is when FETCH_ROWS returns 0, not the NO_DATA_FOUND exception or the %NOTFOUND cursor attribute.

The EXECUTE and the first call to FETCH_ROWS can be combined in one call—EXECUTE_AND_FETCH. When used against a remote database, this can save a network trip and thus improve performance. The syntax for EXECUTE_AND_FETCH is

    FUNCTION EXECUTE_AND_FETCH(c IN INTEGER,
                        exact IN BOOLEAN DEFAULT FALSE)
      RETURN INTEGER;

The parameters are described here:

Parameter	Type	Description
c	INTEGER	Cursor ID number. The cursor should already have a query parsed in it, any input variables bound, and the output variables defined.
exact	BOOLEAN	If TRUE, an exception is raised if the query returns more than 1 row. Even if the exception is raised, the rows are still fetched and can be retrieved.

Return the Results to PL/SQL Variables

Once the data is retrieved into the local buffer by FETCH_ROWS, use COLUMN_VALUE to get the data into PL/SQL variables. Typically, the same variables used in DEFINE_COLUMN are used in COLUMN_VALUE. Each call to DEFINE_COLUMN should be matched by a call to COLUMN_VALUE.

COLUMN_VALUE should be called only after a successful FETCH_ROWS or EXECUTE_AND_FETCH. If the prior FETCH did not return any rows, an exception is raised by COLUMN_VALUE.

Similar to BIND_VARIABLE and DEFINE_COLUMN, COLUMN_VALUE is overloaded on the type of the output variable. These are the calls used for NUMBERs:

```
PROCEDURE COLUMN_VALUE(c IN INTEGER,
                       position IN INTEGER,
                       value OUT NUMBER);

PROCEDURE COLUMN_VALUE(c IN INTEGER,
                       position IN INTEGER,
                       value OUT NUMBER,
                       column_error OUT NUMBER,
                       actual_length OUT INTEGER);
```

These are used for VARCHAR2s:

```
PROCEDURE COLUMN_VALUE(c IN INTEGER,
                       position IN INTEGER,
                       value OUT VARCHAR2);

PROCEDURE COLUMN_VALUE(c IN INTEGER,
                       position IN INTEGER,
                       value OUT VARCHAR2,
                       column_error OUT NUMBER,
                       actual_length OUT INTEGER);
```

The following calls are used for DATEs:

```
PROCEDURE COLUMN_VALUE(c IN INTEGER,
                       position IN INTEGER,
                       value OUT DATE);

PROCEDURE COLUMN_VALUE(c IN INTEGER,
                       position IN INTEGER,
```

```
                              value OUT DATE,
                              column_error OUT NUMBER,
                              actual_length OUT INTEGER);
```

These are used for CHARs:

```
PROCEDURE COLUMN_VALUE_CHAR(c IN INTEGER,
                           position IN INTEGER,
                           value OUT CHAR);

PROCEDURE COLUMN_VALUE_CHAR(c IN INTEGER,
                           position IN INTEGER,
                           value OUT CHAR,
                           column_error OUT NUMBER,
                           actual_length OUT INTEGER);
```

These are the calls used for RAWs:

```
PROCEDURE COLUMN_VALUE_RAW(c IN INTEGER,
                          position IN INTEGER,
                          value OUT RAW);

PROCEDURE COLUMN_VALUE_RAW(c IN INTEGER,
                          position IN INTEGER,
                          value OUT RAW,
                          column_error OUT NUMBER,
                          actual_length OUT INTEGER);
```

These are for MLSLABELs:

```
PROCEDURE COLUMN_VALUE(c IN INTEGER,
                      position IN INTEGER,
                      value OUT MLSLABEL);

PROCEDURE COLUMN_VALUE(c IN INTEGER,
                      position IN INTEGER,
                      value OUT MLSLABEL,
                      column_error OUT NUMBER,
                      actual_length OUT INTEGER);
```

Finally, these calls are used for ROWIDs:

```
PROCEDURE COLUMN_VALUE_ROWID(c IN INTEGER,
                             position IN INTEGER,
                             value OUT ROWID);
```

```
ROCEDURE COLUMN_VALUE_ROWID(c IN INTEGER,
                            position IN INTEGER,
                            value OUT ROWID,
                            column_error OUT NUMBER,
                            actual_length OUT INTEGER);
```

The parameters for these calls are described here:

Parameter	Type	Description
c	INTEGER	Cursor ID number. The cursor should have a query parsed, any placeholders bound, and be executed and fetched.
position	INTEGER	Relative position within the select list. Similar to DEFINE_COLUMN, the first select list item is position 1.
value	NUMBER, DATE, MLSLABEL, CHAR, VARCHAR2, RAW, ROWID	Output variable. The contents of the buffer for this row and column will be returned in the variable. If the type of value differs from the type specified in DEFINE_COLUMN, the error ORA-6562 is raised. The exception DBMS_SQL.INCONSISTENT_TYPE is equivalenced to this error as well.
column_error	NUMBER	Column-level error code. If specified, this variable will return errors such as ORA-1406: fetched column value is truncated. The code is returned as a negative value. The error will be raised as an exception as well, but column_error allows you to determine which column caused the error. If the column was retrieved successfully, column_error is zero.

actual_length INTEGER	If specified, contains the original length of the column (before it is returned). This is useful if the output variable is not long enough and is truncated.

Example

The **DynamicQuery** procedure places the first names, last names, and majors for the students in the majors passed to it into **temp_table**. Although this procedure could have been written statically, it illustrates the processing necessary for queries in DBMS_SQL.

```
CREATE OR REPLACE PROCEDURE DynamicQuery (
   /* Uses DBMS_SQL to query the students table, and puts the
      results in temp_table. The first names, last names, and
      majors are inserted for up to two majors inputted. */
   p_Major1 IN students.major%TYPE DEFAULT NULL,
   p_Major2 IN students.major%TYPE DEFAULT NULL) AS

   v_CursorID   INTEGER;
   v_SelectStmt VARCHAR2(500);
   v_FirstName  students.first_name%TYPE;
   v_LastName   students.last_name%TYPE;
   v_Major      students.major%TYPE;
   v_Dummy      INTEGER;

BEGIN
   -- Open the cursor for processing.
   v_CursorID := DBMS_SQL.OPEN_CURSOR;

   -- Create the query string.
   v_SelectStmt := 'SELECT first_name, last_name, major
                    FROM students
                    WHERE major IN (:m1, :m2)
                    ORDER BY major, last_name';

   -- Parse the query.
   DBMS_SQL.PARSE(v_CursorID, v_SelectStmt, DBMS_SQL.V7);

   -- Bind the input variables.
   DBMS_SQL.BIND_VARIABLE(v_CursorID, ':m1', p_Major1);
```

```
    DBMS_SQL.BIND_VARIABLE(v_CursorID, ':m2', p_Major2);

    -- Define the output variables.
    DBMS_SQL.DEFINE_COLUMN(v_CursorID, 1, v_FirstName, 20);
    DBMS_SQL.DEFINE_COLUMN(v_CursorID, 2, v_LastName, 20);
    DBMS_SQL.DEFINE_COLUMN(v_CursorID, 3, v_Major, 30);

    -- Execute the statement. We don't care about the return
    -- value, but we do need to declare a variable for it.
    v_Dummy := DBMS_SQL.EXECUTE(v_CursorID);

    -- This is the fetch loop.
    LOOP
     -- Fetch the rows into the buffer, and also check for the exit
     -- condition from the loop.
      IF DBMS_SQL.FETCH_ROWS(v_CursorID) = 0 THEN
        EXIT;
      END IF;

      -- Retrieve the rows from the buffer into PL/SQL variables.
      DBMS_SQL.COLUMN_VALUE(v_CursorID, 1, v_FirstName);
      DBMS_SQL.COLUMN_VALUE(v_CursorID, 2, v_LastName);
      DBMS_SQL.COLUMN_VALUE(v_CursorID, 3, v_Major);

      -- Insert the fetched data into temp_table.
      INSERT INTO temp_table (char_col)
        VALUES (v_FirstName || ' ' || v_LastName || ' is a ' ||
                v_Major || ' major.');
    END LOOP;

    -- Close the cursor.
    DBMS_SQL.CLOSE_CURSOR(v_CursorID);

    -- Commit our work.
    COMMIT;
EXCEPTION
  WHEN OTHERS THEN
    -- Close the cursor, then raise the error again.
    DBMS_SQL.CLOSE_CURSOR(v_CursorID);
    RAISE;
END DynamicQuery;
```

The output from this procedure in SQL*Plus is

```
SQL> exec DynamicQuery('History', 'Music')
PL/SQL procedure successfully completed.

SQL> SELECT char_col FROM temp_table;

CHAR_COL
------------------------------------------
Margaret Mason is a History major.
Patrick Poll is a History major.
Timothy Taller is a History major.
David Dinsmore is a Music major.
Rose Riznit is a Music major.
```

Executing PL/SQL

The final type of statement is another anonymous PL/SQL block. One possible use of this statement type would be to call a stored procedure. PL/SQL processing is similar to the processing for DML or DDL statements, in that there is no fetch loop. However, the PL/SQL block could assign to the placeholders. An additional call, VARIABLE_VALUE (similar to COLUMN_VALUE), is used to get the output values for the bind variables. The sequence of calls is

1. Open the cursor (OPEN_CURSOR).

2. Parse the statement (PARSE).

3. Bind any input variables (BIND_VARIABLE).

4. Execute the statement (EXECUTE).

5. Retrieve the value of any output variables (COLUMN_VALUE).

6. Close the cursor (CLOSE_CURSOR).

We will only examine those calls that are used differently or are used only for PL/SQL processing. The other calls behave the same as we've already seen.

Parse the Statement

The string passed to PARSE should contain an anonymous PL/SQL block. The trailing semicolon after the final END *is* included, since it is a syntactic part of the block. The block can contain placeholders, which are bound with BIND_VARIABLE. If they are used as output variables (OUT parameters from a procedure, for example), then their new value can be retrieved after the block is executed with VARIABLE_VALUE. The following are all legal strings that can be passed to PARSE:

```
BEGIN :placeholder := 7; END;

DECLARE
  v_Numeric    NUMBER := :p1;
  v_Character VARCHAR2(50) := :p2;
BEGIN
  INSERT INTO temp_table VALUES (v_Numeric, v_Character);
END;

BEGIN
  SELECT first_name, last_name
    INTO :first_name, :last_name
    FROM students
    WHERE ID = :ID;
END;
```

CAUTION
Don't use the -- comments inside the PL/SQL block. The double dash symbol comments out the following characters, up to a newline. However, since the entire block is within one string, the rest of the block will be commented out. Use the C style /* and */ comments instead.

Retrieve the Value of any Output Variables

After the statement has been executed, the value of any output variables can be retrieved with VARIABLE_VALUE. Similar to a query, the value is stored in a buffer first by EXECUTE, and retrieved from this buffer with VARIABLE_VALUE. Only those bind variables that are used as output need be retrieved. Typically, the same variables used in BIND_VARIABLE are used in VARIABLE_VALUE.

Similar to BIND_VARIABLE and COLUMN_VALUE, VARIABLE_VALUE is overloaded by the type of the output variable.

The following call is used for NUMBERs:

```
PROCEDURE VARIABLE_VALUE(c IN INTEGER,
                         name IN VARCHAR2,
                         value OUT NUMBER);
```

This call is used for VARCHAR2s:

```
PROCEDURE VARIABLE_VALUE(c IN INTEGER,
                         name IN VARCHAR2,
                         value OUT VARCHAR2);
```

Here is the call used for DATEs:

```
PROCEDURE VARIABLE_VALUE(c IN INTEGER,
                         name IN VARCHAR2,
                         value OUT DATE);
```

This call is used for CHARs:

```
PROCEDURE VARIABLE_VALUE_CHAR(c IN INTEGER,
                              name IN VARCHAR2,
                              value OUT CHAR);
```

The following is used for RAWs:

```
PROCEDURE VARIABLE_VALUE_RAW(c IN INTEGER,
                             name IN VARCHAR2,
                             value OUT RAW);
```

This is the call used for MLSLABELs:

```
PROCEDURE VARIABLE_VALUE(c IN INTEGER,
                         name IN VARCHAR2,
                         value OUT MLSLABEL);
```

And here is the call used for ROWIDs:

```
*/PROCEDURE VARIABLE_VALUE_ROWID(c IN INTEGER,
                                 name IN VARCHAR2,
                                 value OUT ROWID);
```

The parameters for these calls are listed here:

Parameter	Type	Description
c	INTEGER	Cursor ID number. The cursor should already have been opened, had a PL/SQL block parsed in it, any placeholders bound, and executed.
name	VARCHAR2	Name of the placeholder whose value is to be retrieved.
value	NUMBER, CHAR, VARCHAR2, DATE, RAW, ROWID, MLSLABEL	Output variable to receive the result. If the type of value does not match the type used in BIND_VARIABLE, the error ORA-6562 is raised. The exception DBMS_SQL.INCONSISTENT_TYPE is equivalenced to this error as well.

Example

The **DynamicPLSQL** procedure executes a PL/SQL block that queries students. Note that we have to pass the maximum length for the output placeholders **:first_name** and **:last_name**. They don't have a value before the block is run, and thus the maximum length can't be determined automatically.

```
CREATE OR REPLACE PROCEDURE DynamicPLSQL (
  /* Executes a PL/SQL block dynamically. The block
     selects from students, and uses p_StudentID as an
     input placeholder. */
  p_StudentID IN students.ID%TYPE) IS

  v_CursorID  INTEGER;
  v_BlockStr  VARCHAR2(500);
  v_FirstName students.first_name%TYPE;
  v_LastName  students.last_name%TYPE;
```

```
    v_Dummy       INTEGER;

BEGIN
  -- Open the cursor for processing.
  v_CursorID := DBMS_SQL.OPEN_CURSOR;

  -- Create the string containing the PL/SQL block.
  -- In this string, the :first_name and :last_name
  -- placeholders are output variables, and :ID is an
  -- input variable.
  v_BlockStr :=
    'BEGIN
       SELECT first_name, last_name
         INTO :first_name, :last_name
         FROM students
         WHERE ID = :ID;
     END;';

  -- Parse the statement.
  DBMS_SQL.PARSE(v_CursorID, v_BlockStr, DBMS_SQL.V7);

  -- Bind the placeholders to the variables. Note that we
  -- do this for both the input and output variables.
  -- We pass the maximum length for :first_name and
  -- :last_name.
  DBMS_SQL.BIND_VARIABLE(v_CursorID, ':first_name', v_FirstName, 30);
  DBMS_SQL.BIND_VARIABLE(v_CursorID, ':last_name', v_LastName, 30);
  DBMS_SQL.BIND_VARIABLE(v_CursorID, ':ID', p_StudentID);

  -- Execute the statement. We don't care about the return
  -- value, but we do need to declare a variable for it.
  v_Dummy := DBMS_SQL.EXECUTE(v_CursorID);

  -- Retrieve the values for the output variables.
  DBMS_SQL.VARIABLE_VALUE(v_CursorID, ':first_name', v_FirstName);
  DBMS_SQL.VARIABLE_VALUE(v_CursorID, ':last_name', v_LastName);

  -- Insert them into temp_table.
  INSERT INTO temp_table (num_col, char_col)
    VALUES (p_StudentID, v_FirstName || ' ' || v_LastName);

  -- Close the cursor.
```

```
   DBMS_SQL.CLOSE_CURSOR(v_CursorID);

   -- Commit our work.
   COMMIT;
EXCEPTION
   WHEN OTHERS THEN
     -- Close the cursor, then raise the error again.
     DBMS_SQL.CLOSE_CURSOR(v_CursorID);
     RAISE;
END DynamicPLSQL;
```

When we run DynamicPLSQL from SQL*Plus, we get

```
SQL> exec DynamicPLSQL(10010)
PL/SQL procedure successfully completed.

SQL> exec DynamicPLSQL(10003)
PL/SQL procedure successfully completed.

SQL> SELECT * FROM temp_table;

  NUM_COL CHAR_COL
--------- ------------------
    10010 Rita Razmataz
    10003 Manish Murgratroid
```

Miscellaneous Procedures

There are additional procedures in DBMS_SQL that are used for fetching LONG
data and for error handling.

Fetching LONG Data

PL/SQL 2.2 ...and HIGHER Since a LONG column can hold up to 2 gigabytes of data, and a
PL/SQL LONG can only hold 32K, DBMS_SQL has the ability to fetch
LONG data in more manageable pieces. This is done through two procedures—
DEFINE_COLUMN_LONG and COLUMN_VALUE_LONG. These procedures
are available starting with PL/SQL 2.2.

They are used the same way as DEFINE_COLUMN and COLUMN_VALUE,
except that COLUMN_VALUE_LONG is typically called in a loop to fetch all of
the pieces.

DEFINE_COLUMN_LONG

The syntax for DEFINE_COLUMN_LONG is

```
PROCEDURE DEFINE_COLUMN_LONG(c IN INTEGER,
                                position IN INTEGER);
```

The parameters are described here:

Parameter	Type	Description
c	INTEGER	Cursor ID number. The cursor should have been opened and parsed with a query that contains a LONG column. Any placeholders should have been bound as well.
position	INTEGER	Relative position within the select list of the LONG item. The first select list item is at position 1.

COLUMN_VALUE_LONG

The syntax for COLUMN_VALUE_LONG is

```
PROCEDURE COLUMN_VALUE_LONG(c IN INTEGER,
                               position IN INTEGER,
                               length IN INTEGER,
                               offset IN INTEGER,
                               value OUT VARCHAR2,
                               value_length OUT INTEGER);
```

The parameters are described here:

Parameter	Type	Description
c	INTEGER	Cursor ID number. The cursor should have been opened, the query parsed, input placeholders bound, the long column defined with DEFINE_COLUMN_LONG and other columns with DEFINE_COLUMN, and executed.
position	INTEGER	Relative position within the select list of the LONG item. The first select list item is at position 1.
length	INTEGER	Length in bytes of this segment.

offset	INTEGER	Byte offset within the data at which the piece starts. The piece will be *length* bytes long. A zero *offset* is the first piece.
value	VARCHAR2	Output variable to receive this piece.
value_length	INTEGER	Actual returned length of the piece. When *value_length* < *length*, the total row has been retrieved.

It is most efficient to start at the beginning of the LONG value and fetch from there, rather than starting in the middle or at the end. Each call to COLUMN_VALUE_LONG will return a piece of the LONG value, starting at *offset*. The length of the piece is specified in *length*. The piece is returned in *value*, and the length of the piece is returned in *value_length*. If *value_length* is less than *length*, the end of the data has been reached.

Additional Error Functions

These functions can be used for additional error reporting and management of DBMS_SQL cursors. Some of the calls are only valid in certain places, and these are noted in the descriptions.

LAST_ERROR_POSITION
This function returns the byte offset within the SQL statement where an error occurred. This is most useful for parse errors such as ORA-911. The function is defined with

```
FUNCTION LAST_ERROR_POSITION RETURN INTEGER;
```

This function should be called only after a PARSE call, before any other calls to DBMS_SQL. In addition, it should only be used if the PARSE was unsuccessful.

LAST_ROW_COUNT
This function returns the cumulative count of the number of rows fetched so far from a cursor, similar to the %ROWCOUNT cursor attribute. It is defined with

```
FUNCTION LAST_ROW_COUNT RETURN INTEGER;
```

It should be called after FETCH_ROWS or EXECUTE_AND_FETCH. If LAST_ROW_COUNT is called after EXECUTE, it will always return zero, since no rows could possibly have been retrieved yet.

LAST_ROW_ID

This function returns the rowid of the last row processed. It is defined with

    FUNCTION LAST_ROW_ID RETURN ROWID;

It should be called after FETCH_ROWS or EXECUTE_AND_FETCH. The value is not defined for EXECUTE, since a DML statement can process many rows.

LAST_SQL_FUNCTION_CODE

Returns the function code for the SQL statement currently being executed. The function codes are subject to change between releases and are listed in Table 10-1.

Code	SQL Function	Code	SQL Function	Code	SQL Function	Code	SQL Function
01	CREATE TABLE	02	SET ROLE	03	INSERT	04	SELECT
05	UPDATE	06	DROP ROLE	07	DROP VIEW	08	DROP TABLE
09	DELETE	10	CREATE VIEW	11	DROP USER	12	CREATE ROLE
13	CREATE SEQUENCE	14	ALTER SEQUENCE	15	(not used)	16	DROP SEQUENCE
17	CREATE SCHEMA	18	CREATE CLUSTER	19	CREATE USER	20	CREATE INDEX
21	DROP INDEX	22	DROP CLUSTER	23	VALIDATE INDEX	24	CREATE PROCEDURE
25	ALTER PROCEDURE	26	ALTER TABLE	27	EXPLAIN	28	GRANT
29	REVOKE	30	CREATE SYNONYM	31	DROP SYNONYM	32	ALTER SYSTEM SWITCH LOG
33	SET TRANSACTION	34	PL/SQL EXECUTE	35	LOCK TABLE	36	(not used)

TABLE 10-1. *SQL Function Codes*

Code	SQL Function	Code	SQL Function	Code	SQL Function	Code	SQL Function
37	RENAME	38	COMMENT	39	AUDIT	40	NOAUDIT
41	ALTER INDEX	42	CREATE EXTERNAL DATATYPE	43	DROP EXTERNAL DATATYPE	44	CREATE DATABASE
45	ALTER DATABASE	46	CREATE ROLLBACK SEGMENT	47	ALTER ROLLBACK SEGMENT	48	DROP ROLLBACK SEGMENT
49	CREATE TABLESPACE	50	ALTER TABLESPACE	51	DROP TABLESPACE	52	ALTER SESSION
53	ALTER USER	54	COMMIT	55	ROLLBACK	56	SAVEPOINT
57	CREATE CONTROL FILE	58	ALTER TRACING	59	create trigger	60	ALTER TRIGGER
61	DROP TRIGGER	62	ANALYZE TABLE	63	ANALYZE INDEX	64	ANALYZE CLUSTER
65	CREATE PROFILE	66	DROP PROFILE	67	ALTER PROFILE	68	DROP PROCEDURE
69	DROP PROCEDURE	70	ALTER RESOURCE COST	71	CREATE SNAPSHOT LOG	72	ALTER SNAPSHOT LOG
73	DROP SNAPSHOT LOG	74	CREATE SNAPSHOT	75	ALTER SNAPSHOT	76	DROP SNAPSHOT

TABLE 10-1. *SQL Function Codes (continued)*

The syntax is

FUNCTION LAST_SQL_FUNCTION_CODE RETURN INTEGER;

This function can be called immediately after the EXECUTE call. If used at another time, the return value is undefined.

IS_OPEN

This boolean function returns TRUE if the cursor identified by *c* is already open and FALSE if not. It is defined with

FUNCTION IS_OPEN(*c* IN INTEGER) RETURN BOOLEAN;

We can use this function in our error handling to make it more robust:

```
DECLARE
  v_CursorID INTEGER;
  ...
BEGIN
  ...
EXCEPTION
  WHEN OTHERS THEN
    IF DBMS_SQL.IS_OPEN(v_CursorID) THEN
      DBMS_SQL.CLOSE_CURSOR(v_CursorID);
    END IF;
    RAISE;
END;
```

Privileges and DBMS_SQL

Several issues arise with privileges when using DBMS_SQL. These include the privilege to execute DBMS_SQL itself, and the way roles interact with DBMS_SQL.

Privileges Required for DBMS_SQL

In order to use DBMS_SQL, you need the EXECUTE privilege on the package. Like the other DBMS packages, DBMS_SQL is owned by SYS. The install script that creates the package typically grants EXECUTE on the package to PUBLIC, so all users will have access to the package. You may want to revoke this privilege from PUBLIC, and grant it only to select users.

Typically, procedures run under the privilege set of their owners. In this case, DBMS_SQL is owned by SYS, which would mean that any commands executed using DBMS_SQL would be run as SYS. Needless to say, this would be a serious security breach. To prevent this, the procedures and functions in DBMS_SQL run under the privilege set of their caller, not SYS. If you connect as **UserA** and call **RecreateTempTable**, for example, **temp_table** would be created under **UserA**'s schema, even though DBMS_SQL is owned by SYS.

Roles and DBMS_SQL

As we discussed in Chapter 5, all roles are disabled inside stored procedures. This applies to DBMS_SQL as well. However, since we can execute arbitrary commands using DBMS_SQL, the user calling DBMS_SQL needs the privileges to execute the dynamic command, as well as EXECUTE on DBMS_SQL itself. Furthermore, the privilege to execute the dynamic command needs to be granted explicitly, and not through a role. The role is disabled inside DBMS_SQL, so the privilege would not be available.

For example, the RESOURCE role is commonly granted to users. This role contains the system privilege CREATE TABLE. Suppose **UserA** has been granted RESOURCE. Then **UserA** can issue commands such as

```
DROP TABLE temp_table;
CREATE TABLE temp_table (num_col NUMBER, char_col VARCHAR2(50));
```

from SQL, since the role is enabled. However, when these same commands are executed using DBMS_SQL (the **RecreateTempTable** procedure, for example), the role is disabled and the error

```
ORA-1031: insufficient privileges
```

is returned. The solution for this is to grant CREATE TABLE directly to **UserA**.

TIP
Whenever you receive the ORA-1031 error when using DBMS_SQL, check the SQL statement or PL/SQL block being executed by DBMS_SQL. Make sure that the user executing this has the appropriate system and object privileges granted directly, not via a role. This is most likely the cause of the problem.

Comparison Between DBMS_SQL and Other Dynamic Methods

Three different tools can perform dynamic SQL and PL/SQL for Oracle: the DBMS_SQL package, OCI, and the Oracle precompilers. The steps required for each are the same—opening cursors, parsing statements, binding input variables, defining output variables, executing and fetching, and closing the cursors at the end.

DBMS_SQL is the newest of these methods and, consequently, has fewer features than the others. In addition, since PL/SQL has no pointer variables, the interface is different.

Feature Comparison

DBMS_SQL differs from the other methods in the lack of a describe function, no array processing, and how it is implemented.

No Way to Describe the Select List

The main thing missing from DBMS_SQL is the ability to describe a select list. Both OCI and the precompilers can do this. Describing the select list of a query allows you to determine at run time what kinds of items will be returned—their lengths and datatypes. This limits the kinds of applications that can be written with DBMS_SQL.

The reason for this has to do with the fact that PL/SQL does not currently allow the user to dynamically allocate and deallocate memory. Typically, after the statement is described, the output variables are dynamically allocated to fit the size of the expected data. Since this isn't currently possible (up through version 2.3), the describe has been left out.

This information can still be determined from PL/SQL, however. The **user_tab_columns** data dictionary view contains information about the type and length of database table columns, so a PL/SQL program can query this table to determine the select list structure.

Array Processing

Both OCI and the precompilers can use the Oracle Array Interface. This method allows data to be inserted into the database directly from C arrays, or fetched from the database directly into C arrays. This is a very useful feature, which can significantly reduce network traffic.

PL/SQL in general does not have this feature. Thus, DBMS_SQL does not. For more information, see Chapter 12.

DBMS_SQL as a Wrapper for OCI

Many of the calls in DBMS_SQL have equivalent calls in OCI. This includes one feature of OCI that is not yet available in the precompilers—fetching from a LONG column in pieces. The COLUMN_VALUE_LONG procedure is similar to the OCI procedure **oflng**, and functions the same way.

Other new features of OCI available in 7.3, such as piecewise insertion and fetching of LONG data, are not yet available in DBMS_SQL as of 2.3.

Interface Differences

Because PL/SQL does not yet (as of 2.3) provide a user-accessible interface for pointer variables, all fetch operations have to be put into a local buffer and then retrieved with COLUMN_VALUE or VARIABLE_VALUE. These extra calls are not necessary with either OCI or the precompilers, since both of these other methods can pass the addresses of program variables directly to the server. When the statement is executed, the database writes directly into the program variables. No buffer is needed.

Tips and Techniques

In this section I suggest several tips for using DBMS_SQL. DBMS_SQL is a powerful feature, but it is also fairly complicated. I recommend using DBMS_SQL when your application demands it. If, however, the application can be implemented using other means (such as cursor variables), those may be a better option.

Reusing Cursors

Whenever possible, cursors should be reused. Avoid unnecessary calls to OPEN_CURSOR and CLOSE_CURSOR. Since different SQL statements can be processed in the same cursor, you can avoid the extra overhead associated with repeatedly opening and closing the cursor. If you are executing the same statement repeatedly, there is no need to rePARSE the statement either—simply reEXECUTE it.

Permissions

Roles are disabled inside packaged procedures, including DBMS_SQL. This can cause strange errors, such as ORA-1031. For more information, see the previous section, "Privileges and DBMS_SQL."

DDL Operations and Hanging

If you are not careful, using DBMS_SQL to dynamically execute DDL statements can cause hanging. For example, a call to a packaged procedure places a lock on the procedure until the call completes. If you try to dynamically drop the package while another user is executing a procedure in that package, the EXECUTE call will hang. The maximum length of the time-out is five minutes.

Summary

In this chapter, we have examined the DBMS_SQL package, which allows dynamic processing of SQL and PL/SQL from a PL/SQL program. Depending on the type of statement being processed (query, DDL or DML, PL/SQL block), different procedures in DBMS_SQL are used. We also compared DBMS_SQL to the dynamic methods available with the precompilers and OCI, and discussed tips and techniques for using dynamic SQL in your programs.

CHAPTER 11

Database Jobs and File I/O

PL/SQL has two additional useful supplied packages. The DBMS_JOB package, available with PL/SQL 2.2 and higher, allows stored procedures to be run periodically by the system, without user intervention. The UTL_FILE package, available with PL/SQL 2.3 and higher, adds the ability to read and write to operating system files. These packages extend PL/SQL and provide functions that are available with other third-generation languages.

Database Jobs

PL/SQL 2.2 ...and HIGHER With PL/SQL 2.2 and higher, you can schedule PL/SQL routines to run at specified times. This is done with the DBMS_JOB package, which implements *job queues*. A job is run by submitting it to a job queue, along with parameters specifying how often the job should be run. Information about currently executing jobs, and the success or failure of previously submitted jobs, is available in the data dictionary. For more information about database jobs, see the *Oracle7 Server Administrator's Guide*, release 7.2 or later.

Background Processes

An Oracle instance is made up of various processes running on the system. Different processes are in charge of running different aspects of the database, such as reading database blocks into memory, writing blocks back to disk, and archiving data to offline storage. These processes are described in Chapter 12. In addition to the processes that manage the database, there are processes known as the SNP processes. SNP processes implement database snapshots, and also job queues.

SNP processes run in the background, like other database processes. Unlike other database processes, however, if an SNP process fails, Oracle7 restarts it without affecting the rest of the database. If other database processes fail, this generally brings down the database. Periodically, an SNP process will wake up and check for a job. If a job is due to be run, the SNP process will execute it and then go back to sleep. A given process can be running only one job at a time. There can be a maximum of ten SNP processes (numbered SNP0 through SNP9), so a maximum of ten database jobs can be running simultaneously.

There are three parameters in the INIT.ORA initialization file that control the behavior of the SNP processes. They are described here:

Parameter	Default Value	Range of Values	Description
JOB_QUEUE_PROCESSES	0	0..10	How many processes to start.
JOB_QUEUE_INTERVAL	60	1..3600	Interval between wake-ups of the process. The process will sleep for the specified number of seconds before checking for a new job.
JOB_QUEUE_KEEP_CONNECTIONS	FALSE	TRUE, FALSE	Controls whether an SNP process closes any remote database connections it makes. If TRUE, all connections will be kept until the process is shut down. If FALSE, the connections are kept only as long as there are jobs to execute.

NOTE

If JOB_QUEUE_PROCESSES is set to zero, no jobs will be executed. Since each process will sleep for JOB_QUEUE_INTERVAL seconds before checking for new jobs, JOB_QUEUE_INTERVAL specifies the minimum amount of time between job executions.

Running a Job

There are two ways of running a job—submitting it to a job queue, or forcing it to run immediately. When a job is submitted to a job queue, an SNP process will run it when it is due. If specified, this job can then be run automatically thereafter. If a job is run immediately, it is run only once.

SUBMIT

A job is submitted to the job queue with the SUBMIT procedure. SUBMIT is defined with

```
PROCEDURE SUBMIT(job OUT BINARY_INTEGER,
                what IN VARCHAR2,
                next_date IN DATE DEFAULT SYSDATE,
                interval IN VARCHAR2 DEFAULT NULL,
                no_parse IN BOOLEAN DEFAULT FALSE);
```

The parameters for SUBMIT are listed here:

Parameter	Type	Description
job	BINARY_ INTEGER	Job number. When the job is created, a unique number is assigned to it. As long as the job exists, its job number will remain the same.
what	VARCHAR2	PL/SQL code that makes up the job. Typically, this is a call to a stored procedure.
next_date	DATE	Date when the job will next run.
interval	VARCHAR2	Function that calculates the time at which the job will run again.
no_parse	BOOLEAN	If TRUE, the job code will not be parsed until the first time it is executed. If FALSE (the default), the job code is parsed when it is submitted. This is useful if the database objects referenced by the job do not yet exist, but you still want to submit it.

For example, suppose we create a procedure **TempInsert** with

```
CREATE SEQUENCE temp_seq
  START WITH 1
  INCREMENT BY 1;

CREATE OR REPLACE PROCEDURE TempInsert AS
BEGIN
    INSERT INTO temp_table (num_col)
      VALUES (temp_seq.nextval);
    COMMIT;
END TempInsert;
```

We can have **TempInsert** run every minute with the following SQL*Plus script:

```
SQL> VARIABLE v_JobNum NUMBER
SQL> BEGIN
  2     DBMS_JOB.SUBMIT(:v_JobNum, 'TempInsert;', sysdate,
  3                      'sysdate + (1/(24*60*60))');
  4  END;
  5  /

PL/SQL procedure successfully completed.
SQL> print v_JobNum

 V_JOBNUM
---------
        2
```

Job Numbers   The job number is assigned to the job when it is first submitted. Job numbers are generated from the sequence SYS.JOBSEQ. Once a job number is assigned to a job, it will never change, unless the job is removed and then resubmitted.

CAUTION
Jobs can be exported and imported, like other database objects. This does *not* change the job number. If you try to import a job whose number already exists, you will receive an error and the job cannot be imported. In this case, simply resubmit the job, which will generate a new job number.

Job Definitions   The *what* parameter specifies the code for the job. Jobs consist of stored procedures, and *what* should be a string that calls the procedure. This procedure can have any number of parameters. All parameters should be IN parameters, since there aren't any actual parameters that could receive the value of an OUT or IN OUT formal parameter. The only exceptions to this rule are the special identifiers **next_date** and **broken**, described next.

TIP
Once the job is submitted, it will be run by one of the SNP processes in the background. In order to see the results, be sure to code a COMMIT at the end of the job procedure.

There are three special identifiers that are valid in a job definition, listed here,:

Identifier	Type	Description
job	BINARY_INTEGER	Evaluates to the number of the current job.
next_date	DATE	Evaluates to the date when the job will next run.
broken	BOOLEAN	Evaluates to the job status—TRUE if the job is broken, FALSE otherwise.

job is an IN parameter, so the job can only read this value. **next_date** and **broken** are IN OUT parameters, so the job itself can modify them. If we modify **TempInsert** as follows,

```
CREATE OR REPLACE PROCEDURE TempInsert
  (p_NextDate IN OUT DATE) AS
  v_CurrVal NUMBER;
BEGIN
  INSERT INTO temp_table (num_col)
    VALUES (temp_seq.nextval);
  SELECT temp_seq.currval
    INTO v_CurrVal
    FROM dual;
  IF v_CurrVal > 15 THEN
    p_NextDate := NULL;
  END IF;
  COMMIT;
END TempInsert;
```

and submit it with

```
BEGIN
  DBMS_JOB.SUBMIT(:v_JobNum, 'TempInsert(next_date);', sysdate,
                  'sysdate + (1/(24*60*60))');
END;
```

then the job will automatically remove itself from the job queue when the sequence number is greater than 15. Because the job can return the value of **next_date** and **broken**, a job can remove itself from the queue when desired.

The *what* parameter is a VARCHAR2 character string. As a result, any character literals that should be used in the call to the job procedure should be delimited by two single quotes. The procedure call should also be terminated with a semicolon. For example, we could call **Register** with the following *what* string:

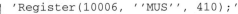

```
'Register(10006, ''MUS'', 410);'
```

Execution Intervals   The first time the job will be run after the SUBMIT call is given by the **next_date** parameter. Just before the job itself is executed, the function given by *interval* is evaluated. If the job is successful, the result returned by **interval** becomes the new **next_date**. If the job is successful and *interval* evaluates to NULL, the job is deleted from the queue. The expression given by *interval* is passed as a character string, but should evaluate to a date. Here are some common expressions and their effects:

Interval Value	Result
'SYSDATE + 7'	Exactly seven days from the last execution. If the job is initially submitted on Tuesday, then the next run will be the following Tuesday. If the second run fails, and it then runs successfully on Wednesday, subsequent runs will be on Wednesdays.
'NEXT_DAY(TRUNC (SYSDATE), ''FRIDAY'') + 12	Every Friday at noon. Notice the use of the two single quotes around the literal 'FRIDAY' within the string.
SYSDATE + 1/24	Every hour.

RUN

The DBMS_ JOB.RUN procedure will run a job immediately. It is defined with

RUN(*job* IN BINARY_INTEGER);

The job must already have been created by calling SUBMIT. Regardless of the current status of the job, it is run immediately by the current process. Note that the job is *not* run by an SNP background process.

Broken Jobs

Oracle will automatically attempt to run a job again if it fails. The job will be run again starting one minute after the first failure. If that attempt also fails, the next attempt is two minutes later. The interval doubles each time, to four minutes, then to eight, and so on. If the retry interval exceeds the execution interval specified for the job, the execution interval is used. Once the job fails 16 times, it is marked as broken. Broken jobs will not be run again automatically.

You can run a broken job with RUN, however. If that call succeeds, then the failure count is reset to zero and the job is marked as not broken. The BROKEN procedure can also be used to change the status of a job. It is defined with

```
BROKEN(job IN BINARY_INTEGER,
       broken IN BOOLEAN,
       next_date IN DATE DEFAULT SYSDATE);
```

The parameters are described in this table:

Parameter	Type	Description
job	BINARY_INTEGER	Job number of the job whose status will be changed.
broken	BOOLEAN	New status of the job. If TRUE, the job is marked as broken. If FALSE, the job is marked as not broken and will be run next at the time specified by next_date.
next_date	DATE	Date at which the job will be run next. Defaults to SYSDATE.

Removing a Job

A job can be removed from a job queue explicitly with the REMOVE procedure,

```
REMOVE(job IN BINARY_INTEGER);
```

where the only parameter is the job number. If the *next_date* for a job evaluates to NULL (either because the job has set it or *interval* evaluates to NULL), then the job will be removed after it has finished executing. If the job is currently running when REMOVE is called, it will be removed from the queue after it has finished.

Altering a Job

The parameters for a job can be altered after the job has been submitted. This is done using one of the following procedures:

```
PROCEDURE CHANGE(job IN BINARY_INTEGER,
                 what IN VARCHAR2,
                 next_date IN DATE,
                 interval IN VARCHAR2);

PROCEDURE WHAT(job IN BINARY_INTEGER,
              what IN VARCHAR2);

PROCEDURE NEXT_DATE(job IN BINARY_INTEGER,
                    next_date IN DATE);

PROCEDURE INTERVAL(job IN BINARY_INTEGER,
                   interval IN VARCHAR2);
```

The CHANGE procedure is used to alter more than one job characteristic at once, and the WHAT, NEXT_DATE, and INTERVAL procedures are used to change the characteristic identified by their respective arguments.

All the arguments behave the same as they do in the SUBMIT procedure. If you change *what* using CHANGE or WHAT, then the current environment becomes the new execution environment for the job. For more information on job environments, see the section "Job Execution Environments," which follows shortly.

Viewing Jobs in the Data Dictionary

There are several data dictionary views that record information about jobs. **dba_jobs** and **user_jobs** return information about a job, such as *what*, *next_date*, and *interval*. Information about the execution environment is also included. The **dba_jobs_running** view describes the jobs that are currently running. These views are described in Appendix D.

Job Execution Environments

When you submit a job to a queue, the current environment is recorded. This includes the settings of NLS parameters such as NLS_DATE_FORMAT. The settings recorded at job creation will be used whenever the job is run. These settings will be changed if the **what** characteristic is changed using CHANGE or WHAT.

NOTE
A job can change its environment by issuing the ALTER SESSION command via the DBMS_SQL package. If this is done, it will only affect the current execution of the job, not future executions. The DBMS_SQL package is described in Chapter 10.

File I/O

PL/SQL 2.3 ...and HIGHER As we have seen, PL/SQL does not have input and output capability built into the language itself, but does have this functionality through supplied packages. Input and output to the screen are implemented with the DBMS_OUTPUT package, described in Chapter 8. PL/SQL 2.3 extends I/O to text files, with the UTL_FILE package. There is no way to output directly to a binary file with this version of UTL_FILE. This restriction will likely be lifted in future versions of PL/SQL.

This section describes how UTL_FILE works. There are three complete examples at the end of the section that demonstrate the package.

Security

Client-side PL/SQL has a package similar to UTL_FILE, known as TEXT_IO. There are different security issues on the client than on the server, however. Files created with the client-side TEXT_IO package can be placed anywhere on the client, subject to operating system privileges. There are no privileges associated with PL/SQL or the database itself for client-side file I/O.

Database Security
On the server, however, a more rigorous security mechanism is needed. This is implemented by restricting the directories into which the package can write. *Accessible* directories are the directories into which UTL_FILE can write. They are defined by the **utl_file_dir** parameter in the INIT.ORA initialization file. Each accessible directory is indicated by a line such as

utl_file_dir = *directory_name*

in the initialization file. The specification of *directory_name* will vary, depending on the operating system. If the operating system is case-sensitive, then *directory_name* is case-sensitive. For example, the following entries in INIT.ORA are legal for a Unix system, assuming that the directories specified actually exist:

```
utl_file_dir = /tmp
utl_file_dir = /home/oracle/output_files
```

In order to access a file with UTL_FILE, the directory name and the filename are passed as separate parameters to the FOPEN function. The directory name is compared against the accessible files list. If it is found, then the operation is allowed. If the directory name specified by FOPEN is not accessible, an error is returned. Subdirectories of accessible directories are not allowed, unless the subdirectory is also listed explicitly as accessible. Given the preceding accessible directories, Table 11-1 describes legal and illegal directory/filename pairs.

NOTE
Even if the operating system is not case-sensitive, the comparison between the specified directory and the accessible directories is always case-sensitive.

If the INIT.ORA file contains

```
utl_file_dir = *
```

Directory Name	Filename	Comment
/tmp	myfile.out	Legal
/home/oracle/ output_files	students.list	Legal
/tmp/1995	january.results	Illegal—subdirectory /tmp/1995 is not accessible
/home/oracle	output_files/ classes.list	Illegal—subdirectory passed as part of the file name
/TMP	myfile.out	Illegal—case different

TABLE 11-1. *Legal and Illegal File Specifications*

then database permissions are disabled. This makes all directories accessible to
UTL_FILE.

CAUTION
Turning off database permissions should be used very carefully.
Oracle does not recommend that you use this option in production
systems, since it can circumvent operating system permissions. In
addition, do not use "." (the current directory on Unix systems) as part
of the accessible directories list. Always use explicit directory paths.

Operating System Security

The file I/O operationsperformed with UTL_FILE will be done by the Oracle user.
(The Oracle user is the owner of the files that are used to run the database, and also
the owner of the processes that make up a database instance.) Consequently, the
Oracle user has to have operating system privileges to read from and write to all of
the accessible directories. If the Oracle user does not have privileges for an
accessible directory, then any operations in that directory will be prohibited by the
operating system.

Any files created by UTL_FILE will be owned by the Oracle user and created
with the default operating system privileges for the Oracle user. If it is necessary for
other users to access these files outside of UTL_FILE, then the system administrator
should change the permissions on the files.

CAUTION
It is also good security practice to prohibit write operations on
directories in the accessible directory list. The only user who should
be given write permission on accessible directories should be the
Oracle user. If users are allowed write permission, they can create
symbolic links to other directories, and thus circumvent operating
system privilege checking.

Exceptions Raised by UTL_FILE

If a procedure or function in UTL_FILE encounters an error, it will raise an
exception. The possible exceptions are listed in Table 11-2. Note that these
exceptions include seven that are defined in UTL_FILE, and two predefined
exceptions (NO_DATA_FOUND and VALUE_ERROR). The UTL_FILE exceptions
can be caught by name or by an OTHERS exception handler. The predefined
exceptions can be identified by their SQLCODE values as well.

Exception	Raised When	Raised By
INVALID_PATH	Directory or filename is invalid or not accessible.	FOPEN
INVALID_MODE	Invalid string specified for file mode.	FOPEN
INVALID_FILEHANDLE	File handle does not specify an open file.	FCLOSE, GET_LINE, PUT, PUT_LINE, NEW_LINE, PUTF, FFLUSH
INVALID_OPERATION	File could not be opened as requested, perhaps because of operating system permissions. Also raised when attempting a write operation on a file opened for read, or a read operation on a file opened for write.	GET_LINE, PUT, PUT_LINE, NEW_LINE, PUTF, FFLUSH
READ_ERROR	Operating system error occurred during a read operation.	GET_LINE
WRITE_ERROR	Operating system error occurred during a write operation.	PUT, PUT_LINE, NEW_LINE, FFLUSH, FCLOSE, FCLOSE_ALL
INTERNAL_ERROR	Unspecified internal error.	All functions
NO_DATA_FOUND	End of file reached during a read.	GET_LINE
VALUE_ERROR	Input line too large for buffer specified in GET_LINE.	GET_LINE

TABLE 11-2. *Exceptions Raised by UTL_FILE*

Opening and Closing Files

All of the operations in UTL_FILE use a file handle. The *file handle* is a value that you use in PL/SQL to identify the file, similar to the cursor ID in DBMS_SQL. All file handles have the type UTL_FILE.FILE_TYPE. FILE_TYPE is defined in the specification of UTL_FILE. File handles are returned by FOPEN.

FOPEN

FOPEN opens a file for input or output. A given file can be opened for input only or output only at any time. A file can't be used for both input and output simultaneously. FOPEN is defined with

```
FUNCTION FOPEN(location IN VARCHAR2,
               filename IN VARCHAR2,
               open_mode IN VARCHAR2)
    RETURN FILE_TYPE;
```

The directory path specified must already exist—FOPEN will not create it. It will, however, overwrite an existing file if the mode is 'w'. The parameters and return value for FOPEN are described here:

Parameter	Type	Description
location	VARCHAR2	Directory path where the file is located. If this directory is not in the accessible directories list, UTL_FILE.INVALID_PATH is raised.
filename	VARCHAR2	Name of the file to be opened. If the mode is 'w', any existing file is overwritten.
open_mode	VARCHAR2	Mode to be used. Valid values are 'r' : Read text 'w': Write text 'a': Append text This parameter is not case-sensitive. If 'a' is specified and the file does not exist, it is created with 'w' mode.
return value	UTL_FILE.FILE_TYPE	File handle to be used in subsequent functions.

FOPEN can raise any of the following exceptions:

- UTL_FILE.INVALID_PATH
- UTL_FILE.INVALID_MODE
- UTL_FILE.INVALID_OPERATION
- UTL_FILE.INTERNAL_ERROR

FCLOSE
When you are finished reading from or writing to a file, it should be closed with FCLOSE. This frees the resources used by UTL_FILE to operate on the file. FLCOSE is defined with

    PROCEDURE FCLOSE(*file_handle* IN OUT FILE_TYPE);

where the only parameter is the file handle. Any pending changes that have yet to be written to the file are done before the file is closed. If there is an error while writing, UTL_FILE.WRITE_ERROR is raised. If the file handle does not point to a valid open file, UTL_FILE.INVALID_FILEHANDLE is raised.

IS_OPEN
This boolean function returns TRUE if the specified file is open, FALSE if not. IS_OPEN is defined as

    FUNCTION IS_OPEN(*file_handle* IN FILE_TYPE)
        RETURN BOOLEAN;

There could still be operating system errors if the file is used, even if IS_OPEN returns TRUE.

FCLOSE_ALL
FCLOSE_ALL will close all open files. It is meant to be used for cleanup, especially in an error handler. The procedure is defined as

    PROCEDURE FCLOSE_ALL;

and does not take any parameters. Any pending changes will be flushed before the files are closed. Because of this, FCLOSE_ALL can raise UTL_FILE.WRITE_ERROR if an error occurs during the write operation.

CAUTION
FCLOSE_ALL will close the files and free the resources used by UTL_FILE. However, it does not mark the files as closed—IS_OPEN will still return TRUE after an FCLOSE_ALL. Any read or write operations on files after FCLOSE_ALL will fail unless the file is reopened with FOPEN.

File Output

There are five procedures used to output data to a file: PUT, PUT_LINE, NEW_LINE, PUTF, and FFLUSH. PUT, PUT_LINE, and NEW_LINE behave very similar to their counterparts in the DBMS_OUTPUT package, which we discussed in Chapter 8. The maximum size for an output record is 1023 bytes.

PUT

PUT will output the specified string to the specified file. The file should have been opened for write operations. PUT is defined with

```
PROCEDURE PUT(file_handle IN FILE_TYPE,
              buffer IN VARCHAR2);
```

The parameters for PUT are described in this table:

Parameter	Type	Description
file_handle	UTL_FILE.FILE_TYPE	File handle returned by FOPEN. If this is not a valid handle, UTL_FILE.INVALID_FILEHANDLE is raised.
buffer	VARCHAR2	Text string to be output to the file. If the file was not opened in 'w' or 'a' mode, UTL_FILE.INVALID_OPERATION is raised.

PUT will not append a newline character in the file. You must use PUT_LINE or NEW_LINE to include the line terminator in the file. If there is an operating system error during the write operation, UTL_FILE.WRITE_ERROR is raised.

NEW_LINE

NEW_LINE writes one or more line terminators to the specified file. It is defined with

```
PROCEDURE NEW_LINE(file_handle IN FILE_TYPE,
                   lines IN NATURAL := 1);
```

The line terminator is system dependent—different operating systems will use different terminators. The parameters for NEW_LINE are described as follows. If there is an operating system error during the write, UTL_FILE.WRITE_ERROR is raised.

Parameter	Type	Description
file_handle	UTL_FILE. FILE_TYPE	File handle returned by FOPEN. If this is not valid, UTL_FILE.INVALID_FILEHANDLE is raised.
lines	NATURAL	Number of line terminators to output. The default value is 1, which outputs a single newline. If the file was not opened in 'w' or 'a' mode, UTL_FILE.INVALID_OPERATION is raised.

PUT_LINE

PUT_LINE outputs the specified string to the specified file, which must have been opened for write operations. After the string is output, the platform-specific newline character is output. PUT_LINE is defined with

```
PROCEDURE PUT_LINE(file_handle IN FILE_TYPE,
                   buffer IN VARCHAR2);
```

The parameters for PUT_LINE are described here:

Parameter	Type	Description
file_handle	UTL_FILE. FILE_TYPE	File handle returned by FOPEN. If this is not a valid handle, UTL_FILE.INVALID_FILEHANDLE is raised.
buffer	VARCHAR2	Text string to be output to the file. If the file was not opened in 'w' or 'a' mode, UTL_FILE. INVALID_OPERATION is raised.

Calling PUT_LINE is equivalent to calling PUT followed by NEW_LINE to output the newline. If there is an operating system error during the write, UTL_FILE.WRITE_ERROR is raised.

PUTF

PUTF is similar to PUT, but it allows the output string to be formatted. PUTF is a limited version of the C function *printf()*, and its syntax is similar to *printf()*. PUTF is defined with

```
PROCEDURE PUTF(file_handle IN FILE_TYPE,
               format IN VARCHAR2,
               arg1 IN VARCHAR2 DEFAULT NULL,
               arg2 IN VARCHAR2 DEFAULT NULL,
               arg3 IN VARCHAR2 DEFAULT NULL,
```

arg4 IN VARCHAR2 DEFAULT NULL,
arg5 IN VARCHAR2 DEFAULT NULL);

The format string contains regular text, along with the special characters %s and \n. Each occurrence of %s in the format string is replaced with one of the optional arguments. Each occurrence of \n is replaced by a newline character. The parameters are described here:

Parameter	Type	Description
file_handle	UTL_FILE. FILE_TYPE	File handle returned by FOPEN. If this is not a valid handle, UTL_FILE.INVALID_FILEHANDLE is raised.
format	VARCHAR2	Format string containing regular text and possibly the special formatting characters '%s' or '\n'. If the file was not opened in 'w' or 'a' mode, UTL_FILE.INVALID_OPERATION is raised.
arg1 ... arg5	VARCHAR2	One to five optional arguments. Each argument will be substituted for the corresponding '%s' format character. If there are more '%s' characters than arguments, the empty string (NULL) is substituted for the format character.

As with PUT and PUT_LINE, if there is an operating system error during the write, UTL_FILE.WRITE_ERROR is raised.

For example, if we were to execute the block

```
DECLARE
  v_OutputFile UTL_FILE.FILE_TYPE;
  v_Name VARCHAR2(10) := 'Scott';
BEGIN
  v_OutputFile := UTL_FILE.FOPEN(...);
  UTL_FILE.PUTF(v_OutputFile,
    'Hi there!\nMy name is %s, and I am a %s major.\n',
    v_Name, 'Computer Science');
  FCLOSE(v_OutputFile);
END;
```

the output file would contain the lines

```
Hi There!
My name is Scott, and I am a Computer Science major.
```

FFLUSH
The data output with PUT, PUT_LINE, PUTF, or NEW_LINE is normally buffered. When the buffer is full, it is then physically output to the file. FFLUSH forces the buffer to be immediately written to the specified file. It is defined with

    PROCEDURE FFLUSH(*file_handle* IN FILE_TYPE);

FFLUSH can raise any of the following exceptions:

- UTL_FILE.INVALID_FILEHANDLE
- UTL_FILE.INVALID_OPERATION
- UTL_FILE.WRITE_ERROR

File Input

GET_LINE is used to read from a file, rather than to write to it. One line of text is read from the specified file and returned in the *buffer* parameter. The newline character is not included in the return string. GET_LINE is defined with

    PROCEDURE GET_LINE(*file_handle* IN FILE_TYPE,
                        buffer OUT VARCHAR2);

When the last line is read from the file, NO_DATA_FOUND is raised. If the line does not fit as an actual parameter into the buffer supplied, VALUE_ERROR is raised. Reading an empty line will return an empty string (NULL). The parameters are:

Parameter	Type	Description
file_handle	UTL_FILE. FILE_TYPE	File handle returned by FOPEN. If this is not a valid handle, UTL_FILE.INVALID_FILEHANDLE is raised.
buffer	VARCHAR2	Buffer into which the line will be written. If the file was not opened for reading ('r'), then UTL_FILE.INVALID_OPERATION is raised.

If an operating system error occurs during the read, UTL_FILE.READ_ERROR is raised. The maximum size of the input line is 1022 bytes.

Examples

This section describes three examples using UTL_FILE. The first example is another implementation of the Debug package, which we have already seen. The second reads student information from a file and loads the table. The third example prints transcripts.

Debug Package

We can implement the Debug package using UTL_FILE, as follows:

```
CREATE OR REPLACE PACKAGE Debug AS

  /* Global variables to hold the name of the debugging file
     and directory. */
  v_DebugDir VARCHAR2(50);
  v_DebugFile VARCHAR2(20);

  PROCEDURE Debug(p_Description IN VARCHAR2,
                  p_Value IN VARCHAR2);

  PROCEDURE Reset(p_NewFile IN VARCHAR2 := v_DebugFile,
                  p_NewDir IN VARCHAR2 := v_DebugDir) ;

  /* Closes the debugging file. */
  PROCEDURE Close;
END Debug;

CREATE OR REPLACE PACKAGE BODY Debug AS

  v_DebugHandle UTL_FILE.FILE_TYPE;

  PROCEDURE Debug(p_Description IN VARCHAR2,
                  p_Value IN VARCHAR2) IS
  BEGIN
    /* Output the info, and flush the file. */
    UTL_FILE.PUTF(v_DebugHandle, '%s: %s\n', p_Description, p_Value);
    UTL_FILE.FFLUSH(v_DebugHandle);
  EXCEPTION
    WHEN UTL_FILE.INVALID_OPERATION THEN
      RAISE_APPLICATION_ERROR(-20102,
                                'Debug: Invalid Operation');
    WHEN UTL_FILE.INVALID_FILEHANDLE THEN
      RAISE_APPLICATION_ERROR(-20103,
                                'Debug: Invalid File Handle');
    WHEN UTL_FILE.WRITE_ERROR THEN
      RAISE_APPLICATION_ERROR(-20104,
                                'Debug: Write Error');
  END Debug;

  PROCEDURE Reset(p_NewFile IN VARCHAR2 := v_DebugFile,
                  p_NewDir IN VARCHAR2 := v_DebugDir) IS
  BEGIN
```

```
    /* Make sure the file is closed first. */
    IF UTL_FILE.IS_OPEN(v_DebugHandle) THEN
      UTL_FILE.FCLOSE(v_DebugHandle);
    END IF;

    /* Open the file for writing. */
    v_DebugHandle := UTL_FILE.FOPEN(p_NewDir, p_NewFile, 'w');

    /* Set the packaged variables to the values just passed in. */
    v_DebugFile := p_NewFile;
    v_DebugDir := p_NewDir;
  EXCEPTION
    WHEN UTL_FILE.INVALID_PATH THEN
      RAISE_APPLICATION_ERROR(-20100, 'Reset: Invalid Path');
    WHEN UTL_FILE.INVALID_MODE THEN
      RAISE_APPLICATION_ERROR(-20101, 'Reset: Invalid Mode');
    WHEN UTL_FILE.INVALID_OPERATION THEN
      RAISE_APPLICATION_ERROR(-20101, 'Reset: Invalid Operation');
  END Reset;

  PROCEDURE Close IS
  BEGIN
    UTL_FILE.FCLOSE(v_DebugHandle);
  END Close;

BEGIN
  v_DebugDir := '/tmp';
  v_DebugFile := 'debug.out';
  Reset;
END Debug;
```

This version of Debug behaves nearly the same as the other versions we examined in Chapters 8 and 9, with only some minor changes. **Debug.Reset** takes the name and location of the debug file as parameters—if they are not specified, the output file defaults to /tmp/debug.out. Every debugging statement will add a line to this file. We've also added a new procedure here, **Debug.Close**, which should be called to close the debugging file. Although **Debug.Debug** flushes the output file, the file should still be closed to free the resources associated with it.

TIP
Notice the exception handlers for the various routines—they identify which errors have actually been raised, and by which procedures. This is a good technique to follow when using UTL_FILE. Otherwise, you would have to trap errors with a WHEN OTHERS handler.

Student Loader

The **LoadStudents** procedure will insert into **students** based on the contents of the file which is passed to it. The file is comma delimited, which means that each record is contained on one line, with commas used to separate the fields. This is a common format for text files. **LoadStudents** is created with

```
CREATE OR REPLACE PROCEDURE LoadStudents (
  /* Loads the students table by reading a comma delimited file.
     The file should have lines which look like:

     first_name,last_name,major

     The student ID is generated from student_sequence.
     The total number of rows inserted is returned by
     p_TotalInserted. */
  p_FileDir  IN VARCHAR2,
  p_FileName IN VARCHAR2,
  p_TotalInserted IN OUT NUMBER) AS

  v_FileHandle UTL_FILE.FILE_TYPE;
  v_NewLine  VARCHAR2(100); -- Input line
  v_FirstName students.first_name%TYPE;
  v_LastName students.last_name%TYPE;
  v_Major students.major%TYPE;
  /* Positions of commas within input line. */
  v_FirstComma NUMBER;
  v_SecondComma NUMBER;

BEGIN
  -- Open the specified file for reading.
  v_FileHandle := UTL_FILE.FOPEN(p_FileDir, p_FileName, 'r');

  -- Initialize the output number of students.
  p_TotalInserted := 0;

  -- Loop over the file, reading in each line. GET_LINE will
  -- raise NO_DATA_FOUND when it is done, so we use that as the
  -- exit condition for the loop.
  LOOP
    BEGIN
      UTL_FILE.GET_LINE(v_FileHandle, v_NewLine);
    EXCEPTION
      WHEN NO_DATA_FOUND THEN
        EXIT;
    END;
```

```
    -- Each field in the input recod is delimited by commas. We
    -- need to find the locations of the two commas in the line,
    -- and use these locations to get the fields from v_NewLine.
    -- Use INSTR to find the locations of the commas.
    v_FirstComma := INSTR(v_NewLine, ',', 1, 1);
    v_SecondComma := INSTR(v_NewLine, ',', 1, 2);

    -- Now we can use SUBSTR to extract the fields.
    v_FirstName := SUBSTR(v_NewLine, 1, v_FirstComma - 1);
    v_LastName := SUBSTR(v_NewLine, v_FirstComma + 1,
                         v_SecondComma - v_FirstComma - 1);
    v_Major := SUBSTR(v_NewLine, v_SecondComma + 1);

    -- Insert the new record into students.
    INSERT INTO students (ID, first_name, last_name, major)
      VALUES (student_sequence.nextval, v_FirstName,
              v_LastName, v_Major);

    p_TotalInserted := p_TotalInserted + 1;
  END LOOP;

  --Close the file.
  UTL_FILE.FCLOSE(v_FileHandle);

  COMMIT;
EXCEPTION
  -- Handle the UTL_FILE exceptions meaningfully, and make sure
  -- that the file is properly closed.
  WHEN UTL_FILE.INVALID_OPERATION THEN
    UTL_FILE.FCLOSE(v_FileHandle);
    RAISE_APPLICATION_ERROR(-20051,
                            'LoadStudents: Invalid Operation');
  WHEN UTL_FILE.INVALID_FILEHANDLE THEN
    UTL_FILE.FCLOSE(v_FileHandle);
    RAISE_APPLICATION_ERROR(-20052,
                            'LoadStudents: Invalid File Handle');
  WHEN UTL_FILE.READ_ERROR THEN
    UTL_FILE.FCLOSE(v_FileHandle);
    RAISE_APPLICATION_ERROR(-20053,
                            'LoadStudents: Read Error');
  WHEN OTHERS THEN
    UTL_FILE.FCLOSE(v_FileHandle);
```

```
    RAISE;
END LoadStudents;
```

A sample input file for **LoadStudents** could look like this:

```
Scott,Smith,Computer Science
Margaret,Mason,History
Joanne,Junebug,Computer Science
Manish,Murgratroid,Economics
Patrick,Poll,History
Timothy,Taller,History
Barbara,Blues,Economics
David,Dinsmore,Music
Ester,Elegant,Nutrition
Rose,Riznit,Music
Rita,Razmataz,Nutrition
```

Printing Transcripts

We first saw **PrintTranscript** in Chapter 8. Now that we know how to use
UTL_FILE, we can complete the procedure. We first need the **CalculateGPA**
procedure:

```
CREATE OR REPLACE PROCEDURE CalculateGPA (
  /* Returns the grade point average for the student identified
     by p_StudentID in p_GPA. */
  p_StudentID IN students.ID%TYPE,
  p_GPA OUT NUMBER) AS

  CURSOR c_ClassDetails IS
    SELECT classes.num_credits, rs.grade
      FROM classes, registered_students rs
      WHERE classes.department = rs.department
      AND classes.course = rs.course
      AND rs.student_id = p_StudentID;

  v_NumericGrade NUMBER;
  v_TotalCredits NUMBER := 0;
  v_TotalGrade NUMBER := 0;

BEGIN
  FOR v_ClassRecord in c_ClassDetails LOOP
    -- Determine the numeric value for the grade.
    SELECT DECODE(v_ClassRecord.grade, 'A', 4,
```

```
                                           'B', 3,
                                           'C', 2,
                                           'D', 1,
                                           'E', 0)
        INTO v_NumericGrade
        FROM dual;

      v_TotalCredits := v_TotalCredits + v_ClassRecord.num_credits;
      v_TotalGrade := v_TotalGrade +
                        (v_ClassRecord.num_credits * v_NumericGrade);
    END LOOP;

    p_GPA := v_TotalGrade / v_TotalCredits;
END CalculateGPA;
```

PrintTranscript is created with

```
CREATE OR REPLACE PROCEDURE PrintTranscript (
    /* Outputs a transcript for the indicated student. The
       transcript will consist of the classes for which the
       student is currently registered and the grade received
       for each class. At the end of the transcript, the student's
       GPA is output. */
    p_StudentID IN students.ID%TYPE,
    p_FileDir IN VARCHAR2,
    p_FileName IN VARCHAR2) AS

    v_StudentGPA NUMBER;
    v_StudentRecord  students%ROWTYPE;
    v_FileHandle UTL_FILE.FILE_TYPE;
    v_NumCredits NUMBER;

    CURSOR c_CurrentClasses IS
      SELECT *
        FROM registered_students
        WHERE student_id = p_StudentID;

BEGIN
    -- Open the output file in append mode.
    v_FileHandle := UTL_FILE.FOPEN(p_FileDir, p_FileName, 'w');

    SELECT *
      INTO v_StudentRecord
```

```
   FROM students
   WHERE ID = p_StudentID;

-- Output header information. This consists of the current
-- date and time, and information about this student.

UTL_FILE.PUTF(v_FileHandle, 'Student ID: %s\n',
  v_StudentRecord.ID);
UTL_FILE.PUTF(v_FileHandle, 'Student Name: %s %s\n',
  v_StudentRecord.first_name, v_StudentRecord.last_name);
UTL_FILE.PUTF(v_FileHandle, 'Major: %s\n',
  v_StudentRecord.major);
UTL_FILE.PUTF(v_FileHandle, 'Transcript Printed on: %s\n\n\n',
  TO_CHAR(SYSDATE, 'Mon DD,YYYY HH24:MI:SS'));

UTL_FILE.PUT_LINE(v_FileHandle, 'Class   Credits Grade');
UTL_FILE.PUT_LINE(v_FileHandle, '------- ------- -----');
FOR v_ClassesRecord in c_CurrentClasses LOOP
  -- Determine the number of credits for this class.
  SELECT num_credits
    INTO v_NumCredits
    FROM classes
    WHERE course = v_ClassesRecord.course
    AND department = v_ClassesRecord.department;

  -- Output the info for this class.
  UTL_FILE.PUTF(v_FileHandle, '%s %s %s\n',
    RPAD(v_ClassesRecord.department || ' '  ||
        v_ClassesRecord.course, 7),
    LPAD(v_NumCredits, 7),
    LPAD(v_ClassesRecord.grade, 5));
END LOOP;

-- Determine the GPA.
CalculateGPA(p_StudentID, v_StudentGPA);

-- Output the GPA.
UTL_FILE.PUTF(v_FileHandle, '\n\nCurrent GPA: %s\n',
  TO_CHAR(v_StudentGPA, '9.99'));

-- Close the file.
UTL_FILE.FCLOSE(v_FileHandle);
```

```
EXCEPTION
  -- Handle the UTL_FILE exceptions meaningfully, and make sure
  -- that the file is properly closed.
  WHEN UTL_FILE.INVALID_OPERATION THEN
    UTL_FILE.FCLOSE(v_FileHandle);
    RAISE_APPLICATION_ERROR(-20061,
                        'PrintTranscript: Invalid Operation');
  WHEN UTL_FILE.INVALID_FILEHANDLE THEN
    UTL_FILE.FCLOSE(v_FileHandle);
    RAISE_APPLICATION_ERROR(-20062,
                        'PrintTranscript: Invalid File Handle');
  WHEN UTL_FILE.WRITE_ERROR THEN
    UTL_FILE.FCLOSE(v_FileHandle);
    RAISE_APPLICATION_ERROR(-20063,
                        'PrintTranscript: Write Error');
  WHEN OTHERS THEN
    UTL_FILE.FCLOSE(v_FileHandle);
    RAISE;
END PrintTranscript;
```

If the **registered_students** table looks like this,

```
SQL> select * from registered_students;
STUDENT_ID DEP    COURSE G
---------- ---    ---------- -
     10002 CS        102 B
     10002 HIS       101 B
     10002 ECN       203 A
     10002 CS        101 A
     10009 HIS       101 D
     10009 MUS       410 B
     10009 HIS       301 C
     10009 MUS       410 B

8 rows selected.
```

and we call **PrintTranscript** for students 10002 and 10009, we get the following two output files:

```
Student ID: 10002
Student Name: Joanne Junebug
Major: Computer Science
```

```
Transcript Printed on: Jan 27,1996 17:37:43


Class   Credits Grade
------- ------- -----
CS  102       4     B
HIS 101       4     B
ECN 203       3     A
CS  101       4     A


Current GPA:   3.47




Student ID: 10009
Student Name: Rose Riznit
Major: Music
Transcript Printed on: Jan 27,1996 17:38:56


Class   Credits Grade
------- ------- -----
HIS 101       4     D
MUS 410       3     B
HIS 301       4     C
MUS 410       3     B


Current GPA:   2.14
```

Summary

We have examined two more utility packages in this chapter: DBMS_JOB and UTL_FILE. Database jobs allow procedures to be automatically run by the database at predefined times. UTL_FILE adds file I/O capability to PL/SQL, subject to security issues on the server. Each of these packages provides useful functionality that is not inherent to the language.

CHAPTER 12

Performance and Tuning

I t is important that your application do what it is expected to. It is equally as important, however, that it perform the necessary processing as fast and efficiently as possible. Developing a properly tuned PL/SQL application is not difficult, as long as you keep in mind a few concepts. These are the shared pool, properly designed SQL statements, and an understanding of network issues. We will discuss all of these in this chapter, with advice on how to utilize them in your own applications.

The Shared Pool

The shared pool is an area of memory in which Oracle stores information about SQL statements and stored subprograms. Setting the size of the shared pool and using it properly are key components of a properly tuned PL/SQL application.

Structure of an Oracle Instance

In order to discuss how the shared pool works and its implications for PL/SQL programming, we first need to examine the structure of a running Oracle *instance*. An instance consists of processes, memory, and operating system files, all running on the server. Additional client processes can connect to the database as well. Figure 12-1 illustrates the structure of an instance.

NOTE
On some systems (such as Windows 3.1) an Oracle instance consists of a single process only. This process is responsible for all database administration, in addition to serving as a shadow process. The shared pool behaves the same, however.

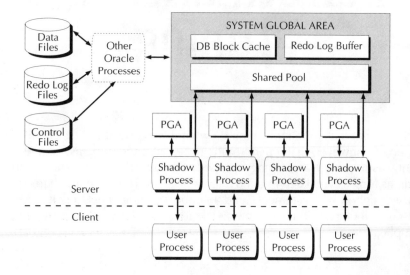

FIGURE 12-1. *An Oracle instance*

Processes

When an instance is started, a number of Oracle background processes are started. These processes communicate with each other via shared memory, known as the SGA (*system global area*). All of the Oracle processes can read and write to various data structures in the SGA. Each process is in charge of a different aspect of running the database. Some of these processes are described in Table 12-1. A full discussion of how these processes work is beyond the scope of this book; for more information, see *Oracle7 Server Concepts*. Here, we will examine user and shadow processes.

User Processes   A user process is an application that sends SQL and PL/SQL to the server to be processed. These applications can be developed using any of Oracle's development tools, including the precompilers, OCI, SQL*Plus, and the Developer 2000 suite. The user process communicates with the shadow process over the network using SQL*Net. This communication and its implications are discussed later in this chapter, in the "Network Issues" section.

Shadow Processes   The shadow process is responsible for passing information back and forth between a user process and the rest of the instance. Without the multithreaded server, there is one shadow process per user process. With the multithreaded server, a single shadow process can manage multiple user processes, with the help of the dispatcher processes. For more information on the multithreaded server and how to configure it, see *Oracle7 Server Concepts*.

Memory

The memory used by the instance is partitioned into different areas, which are used by different processes. There are four different kinds of memory: the shared pool, DB block cache, redo log buffer, and the process global area (PGA). All but the PGA are allocated as part of the SGA, and are thus available to all processes. The SGA is completely allocated when the instance starts up. Its size is determined by various INIT.ORA parameters, including SHARED_POOL_SIZE, LOG_BUFFER, and DB_BLOCK_BUFFERS. For more information on these and other INIT.ORA parameters, see the *Oracle7 Server Reference*.

Shared Pool   The shared pool is the memory structure that most affects the performance of PL/SQL. The shared pool contains the text of SQL statements and PL/SQL blocks sent to the database, along with the parsed representation of them. Items in the shared pool do not necessarily remain there forever—they are aged out of the pool when they are no longer necessary. Later in this section we will see how this works and examine the shared pool in detail.

Process	Description
Database Writer (DBWR)	Writes changed information from the buffer cache in the SGA to the database files.
Process Monitor (PMON)	Cleans up after failed user processes, such as releasing locks and rolling back any uncommitted SQL statements.
System Monitor (SMON)	Performs instance recovery (if necessary) when the instance is started. Also responsible for freeing temporary segments and coalescing free space in the SGA.
Recover (RECO)	Resolves failures with distributed transactions. RECO is only present when the Distributed Option is used.
Log Writer (LGWR)	Writes the redo log buffer to the redo log on disk. LGWR and DBWR work together to ensure that all committed information is properly written before the commit is successful.
Archiver (ARCH)	Copies full redo logs to an offline storage device, such as a tape drive. ARCH is only running when the database is in ARCHIVELOG mode.
Snapshot Refresh (SNP)	Refreshes table snapshots and runs database jobs. (See Chapter 11).
Shadow Process	Manages the information transfer between the user process and other database resources.
User Process	Runs a user application, sending SQL statements and PL/SQL blocks to the database.
Dispatcher Process	Allows multiple user processes to share a single shadow process, as part of the multithreaded server. The user processes connect to the dispatcher, which in turn passes information on to the shadow process. The connections between the user and dispatcher process must use SQL*Net version 2.

TABLE 12-1.   *Database Processes*

DB Block Cache   Data is read from and written to database files in *blocks*. The size of data blocks is usually a multiple of the operating system block size, for maximum efficiency, and is specified by the INIT.ORA parameter DB_BLOCK_SIZE. Typical values for DB_BLOCK_SIZE are 2048 and 4096, since operating system blocks are often 1024 bytes. The shadow processes read data blocks from the data files. These are stored in the DB block cache and manipulated there. If the contents of a block are changed, DBWR will write the block back to the file.

Redo Log Buffer   The redo log buffer behaves the same as the DB block cache, except that it contains redo blocks, rather than data blocks. Redo information is generated by SQL statements and PL/SQL blocks as they are processed. This redo information is used in case of instance failure and for read consistency. LGWR is responsible for writing the blocks in the redo log buffer to the online redo logs.

PGA   Each shadow process allocates memory for its own use. This memory is known as the *process global area* (PGA). Information in the PGA includes the active sets for any currently open cursors, pointers to the parsed SQL statements and PL/SQL blocks in the shared pool, and memory used to execute PL/SQL. The PGA is allocated when the shadow process is started and remains as long as the connection does.

Files

The database uses three different kinds of operating system files, each of which stores different kinds of information. Different processes are in charge of maintaining different files. The three kinds of files are database files, redo log files, and control files.

Database Files   These files store the actual data found in the database. This includes table and index data, code for stored subprograms, view definitions, and sequence information, along with the data dictionary itself. DBWR is responsible for writing to database files, and the shadow processes can read from them.

Redo Log Files   The redo log records all of the changes made to database objects. This information is used to generate a read-consistent view of the data for queries, and to perform rollbacks. LGWR is responsible for writing to the redo log. If archiving is enabled (the database is running in ARCHIVELOG mode), then the ARCH process is responsible for reading the redo logs and copying them to offline storage.

Control Files   The current state of the statement is stored in the one or more control files. If there is more than one file, they are all *mirrored,* which means they are kept in the same state, to ensure recovery in case one is lost. The database state includes the number of data and redo files, and how much information has been written to each. LGWR also modifies the control files, and ARCH is responsible for recording these changes in the offline storage.

How the Shared Pool Works

Whenever a SQL statement is received by the database, it is parsed and the execution plan determined. This information is then stored in the shared pool. If the same SQL statement is received by the database at a later point (issued by the same user process, or a different user process), the database does not have to reparse the statement. The parsed form is already there in the shared pool. This performance enhancement can significantly reduce the amount of work done by the server, especially in environments with a large number of users running the same application.

When the database receives a SQL statement from a client application, it first checks to see if the statement already exists in the shared pool. If so, then the parsed form and execution plan are immediately available. If the statement is not in the shared pool, it will be placed there after it is parsed. The important thing to note about this process is that the database has to receive the statement before it can be compared. Even if the statement is found in the shared pool, it will still travel over the network each time. Although the database may not have to do any work with the statement (since it's in the pool already), it does have to receive the entire statement first. For long SQL statements, this can be significant. Because a pointer to the parsed statement is returned to the client the first time the statement is issued, the client application can be written to avoid subsequent parse calls altogether. See the section "Avoiding Unnecessary Reparsing" later in this chapter for more information.

Besides the parsed form of SQL statements, the shared pool also holds the compiled p-code for stored subprograms and the contents of database pipes. When a stored subprogram is called for the first time, the p-code is retrieved from disk and kept in the shared pool. The next time the same object is referenced, the disk access can be avoided since the p-code is already in memory.

When the shared pool fills up, objects within it are aged out according to an LRU (least recently used) algorithm. The object that hasn't been accessed for the longest time is removed from the pool, and the space it took up is used for a new object. Only those objects that are not currently being used are eligible for aging. If a subprogram is still being executed, for example, it will not be aged out. Since all objects are not the same size, this can result in shared pool fragmentation—the space for a new object may be available, but it is not contiguous. When there is not enough memory in the shared pool for a new object, the following Oracle error is returned:

ORA-4031: unable to allocate X bytes of shared memory

This can happen either because the shared pool is not big enough, or because the space in it has become fragmented.

Flushing the Shared Pool

If you receive the ORA-4031 error, one solution is to flush the shared pool. This will remove all eligible objects (those that are not currently being used). The command to do this is

ALTER SYSTEM FLUSH SHARED POOL;

You can issue this command from any account with the ALTER SYSTEM system privilege. The shared pool can be flushed while the database is still running without affecting current applications.

The shared pool is also flushed when the instance is brought down. When an instance is brought up, the shared pool is empty because no SQL has been executed yet.

Triggers and the Shared Pool

The p-code is only cached if the subprogram is stored. In releases of Oracle7 earlier than 7.3, this does not include triggers; in these versions, the compiled p-code for triggers is not stored in the data dictionary—only the source is. Consequently, when a trigger is fired for the first time, it must be compiled. The compiled code is then stored in the shared pool for subsequent trigger firings. However, if the trigger gets aged out of the shared pool, it must be recompiled before it can be executed again.

It is a good idea to keep your trigger code as small as possible, to minimize the time spent compiling it. This can be accomplished by moving the work done in a trigger into a packaged subprogram and then calling the package from the trigger. The trigger thus consists only of the call to the package, which is comparatively short.

 PL/SQL 2.3 ...and HIGHER Packaging your triggers is not necessary in Oracle7 Release 7.3 because triggers are stored in compiled form with this release of PL/SQL and the database. Calling packaged procedures from a trigger is still a good idea, however. This way the code can be called from other places as well.

The Shared Pool and the Multithreaded Server

When using the multithreaded server, some of the session information that is normally kept in the PGA is moved to the shared pool in the SGA. This is necessary because a database session may be handled by different shadow processes. If a session is migrated to a different shadow, the new shadow needs to have access to the session information. Thus it has to be accessible to both processes in the shared pool. This means that the shared pool needs to be larger when using the multithreaded server. For more information, see the *Oracle7 Server Reference*.

Estimating the Size of the Shared Pool

The size of the shared pool is specified by the INIT.ORA parameter SHARED_POOL_SIZE. The default value is 3.5MB. This amount of memory is allocated when the instance is started, and it will not grow or shrink. If there is not enough contiguous memory available at startup time, the database will not come up.

Since the shared pool is a fixed size, it is important to set the size properly. The best way to do this is to examine the size of the objects you use frequently, and make sure that they can all fit in the shared pool simultaneously. If not, then they will be aged in and out, resulting in a fragmented pool and the ORA-4031 error.

There are various methods for sizing the shared pool properly. They will not be discussed in full detail here—for more information see *Oracle7 Server Tuning*. Essentially, you determine the size for each of the objects you commonly access. Add these together, and you have the minimum shared pool size. If you are using the multithreaded server, you also need to include the size of the session information.

Size of Stored Subprograms

The **dba_object_size** data dictionary view records the size of stored PL/SQL objects. For example, the following query returns the size of several internal packages:

```
SQL> SELECT name, type, code_size
  2    FROM dba_object_size
  3    WHERE name IN ('DBMS_PIPE', 'STANDARD', 'DBMS_OUTPUT')
  4    ORDER BY name, type;
```

NAME	TYPE	CODE_SIZE
DBMS_OUTPUT	PACKAGE	388
DBMS_OUTPUT	PACKAGE BODY	6217
DBMS_OUTPUT	SYNONYM	0
DBMS_PIPE	PACKAGE	699
DBMS_PIPE	PACKAGE BODY	6427
DBMS_PIPE	SYNONYM	0
STANDARD	PACKAGE	10494
STANDARD	PACKAGE BODY	22400

The **code_size** column in this view will contain the size of the object. You can query **dba_object_size** for all of the objects you commonly access.

Session Memory

The session memory usage for a particular database session can be determined from the **v$sesstat** and **v$statname** views. In order to do this, you first need to identify a database SID (session identifier) with a query such as:

```
SQL> SELECT sid
  2     FROM v$process p, v$session s
  3     WHERE p.addr = s.paddr
  4     AND s.username = 'SYSTEM';

      SID
---------
        6
```

This query gives the SID for the session connected as the Oracle user SYSTEM (you can specify a different user as well). Now that we know the SID, we can determine the session memory for this SID with

```
SQL> SELECT value
  2     FROM v$sesstat s, v$statname n
  3     WHERE s.statistic# = n.statistic#
  4     AND n.name = 'session uga memory max'
  5     AND SID = 6;

    VALUE
---------
    94704
```

Thus the memory usage for this session so far is 94,704 bytes. This query should be run for a session after it has been running for some time, since it returns the maximum amount of memory used by a session so far, not the maximum amount it will use. Multiply this by the number of sessions to determine the necessary shared pool size.

Pinning Objects

Sizing the shared pool properly is only the first step in shared pool tuning. You should also pin commonly used objects in the shared pool. When an object is *pinned*, it will never be aged out until you request it, no matter how full the pool gets or how often the object is accessed. Pinning objects is controlled with the DBMS_SHARED_POOL package. This package has three procedures: DBMS_SHARED_POOL.KEEP, DBMS_SHARED_POOL.UNKEEP, and DBMS_SHARED_POOL.SIZES.

KEEP

The DBMS_POOL.KEEP procedure is used to pin objects into the pool. Packages and SQL statements can be pinned. KEEP is defined with

```
PROCEDURE KEEP(name VARCHAR2,
              flag CHAR DEFAULT 'P');
```

The parameters are described here:

Parameter	Type	Description
name	VARCHAR2	Name of the object. This can be a package name or the identifier associated with a SQL statement. The SQL identifier is the concatenation of the **address** and **hash_value** fields in the **v$sqlarea** view, and is returned by the SIZES procedure.
flag	CHAR	Determines whether the object is a package or a SQL statement. If 'P' (the default), then **name** should match a package name. If not, then **name** should match a shared SQL statement.

Once an object has been kept, it will not be removed until the database is shut down or the DBMS_SHARED_POOL.UNKEEP procedure is used.

UNKEEP

UNKEEP is the only way to remove a kept object from the shared pool. Kept objects are never aged out automatically. UNKEEP is defined with

```
PROCEDURE UNKEEP(name VARCHAR2,
                flag CHAR DEFAULT 'P');
```

The arguments are the same as for KEEP. If the specified object does not already exist in the shared pool, an error is raised.

SIZES

SIZES will echo the contents of the shared pool to the screen. It is defined with

    PROCEDURE SIZES(*minsize* NUMBER);

Objects with a size greater than *minsize* will be returned. SIZES uses DBMS_OUTPUT to return the data, so be sure to use "set serveroutput on" in SQL*Plus or Server Manager before calling the procedure. For more information on DBMS_OUTPUT, see Chapter 8.

SQL Statement Tuning

In order to execute a SQL statement, the database must determine the *execution plan*. An execution plan is the method by which the database will actually process the statement—what tables and indexes it needs to access, whether or not a sort operation needs to be done, and so on. The execution plan can have a large impact on the length of time it takes to execute a SQL statement. This section describes how to tune SQL statements in general, whether or not they are inside a PL/SQL block.

Determining the Execution Plan

There are two different methods for determining the execution plan. The EXPLAIN PLAN statement is a good method for querying the plan quickly and easily. The TKPROF utility will also give you the execution plan, along with additional statistics about the SQL processing.

EXPLAIN PLAN

The EXPLAIN PLAN SQL statement will determine an execution plan for a given statement, and insert it into another database table. The format for EXPLAIN PLAN is

    EXPLAIN PLAN [SET STATEMENT_ID = '*statement_info*'
        [INTO *plan_table*] FOR *sql_statement*;

where *sql_statement* is the statement which you want to explain. The plan will be inserted into *plan_table*. If *plan_table* isn't specified, then it defaults to PLAN_TABLE. The table should look like this:

```
CREATE TABLE plan_table (
    statement_id    VARCHAR2(30),
    timestamp       DATE,
    remarks         VARCHAR2(80),
    operation       VARCHAR2(30),
    options         VARCHAR2(30),
    object_node     VARCHAR2(30),
    object_owner    VARCHAR2(30),
    object_name     VARCHAR2(30),
    object_instance NUMBER,
    object_type     VARCHAR2(30),
    search_columns  NUMBER,
    id              NUMBER,
    parent_id       NUMBER,
    position        NUMBER,
    other           LONG);
```

In order to use EXPLAIN PLAN, you should either have **plan_table** in your own schema, or specify another plan table (with the above definition) in the EXPLAIN PLAN statement. The *statement_id*, if specified in EXPLAIN PLAN, will be inserted into the **statement_id** column of **plan_table**. This is used to store multiple plans in the same table—the statement id is the key for each statement. If the *statement_id* already exists in the plan table, its plan is replaced.

TIP
The **utlxplan.sql** file will create a plan_table for you. The location of this file is operating system-specific. On Unix systems, it is located with the other data dictionary scripts in $ORACLE_HOME/rdbms/admin.

For example, we can determine an execution plan for a query against **registered_students** and **classes** with:

```
EXPLAIN PLAN
  SET STATEMENT_ID = 'Query 1' FOR
    SELECT rs.course, rs.department, students.ID
      FROM registered_students rs, students
      WHERE rs.student_id = students.id
      AND students.last_name = 'Razmataz';
```

Once we issue this statement, we can query the plan table with the following SQL statement:

```
SELECT LPAD(' ', 2 * (LEVEL - 1)) || operation ||
       ' ' || options || ' ' || object_name || ' ' ||
       DECODE(id, 0, 'Cost = ' || position) "Execution Plan"
  FROM plan_table
  START WITH id = 0
    AND statement_id = 'Query 1'
  CONNECT BY PRIOR id = parent_id
    AND statement_id = 'Query 1';
```

Notice that the same statement id is used both in the EXPLAIN PLAN statement and the query of the plan table. The preceding query returns the following output:

```
Execution Plan
-------------------------------------------
SELECT STATEMENT    Cost =
  NESTED LOOPS
    TABLE ACCESS FULL REGISTERED_STUDENTS
    TABLE ACCESS BY ROWID STUDENTS
      INDEX UNIQUE SCAN SYS_C00859
```

We will discuss how to interpret the execution plan later in this chapter, in the section "Using the Plan."

TKPROF Utility

The EXPLAIN PLAN statement is useful for determining the execution plan, as we saw in the previous section. The TKPROF utility, however, can give us the execution plan along with statistics about how well the SQL statement actually performs. In order to use TKPROF, you first need to get a SQL trace file for your session. TKPROF is then used to format the trace file and make it readable. In order to generate a trace file, issue the SQL command

ALTER SESSION SET SQL_TRACE = TRUE;

before any SQL statements you want to examine. This will start a trace file, which will contain information about any subsequent SQL statements or PL/SQL blocks submitted to the database. Information will be dumped to the trace file until the session ends or tracing is turned off with

ALTER SESSION SET SQL_TRACE = FALSE;

The location of the trace file is determined by the USER_DUMP_DEST parameter in INIT.ORA. The name of the trace file is system-specific, but will usually start with "ora" and contain the process identifier of the shadow process.

For example, a trace file name could be "ora_12345.trc". The easiest way to determine the correct trace file is to look in USER_DUMP_DEST for the newest file immediately after issuing the trace.

> **CAUTION**
> ALTER SESSION is not allowed in a PL/SQL block, since it is not a DML statement. You can issue the ALTER SESSION before issuing the block, however. Alternatively, you can trace SQL statements outside of a block.

For example, we can issue the following statements from SQL*Plus:

```
SQL> ALTER SESSION SET SQL_TRACE = TRUE;
Session Altered.
SQL> SELECT rs.course, rs.department, students.ID
     FROM registered_students rs, students
     WHERE rs.student_id = students.id
     AND students.last_name = 'Razmataz';
   COURSE DEP        ID
---------- --- ----------
      101 HIS      10010
      307 NUT      10010

SQL> ALTER SESSION SET SQL_TRACE = FALSE;
Session altered.
```

This produced a file "ora_29338.trc" in USER_DUMP_DEST. We now need to format this trace file, to produce a readable output. We use TKPROF to do this. TKPROF is a utility which is run from the operating system. Its location is system dependent, but it is usually found in the same directory as other Oracle executables such as SQL*Plus itself. The format for TKPROF is

> TKPROF *input_file output_file* [SORT = *sort_options*] [PRINT = *num_print*]
>   [EXPLAIN = *user/password*]

where *input_file* is the name of the generated trace file (ora_29338.trc in this case) and *output_file* will contain the formatted trace file. If SORT is not specified, the SQL statements will appear in the order they are submitted in. Otherwise, you can sort based on one or more of the options listed in Table 12-2. To specify more than one sort option, use this syntax:

> SORT = (*option1, option2, ...*)

Sort Option	Description
PRSCNT	Parse count
PRSCPU	Amount of CPU time spent parsing
PRSELA	Elapsed time during the parse
PRSDSK	Number of disk reads during the parse
PRSQRY	Number of consistent block reads during the parse
PRSCU	Number of current block reads during the parse
PRSMIS	Number of library cache misses during the parse
EXECNT	Number of executes
EXECPU	Amount of CPU time spent during the execute
EXEELA	Elapsed time during the execute
EXEDSK	Number of physical disk reads during the execute
EXEQRY	Number of consistent block reads during the execute
EXECU	Number of current block reads during the execute
EXEROW	Number of rows processed during the execute
EXEMIS	Number of library cache misses during the execute
FCHCNT	Number of fetches
FCHCPU	Amount of CPU time spent during the fetch
FCHELA	Elapsed time during the fetch
FCHDSK	Number of physical disk reads during the fetch
FCHQRY	Number of consistent block reads during the fetch
FCHCU	Number of current block reads during the fetch
FCHROW	Number of rows fetched

TABLE 12-2. *TKPROF Sort Options*

To include an execution plan in the trace file, specify a username and password in the EXPLAIN option. TKPROF will create a plan table, run EXPLAIN PLAN into this table, select the output into the file, and drop the table. If specified, only *num_print* statements will be included in the file, after sorting.

We can format our trace file with

TKPROF ora_29338.trc trace.out EXPLAIN=*example/example*

which produces an output file "trace.out". A portion of this file is given below.

```
SELECT rs.course, rs.department, students.ID
     FROM registered_students rs, students
     WHERE rs.student_id = students.id
     AND students.last_name = 'Razmataz'
```

call	count	cpu	elapsed	disk	query	current	rows
Parse	1	0.00	0.00	0	0	0	0
Execute	1	0.00	0.00	0	0	0	0
Fetch	1	0.00	0.00	0	55	3	2
total	3	0.00	0.00	0	55	3	2

```
Misses in library cache during parse: 1
Optimizer hint: CHOOSE
Parsing user id: 9   (EXAMPLE)
```

Rows	Execution Plan
0	SELECT STATEMENT OPTIMIZER HINT: CHOOSE
2	NESTED LOOPS
18	TABLE ACCESS (FULL) OF 'REGISTERED_STUDENTS'
18	TABLE ACCESS (BY ROWID) OF 'STUDENTS'
18	INDEX (UNIQUE SCAN) OF 'SYS_C00859' (UNIQUE)

```
*****************************************************************
```

The statement itself, statistics about the execution of the statement, and the execution plan are all included in the output. In this case, no CPU time was necessary for the parse, since this statement had been executed already, and thus was already in the shared pool. Notice, however, that the parse count is still 1, because a parse call was issued to the database.

NOTE
The trace file will also show the recursive SQL statements generated automatically by your SQL. For any given statement, Oracle can issue up to 6 recursive statements, which do such things as check the NLS settings and verify object privileges. Because the trace file shows all of the SQL statements, recursive and otherwise, it can be a useful debugging technique.

Using the Plan

The execution plan is the same whether it is determined via EXPLAIN PLAN or TKPROF. A plan is composed of individual *operations*. Operations (such as a full table scan or an index scan) are executed individually. Each operation will produce a set of rows as its output. It can determine this set by querying a table or index, or by accepting the output of another operation. The results of the final operation are the result set of the query. Each operation does some of the work for the entire query. A full discussion of the operations and their efficiency is beyond the scope of this chapter. We will briefly discuss some of the main operations, however. For more information, see *Oracle7 Server Tuning*.

The execution plan in the prior two sections has three operations—NESTED LOOPS and two different kinds of TABLE ACCESSes.

NESTED LOOP

A NESTED LOOP operation combines the result sets from two other operations, **a** and **b**. Rows in **a** and **b** are compared according to a condition, and those that match are kept. In our example, the condition is the join condition "rs.student_id = students.id" given in the statement. Whenever a join is used, a NESTED LOOP operation is required for execution.

TABLE ACCESS(FULL)

A full table scan simply retreives all rows from a table. In our example, a full table scan is necessary for **registered_students** since there are no indexes created on this table.

TABLE ACCESS (BY ROWID)

This is the fastest way to retrieve an individual row. In our example, the results from the INDEX SCAN operation are sent to the TABLE ACCESS BY ROWID operation. The index scan is available since there is an index defined for the **ID** column of **students**.

Network Issues

Once the SQL statement has made it to the database, the structure of the statement determines the execution plan and the resultant performance. However, the SQL statement has to be sent to the database first, from the user process to the shadow process. Even if the user and shadow processes are running on the same machine, the SQL statement or PL/SQL block still needs to be passed between them. In most applications, the majority of the processing time is spent in the network. Thus, reducing network traffic is a prime component for application tuning. There are three techniques available for reducing network traffic: utilizing client-side PL/SQL, avoiding unnecessary reparsing, and the Oracle array interface. Although the latter two methods are primarily applicable when using OCI or the Oracle precompilers, they are still relevant to PL/SQL.

Using Client-side PL/SQL

If the application is written using the Developer or Designer 2000 suite of tools, then there is a PL/SQL engine on the client. This execution environment is discussed in more detail in Chapter 7. Any work that can be done on the client reduces the load on the server. In addition, if many users are running the application simultaneously, they can process on their individual client machines in parallel without bogging down the server.

This PL/SQL engine should be used as much as possible. For example, validation of input data can be done before the data is sent to the server.

Avoiding Unnecessary Reparsing

When a SQL statement or PL/SQL block is sent from the client to the server, the client can keep a reference to the parsed statement. This reference is the cursor data area when using OCI, or the cursor cache entry when using the precompilers. If your application issues the same statement more than once, it only needs to parse the statement the first time. For all subsequent executions, the original parsed statement can be used, possibly with different values for the bind variables.

This technique is available primarily with OCI or the precompilers, since they give you more control over cursor processing. In OCI, cursors are controlled directly with a cursor data area. You make explicit calls to parse (**oparse**) and execute (**oexec**) the statement. With the precompilers, the HOLD_CURSOR and RELEASE_CURSOR options control the behavior.

The most obvious place for this technique directly in PL/SQL is with the DBMS_SQL package, where the interface is similar to OCI. Once a statement is parsed with DBMS_SQL.PARSE, it can be executed multiple times. For more information, see Chapter 10.

Array Processing

The precompilers and OCI have the ability to send and retrieve data using host arrays. This technique, known as the Oracle *array interface,* is very useful because it allows large amounts of data to travel over the network as one unit rather than taking several trips. For example, if you are retreiving 100 rows, you can do it in one fetch which brings back all 100 rows, rather than 100 fetches, each of which returns one row. This approach is used in SQL*Plus.

PL/SQL does not directly use the Oracle array interface, since it does not store arrays in the same way as a host array. PL/SQL tables are implemented differently, as discussed in Chapter 3. However, the array interface should be used whenever possible. If you are issuing PL/SQL commands from OCI or the precompilers, use the array interface for the other SQL statements in your application. For more information on how to use host arrays, consult the precompiler and/or OCI documentation.

Summary

A good application is designed for performance. In this chapter we have examined several different aspects of performance and tuning. We first discussed the structure of an Oracle instance and the process of executing SQL statements. Once the statement gets to the server, it is processed according to its execution plan, as determined with EXPLAIN PLAN or the TKPROF utility. We also discussed how to minimize network traffic by using client-side PL/SQL, avoiding unnecessary reparsing, and taking advantage of the Oracle array interface.

APPENDIX A

Reserved Words
in PL/SQL

The words listed in this appendix are reserved by PL/SQL. Reserved words have special syntactic meaning to the language and, thus, can't be used as identifiers (for variable names, procedure names, and so on). Some of these words are reserved by SQL as well. These words cannot be used to name database objects such as tables, sequences, or views.

Table of Reserved Words

The following table lists the reserved words for PL/SQL version 2.3. Not all of these words are reserved by earlier versions, but their use should still be avoided in these versions, since they will conflict if you ever import your programs into version 2.3. Entries with an asterisk (*) are also reserved by SQL.

ABORT	ACCEPT	ACCESS*	ADD*
ALL*	ALTER*	AND*	ANY*
ARRAY	ARRAYLEN	AS*	ASC*
ASSERT	ASSIGN	AT	AUDIT*
AUTHORIZATION	AVG	BASE_TABLE	BEGIN
BETWEEN*	BINARY_INTEGER	BODY	BOOLEAN
BY*	CASE	CHAR*	CHAR_BASE
CHECK*	CLOSE	CLUSTER*	CLUSTERS
COLAUTH	COLUMN*	COLUMNS	COMMENT
COMMIT	COMPRESS*	CONNECT*	CONSTANT
CRASH	CREATE*	CURRENT*	CURRVAL
CURSOR	DATABASE	DATA_BASE	DATE*
DBA	DEBUGOFF	DEBUGON	DECIMAL*
DECLARE	DEFAULT*	DEFINITION	DELAY
DELETE*	DELTA	DESC*	DIGITS
DISPOSE	DISTINCT*	DO	DROP*
ELSE*	ELSIF	END	ENTRY
EXCEPTION	EXCEPTION_INIT	EXISTS*	EXIT
FALSE	FETCH	FILE*	FLOAT*
FOR*	FORM	FROM*	FUNCTION
GENERIC	GOTO	GRANT*	GROUP*
HAVING*	IDENTIFIED*	IF	IMMEDIATE*
IN*	INCREMENT*	INDEX*	INDEXES
INDICATOR	INITIAL*	INSERT	INTERFACE
INTEGER*	INTERSECT*	INTO*	IS*
LEVEL*	LIKE*	LIMITED	LOCK*
LONG*	LOOP	MAX	MAXEXTENTS*
MIN	MINUS*	MLSLABEL	MOD
MODE*	MODIFY*	NATURAL	NATURALN
NEW	NEXTVAL	NOAUDIT*	NOCOMPRESS*
NOT*	NOWAIT*	NULL*	NUMBER*
NUMBER_BASE	OF*	OFFLINE*	ON*
ONLINE*	OPEN	OPTION*	OR*

ORDER*	OTHERS	OUT	PACKAGE
PARTITION	PCTFREE*	PLS_INTEGER	POSITIVE
PRAGMA	PRIOR*	PRIVATE	PRIVILEGES*
PROCEDURE	PUBLIC*	RAW*	RAISE
RANGE	REAL	RECORD	REF
RELEASE	REMR	RENAME*	RESOURCE*
RETURN	REVERSE	REVOKE*	ROLLBACK*
ROW*	ROWID*	ROWLABEL*	ROWNUM*
ROWS*	ROWTYPE	RUN	SAVEPOINT
SCHEMA	SELECT*	SEPARATE	SET*
SHARE*	SIZE*	SMALLINT	SPACE
SQL	SQLCODE	SQLERRM	START*
STATEMENT	STDDEV	SUBTYPE	SUCCESSFUL*
SUM	SYNONYM*	SYSDATE*	TABAUTH
TABLE*	TABLES	TASK	TERMINATE
THEN*	TO*	TRIGGER*	TRUE
TYPE	UID*	UNION*	UNIQUE*
UPDATE*	USE	USER*	VALIDATE*
VALUES*	VARCHAR*	VARCHAR2*	VARIANCE
VIEW*	VIEWS	WHEN	WHENEVER*
WHERE	WHILE	WITH*	WORK
WRITE	XOR		

If you want to use a reserved word, it must be enclosed in double quotation marks. For example, the following block is legal:

```
DECLARE
   "BEGIN" NUMBER;
BEGIN
   "BEGIN" := 7;
END;
```

However, even though this block is legal, it is not recommended. For more information, see Chapter 2.

APPENDIX B

Guide to Supplied Packages

This appendix catalogs the built-in packages that are available for use with PL/SQL. Each package is described briefly, including the syntax for the procedures and functions within it.

Creating the Packages

All of the supplied packages are owned by the database user SYS. There are public synonyms for them as well, so they can be called without prefixing SYS to the package name. EXECUTE permission on the package is necessary for users other than SYS to call the procedures and functions within the packages. The script that creates the data dictionary, **catproc.sql**, also creates these packages. You can look online in your Oracle system to find additional information—the individual packages are created in separate files. The location of the files is system dependent; for example, on Unix systems they are usually located in the $ORACLE_HOME/rdbms/admin directory. The files to create each package contain comments that provide further information about how to use them.

The packages described in this appendix are listed in Table B-1. The packages discussed in earlier chapters are indicated by asterisks (*) in the table; these packages are discussed only briefly in this appendix.

Package Descriptions

Each of the supplied packages is described in the following sections. The procedures and functions are described following a general introduction to the package itself. Some of the packages, or the procedures within the packages, are available in certain PL/SQL releases only. This is also indicated.

Package Name	Description
DBMS_ALERT*	Synchronous intersession communication
DBMS_DDL	PL/SQL equivalents for some DDL commands
DBMS_DESCRIBE	Describes stored subprograms
DBMS_JOB*	Allows scheduling of PL/SQL procedures
DBMS_LOCK	User-defined locks
DBMS_OUTPUT*	Provides screen output in SQL*Plus or Server Manager
DBMS_PIPE*	Asynchronous intersession communication
DBMS_SESSION	PL/SQL equivalents for ALTER SESSION
DBMS_SHARED_POOL*	Control of the shared pool
DBMS_SQL*	Dynamic PL/SQL and SQL
DBMS_TRANSACTION	Transaction management commands
DBMS_UTILITY	Additional utility procedures
UTL_FILE*	Provides File I/O

TABLE B-1. *Packages Supplied with PL/SQL*

DBMS_ALERT

The DBMS_ALERT package is used to send messages between sessions connected to the same database. Alerts are synchronous, meaning that they are sent when the transaction commits. If the transaction rolls back, the alert is not sent. For more information on alerts, see Chapter 9.

DBMS_DDL

```
PROCEDURE ALTER_COMPILE(type VARCHAR2,
                        schema VARCHAR2,
                        name VARCHAR2);
```

This procedure is equivalent to the SQL commands ALTER PROCEDURE COMPILE, ALTER PACKAGE COMPILE, ALTER PACKAGE BODY COMPILE, and ALTER FUNCTION COMPILE. The parameters are described in the following table:

Parameter	Type	Description
type	VARCHAR2	Type of object to compile. Must be one of 'PROCEDURE', 'FUNCTION', 'PACKAGE', or 'PACKAGE BODY'.
schema	VARCHAR2	Schema that owns the object. This is case-sensitive.
name	VARCHAR2	Name of the object to compile. Also case-sensitive.

ALTER_COMPILE can raise any of the following errors:

- ORA-20000: Insufficient privileges or object does not exist.
- ORA-20001: Remote object, cannot compile.
- ORA-20002: Bad value for object type.

ANALYZE_OBJECT

```
PROCEDURE ANALYZE_OBJECT (type VARCHAR2,
                          schema VARCHAR2,
                          name VARCHAR2,
                          method VARCHAR2,
                          estimate_rows NUMBER DEFAULT NULL,
                          estimate_percent NUMBER DEFAULT NULL);
```

This procedure is equivalent to the SQL commands ANALYZE TABLE, ANALYZE CLUSTER, and ANALYZE INDEX. The parameters are described in the following table:

Parameter	Type	Description
type	VARCHAR2	Type of object to analyze. Should be one of 'TABLE', 'CLUSTER', or 'INDEX'.
schema	VARCHAR2	Schema that owns the object. This parameter is case-sensitive.
name	VARCHAR2	Name of the object to analyze. This parameter is also case-sensitive.
method	VARCHAR2	Analyze method—NULL or 'ESTIMATE'. If 'ESTIMATE', then one of estimate_rows or estimate_percent must be non-zero.
estimate_rows	NUMBER	Number of rows to estimate.
estimate_percent	NUMBER	Percentage of rows to estimate. If estimate_rows is non-zero, this parameter is ignored.

DBMS_DESCRIBE

The DBMS_DESCRIBE package has only one procedure—DESCRIBE_PROCEDURE. Given the name of a stored procedure or function, it will return information about the parameters that the subprogram takes. If the subprogram is overloaded as part of a package, information about all the overloaded versions is returned. Two table types are used in the procedure specification:

```
TYPE varchar2_table IS TABLE OF VARCHAR2(30)
    INDEX BY BINARY_INTEGER;
TYPE number_table   IS TABLE OF NUMBER
    INDEX BY BINARY_INTEGER;
```

DESCRIBE_PROCEDURE

```
PROCEDURE DESCRIBE_PROCEDURE (object_name IN VARCHAR2,
                             reserved1 IN VARCHAR2,
                             reserved2 IN VARCHAR2,
```

overload OUT number_table,
position OUT number_table,
level OUT number_table,
argument_name OUT varchar2_table,
datatype OUT number_table,
default_value OUT number_table,
in_out OUT number_table,
length OUT number_table,
precision OUT number_table,
scale OUT number_table,
radix OUT number_table,
spare OUT number_table);

The procedure that is to be described is specified by *object_name*. Information about each parameter is returned in the PL/SQL tables. For example, the name of the first parameter is in *argument_name*(1), and its datatype is in *datatype*(1). The name of the second parameter is in *argument_name*(2), and so on. The OCI procedure **odessp** provides the same functionality as DBMS_DESCRIBE. The parameters are described in the following table:

Parameter	Datatype	Description
object_name	VARCHAR2	Procedure or function to describe. Can be owned by a different schema, or be in a package.
reserved1	VARCHAR2	Not used currently. Pass as NULL.
reserved2	VARCHAR2	Not used currently. Pass as NULL.
overload	number_table	Sequence number for overloaded procedures. Information about the first version has *overload* = 0, the second has *overload* = 1, and so on.
position	number_table	Position within the argument list. Function return values have position 0.
level	number_table	For composite types such as a record or table, level increases by 1 with each level of nesting. If a record declaration is at level 2, then the fields within the record will be at level 3.
argument_name	varchar2_table	Name of this parameter.

Parameter	Datatype	Description
datatype	number_table	Datatype code for this parameter. Available values are listed in Table B-2. Note that subtypes are returned the same as their base type; for example, INTEGER and REAL are subtypes of NUMBER, and thus would return 2.
default_value	number_table	1 if the argument has a default value, 0 otherwise.
in_out	number_table	Indicates the mode of the parameter. 0 means IN, 1 means OUT, and 2 signifies IN OUT.
length	number_table	Length of the argument (for CHAR or VARCHAR2).
precision	number_table	Precision of the argument (for NUMBER).
scale	number_table	Scale of the argument (for NUMBER).
radix	number_table	Radix of the argument (for NUMBER).
spare	number_table	Not currently used—this parameter is reserved for future functionality.

DBMS_ JOB

PL/SQL 2.2 ...and HIGHER The DBMS_JOB package is used to schedule PL/SQL jobs to run in the background. Jobs are scheduled to run at certain times by background processes. A job is just a stored procedure. If a job fails, PL/SQL will try up to 16 times to run the job again until it succeeds. For more information, see Chapter 11.

DBMS_LOCK

The DBMS_LOCK package is used to create your own user-defined locks. These locks are managed the same way as other Oracle locks. This means that they can be viewed in the fixed views in the data dictionary. User locks are prefixed with 'UL' so they do not conflict with Oracle locks. For more information on the DBMS_LOCK package, see the *Oracle7 Server Application Developer's Guide* and the *Oracle7 Server Reference*.

Several of these procedures use lock modes, which are specified by number. These numbers and their meanings are listed in Table B-3.

Datatype Value	Meaning
1	VARCHAR2
2	NUMBER
3	BINARY_INTEGER
8	LONG
11	ROWID
12	DATE
23	RAW
24	LONG RAW
96	CHAR
106	MLSLABEL
250	PL/SQL Record
251	PL/SQL Table
252	BOOLEAN

TABLE B-2. *Datatype Codes Used for DBMS_DESCRIBE.DESCRIBE_PROCEDURE*

Identifier	Meaning
1	Null mode
2	Row Share mode (ULRS)
3	Row Share Exclusive mode (ULRX)
4	Share mode (ULS)
5	Share Row Exclusive mode (ULRSX)
6	Exclusive mode (ULX)

TABLE B-3. *Lock Mode Identifiers*

ALLOCATE_UNIQUE

PROCEDURE ALLOCATE_UNIQUE(*lockname* IN VARCHAR2,
                     lockhandle OUT VARCHAR2,
                     expiration_secs IN INTEGER DEFAULT 864000);

This procedure will generate a unique lock ID from a lock name. A handle to the lock ID is returned in *lockhandle*, which can be up to 128 bytes. Lock IDs are numbers ranging from 0 to 1073741823. Either lock IDs or lock handles are used in subsequent calls. This procedure always issues a COMMIT. *expiration_secs* specifies the minimum time before the lock is subject to cleanup, in seconds.

CAUTION
Lock names beginning with 'ORA$' are reserved for use by Oracle. The lock name has a maximum length of 128 bytes and is case-sensitive.

REQUEST

FUNCTION REQUEST(*id* IN INTEGER,
                  lockmode IN INTEGER DEFAULT X_MODE,
                  timeout in INTEGER DEFAULT MAXWAIT,
                  release_on_commit IN BOOLEAN DEFAULT FALSE)
    RETURN INTEGER;
FUNCTION REQUEST(*lockhandle* IN VARCHAR2,
                  lockmode IN INTEGER DEFAULT X_MODE,
                  timeout IN INTEGER DEFAULT MAXWAIT,
                  release_on_commit IN BOOLEAN DEFAULT FALSE)
    RETURN INTEGER;

This function is used to request a lock with a particular mode. It is overloaded on the first parameter—the lock handle or lock ID. The parameters are described in the following table:

Parameter	Type	Description
id	INTEGER	Lock ID of the lock to request. Ranges from 0 to 1073741823.
lockhandle	VARCHAR	Lock handle, as returned by ALLOCATE_UNIQUE. Either *lockhandle* or *id* should be specified, but not both.

lockmode	INTEGER	Lock mode to request. Valid values are listed in Table B-3.
timeout	INTEGER	Maximum time (in seconds) to wait for the lock to be granted. If the lock can't be granted within this period, REQUEST returns 1.
release_on_commit	BOOLEAN	If TRUE, the lock will be released when the transaction issues a COMMIT. If FALSE, the lock is held until it is explicitly released.

The return values are described here:

REQUEST Return Value	Meaning
0	Success
1	Timeout
2	Deadlock detected
3	Parameter error
4	Already own the lock
5	Illegal lock handle

CONVERT

```
FUNCTION CONVERT(id IN INTEGER,
                 lockmode IN INTEGER,
                 timeout IN NUMBER DEFAULT MAXWAIT)
    RETURN INTEGER;
FUNCTION CONVERT(lockhandle IN VARCHAR2,
                 lockmode IN INTEGER,
                 timeout IN NUMBER DEFAULT MAXWAIT)
    RETURN INTEGER;
```

CONVERT is used to change a lock from one mode to another. The arguments and return values are similar to REQUEST, and are described in the following tables:

Parameter	Type	Description
id	INTEGER	User assigned lock identifier, from 0 to 1073741823.
lockhandle	VARCHAR2	Lock handle, as returned by ALLOCATE_UNIQUE. Either *id* or *lockhandle* can be specified, but not both.

lockmode	INTEGER	Lock mode requested, as defined in Table B-3.
timeout	NUMBER	Maximum number of seconds to wait before timing out.

Like REQUEST, CONVERT is overloaded on the first parameter.

CONVERT Return Value	Meaning
0	Success
1	Time out
2	Deadlock detected

CONVERT Return Value	Meaning
3	Parameter error
4	Don't own the specified lock
5	Illegal lock handle

RELEASE

```
FUNCTION RELEASE(id IN INTEGER) RETURN INTEGER;
FUNCTION RELEASE(lockhandle IN VARCHAR2) RETURN INTEGER;
```

This function releases a lock that was acquired by REQUEST. It is overloaded on the type of its argument—the lock can be specified either by ID or by a lock handle. The return values are listed here:

RELEASE Return Value	Meaning
0	Success
3	Parameter error
4	Don't own the specified lock
5	Invalid lock handle

SLEEP

```
PROCEDURE SLEEP(seconds IN NUMBER);
```

SLEEP suspends the current session for the specified number of seconds. The maximum resolution is hundredths of a second, so *seconds* can be fractional.

DBMS_OUTPUT

The DBMS_OUTPUT package provides limited output capability to PL/SQL, when used in conjunction with SQL*Plus or Server Manager. It is useful for debugging and testing your PL/SQL code. For more information, see Chapter 8.

DBMS_PIPE

The DBMS_PIPE package is similar to DBMS_ALERT, in that it allows communication between different sessions connected to the same database. Messages sent over pipes, however, are asynchronous. Once a message is sent, it will go through even if the transaction that sent it rolls back. For more information, see Chapter 9.

DBMS_SESSION

The ALTER SESSION command is DDL, and thus is not allowed directly in PL/SQL. The DBMS_SESSION package provides an interface to some of the options available with ALTER SESSION, callable from PL/SQL blocks. The DBMS_SQL package can be used as an alternative to DBMS_SESSION, since it allows execution of arbitrary statements, including ALTER SESSION.

SET_ROLE

PROCEDURE SET_ROLE(*role_cmd* VARCHAR2);

SET_ROLE is equivalent to the SQL command SET ROLE. The text of *role_cmd* is appended to 'SET ROLE', and then the string is executed. Since roles are disabled inside stored procedures, calling SET_ROLE in a stored subprogram or trigger will have no effect. If the role requires a password, you include it in the call. For example, the following code enables the role **Administrator** with the password 'admin':

```
DBMS_SESSION.SET_ROLE('Administrator IDENTIFIED BY admin');
```

SET_SQL_TRACE

PROCEDURE SET_SQL_TRACE(*sql_trace* BOOLEAN);

This procedure is used to turn SQL tracing on or off. It is equivalent to ALTER SESSION SET SQL_TRACE = *sql_trace*. For more information on tracing, see Chapter 12.

SET_NLS

PROCEDURE SET_NLS(*param* VARCHAR2, *value* VARCHAR2);

This command is equivalent to ALTER SESSION SET *param* = *value*, where *param* is a valid NLS parameter, and *value* is the value to which it should be set. This procedure is not valid in triggers. *param* and *value* will be used directly in the resulting ALTER SESSION command, so if *value* is a text literal it must contain the embedded single quotes. For example, we can change the date format with

```
DBMS_SESSION.SET_NLS('nls_date_format', '''DD-MON-YY
                      HH24:MI:SS''');
```

CLOSE_DATABASE_LINK

PROCEDURE CLOSE_DATABASE_LINK(*dblink* VARCHAR2);

This procedure is equivalent to ALTER SESSION CLOSE DATABASE LINK *dblink*. It closes an implicit connection to a remote database.

SET_LABEL

PROCEDURE SET_LABEL(*lbl* VARCHAR2);

This procedure is valid in Trusted Oracle and is equivalent to ALTER SESSION SET LABEL = *lbl*. *lbl* can be 'DBHIGH', 'DBLOW', or another text label.

SET_MLS_LABEL_FORMAT

PROCEDURE SET_MLS_LABEL_FORMAT(*fmt* VARCHAR2);

Also valid in Trusted Oracle, SET_MLS_LABEL_FORMAT is equivalent to ALTER SESSION SET MLS_LABEL_FORMAT = *fmt*. It changes the default label format for the current session.

RESET_PACKAGE

PROCEDURE RESET_PACKAGE;

There is no SQL equivalent for RESET_PACKAGE. It will free the memory used to store the package state and deinstantiate all packages for the session. This is the situation at the beginning of a session.

UNIQUE_SESSION_ID

    FUNCTION UNIQUE_SESSION_ID RETURN VARCHAR2;

This function returns a string with a maximum length of 24 bytes, which is unique among all sessions currently connected to the database. Multiple calls to UNIQUE_SESSION_ID from the same session always return the same result. There is no SQL equivalent.

IS_ROLE_ENABLED

    FUNCTION IS_ROLE_ENABLED(*rolename* VARCHAR2)
       RETURN BOOLEAN;

This function returns TRUE if *rolename* is enabled for this session and FALSE otherwise. If IS_ROLE_ENABLED is called from a stored subprogram or trigger, it will always return FALSE since all roles are disabled there.

DBMS_SHARED_POOL

The DBMS_SHARED_POOL package is used to manage the shared pool. You can pin packages and procedures in the shared pool, so they won't get aged out. This is a key component of a properly tuned PL/SQL environment. For more information, see Chapter 12.

DBMS_SQL

PL/SQL 2.1 ...and HIGHER DBMS_SQL implements dynamic PL/SQL. Using this package, your program can construct SQL statements and PL/SQL blocks at run time and execute them. DBMS_SQL can also be used to execute DDL statements from PL/SQL, which are not permitted otherwise. For more information, see Chapter 10.

DBMS_TRANSACTION

The DBMS_TRANSACTION package provides procedures for transaction management. Many of the commands available here are also available in their SQL equivalents directly in PL/SQL. They are included for completeness.

SET TRANSACTION Commands

```
PROCEDURE READ_ONLY;
PROCEDURE READ_WRITE;
PROCEDURE USE_ROLLBACK_SEGMENT(rb_name VARCHAR2);
```

These procedures are equivalent to the SQL commands SET TRANSACTION READ ONLY, SET TRANSACTION READ WRITE, and SET TRANSACTION USE ROLLBACK SEGMENT *rb_name*. Each must be executed as the first statement in a transaction.

ALTER SESSION ADVISE Commands

```
PROCEDURE ADVISE_COMMIT;
PROCEDURE ADVISE_ROLLBACK;
PROCEDURE ADVISE_NOTHING;
```

These procedures are equivalent to ALTER SESSION ADVISE COMMIT, ALTER SESSION ADVISE ROLLBACK, and ALTER SESSION ADVISE NOTHING. They are used to send advice for a distributed transaction. This advice will be in the **advice** column of the **dba_2pc-pending** data dictionary view in the remote database in case the transaction is in doubt.

COMMIT Commands

```
PROCEDURE COMMIT;
PROCEDURE COMMIT_COMMENT(cmnt VARCHAR2);
PROCEDURE COMMIT_FORCE(xid VARCHAR2,
                       scn VARCHAR2 DEFAULT NULL);
```

These commands are equivalent to the SQL commands COMMIT, COMMIT COMMENT *cmnt*, and COMMIT FORCE *xid, scn*. COMMIT COMMENT and COMMIT FORCE are typically used in distributed transactions.

ROLLBACK and SAVEPOINT Commands

```
PROCEDURE SAVEPOINT(savept VARCHAR2);
PROCEDURE ROLLBACK;
PROCEDURE ROLLBACK_SAVEPOINT(savept VARCHAR2);
PROCEDURE ROLLBACK_FORCE(xid VARCHAR2);
```

These procedures are equivalent to the SQL commands SAVEPOINT *savept,* ROLLBACK, ROLLBACK TO SAVEPOINT *savept,* and ROLLBACK FORCE *xid. xid* is the local or global transaction ID. ROLLBACK_FORCE is typically used in distributed transactions.

BEGIN_DISCRETE_TRANSACTION

PROCEDURE BEGIN_DISCRETE_TRANSACTION;

This procedure is used to mark the current transaction as discrete. A discrete transaction can run faster than a regular transaction, because no undo information is written. All changes to the database are buffered and actually applied at COMMIT time. There are a number of restrictions on discrete transactions, and they should be used with care. For more information, see the *Oracle7 Server Application Developer's Guide.*

PURGE_MIXED

PROCEDURE PURGE_MIXED(*xid* VARCHAR2);

This procedure can be used to purge mixed transactions, which are distributed transactions in which some sites have committed and others rolled back. It should be used with care by the DBA or application. *xid* should be set to the transaction ID as stored in the **local_tran_id** column in **dba_2pc_pending**.

LOCAL_TRANSACTION_ID

FUNCTION LOCAL_TRANSACTION_ID(*create_transaction* BOOLEAN
                                    DEFAULT FALSE)
    RETURN VARCHAR2;

Returns a unique identifier for the current transaction or NULL if there is no current transaction. The identifier is unique to the local instance. If *create_transaction* is TRUE, a transaction is created if it does not already exist.

STEP_ID

FUNCTION *step_id* RETURN NUMBER;

This function returns a unique positive integer that orders the DML operations of the current transaction. The value returned is unique with respect to the current transaction only.

DBMS_UTILITY

The DBMS_UTILITY package provides additional functionality for managing procedures, reporting errors, and other information.

COMPILE_SCHEMA

> PROCEDURE COMPILE_SCHEMA(*schema* VARCHAR2);

This procedure will compile all procedures, functions, and packages in the specified schema, equivalent to the SQL commands ALTER PROCEDURE COMPILE, ALTER FUNCTION COMPILE, and ALTER PACKAGE COMPILE. If you don't have ALTER privileges for one or more objects in *schema*, an ORA-20000 error is raised.

ANALYZE_SCHEMA

> PROCEDURE ANALYZE_SCHEMA(*schema* VARCHAR2,
>   *method* VARCHAR2,
>   *estimate_rows* NUMBER DEFAULT NULL,
>   *estimate_percent* NUMBER DEFAULT NULL);

This procedure will analyze all the tables, clusters, and indexes in the schema. The parameters are defined by the following table:

Parameter	Type	Description
schema	VARCHAR2	Schema whose objects should be analyzed.
method	VARCHAR2	Analyze method—either NULL or 'ESTIMATE'. If 'ESTIMATE', then one of *estimate_rows* or *estimate_percent* should be non-zero.
estimate_rows	NUMBER	Number of rows to estimate.
estimate_percent	NUMBER	Percentage of rows to estimate. If *estimate_rows* is specified, this parameter is ignored.

FORMAT_ERROR_STACK

> FUNCTION FORMAT_ERROR_STACK RETURN VARCHAR2;

This function will return the entire error stack, with a maximum length of 2000 bytes. It is useful in exception handlers.

FORMAT_CALL_STACK

FUNCTION FORMAT_CALL_STACK RETURN VARCHAR2;

This function returns a string consisting of the current call stack—all of the procedures that are currently executing. The maximum length is 2000 bytes.

IS_PARALLEL_SERVER

FUNCTION IS_PARALLEL_SERVER RETURN BOOLEAN;

This function returns TRUE if the instance is running in parallel server mode and FALSE otherwise.

GET_TIME

FUNCTION GET_TIME RETURN NUMBER;

Returns elapsed time in hundredths of a second. This is useful for timing a procedure. For example:

```
DECLARE
  v_Start NUMBER;
  v_End NUMBER;
BEGIN
  v_Start := DBMS_UTILITY.GET_TIME;
  /* Do some work here */
  v_End := DBMS_UTILITY.GET_TIME;
  /* The work took (v_Start - v_End) * 100 seconds to execute. */
END;
```

NAME_RESOLVE

PROCEDURE NAME_RESOLVE(*name* in VARCHAR2,
                      context IN NUMBER,
                      schema OUT VARCHAR2,
                      part1 OUT VARCHAR2,
                      part2 OUT VARCHAR2,
                      dblink OUT VARCHAR2,

part1_type OUT NUMBER,
object_number OUT NUMBER);

NAME_RESOLVE is used to resolve a given reference into its components. Given input of "example.Debug.Reset@dblink", for example, the output will be separated into 'example', 'Debug', 'Reset', and 'dblink', and returned in *schema*, *part1*, *part2*, and *dblink*, respectively. The parameters are described in the following table:

Parameter	Datatype	Description
name	VARCHAR2	Name of the object to resolve.
context	NUMBER	Reserved for future use—must be passed as 1.
schema	VARCHAR2	Schema of the object, if specified as part of *name*.
part1	VARCHAR2	First part of the name. This would be the package name if the object is a packaged procedure. If it is not a packaged procedure, this is the entire name. This is also determined by *part1_type*.
part2	VARCHAR2	Second part of the name, if applicable.
dblink	VARCHAR2	Database link name, if applicable.
part1_type	NUMBER	Determines the meaning of part1. Valid values are 5 - synonym 7 - procedure 8 - function 9 - package
object_number	NUMBER	If the object is successfully resolved, this is the object number as recorded in the data dictionary.

PORT_STRING

FUNCTION PORT_STRING RETURN VARCHAR2;

This function returns a string that uniquely identifies both the version of Oracle and the operating system. The maximum length is dependent on the operating system.

UTL_FILE

PL/SQL 2.3 ...and HIGHER The UTL_FILE procedure implements file I/O in PL/SQL. Using this package, PL/SQL programs can read from and write to operating system files located on the server. The accessible files and directories are limited by parameters in the INIT.ORA database initialization file, for security. For more information, see Chapter 11.

APPENDIX C

Glossary of PL/SQL Features

This appendix briefly describes essential PL/SQL features, with references to chapters where you can find more detailed information. Table C-1 first lists the features; following the table is an alphabetical glossary.

Assignment	Blocks	Comments
COMMIT Statement	Conditions	CURSOR_ALREADY_OPEN Exception
Cursor Variables	Cursors	Datatypes
DDL	DELETE Statement	DUP_VAL_ON_INDEX Exception
EXCEPTION_INIT Pragma	Exceptions	EXIT Statement
Expressions	FETCH Statement	%FOUND Attribute
Functions	GOTO Statement	Identifiers
IF Statement	INSERT Statement	INVALID_CURSOR Exception
INVALID_NUMBER Exception	I/O	%ISOPEN
Literals	LOCK TABLE Statement	LOGIN_DENIED Exception
Loops	NO_DATA_FOUND Exception	NOT_LOGGED_ON Exception
%NOTFOUND	NULL Statement	NULL Value
OPEN Statement	Packages	Procedural Statements
Procedures	PROGRAM_ERROR Exception	RAISE Statement
Records	RESTRICT_REFERENCES Pragma	RETURN Statement
ROLLBACK Statement	%ROWCOUNT Attribute	%ROWTYPE Attribute
ROWTYPE_MISMATCH Exception	SAVEPOINT Statement	SELECT..INTO Statement
SET TRANSACTION Statement	SQL Cursor	SQL Statements
SQLCODE Function	SQLERRM Function	STANDARD Package
Statements	STORAGE_ERROR Exception	Tables
TIMEOUT_ON_RESOURCE Exception	TOO_MANY_ROWS Exception	TRANSACTION_BACKED_OUT Exception
Triggers	%TYPE Attribute	UPDATE Statement
VALUE_ERROR Exception	Variables and Constants	ZERO_DIVIDE Exception

TABLE C-1. *PL/SQL Features*

Assignment   Assignment statements are used to place a value into a PL/SQL variable. The syntax is

> *variable := expression;*

where *variable* is an identifier for a PL/SQL variable, and *expression* is a PL/SQL expression. *expression* is considered an rvalue and *variable* an lvalue. If *expression* and *variable* are not of the same type, PL/SQL will attempt to convert the type of *expression* to the type of *variable*. If the conversion fails, an error is raised. For more information, see Chapter 2.

Blocks   All PL/SQL programs are made up of blocks. A PL/SQL block consists of declarative, executable, and exception-handling sections. The syntax for a block is

```
DECLARE
    declarative section here
BEGIN
    executable section here
EXCEPTION
    exception-handling section here
END;
```

The DECLARE, BEGIN, EXCEPTION, and END keywords delimit the sections. Only the executable section is required. For more information, see Chapter 2.

Comments   Comments are used to document your code and make it more readable. The PL/SQL compiler ignores them. There are two types of comments: single line and multiline or C-style. Single-line comments start with two dashes (--) and continue to the end of the line (delimited by a newline character). Multiline comments start with /* and end with */. See Chapter 2 for more information. For example:

```
    -- This is a single line comment.
/* This is a multiline
    comment, continued over two lines. */
```

COMMIT Statement   The COMMIT SQL statement is used to end a transaction and make all changes permanent. Until a transaction is committed, other users cannot see the changes made to the database by the transaction. COMMIT also releases any locks acquired by the transaction. The syntax is

> COMMIT [WORK];

where the WORK keyword is optional. For more information, see Chapter 3.

Conditions A condition is an expression that evaluates to a BOOLEAN value. Conditions are used in IF..THEN, EXIT..WHEN, WHILE..LOOP, and the WHERE clause of SQL statements. Conditions can be combined using the logical operators AND, OR, and NOT. They can be constructed using logical operators such as =, >=, LIKE, IN, and BETWEEN. For more information, see Chapter 2.

CURSOR_ALREADY_OPEN Exception This predefined exception corresponds to "ORA-6511: PL/SQL: cursor already open." It is raised when you try to open a cursor that is already open. You can determine the open status of a cursor with the %ISOPEN attribute. For more information about cursors, see Chapter 4.

Cursor Variables

PL/SQL 2.2 ...and HIGHER Cursor variables are dynamic cursors. A given cursor variable can be opened for different queries using the OPEN..FOR syntax. Typically, a cursor variable is opened on the server and fetched from and then closed on the client. Cursor variables are available in PL/SQL 2.2 and higher. With release 2.2, you must use a client program such as SQL*Plus, or one written using the precompilers or OCI, to access cursor variables. PL/SQL 2.3 can process cursor variables entirely on the server. A cursor variable is declared with type REF CURSOR and is the only pointer type available in PL/SQL up to release 2.3. For more information, see the "Cursor Variables" section in Chapter 4.

Cursors Cursors are used to control the processing for queries that return more than one row. A cursor is declared using the CURSOR..IS syntax, then processed with OPEN, FETCH, and CLOSE. Cursor attributes are used to determine the current status of a cursor, with information about how many rows the cursor has returned, whether the cursor is open, and whether the last fetch was successful. For more information, see Chapter 4.

Datatypes PL/SQL supports all of the datatypes provided by the Oracle7 server, plus a number of additional ones. The types are described in detail in Chapter 2, and listed here by category and family:

Category	Family	Types
Reference Types	N/A	REF CURSOR
Composite Types	N/A	RECORD, TABLE
Scalar Types	Numeric	NUMBER, DEC, DECIMAL, DOUBLE PRECISION, INTEGER, INT, NUMERIC, REAL, SMALLINT, BINARY_INTEGER, NATURAL, POSITIVE

Boolean	BOOLEAN
Trusted	MLSLABEL
Character	VARCHAR2, VARCHAR, CHAR, CHARACTER, LONG
Raw	RAW, LONG RAW
Date	DATE
Rowid	ROWID

DDL (Data Definition Language)

PL/SQL 2.1 ...and HIGHER PL/SQL does not allow DDL statements to be used directly, because the compiler is implemented using early binding. PL/SQL 2.1, however, allows the use of DDL statements with the DBMS_SQL package. This package allows statements to be constructed at run time rather than compile time. For more information, see Chapter 10.

DELETE Statement   The DELETE SQL statement is used to remove rows from a table. It is defined with

```
DELETE [FROM] table [alias]
   WHERE {where_clause | CURRENT OF cursor;};
```

Table specifies the table from which the rows should be deleted. An alias for the table name can also be specified if desired. The *where_clause* determines which rows will be deleted. If the CURRENT OF *cursor* clause is used, then the last row fetched from *cursor* will be deleted. After a delete that removes one or more rows, SQL%NOTFOUND is FALSE, SQL%FOUND is TRUE, and SQL%ROWCOUNT contains the number of rows deleted. If the *where_clause* does not match any rows, no rows are deleted and SQL%NOTFOUND is TRUE, SQL%FOUND is FALSE, and SQL%ROWCOUNT equals 0. For more information, see Chapter 3.

DUP_VAL_ON_INDEX Exception   This predefined exception corresponds to the Oracle error "ORA-1: unique constraint violated." It is raised when you try to insert a row into a table with a unique index defined for a particular field, and the value for the field you are trying to insert already exists in the table.

EXCEPTION_INIT Pragma   Pragma EXCEPTION_INIT is used to associate a named exception with an Oracle error. This provides named exceptions in addition to the predefined ones. The syntax is

```
PRAGMA EXCEPTION_INIT(exception_name, error_number);
```

where *exception_name* is an exception currently in scope, and *error_number* is the SQLCODE value corresponding to an Oracle error. For example, the following code will raise **e_NonExistentTable** whenever the error "ORA-942: table or view does not exist" is returned:

```
DECLARE
  e_NonExistentTable  EXCEPTION;
  PRAGMA EXCEPTION_INIT(e_NonExistentTable, -942);
  . . .
```

For more information, see Chapter 6.

Exceptions   Exceptions are used to trap run-time errors. When an error occurs, an exception is raised, and control immediately passes to the exception-handling section of the block. If there is no exception-handling section in the current block, the exception is propagated out to the enclosing block. Predefined exceptions are defined in package STANDARD, and you can define your own exceptions as well. For more information, see Chapter 6.

EXIT Statement   EXIT is used to pass control out of a currently executing loop. It is defined with

> EXIT [*loop_name*] [WHEN *condition*];

where *condition* is a boolean expression. If there is no WHEN clause, the loop is exited immediately. If there is a WHEN clause, the loop is exited only if *condition* evaluates to TRUE. If specified, *loop_name* should match a label at the beginning of a loop. For more information, see Chapter 3.

Expressions   An expression is a combination of variables, constants, literals, operators, other expressions, and function calls. An expression evaluates to an rvalue. Expressions can be used in a variety of PL/SQL statements, including the WHERE clause of SELECT, UPDATE, and DELETE statements. Expressions are combined using operators such as +, −, NOT, OR, ||, and -. If an expression is composed of items that have different types, they are converted to the same type first, and then the operators are applied. For more information, see Chapter 2.

FETCH Statement   FETCH is used to retrieve rows from a cursor or cursor variable into PL/SQL variables or a PL/SQL record. It is defined with

> FETCH *cursor* | *cursor_variable*
>   INTO *record* | *list_of_variables*;

where *cursor* is the name of a previously opened cursor, or *cursor_variable* is the name of a previously opened cursor variable (PL/SQL 2.2 and higher). The *list_of_variables* or the fields in *record* should match the select list of the query. Typically, FETCH is called in a loop whose exit condition is determined by the %NOTFOUND attribute. Each call to FETCH will retrieve one more row and increment *cursor*%ROWCOUNT by one. For more information, see Chapter 4.

%FOUND Attribute   This boolean cursor attribute is used to determine whether the last FETCH for a cursor or cursor variable (PL/SQL 2.3 and higher) returned a row. It is defined with

>   *cursor*%FOUND | *cursor_variable*%FOUND

where *cursor* is the name of a cursor, and *cursor_variable* is the name of a cursor variable. If the last FETCH returned a row, then %FOUND evaluates to TRUE. After a cursor is opened, but before the first FETCH, %FOUND evaluates to NULL. %FOUND is the opposite of the %NOTFOUND cursor attribute. For more information, see Chapter 4.

Functions   Functions are named PL/SQL blocks that return a value and can be called with arguments. They can be used as part of an expression. They are legal in procedural statements, and certain functions can be used in SQL statements in PL/SQL 2.1 and higher. Functions can be stored in the database with the CREATE [OR REPLACE] FUNCTION command, or they can be located in the declarative section of another block. For more information, see Chapter 5.

GOTO Statement   GOTO passes control to a statement identified by a label. The syntax is

>   GOTO *label*;

where *label* is delimited by double angle brackets **<<** and **>>**. It is illegal to branch into or out of an exception handler, or into an IF statement, loop, or sub-block. For more information, see Chapter 2.

Identifiers   The name of any PL/SQL object is an identifier. Identifiers are not case-sensitive, and consist of up to 30 characters in the PL/SQL character set. Identifiers must begin with a letter. For more information, see Chapter 2.

IF Statement   The IF statement is used to conditionally execute a sequence of statements. It is defined with

```
IF condition1 THEN
  sequence_of_statements1;
[ELSIF condition2 THEN
  sequence_of_statements2;]
...
[ELSE
  sequence_of_statements3;]
END IF;
```

The *sequence_of_statements* under the first *condition* that evaluates to TRUE is executed. At most, one *sequence_of_statements* will be executed. For more information, see Chapter 2.

INSERT Statement   INSERT is used to add a row to a table. It is defined with

```
INSERT INTO table [(column_list)]
  VALUES (expression_list);
```

where *table* is a reference to the table into which the rows will be inserted, and *expression_list* is a comma-separated list of expressions that make up the fields of the new row. If *column_list* is specified, then it determines the columns that will have values. Columns that are not specified will have a value of NULL. If *column_list* is not specified, then *expression_list* should correspond to all the columns in the table. For more information, see Chapter 4.

INVALID_CURSOR Exception   This predefined exception corresponds to the Oracle error "ORA-1001: invalid cursor." It is raised when a cursor is invalid but you try to use it regardless. This can occur if you try to fetch from a cursor before it has been opened, or if you fetch from a cursor declared for update after a commit. For more information on cursor processing, see Chapter 4.

INVALID_NUMBER Exception   This predefined exception corresponds to the Oracle error "ORA-1722: invalid number." It is raised when an attempted conversion to a NUMBER value failed. For example, the string 'Nineteen Hundred and Ninety Five' cannot be converted into a NUMBER since it does not contain only digits, a decimal point, or an optional sign. For more information on number conversions, see Chapters 2 and 3.

I/O   PL/SQL does not have support for input/output directly in the language. The DBMS_OUTPUT package, when used with SQL*Plus, Server Manager, or SQL*DBA, provides output capability. SQL*Plus provides input capability via substitution variables. PL/SQL 2.3 remedies this situation with the UTL_FILE package, which provides file I/O. DBMS_OUTPUT is discussed in Chapter 8, and UTL_FILE in Chapter 11.

ISOPEN   The %ISOPEN cursor attribute is used to determine whether a cursor or cursor variable (PL/SQL 2.3 and higher) is open. It is defined with

> *cursor*%ISOPEN | *cursor_variable*%ISOPEN

where *cursor* is the name of an explicit cursor, or *cursor_variable* is the name of a cursor variable. If the cursor or cursor variable has been opened with the OPEN or OPEN..FOR statement, and has not yet been closed, %ISOPEN will return TRUE. SQL%ISOPEN always returns FALSE, since the implicit cursor is always closed after execution of the SQL statement. For more information, see Chapter 4.

Literals   Literals can be classified as either numeric or character. A numeric literal is composed of the digits 0 through 9, with an optional sign and/or decimal point. Numeric literals can also be specified in scientific notation. All numeric literals have datatype NUMBER. A character literal is any sequence of characters enclosed in single quotes. A double-quoted string is not treated as a literal, but as a case-sensitive identifier. Character literals have datatype CHAR, not VARCHAR2. For more information, see Chapter 2.

LOCK TABLE Statement   LOCK TABLE is a DML statement that can be used to lock an entire table. The SELECT..FOR UPDATE statement is used to lock selected rows within a table. The syntax for LOCK TABLE is

> LOCK TABLE *table* in *lock_mode* [NOWAIT];

where *table* is a reference to the desired table, and *lock_mode* specifies the mode. Available modes include ROW EXCLUSIVE, ROW SHARE, SHARE UPDATE, SHARE, SHARE ROW EXCLUSIVE, and EXCLUSIVE. If NOWAIT is specified, the statement will return immediately either with the lock acquired or with TIMEOUT_ON_RESOURCE raised if the lock cannot be acquired. If NOWAIT is not specified, then the LOCK TABLE will wait until the lock can be acquired. For more information, see the *Oracle7 Server SQL Reference*.

LOGIN_DENIED Exception   This predefined exception corresponds to the Oracle error "ORA-1017: invalid username/password; logon denied." It is raised when an incorrect user name/password combination is specified.

Loops   There are four different kinds of looping structures in PL/SQL. Basic loops are delimited with the LOOP and END LOOP keywords. WHILE loops start with the WHILE..LOOP keywords and end with END LOOP. Numeric and cursor FOR loops use the FOR *index* IN..LOOP and END LOOP keywords. All loops can optionally begin with a label, which can be used in the EXIT statement within the loop if desired. For more information on simple, WHILE, and numeric FOR loops, see Chapter 3. For more information on cursor FOR loops, see Chapter 4.

NO_DATA_FOUND Exception   This predefined exception corresponds to the Oracle error "ORA-1403: no data found." It is raised if a SELECT..INTO statement matches no rows, or if you reference a row in a PL/SQL table that has not yet been assigned. For more information on SELECT..INTO, see Chapter 3. For more information on PL/SQL tables, see Chapter 2.

NOT_LOGGED_ON Exception   This predefined exception corresponds to the Oracle error "ORA-1012: not connected to Oracle." It is raised if an SQL statement is issued before a valid connection has been established.

%NOTFOUND   The %NOTFOUND cursor attribute is used to determine whether the last FETCH from a cursor or cursor variable (PL/SQL 2.3 and higher) did not return a row. It is defined with

   cursor%NOTFOUND | *cursor_variable*%NOTFOUND

where *cursor* is an identifier for a cursor, or *cursor_variable* is an identifier for a cursor variable (PL/SQL 2.3 and higher). If the prior FETCH did not return a row because the end of the active set has been reached, %NOTFOUND will return TRUE. %NOTFOUND is the opposite of %FOUND. For more information, see Chapter 4.

NULL Value   All PL/SQL expressions can evaluate to NULL, unless they are constrained not to when a variable is declared. A NULL means "missing or unknown value." Many expressions will evaluate to NULL if one of the operands evaluates to NULL. This includes BOOLEAN expressions—the logical operators in PL/SQL implement a three-valued logic, not a two-valued logic. For more information on NULL and its implications, see Chapter 2.

NULL Statement   The NULL statement, specified with

   NULL;

performs no work. It is useful for indicating that no action is to be taken at a point where PL/SQL syntax demands a statement. For more information, see Chapter 2.

OPEN Statement   The OPEN statement is used to open a cursor (or cursor variable, in release 2.2 and higher). When a cursor is opened, any bind variables in the WHERE clause are evaluated, and the active set is determined. The bind variables will not be examined, nor will the active set change unless the cursor is closed and then reopened. The syntax for OPEN is

> OPEN cursor_name; | OPEN cursor_variable FOR select_statement;

where cursor_name specifies a previously defined static cursor, and cursor_variable specifies a previously defined cursor variable. For a cursor variable, the query is specified with select_statement. For more information, see Chapter 4.

Packages   Packages are defined as two separate data dictionary objects—the package header (or specification) and the package body. The header is created with the CREATE OR REPLACE PACKAGE command, the body with the CREATE OR REPLACE PACKAGE BODY command. Packages must be stored in the database; they cannot be placed in a declarative section like procedures and functions. Packages themselves can contain procedures, functions, variables, types, cursors, and exceptions. Items declared in the package header will be visible outside the package, while items defined only in the package body will be private to the package. Packages also break the dependency chain because the package body can be recompiled without affecting the package specification. For more information, see Chapter 5.

Procedural Statements   Procedural statements, as opposed to SQL statements, control the processing of a PL/SQL block. They are processed by the PL/SQL engine and are not sent to the SQL statement executor in the database. Procedural statements include calls to procedures, assignments, conditional control statements such as IF..THEN, and loops. For more information, see Chapter 2.

Procedures   Procedures can be stored in the database with the CREATE OR REPLACE PROCEDURE statement, or they can be declared in the declarative section of a block. A procedure is a named block that can be called with parameters. The parameters can either accept a value from the calling environment (IN), return a value to the calling environment (OUT), or both (IN OUT). For more information, see Chapter 5.

PROGRAM_ERROR Exception   This predefined exception corresponds to the Oracle error " PL/SQL: internal error *mmm*, arguments [*mmm*], [*mmm*], [*mmm*], [*mmm*], [*mmm*], [*mmm*]", where *mmm* represents the code associated with this particular internal error. This error is raised when an internal PL/SQL error has occurred, which should not normally occur.

RAISE Statement   RAISE is used to signal that an error has occurred by raising an exception. The exception can be user-defined or predefined. The syntax for RAISE is

>   RAISE [*exception_name*];

where *exception_name* specifies the exception to be raised. The only place where it is legal to issue a RAISE statement without a named exception is in an exception handler. In this case, the current exception is raised again. For more information, see Chapter 6.

Records   PL/SQL records are used to group logically related information of different types. As with PL/SQL tables, you must first define a record type and then declare a variable of that type. For example, the following declarative section declares a record to hold some of the student information:

```
DECLARE
  TYPE t_StudentType IS RECORD (
    FirstName students.first_name%TYPE;
    LastName  students.last_name%TYPE;
    ID        students.ID%TYPE);
  v_StudentInfo t_StudentType;
```

The %ROWTYPE attribute returns a PL/SQL record as well. For more information, see Chapter 2.

RESTRICT_REFERENCES Pragma

PL/SQL **2.1** ...and **HIGHER**   The RESTRICT_REFERENCES pragma is used to assert the purity level for user-defined functions. In order to be used in SQL statements, you must guarantee to the PL/SQL engine that the function does not modify any database or package state. The pragma is specified with

>   PRAGMA RESTRICT_REFERENCES(*function_name*,
>   [RNDS] [,WNDS] [,RNPS] [,WNPS])

where *function_name* is the function whose purity you are asserting. The purity levels, defined in the following table, can be specified in any order. For more information, see Chapter 5.

Purity Level	Meaning
RNDS	Reads no database state
WNDS	Writes no database state

> RNPS   Reads no package state
>
> WNPS   Writes no package state

RETURN Statement   RETURN can be used in two ways: to return from a function or from a procedure. It is specified with

> RETURN [*return_value*];

RETURN causes control to pass from a function or procedure back to the calling environment. The *return_value* must be specified for a function, and not for a procedure. RETURN is optional for procedures, but it is required for functions, since a function must pass a value back to the calling environment. For more information, see Chapter 5.

ROLLBACK Statement   The ROLLBACK statement is used to end a transaction and undo the work done by that transaction. It is as if the transaction was never begun. The syntax is

> ROLLBACK [WORK] [TO SAVEPOINT *savepoint*];

The WORK keyword is optional. Like COMMIT, ROLLBACK also releases any locks acquired by the transaction. If a savepoint is specified, only the work done after *savepoint* is rolled back. For more information, see Chapter 3.

%ROWCOUNT Attribute   This cursor attribute returns the number of rows fetched so far for an explicit cursor, and the number of rows affected by the last statement for the implicit SQL cursor. Each explicit FETCH for a cursor will increment its %ROWCOUNT value by one. For more information, see Chapter 3.

%ROWTYPE Attribute   The %ROWTYPE attribute can be applied to a database table. It will return the type of a PL/SQL record consisting of all the columns in the table, in the order in which they were specified at table creation. For example, the following block declares a record that can hold a row in the **classes** table:

```
DECLARE
  v_ClassInfo classes%ROWTYPE;
```

For more information, see Chapter 2.

ROWTYPE_MISMATCH Exception

PL/SQL 2.2 ...and HIGHER   This predefined exception corresponds to the Oracle error "ORA-6504: PL/SQL: return types of result set variables or query do not match." This

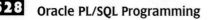

error is raised when you open a cursor variable for a different type of query than it was defined for, using the OPEN..FOR syntax. For more information, see Chapter 4.

SAVEPOINT Statement   SAVEPOINT is used to mark the place in a transaction. The syntax is

        SAVEPOINT savepoint_name;

where *savepoint_name* is the name of the savepoint to be defined. Once the savepoint is defined, you can roll back to it using the ROLLBACK TO SAVEPOINT command. For more information, see Chapter 3.

SELECT..INTO Statement   SELECT..INTO is used to retrieve one row from the database. The syntax is

        SELECT select_list
            INTO variable_list | record
            FROM table
            [WHERE where_clause]
            [GROUP BY group_clause]
            [ORDER BY order_clause]
            [HAVING having_clause];

The variables in *variable_list* should match the items in *select_list*, or the fields in the *record* should match. The row will be retrieved from the table identified by *table*. The rest of the clauses determine which row will be retrieved. If the query returns more than one row, use an explicit cursor. If the query does not return any rows, the NO_DATA_FOUND exception is raised. For more information, see Chapter 3.

SET TRANSACTION Statement   SET TRANSACTION is used to specify the properties of the transaction. It must be called as the first statement in the transaction. The syntax for SET TRANSACTION is

        SET TRANSACTION
            USE ROLLBACK SEGMENT segment | READ ONLY;

    SET TRANSACTION can be used both to assign a particular rollback segment to the transaction and to allow only read operations (queries and LOCK TABLE statements). All queries in a read-only transaction will be read consistently from the beginning of the transaction, rather than for each statement. For more information, see the *Oracle7 Server SQL Reference*.

SQL Cursor   All SQL statements are processed in a cursor. Explicit cursors are used for multirow queries, and they are processed using the OPEN, FETCH, and CLOSE commands. For other SQL statements, an implicit cursor, known as the SQL cursor, is used. The four cursor attributes are available, referenced with SQL%FOUND, SQL%NOTFOUND, SQL%ROWCOUNT, and SQL%ISOPEN. SQL%ISOPEN will always return FALSE since the implicit cursor is opened, the statement is executed within it, and the cursor is closed before %ISOPEN can be checked. For more information, see Chapter 3.

SQL Statements   SQL statements, as opposed to procedural statements, are used to issue commands to the database. Only DML (data manipulation language) and transaction control statements are allowed directly in PL/SQL. The DBMS_SQL package, available with PL/SQL 2.1 and higher, can be used to issue DDL statements from PL/SQL. For more information, see Chapter 3.

SQLCODE Function   SQLCODE is used to return the error code associated with the current error. It is typically used in a WHEN OTHERS handler, to determine which Oracle error raised the exception. SQLCODE returns an INTEGER value. For more information, see Chapter 6.

SQLERRM Function   SQLERRM returns the error message text associated with an Oracle error code. If no error code is specified, SQLERRM returns the error message text for the current error. Typically, SQLERRM is used along with SQLCODE in a WHEN OTHERS handler, to determine the text of the error that raised the exception. The maximum length of an error message is 512 characters. For more information, see Chapter 6.

STANDARD Package   The predefined exceptions (such as NO_DATA_FOUND or INVALID_CURSOR), types (such as NUMBER or DATE), and functions (such as TO_CHAR or ADD_MONTHS) are all defined in a PL/SQL package known as STANDARD. It is owned by the database user SYS and is created when the data dictionary is created by the **catproc.sql** script. EXECUTE permission on STANDARD is granted to PUBLIC by **catproc.sql** as well. Unlike other PL/SQL packages, you can refer to objects within STANDARD without prefixing them with the package name.

Statements   There are two kinds of statements: procedural and SQL. Procedural statements consist of assignments, procedure calls, loops, or IF statements, for example. SQL statements can be divided into DML (data manipulation language), DDL (data definition language), transaction control, session control, and system control statements. For more information, see Chapters 2 and 3.

STORAGE_ERROR Exception   This predefined exception corresponds to the Oracle error "ORA-6500: PL/SQL: storage error." This error is raised when PL/SQL cannot allocate enough memory to continue. It is an internal error, which should not normally occur.

Tables   PL/SQL tables are syntactically treated similar to arrays in other third-generation languages. To declare a PL/SQL table, first you define a new table type and then a variable of that type. For example, the following declarative section defines a table of dates:

```
DECLARE
  TYPE t_DateTable IS TABLE OF DATE
    INDEX BY BINARY_INTEGER;
  v_Dates t_DateTable;
```

Although a table is treated syntactically like an array, it is not implemented like an array. For more information, see Chapter 2.

TIMEOUT_ON_RESOURCE Exception   This predefined exception corresponds to the Oracle error "ORA-51: timeout occurred while waiting for resource." It can be raised if you specify the NOWAIT clause in a SELECT..FOR UPDATE statement, and another session already has a lock on the requested rows.

TOO_MANY_ROWS Exception   This predefined exception corresponds to the Oracle error "Oracle 1422: exact fetch returns more than requested number of rows." It is raised if a SELECT..INTO statement matches more than one row. In this case, a cursor should be used to retrieve the entire active set. For more information, see Chapter 4.

TRANSACTION_BACKED_OUT Exception   This predefined exception corresponds to the Oracle error "ORA-61: another instance has a different DML_LOCKS setting." This exception is predefined only in PL/SQL 2.0 and 2.1, not in 2.2 or higher. It is raised if a transaction has to be rolled back by the database due to a deadlock situation.

Triggers   A trigger is similar to a procedure, in that it is a named, callable block that is stored in the database. However, a trigger is not called explicitly. Rather, it is called (or fired) implicitly whenever the triggering event occurs. The event is a DML operation on a database table. There are 12 different kinds of triggers, based on the type of statement (INSERT, UPDATE, DELETE), the type of trigger (ROW, STATEMENT), and the triggering time (BEFORE, AFTER). For more information, see Chapter 5.

%TYPE Attribute   The %TYPE attribute can be applied to a variable or a table column. It returns the type of the object and is used to make your program more flexible. For example, in the following block, **v_FirstName** is declared with type VARCHAR2(20), and **v_CurrentCredits** is defined with type NUMBER(3), since these are the types of **students.first_name** and **students.current_credits**, respectively.

```
DECLARE
  v_FirstName        students.first_name%TYPE;
  v_CurrentCredits   students.current_credits%TYPE;
```

Only the length or precision/scale constraint is taken from the column definition. Even if the column is constrained to be NOT NULL, the variable can contain NULLs (unless it is also constrained). For more information, see Chapter 2.

UPDATE Statement   The UPDATE statement is used to modify existing rows in a database table. The syntax is

> UPDATE *table* SET *column1* = *value1*, *column2* = *value2*, ...
>   [WHERE *where_clause*];

where *table* is a reference to the table to be modified, and *where_clause* specifies the rows to change. The columns specified by *column1*, *column2*, and so on, will be set to their corresponding *value*s. If an UPDATE statement affects one or more rows, SQL%FOUND will be TRUE, SQL%NOTFOUND will be FALSE, and SQL%ROWCOUNT will contain the number of rows modified after the statement executes. If the statement does not match any rows, SQL%FOUND will be FALSE, SQL%NOTFOUND will be TRUE, and SQL%ROWCOUNT will be zero.

VALUE_ERROR Exception   This predefined exception corresponds to the Oracle error "ORA-6502: numeric or value error." It is raised if an attempted conversion of a character value to a NUMBER fails. VALUE_ERROR is generally raised for a procedural statement; for a SQL statement, an error such as INVALID_NUMBER is raised instead. For more information on datatype conversion, see Chapters 2 and 3.

Variables and Constants   Variables and constants are defined in the declarative section of a PL/SQL block. A declaration looks like

> *variable_name type* [CONSTANT] [NOT NULL] := *initial_value*;

where *variable_name* is the name of the new variable or constant, and *type* is its type. *Type* can be either a predefined type, such as DATE or ROWID, or a user-defined type. If CONSTANT is specified, the value of the variable cannot be changed; it is a constant. The variable or constant will be assigned *initial_value* if it is specified or NULL if no initial value is specified. For more information, see Chapter 2.

ZERO_DIVIDE Exception   This predefined exception corresponds to the Oracle error "ORA-1476: divisor is equal to zero." It is raised whenever an attempt to divide by zero is performed.

A P P E N D I X D

The Data Dictionary

This appendix describes some of the views in the data dictionary that are relevant to PL/SQL programmers. It does not include all of the views, just the more commonly used ones. A brief description of the data dictionary and how it works is also included.

What Is the Data Dictionary?

The data dictionary is where Oracle stores information about the structure of the database. The data itself is located in other areas—the data dictionary describes how the actual data is organized. The dictionary consists of tables and views that you can query, like any other database table or view. The views are owned by the Oracle user SYS.

The data dictionary is typically created when the database is created and installed for the first time. Without the dictionary, no PL/SQL work can be done.

On most systems, there is a script called **catproc.sql** that creates the dictionary views. This script should be run while connected as SYS, or connected as internal in SQL*DBA or Server Manager.

In addition to creating the data dictionary itself, **catproc.sql** creates the standard PL/SQL and DBMS packages, which are stored in the data dictionary. For more information on the data dictionary views (including views not discussed here and the v$ performance views), see the *Oracle7 Server Reference*. For more information on the built-in packages, see Appendix B.

Naming Conventions

Many of the views have three different instantiations. These are known as **user_***, **all_***, and **dba_***. For example, there are three instantiations of the information about the source for stored objects. The views that represent this are **user_source**, **all_source**, and **dba_source**. In general, the **user_*** views contain information about objects owned by the current user, the **all_*** views contain information about all objects accessible to the current user (not necessarily owned by them), and the **dba_*** views contain information about all objects in the database.

SQL and PL/SQL are not case-sensitive. In order to implement this, all objects are converted into uppercase before they are stored. Therefore, you should use uppercase when querying the data dictionary. For example, the **user_objects** view has a column **object_name** that contains the name of the object. These names are always stored in uppercase. You could query **user_objects** with

```
SQL> SELECT object_type, status
  2    FROM user_objects
  3   WHERE object_name = UPPER('ClassPackage');

OBJECT_TYPE    STATUS
-------------  -------
PACKAGE        VALID
PACKAGE BODY   VALID
```

Notice the use of the UPPER function; it ensures that the query will return the desired rows.

Permissions

The data dictionary views are owned by SYS. By default, only SYS and users with the DBA system privilege can see all of the views. Users without the DBA privilege can see the **user_*** and **all_*** views, in addition to some others. They cannot see the **dba_*** views unless they have been granted specific SELECT privileges on them.

The data dictionary views should *never* be updated, even by SYS. They are updated automatically by the database as their relevant information changes. Oracle also provides scripts to modify the data dictionary tables when a database is upgraded or downgraded. These scripts can be found in the same directory as **catproc.sql**.

All/User/DBA Dictionary Views

This section describes the data dictionary views that have the **user_***, **dba_***, and **all_*** instantiations. Since the three instantiations have many columns in common, they are listed together. Each category is listed in Table D-1 for reference and described in detail in the following sections.

Dependency Information

The **all_dependencies**, **dba_dependencies**, and **user_dependencies** views document the dependency relationship between stored objects.

Category	Views
Dependency Information	all_dependencies, dba_dependencies, user_dependencies
Compile Error Information	all_errors, dba_errors, user_errors
Object Information	all_objects, dba_objects, user_objects
Job Information	all_jobs, dba_jobs, user_jobs
Source Code	all_source, dba_source, user_source
Table Column Information	all_tab_columns, dba_tab_columns, user_tab_columns
Table Information	all_tables, dba_tables, user_tables, all_catalog, dba_catalog, user_catalog
Trigger Information	all_triggers, dba_triggers, user_triggers
Trigger Column Information	all_trigger_cols, dba_trigger_cols, user_trigger_cols
View Information	all_views, dba_views, user_views

TABLE D-1. *Data Dictionary Views in This Appendix*

Column	Null?	Type	Description
OWNER	NOT NULL	VARCHAR2(30)	Schema that owns the object (**all_dependencies** and **dba_dependencies** only).
NAME	NOT NULL	VARCHAR2(30)	Name of the object (in uppercase).
TYPE		VARCHAR2(12)	Type of the object—one of PROCEDURE, FUNCTION, PACKAGE, PACKAGE BODY.
REFERENCED_ OWNER		VARCHAR2(30)	Schema that owns the referenced object.
REFERENCED_ NAME		VARCHAR2(30)	Name of the referenced object.
REFERENCED_ TYPE		VARCHAR2(12)	Type of the referenced object—one of PROCEDURE, FUNCTION, PACKAGE, PACKAGE BODY.
REFERENCED_ LINK_NAME		VARCHAR2(128)	Name of the database link to the referenced object (if the referenced object is in a remote database).

Compile Error Information

The **all_errors**, **dba_errors**, and **user_errors** views contain the text of compile errors for stored objects and views. If there is an entry in one of the **_errors** views, then the object is necessarily invalid (indicated in **all_objects**, **dba_objects**, and **user_objects**).

A typical query of **user_errors** could be

```
SELECT line, position, text
  FROM user_errors
 WHERE name = object_name
 ORDER BY sequence;
```

Column	Null?	Type	Description
OWNER	NOT NULL	VARCHAR2(30)	Schema that owns the object (**all_errors** and **dba_errors** only).

NAME	NOT NULL	VARCHAR2(30)	Name of the object (in uppercase).
TYPE		VARCHAR2(12)	Type of the object—one of VIEW, PROCEDURE, FUNCTION, PACKAGE, PACKAGE BODY.
SEQUENCE	NOT NULL	NUMBER	Sequence number, used to order the errors.
LINE	NOT NULL	NUMBER	Line number at which the error occurs.
POSITION	NOT NULL	NUMBER	Zero-based offset within the line at which the error occurs.
TEXT	NOT NULL	VARCHAR2(2000)	Text of the error, including both the error code and the error message.

Object Information

The **all_objects**, **dba_objects**, and **user_objects** views contain information about all types of objects, including tables, stored subprograms, views, sequences, and indexes.

Column	Null?	Type	Description
OWNER	NOT NULL	VARCHAR2(30)	Schema that owns the object (**all_objects** and **dba_objects** only).
OBJECT_ NAME	NOT NULL	VARCHAR2(30)	Name of the object (in uppercase).
OBJECT_ID	NOT NULL	NUMBER	Object number. Every database object is assigned a unique ID.
OBJECT_ TYPE		VARCHAR2(12)	Type of the object (TABLE, PACKAGE BODY, SEQUENCE, PROCEDURE, etc.).
CREATED	NOT NULL	DATE	Timestamp when the object was created.
LAST_DDL_ TIME	NOT NULL	DATE	Timestamp when the last DDL operation (such as an ALTER) was performed on the object. GRANTs and REVOKEs also modify this timestamp.

TIMESTAMP	VARCHAR2(75)	Creation timestamp, in YYYY-MM-DD:HH24:MI:SS format.
STATUS	VARCHAR2(7)	Object status—VALID, INVALID, or N/A.

Job Information

PL/SQL 2.2 ...and HIGHER The **all_jobs**, **dba_jobs**, and **user_jobs** views contain information about database jobs.

Column	Null?	Type	Description
JOB	NOT NULL	NUMBER	Job ID number. As long as the job exists, this ID will remain the same.
LOG_USER	NOT NULL	VARCHAR2(30)	User who submitted the job.
PRIV_USER	NOT NULL	VARCHAR2(30)	User whose default privileges apply for this job.
SCHEMA_ USER	NOT NULL	VARCHAR2(30)	Default schema for the job.
LAST_DATE		DATE	Date when the job last successfully executed.
LAST_SEC		VARCHAR2(8)	Same as **last_date**, in HH24:MI:SS format.
THIS_DATE		DATE	Date the job started executing. NULL if the job is not currently running.
THIS_SEC		VARCHAR2(8)	Same as **this_date**, in HH24:MI:SS format.
NEXT_DATE	NOT NULL	DATE	Date when the job will next be executed.
NEXT_SEC		VARCHAR2(8)	Same as **next_date**, in HH24:MI:SS format.
TOTAL_TIME		NUMBER	Total time in seconds spent by the system on this job.
BROKEN		VARCHAR2(1)	Y if the job is broken, N if not.

INTERVAL	NOT NULL	VARCHAR2(200)	Date function which is used to calculate the next value of **next_date**.
FAILURES		NUMBER	Number of failures since the last successful run of this job.
WHAT		VARCHAR2(2000)	Body of the anonymous PL/SQL block making up the job.
CURRENT_ SESSION_ LABEL		RAW MLSLABEL	Trusted Oracle7 Server label of the current job session.
CLEARANCE_ HI		RAW MLSLABEL	Highest clearance level available for the job (Trusted Oracle7 only).
CLEARANCE_ LO		RAW MLSLABEL	Lowest clearance level available for the job (Trusted Oracle7 only).
NLS_ENV		VARCHAR2(2000)	NLS environment for the job (as specified by ALTER SESSION).
MISC_ENV		RAW(32)	Other session parameters for the job.

Source Code

The **all_source**, **dba_source**, and **user_source** views contain the source code for stored procedures, functions, packages, and package bodies. Trigger source code is in the **all_triggers**, **dba_triggers**, and **user_triggers** views. If the stored object is wrapped, these views contain the encoded source rather than clear text.

A typical query of the **user_source** table could be

```
SELECT text
  FROM user_source
  WHERE NAME = object_name
  ORDER BY LINE;
```

Column	Null?	Type	Description
OWNER	NOT NULL	VARCHAR2(30)	Schema that owns the object (**all_source** and **dba_source** only).
NAME	NOT NULL	VARCHAR2(30)	Name of the stored object.

TYPE		VARCHAR2(12)	Type of the object. Valid values are PACKAGE, PACKAGE BODY, PROCEDURE, and FUNCTION.
LINE	NOT NULL	NUMBER	Line number for this line of source code.
TEXT		VARCHAR2(2000)	Text source at this line.

Table Column Information

The **all_tab_columns**, **dba_tab_columns**, and **user_tab_columns** views contain information about columns in database tables, views, and clusters. When an object is described, this table is queried.

Column	Null?	Type	Description
OWNER	NOT NULL	VARCHAR2(30)	Schema that owns the object (**all_tab_columns** and **dba_tab_columns** only).
TABLE_ NAME	NOT NULL	VARCHAR2(30)	Name of the table, view, or cluster.
COLUMN_ NAME	NOT NULL	VARCHAR2(30)	Name of the column.
DATA_TYPE		VARCHAR2(9)	Datatype of the column (NUMBER, CHAR, DATE, etc.).
DATA_ LENGTH	NOT NULL	NUMBER	Maximum length of the column in bytes.
DATA_ PRECISION		NUMBER	Decimal precision for NUMBER columns, binary precision for FLOAT columns. NULL for other datatypes or when the precision is not specified.
DATA_ SCALE		NUMBER	Scale for NUMBER columns. NULL for other datatypes or when the scale is not specified.
NULLABLE		VARCHAR2(1)	Y if the column allows NULLs, N if not.
COLUMN_ ID	NOT NULL	NUMBER	Unique value assigned to the column. All columns have an ID associated with them.
DEFAULT_ LENGTH		NUMBER	Length of the default value for the column, if specified.

DATA_ DEFAULT	LONG	Default value for the column, if specified.
NUM_ DISTINCT	NUMBER	Number of distinct values in the column.
LOW_ VALUE	RAW(32)	Second lowest value in the table (4 rows or more), or lowest value in the table (3 rows or less). Stored as the internal representation of the first 32 bytes of the column.
HIGH_ VALUE	RAW(32)	Second highest value in the table (4 rows or more), or highest value in the table (3 rows or less). Stored as the internal representation of the first 32 bytes of the column.
DENSITY	NUMBER	Density of the column.
NUM_NULLS	NUMBER	Number of rows that contain NULL values.
NUM_ BUCKETS	NUMBER	Number of buckets used when ANALYZing the table.
LAST_ ANALYZED	DATE	Timestamp when the table was last ANALYZEd.
SAMPLE_ SIZE	NUMBER	Sample size used during the last ANALYZE.

Table Information

The **all_tables**, **dba_tables**, and **user_tables** views contain information about database tables. This information is for the table itself. Column information is stored in **all_tab_columns**, **dba_tab_columns**, and **user_tab_columns**.

Column	Null?	Type	Description
OWNER	NOT NULL	VARCHAR2(30)	Schema that owns the table (**all_tables** and **dba_tables** only).
TABLE_NAME	NOT NULL	VARCHAR2(30)	Name of the table (in uppercase).
TABLESPACE_ NAME	NOT NULL	VARCHAR2(30)	Name of the tablespace containing the table.

CLUSTER_NAME		VARCHAR2(30)	Name of the cluster to which the table belongs. NULL if the table is not clustered.
PCT_FREE	NOT NULL	NUMBER	Minimum percentage of free space in a block, specified at table creation, or when the table was last ALTERed.
PCT_USED	NOT NULL	NUMBER	Minimum percentage of used space in a block, specified at table creation, or when the table was last ALTERed.
INI_TRANS	NOT NULL	NUMBER	Initial number of transactions, specified at table creation, or when the table was last ALTERed.
MAX_TRANS	NOT NULL	NUMBER	Maximum number of transactions, specified at table creation, or when the table was last ALTERed.
INITIAL_EXTENT		NUMBER	Size of the initial extent in bytes, if specified.
NEXT_EXTENT		NUMBER	Size of the next extent in bytes, if specified.
MIN_EXTENTS		NUMBER	Minimum number of extents allowed in the segment, if specified.
MAX_EXTENTS		NUMBER	Maximum number of extents, if specified.
PCT_INCREASE		NUMBER	Percentage increase allowed in extent size, if specified.
FREELISTS		NUMBER	Number of process freelists allocated to the segment, if specified.
FREELIST_GROUPS		NUMBE	Number of freelist groups allocated to the segment, if specified.
BACKED_UP		VARCHAR2(1)	Y if the table has been backed up since the last change, N if not.

NUM_ROWS	NUMBER	Number of rows in the table.
BLOCKS	NUMBER	Number of data blocks allocated to the table.
EMPTY_BLOCKS	NUMBER	Number of data blocks allocated that contain no data. (**empty_blocks** / **blocks**) * 100 is the percentage used.
AVG_SPACE	NUMBER	Average amount of free space in an allocated data block, in bytes.
CHAIN_CNT	NUMBER	Number of rows in the table that are chained over more than one block.
AVG_ROW_LEN	NUMBER	Average row length, in bytes.
DEGREE	VARCHAR2(10)	Number of threads per instance for scanning the table (parallel server only).
INSTANCES	VARCHAR2(10)	Number of instances across which the table will be scanned (parallel server only).
CACHE	VARCHAR2(5)	Y if the table is cached in the buffer cache, N if not.
TABLE_LOCK	VARCHAR2(8)	ENABLED if table locking is enabled, DISABLED if not.

The **all_catalog**, **dba_catalog**, and **user_catalog** views provide a subset of the information in **all_tables**, **dba_tables**, and **user_tables**.

Column	Null?	Type	Description
OWNER	NOT NULL	VARCHAR2(30)	Schema that owns the object (**all_catalog** and **dba_catalog** only)
TABLE_NAME	NOT NULL	VARCHAR2(30)	Name of the object (in uppercase)
TABLE_TYPE		VARCHAR2(11)	Type of the object (TABLE, VIEW, SYNONYM, SEQUENCE)

Trigger Information

The **all_triggers**, **dba_triggers**, and **user_triggers** views describe the database triggers accessible to the user. All of the different components in the CREATE TRIGGER statement are columns in these views.

Column	Null?	Type	Description
OWNER	NOT NULL	VARCHAR2(30)	Schema that owns the trigger (**all_triggers** and **dba_triggers** only).
TRIGGER_NAME	NOT NULL	VARCHAR2(30)	Name of the trigger (in uppercase).
TRIGGER_TYPE		VARCHAR2(16)	Trigger type—BEFORE ROW, BEFORE STATEMENT, AFTER ROW, AFTER STATEMENT.
TRIGGERING_EVENT		VARCHAR2(26)	DML statement that fires the trigger—one or more of INSERT, UPDATE, DELETE.
TABLE_OWNER	NOT NULL	VARCHAR2(30)	Owner of the table on which the trigger is defined.
TABLE_NAME	NOT NULL	VARCHAR2(30)	Name of the table on which the trigger is defined.
REFERENCING_NAMES		VARCHAR2(87)	If specified, names used for referencing :old and :new in row-level triggers.
WHEN_CLAUSE		VARCHAR2(2000)	WHEN clause of the trigger, if specified.
STATUS		VARCHAR2(8)	ENABLED if the trigger is enabled, DISABLED if not.
DESCRIPTION		VARCHAR2(2000)	Character string containing the trigger name, trigger type, WHEN clause, and referencing clause, as specified in the CREATE TRIGGER statement. Useful for re-creating the statement if the source file is lost.
TRIGGER BODY		LONG	PL/SQL block making up the body of the trigger.

Trigger Column Information

The **all_trigger_cols**, **dba_trigger_cols**, and **user_trigger_cols** views show the usage of columns in database triggers. These views complement the **all_triggers**, **dba_triggers**, and **user_triggers** views.

Column	Null?	Type	Description
TRIGGER_OWNER	NOT NULL	VARCHAR2(30)	Schema that owns the trigger.
TRIGGER_NAME	NOT NULL	VARCHAR2(30)	Name of the trigger (in uppercase).
TABLE_OWNER	NOT NULL	VARCHAR2(30)	Schema that owns the table on which the trigger is defined.
TABLE_NAME	NOT NULL	VARCHAR2(30)	Name of the table on which the trigger is defined (in uppercase).
COLUMN_NAME	NOT NULL	VARCHAR2(30)	Name of the column used in the trigger.
COLUMN_LIST		VARCHAR2(3)	YES if the column is specified in the UPDATE clause, NO if not.
COLUMN_USAGE		VARCHAR2(17)	Specifies how the column is referenced in the trigger. All applicable combinations of NEW, OLD, IN, OUT, and IN OUT.

View Information

The **all_views**, **dba_views**, and **user_views** views describe the views in the database.

Column	Null?	Type	Description
OWNER	NOT NULL	VARCHAR2(30)	Schema that owns the view (**all_views** and **dba_views** only).
VIEW_NAME	NOT NULL	VARCHAR2(30)	Name of the view (in uppercase).
TEXT_LENGTH		NUMBER	Length of the view text.
TEXT		LONG	Text of the view—the body of the CREATE VIEW statement.

Other Dictionary Views

In addition to the views described in the previous section, there are two other data dictionary views that are useful to the PL/SQL programmer. They are described in this section, listed alphabetically.

DICT_COLUMNS

The **dict_columns** view describes all of the columns in the data dictionary.

Column	Null?	Type	Description
TABLE_ NAME		VARCHAR2(30)	Name of the data dictionary view.
COLUMN_ NAME		VARCHAR2(30)	Column in the view.
COMMENTS		VARCHAR2(2000)	Description of the column.

DBMS_ALERT_INFO

The **dbms_alert_info** view contains information about sessions that have registered interest in alerts.

Column	Null?	Type	Description
NAME	NOT NULL	VARCHAR2(30)	Name of the alert for which the session has registered interest.
SID	NOT NULL	VARCHAR2(30)	Session identifier.
CHANGED		VARCHAR2(30)	Y if the alert has been signaled, N if not.
MESSAGE		VARCHAR2(1800)	Message that is included in the SIGNAL call, if any.

Index